ASSESSMENT OF DEMOCRATIC TRENDS IN NIGERIA

ASSESSMENT OF DEMOCRATIC TRENDS IN NIGERIA

Editors
Sarafa I. Ogundiya
Olanrewaju A. Olutayo
Jimoh Amzat

GYAN

Assessment of Democratic Trends in Nigeria

ISBN: 978-81-212-1136-9

Published in 2011 in India by
Gyan Publishing House
23, Main Ansari Road, Darya Ganj
New Delhi-110002
Phones : 23282060, 23261060
Fax : 011-23285914
E-mail: books@gyanbooks.com
Website: www.gyanbooks.com

Laser Type Setting by: Rudra Computer Graphics, Delhi
Printed at : Chawla Offset Printers, Delhi

Contents

Preface

After a number of failed/aborted republican governments, Nigeria eventually 're-democratized' in 1999 with the emergence of Chief Olusegun Obasanjo as the President. And for the first time in her political history, the Nigeria experienced a successful civilian to civilian transition. The emergence of 'democratic' rule brought the fragile state a lot of hope and expectations. At least, after a long period of military rule, Nigerians were able to decide who should govern them through election (though the question of its fairness is still a debate). With eventual transformation to 'democratic administration', there are still controversies on whether Nigeria is truly operating democracy or civil rule. The contention has been brought to the fore because of the questions of legitimacy, accountability, rule of law and the self-centered practices of Nigerian leaders which are inimical to democratic principles. Therefore, there are more questions than answers - although hope still abounds more than never before as Nigerians now prefer the civil to the military which is devoid of people's mandate.

Consequent on the agitations, contentions and controversies, there have been numerous responses (to the crisis of underdevelopment) from the Nigerian 'democratic' government. This is a period in the history of Nigeria that the polity is laden with policy debates, reforms and instituted programmes to address the plights of the Nigerian population. The questions of the effectiveness of the government responses, alternative plans of action that could enhance the national drive for development, especially in terms of enabling the government to meet the expectations of Nigerians are of greatest concern. The contentions and controversies are paramount because most of the problems or challenges of the Nigerian state (since independence in 1960) are still endemic, making the 'rich' country to be poor.

The interdependence of the three arms of government and their shared orientation to contribute to governance is yet another issue of concern. More than ever before, Nigeria has recorded a number of landmark judgments (from the judiciary), various legislative enquiries, hearings and bills, and executive machineries in the pursuit of good governance, justice and development. All these efforts have however not really yielded desired results. The country is still fraught with ethno-political agitations, infrastructural decay, health problems, poverty, corruption and so on. Meanwhile, regarding the crisis of underdevelopment, the government is now driving towards the MDGs and vision 2020. The question is: would these goals be achieved based on the prevailing structures of the state?

From the foregoing, Nigeria, looking back to date (1999-2009), several questions have been raised. Has Nigeria really democratized? How has civil rule fared in the last ten years and does democracy have a future in Nigeria? What are the contributions of political parties to democratic stability and survival? What are the major impediments to development? What are the contributions of the arms of government towards democratic consolidation? What are the alternative lines of action for the government in order to enhance democratic dividends? This book project is devoted to providing answers these and other nosy questions.

Foreword

I feel highly honoured and privileged to be called upon to write the foreword to this timely, highly readable and engaging book on the social, political and economic problems and prospects of Nigeria.

Although the book consists of chapters written by different authors from different disciplines and with slightly different styles, a common theme runs through the entire volume, that is, a critical interrogation of the causes, course and consequences of the myriad of problems impeding democratic stability and the all round accelerated development of Nigeria, in spite of her size, human and material resources.

In the five sections into which the book is divided, the authors identified and discuss these problems ranging from the structure of the state, democracy and democratisation, the crisis of legitimacy and governance, the rule of law and the protection of human rights, corruption, endemic poverty, citizens' access to political participation and public goods, and, the interface of internal democracy and external relations. The authors not only discuss these problems lucidly, parsimoniously, analytically and, in most cases, forcefully but also proffer theoretically informed and / or empirically derived solutions to them. By so doing, they have provided a template for dealing with the quality of governance in the various spheres of the nation's corporate existence.

Moreover, by touching on a wide variety of oftentimes controversial issues and providing a rich and up-to-date bibliography for each chapter, the authors will no doubt promote further debate and scholarship on these issues.

These two qualities, I believe, will commend the book to not only the community of scholars in the social sciences but also to the general public and friends of Nigeria who desire to see the slumbering giant assume her rightful place in the community of civilized and progressive nations.

The authors and the editors richly deserve to be commended for their efforts.

Professor Dejo A. Abdulrahaman
Dean, Faculty of Social Sciences,
Usmanu Danfodiyo University
Sokoto.

List of Contributors

Ogundiya I.S. (PhD) is a senior lecturer at the Department of Political Science, Usmanu Danfodiyo University, Sokoto, Nigeria. Contact : geatjoa@yahoo.co.uk

Olutayo A.O. (PhD) is a senior lecturer and currently the Head of Department of Sociology, University of Ibadan, Nigeria. Contact : lantopamtu@yahoo.com.

Amzat, J. (PhD) is a lecturer at the Department of Sociology, Usmanu Danfodiyo University, Sokoto, Nigeria. Contact : greatjoa@yahoo.co.uk

Habu Mohammed (PhD) is a senior lecturer in the Department of Political Science, Bayero University, Kano, and Assistant Director (Research and Documentation), Aminu Kano Centre for Democratic Research and Training, Mambayya House, B.U.K. Contact : habuum@yahoo.co.uk

Tunde Abisoye (PhD) has just fininshed his doctoral research at the Department of Sociology, University of Ibadan, Nigeria. Contact : lantopamtu@yahoo.com

Azeez O. Olaniyan (PhD) is a lecturer, Department of Political Science, University of Ado-Ekiti, Ado-Ekiti, Nigeria. Contact : olaniyan444@yahoo.com

Yahaya T.K. Baba (PhD) is a doctoral candidate and lecturer at the Department of Political Science, Usmanu Danfodiyo University, Sokoto, Nigeria. Contact : tkbabayaha@yahoo.com, jafarhajar14@gmailcom

Olayinka Akanle is a doctoral candidate, Department of Sociology, University of Ibadan, Nigeria. Contact : yakanle@yahoo.com

Dele Ashiru is a PhD student and a lecturer at the Department of Political Science, University of Lagos, Akoka, Lagos. Contact : ashirudele@yahoo.co.uk

Sulaiman Y. Balarabe Kura (PhD) is a lecturer at the Department of Political Science, Usmanu Danfodiyo University, Sokoto, Nigeria. Contact : sulaimankura@yahoo.co.in, sybkura@gmail.com.

Freedom C. Onuoha is a Research Fellow at the African Centre for Strategic Research and Studies, National Defence College, Abuja, Nigeria. Contact : chufreedom@yahoo.com

Omotosho, Babatunde Joshua (PhD) is a lecturer at the Department of Sociology, Faculty of the Social Sciences, University of Ado-Ekiti, Nigeria. Contact : babatundeomotosho@gmail.com, tuntoy20032003@yahoo.com

Emmanuel O. Ojo (PhD) is a senior lecturer at the Department of Political Science, University of Ilorin, Ilorin, Nigeria. Contact : eojo12000@yahoo.com

Muhammad Zaiyan Umar (PhD) is a senior lecturer at the Department of Political Science, Usmanu Danfodiyo University, Sokoto, Nigeria.

Folashade B. Okeshola, Mrs (PhD) is a lecturer at the Department of Sociology, Ahmadu Bello University, Zaria, Nigeria.

Musibau Adetunji Babatunde (PhD) is a lecturer at the Department of Economics, University of Ibadan, Ibadan, Nigeria. Contact : tunjiyusuf19@yahoo.com

Emeka Emmanuel Okafor (PhD) is a lecturer at the Department of Sociology, University of Ibadan, Ibadan, Nigeria. Contact : eemfor@yahoo.com

Kehinde A. Bolaji is a Research Assistant, Democracy and Good Governance Unit, ECOWAS Commission, Abuja and a doctoral candidate at the University of Ibadan, Ibadan, Nigeria. Contact : ayodeji_bolaji@yahoo.com, kbolaji@ecowas.int

Enemaku Idachaba (PhD) is a lecturer at the Department of Political Science, University of Ibadan, Nigeria.

SECTION-I

DEMOCRACY AND DEMOCRATIZATION

1

From Civil Rule to Democracy: What is Needed?

Habu Mohammed

Introduction

There is no single pattern in the development of democracy as political systems differ, much as value orientation of civil society and their political culture diverge (Wiard, 2002: 2) and as changes in the perception and conception of what democracy stands for differ from one person to another and among social groups/organizations (Jega, 2007: 27). The single most important factor in the differential patterns of democratization is, therefore, found in the civic/political value preferences of the people and the maturity of the political system in which democracy thrives. Thus, as time passes by and as democracy flourishes what is most important is the extent to which civil society imbibes democratic ethos and the degree to which political institutions are entrenched and made to deepen democratic values in the conduct of public policy. At another level, the extent to which the system provides what is usually referred to as 'dividends of democracy' is a correlate of the longevity of the democratic rule process. In developing democracies, to be specific, 'third wave' democratic societies of Africa, Asia and Latin America, the dividends of democracy is much aspired for, and it is invariably translated to mean 'human face' of democracy, defined as the improvement in the quality of life of the people in terms of welfare and social service provision. This is to say that the extent to which 'democracy' is able to provide public goods for the greater number of people and the ability of its various institutions to promote and protect their fundamental human rights, in addition to entrenching the constitutionality of the rule of law, is what places a democratic system of government higher than any other forms of modern government.

This chapter examines critically the civil rule in Nigeria with a view to elucidating its dynamics, and it provides an assessment of the system and how far it has fared. The aim is to embark on an in-depth assessment of what is on the ground rather than what the operators of the system promise the process of democratic consolidation in the country. In order to begin to assess the process of democracy in Nigeria which by any means is not an easy task as areas to be covered are boundless as scientifically and systematically as possible, a thematic overview becomes necessary. Hence, for the purposes of this chapter, four sections are provided. In Section One a distinction is drawn between the concept of democracy and the term 'civil rule'. The section also highlights the framework of analyzing civilian rule in Nigeria. In the second section, a prelude to civil rule is examined and contextualized in order to shape our understanding of its (civil rule) dynamics in the last ten years. Section Three examines the dynamics of civil rule in Nigeria, its ironies and areas of development for present and future consolidation, while Section Four, and the last, deals with what is to be done in Nigeria's journey to democracy and its consolidation.

Civil Rule, Democracy and Democratization: Conceptual Issues

Though interconnected and mutually reinforcing, civil rule and democracy are not the same; the former is the precondition of reaching the latter. Democratic system of government provides the process of 'civilianization' of rule. In its simplest definition, democracy is a limited government (Weingast, 1997: 245). It involves a process of electing leaders who will form a government of the people with a view to representing the interest of the generality of members of the society. Democracy is aimed at realizing "the organization of people, by the people themselves, to attain the collectively self-defined, and ever improving, higher levels of civilization" (Asobie, 2007: 4). This conception of democracy suggests that it is a representational government which is based on the consent and will of the people, a responsive and responsible government in which the majority upholds power without suppressing the interest of the minority.

Democracy is different from a civilian rule in various aspects of governance as well as in forms and content; however, the prime mover of democracy is civil rule. On the one hand, democracy thrives on enabling ethos, practices and institutions that are fully or virtually matured so as to guarantee continuity through fair play, debate, compromise and opposition. On the other hand, there may be a civilian rule in a country without the necessary conditions for democracy to thrive. In such a situation, a government is a product of a civil society, not led by comrades-in-arms but by elected civilians, and yet it would neither exhibit democratic credentials and tendencies nor govern on the basis of the principle of rule of law. In some cases, a civilian rule, in contrast to democratic rule, bears many semblances of democracy but the government may not be considered as democratic. In civil rule, democratic institutions exist and they take some time to mature. In the process of permutation towards the maturity level of these institutions, mistakes are made by both the political class and civil society. In this vein, Nigeria is still under a civilian rule and is in the process of democratization. Therefore, the country has not reached a stage in which one can aptly say the conduct of democratic institutions and civil society is as it abounds in matured democracies of western societies.

The problem of operationalisation and adaptability of democratic practices is still apparent. The word "democracy" is a very fluid concept with varying forms: direct, representative or indirect, republican or liberal, and socialist democracies. Still, it is very clear that the model Nigeria is trying to adopt is liberal democracy based on the pattern of government (presidential system) established in the United States of America. In this regard, Nigeria is utilizing the environment of civilian rule after a prolonged period of military rule to democratize. If the country is successful in the democratization process and finally attains democratic consolidation, as in the case of Senegal, South Africa, and recently Ghana, then the country will be said to have been a democratic state.

For example, like many other African states after independence, Ghana, formerly known as Gold Coast, had parted ways with the then promising democracies in the continent following the overthrow of the country's independent nationalist leader, Kwame Nkrumah in a military coup in 1966. From then, government in Ghana alternated between military and civilian rule until 1992 when Flight Lieutenant Jerry (Rtd) Rawlings was elected as President in one of the freest and fairest change of government in Africa. Rawlings was re-elected in another round of elections in 1996 to serve his second term in office as Ghana's President on the platform of the party National Democratic Congress (NDC). The party lost power to New Patriotic Party (NPP) in 1999 and later NDC returned to power after December 7, 2008 national election and two presidential run-offs on December 28 and January 2, 2009. The outcome of these elections saw the emergence of Professor John Evans Atta-Mills as President of the Republic of Ghana, elected under the platform of the NDC.

The 2008 election was Ghana's fifth since her return to multiparty democracy in 1992. The country is now a stable democratic state not only because of its successful systematic transfer of power from one legitimately elected government to another, but also for the fact that the political *dramatis personae* and the civil society in the country have learnt to be governed by democratic norms. They have imbibed and developed the mind-set of adopting political tolerance, participation and the rules of competitive politics. The lessons to learn from the Ghanaian experience, particularly by Nigerian political actors are quite enormous. Rather in comparison, in the latter politics is not transparent; elections since the return to democracy in 1999 have been heavily rigged, especially by the ruling party, the Peoples Democratic Party (PDP); over fifty political parties exist, but many of them are weak and dysfunctional without ideology; politics of godfatherism has overtaken that of principle and renewal; the electoral body (INEC) is politicized and has become a partisan institution; politics as business and wealth acquisition has hijacked selfless service and patriotism. In fact, the democratization process in Nigeria since 1999 leaves much to be desired.

Thus, democracy is essentially based on fulfillment of conditions which are not similar in all cases but profoundly noticeable; it is not an event but a development from various practices not just periodic elections. The successive transfer of power from civilian to civilian administration in Nigeria since 1999 does not guarantee democracy in the country, because elections have been marred by overt and covert rigging and contestations. As a result, various governments at different levels lack legitimacy as they clearly lose the democratic basis of their mandate, and this, in turn, make them overlook various aspects of democratic ethos.

In a country where a prolonged period of military authoritarian rule has made delicate processes of goal attainment and difficult the entrenchment of democratic values, civilian rule, if well utilized and sustained, is a prelude, a stepping stone, indeed a means of reaching a stage in which the society is said to have attained a democratic system of government. This process of 'utilization' and 'sustenance' of democratic values and cultures in the state, democratic institutions and the civil society is a democratization process. The large number of 'third wave' democracies that have passed through a one-party system or military authoritarian governments and are striving to entrench democracy through a series of programmes called transition are undergoing the process of democratization.

Thus, despite the return to civil rule in 1999, Nigeria has not yet attained the status of full-fledged democratic nation, which is to say the country is not disengaging from her so long democratization process, which Omotola defines "as the process of transition to a stable/consolidated democracy" (2007: 247). As a process, the journey to democratization is a long one; its beginning may be known, its ending however is undeterminable. Depending on how fast a political system and its various institutions embrace the democratic project and are committed to it, democratization may last for a decade, or a century or so, and all this long it is often characterized by some pitfalls, ironies, and even sad mixed with gladsome developments created by its various movers and shakers, especially the political actors.

balkanization during the years of the military terror. Thus, only the existing politicians who were anxious for power and already enriched by the neo-patrimonial, military clientele politics were able to seize the opportunity of General Abdulsalam Abubakar's transition to civil rule. The G-34 politicians was one of these groups; they comprise the crops of leaders that steered the helm of the Nigerian political affairs from 1999 to 2003, and General Obasanjo was a member who contested and won the presidential election under the platform of the PDP.

The rush transition plan thus occasioned the hasty formation of political parties which included United Nigeria Peoples Party (UNPP), the Peoples Democratic Party (PDP), Alliance for Democracy (AD), the Peoples Liberty Party (PLP), All Peoples Party (ANPP) and the Liberal Democratic Party (LDP). In 1998, the Independent National Electoral Commission (INEC) eventually registered only three political parties, the PDP, the APP (later ANPP) and the AD on the basis of 10% votes for the three parties in at least 24 states of the federation in the 1998 local government elections (Obiyan, 1999: 41; Apam, 2007: 5).

Thus, although the take-off of the civilian rule in 1999 has bequeathed Nigeria new political culture and direction, scholars have different perceptions about what exactly went wrong? A dominant explanation, especially held by political economists, is the military culture. According to them, the political ethos of the crops of politicians that emerged from the prolonged turbulent period of military rule are inescapably would definitely be prone to anti-democratic politics or governance. It is no doubt a fact that the 1999 constitution put together by the military is undemocratic in its essence, in some of its fundamental provisions, as well as by virtue of its lack of consultation of the civil society; consequently, militarization of the political culture under civilian rule is inevitable. The military political culture of primitive accumulation, lack of expansion of the democratic space, crony politics, neo-patrimonial tendencies, etc. have permeated the civilian political class, some of whom served in various capacities under the military regimes in the country. These crops of politicians have been euphemistically called "militicians" (Jega, 2007; Momoh, 2007), and their style of leadership is referred to as "garrison democracy" (Bako, 2007), "authoritarian democracy" (Momoh, 2007) or "civilian dictatorship" (Sani, 2008).

It is important to note that a democracy founded by the militicians cannot easily accommodate changes needed for faster democratization and democratic consolidation. The failure to entrench a vibrant democratic ethos from the start has come to affect the Nigeria's democratization journey. It is in this light that the contradictions in the process earlier stated can be understood. In the contradictions is basically the militicians' inability to provide a quick political terrain for democratic consolidation. More often than not, the Nigerian polity is embroiled with systemic and constitutional lapses, attitudinal inappropriateness and the culture of primitive capitalist accumulation which informs the tendency of political leaders to remain in power by all means until they want to quit politics or end their tenure.

Civil Rule and Contradictions between the Institutions of Democracy and Expectations on the Enrichment of Democratic Values

The most vital institutions of democracy in any society are the three arms of government: the executive, the legislature and the judiciary. The workings of these institutions in line with the provisions of the rule of law provide the much needed checks and balances in the government. As one of the three arms of government, the legislature occupies a central position in the process of democratic consolidation, because it plays a pivotal role in the operation of the separation of powers in a presidential system of government. It determines the content and intent of public policies and their relevance to the needs of national development. Through open debates and constructive ideas, the legislature has come to play a significant role in modern democratic states as it nurtures a culture of free flow of ideas and information in addition to accommodating the interests of the various constituencies which its members represent and that of the nation at large (Johnson, 1992).

The experience of the first four years of military rule in Nigeria was characterized by excessive tussles between the legislature and the executive, while the judiciary was overlooked and often sidelined on various aspects that affected the process of democratization in the country. The Nigeria's leadership under President Olusegun Obasanjo was replete with executive lawlessness, undermining the natural process of evolving strong institutions for the entrenchment of democracy. The legislature was one institution that the executive pocketed and robbed of its democratic essence by winning over some of the membership's loyal support. In the first two years of Obasanjo's administration, as Bako (2001: 1) notes, the presidency "has been busy systematically destroying all democratic institutions". He further notes that the chief of the executive arm of government was able to occupy the political space not suitable for one person, "concentrating powers in the hands of the president in an effort to secure a second-term and perhaps perpetuate his regime even at the expense of democracy". The usurpation of the powers of the legislature by the executive has engendered a situation of virtual democratic failure. A notable unconstitutional exercise of power by the regime was the monopolization of the oil sector and its associated revenue which was unlawfully withdrawn by the presidency in defiance of due process. Between October 2005 and April 2006 alone, the President withdrew the sum of US$1.2 billion from the excess crude oil account in order to meet part of the cost of conducting the 2006 population census (Sani, 2008: 234). Thus, the first set of members of the National Assembly had to work under the intense pressure by the executive which knew very little about the virtues of debate, dialogue and consultation in the making and passing of bills. The executive nearly had the field day through its carrot and stick approach, fomentation of internal schisms in the National Assembly and cooptation. The efforts of the then Speaker of the House of Representatives, Hon. Ghali Umar Na'Abba, to check the excesses of the executive proved abortive as some of his fellow members lacked the political will to resist the advances of the presidency.

The feud between the executive and legislature was no child's play. However, the central issue in their conflict was appropriation process, and later, the attempt by the President to get tacit support for a-third-term tenure of his government. While the 1999 constitution explicitly states that all funds belonging to the federation cannot be spent except in the manner prescribed by the National Assembly, the executive hardly see the oversight functions of the legislature on appropriation as normal in the scheme of the rule of law. Be that as it may, the 300-page reports of the Auditor General, Vincent Azie, released in January 2003, which covers the 2001 fiscal year, vindicated the National Assembly because a number of suspicious payments and high level political corruption was unveiled in the Presidency. Although there has been a temporary respite in the loggerhead between the executive and the legislature since the end of Obasanjo's government in May, 2007, political corruption and internal wrangling within the legislature has become a norm in Nigeria's Fourth Republic. This was more pronounced when the government divided the National Assembly on the issue of the third term agenda which was eventually rejected by a majority opposition in the two Houses.

The hallmark of modern democracy is the process of selecting leaders who are expected to be responsive and responsible to those who elected them, i.e., the electorate. In addition to providing good leadership and governance, transparent conduct of public office and a selfless leadership devoid of corrupt practices or political vindictiveness against the opposition, election is central to any democratic process. It provides a peaceful transfer of power from one government to another and thus a peaceful coexistence among the different people and social groups that make up a society. A free and fair election is an important yardstick for determining the viability of any democratic process. It is in this vein that in Nigeria's journey to democratic consolidation and sustenance the conduct of free, fair, credible and transparent elections is badly needed. Instead of gaining political legitimacy by acceptable and popular transfer of power, elections in Nigeria serve as bedrock to political corruption, which, in Aiyede's words, is "the abuse or misuse of public or governmental power for illegitimate private advantage" (Aiyede, 2008: 40).

The experience of civilian rule in Nigeria since 1999 has shown that political corruption has been deeply embedded in the country's political process. Once politicians get to power they always want to exploit it for private ends by whatever means possible. The politics of godfatherism has profoundly increased as control of public offices becomes an avenue for personal enrichment through a process of primitive accumulation (see Ayoade, 1998). Thus, despite establishing institutions designed to check political corruption, such as the Independent Corrupt Practices and Other Related Offenses (ICPC) and the Economic and Financial Crimes Commission (EFCC), the phenomenon of corruption continues and has become a culture, endemic in the country. In most cases, these institutions are incapacitated through politicization. They therefore become very selective and discriminatory in their dealings with corrupt public officers and politicians. With particular reference to election of leaders at the local, states and national government levels, many of the emerged state governors especially in the 2007 elections lack political legitimacy because of electoral malpractices and the federal government has been rendered weak by political corruption. Aiyede (2008: 41) aptly notes:

> In Nigeria, corruption has made election results to have very little or nothing to do with the performance in office of politicians. Precisely because performance is not a critical factor in electoral outcome, the incentive to perform is very weak. And because corruption is effective in achieving electoral victory the incentive to resort to corrupt practices is very high.

The case of Anambra State in the aftermath of the 2003 elections illustrates how brazenly rooted corruption has become in Nigeria's democratic process. Chris Uba, the 'godfather' of Anambra State politics and the Special Adviser to President Obasanjo ran into problems with his protégé, the state Governor, Chris Ngige, and he (Uba) therefore insisted that the governor must either dance to his tune and respect the 'pay-off' deals between them or lose his appointment. The political brouhaha between the two politicians put the state in a political stalemate until the legal battle was finally settled when the Supreme Court invalidated Ngige's election and Mr. Peter Obi who won the election in the first instance was declared the Governor of the state. Noteworthy in the Anambra State political imbroglio is the weak position of INEC vis-à-vis the 'power' of 'political entrepreneurs' in the country. In the issued debacle in Anambra state, the People's Democratic Party (PDP) on whose platform Ngige contested the State Gubernatorial election in 2003 admitted that he was not duly elected (Smah, 2008: 68), affirming that his 'victory' was but for the influence and money politics of his 'godfather', Chris Uba. This implies that the institution, INEC on whose shoulder rests the responsibility of organizing and conducting elections in the country is equally not immune to political corruption, it lacks independence to conduct a credible election, and it really facilitated it (Aiyede, 2008; CDP/CDRT Report on Financing Political Parties in Nigeria, 2008).

The journey so far in Nigeria's democratization process also reveals the dominance of one political party over many others, in both electoral outcomes and control of public offices. The ruling party, PDP has overly dominated in the political competition for power. Despite the formation of the Conference on Nigerian Political Parties (CNPP) in 2003 as a coalition of opposition against the ruling party, the supremacy of the party (PDP) in the struggles for power has remained uncontested. The registration of fifty political parties to contest the 2007 elections, with only the All Nigeria Peoples Party (ANPP) and the newly formed but lately registered Action Congress (AC), seemed to have, on the surface, created the strongest opposition against the PDP. However, in reality the political landscape was clear for PDP and it had itself shielded with all the mechanisms for the control of power in the country. Public opinion does not support but rather laments the situation in which one party controls power to the disadvantage of 'weak' political parties, regarding it as dangerous to Nigeria's democracy. This view has been seriously expressed by the civil society in various public hearings held across the country during the visit of the National Electoral Reform Committee, which was set up by President Umaru Musa Yar'adua in 2008, to the nation's six geo-political zones. In fact, CAN President, Archbishop Onaiyekan, well expresses the minds of civil society about party politics in the country thus: "Democracy does not exist in Nigeria...I always say that what we have been running in Nigeria for the past ten years is not democracy, but *partitocracy*: the government of the people by the party, for the party" (*Leadership*, March, 2009:1-2).

This scenario was reinforced by the disposition and political proclivity of the President who served as a gatekeeper and presided over what Bako (2007) euphemistically referred to as "garrison democracy" which "is a reverse liberal democracy operating as a neo-liberal movement by abusing the rule of law and constitutionalism" (Bako, 2007: 4). For example, in one of the party's presidential campaigns, Obasanjo made it point blank that as far as his party is concerned the 2007 general elections was a "do or die" affair in which by all means the PDP would win.

Other political parties likewise perpetrated in their own ways corruption in both the primary and state elections, thereby generating the allegations and counter-allegations of election rigging. With a few exceptions, the incumbent state governors clung to power and have returned for a second term by virtue of the wealth they have amassed, while in the crudest form some of them installed their puppets as governors by ensuring that they get their party's mandate in the primary and the main elections. Marx Van Berg, Head of the European Union Election Monitoring Team remarked about the 2007 election thus: "I can compare it of course with 2003, when I was the chief observer, and I had expected, really, after that was a very disappointing election, that we would see now something better. But we have not seen that, and the credibility is not there (BBC News, Monday, April, 2007). 'Money politics' and other related forms of nasty politicking such as the use of hired assassins to kill strong opposition party candidates as well as the use of thugs to cause political havoc on supporters of opposition parties pervade the country.

In the area of intergovernmental relations (IGRs), the federal government overlooks the principle of balanced federation as it erodes the sovereignty of states in their daily political and administrative processes as well as in their capacity to exercise their constitutional autonomy to initiate and undertake policy action that would change the lives of their peoples. Thus, the practice of a more-difficult-to-classify pattern of federalism under military rule (Tamuno, 1997: 16), vaguely described in different quarters as "quasi-federal", "militarist", "centralist", or "pseudo" federalism, resonated in the period of civilian regime in Nigeria, sometimes with profound effect on the independence status of the states. When constitutionally empowered states decide to create more local governments in their localities, such efforts are often thwarted by the central government often for political reasons, threatening that doing so would be met with not only the non-payment of federal grants to the newly created local governments but also their illegalization, as in the experience of Lagos State in 2003 amply demonstrated.

Moreover, a constitutional bottleneck that stipulates confirmation by the National Assembly of any local government created in the country further erodes the autonomy of states to act independently on matters that affect them. The result is that since 1967 when 12 states were created by the federal military government led by General Gowon, states and local governments have been subsequently created leading to the present thirty-six states federal structure, but all have been created by the successive military regimes. In other words, there has never been a time when a civilian government created local governments and successfully secured the approval of the federal government, be it under military or civilian rule. Suffice it to say that in post-military period the fear of dependence on the centre for grants has been a compelling reason by the federal government to deny states any attempt to create local governments.

Civil Rule and Contradictions between Expectations on Good Governance and Realization of Democratic Dividends

Despite greater freedom of speech and improved respect for the rule of law, the government effort at establishing a peaceful democratic society has been associated with a lot of problems. Some of them are systemic and therefore have much to do with the way the institutions of democracy are used. Others are attitudinal in which the failure of the Nigerian state and its political elites to change their attitude of "business-as-usual" and cultivate a new mindset that conforms to democratic demands (Mohammed, 2005: 92). The result is that Nigerians, and the Nigerian diaspora, are not only disenchanted and disillusioned with the manner the government is toying with public affairs but they have also lost hope in the nation's leadership. The Nigerian social critic, scholar and novelist Chinua Achebe for instance demonstrated this fact when he refused to accept national honour award from the directionless Nigerian government.

The failure of the state to provide a workable compromise with the aggrieved communities on resource revenue allocation has created a lot of skirmishes in the Niger Delta region. The situation today in the region is frightening; it takes a dimension of abduction and murder of security personnel, the armed policemen and military personnel, as well as the local and foreign oil workers. The Niger Delta Development Corporation (NDDC), Oil Minerals Producing Areas Development Commission (OMPADEC) and the Ministry of Niger Delta lately created by the Yar'adua administration are hoax. The Ministry not only lacks the support of the people of the Niger Delta Region, but even the militants are distancing themselves from it. This is to say that the bone of contention in this region has not been addressed, thus, the institutions which are established to oversee the social service provision and infrastructural development of the areas will definitely suffer the inimical problem of legitimacy and consequently may little or no difference from similar institutional efforts in the region.

Again, as Jega (2002: 6) argues: "instead of democracy yielding peace, stability and security to lives and property, it seems to have yielded a return, full circle, to the spate of ethno-religious conflicts and violent eruptions, which characterized military rule, especially under Generals Babangida and Abacha". Such conflicts include, among others, Hausa and Fulani pastoralists, Umuleri and Aguleri in Anambra state, Urhobo and Itsekiri in Delta State, Muslims and Christians in different parts of the country, Birom and Hausa in Plateau state, Tiv and Jukun in Taraba state, Tiv and Azara in Benue state, and Ife and Modakeke in Osun state. The occurrences of these conflicts have created a serious dilemma for Nigeria, particularly in her quest for attracting foreign investment and tourism.

Furthermore, the critical role of the state as the arbiter of conflict creates a different meaning in Nigeria's Fourth Republic. Either because of the state's failure to adhere to the rule of law or engage interactive problem-solving mechanisms in the resolution of conflict, the government tends to fuel crisis and create havoc in sensitive communities. The swift deployment and use of brutal force in the towns of Odi and Zaki Biam in Bayelsa and Benue states in 1999 and 2000, respectively, testifies to the argument that the Nigerian state in the post-military period has not disentangled itself from its military culture of yesteryears.

Since the end of military rule, the dream of Nigerians has been a civilian government which would turn around the fate of the crippled economy inherited from the past authoritarian regimes and would establish the process of development for economic prosperity and greater democratic dividends. In other words, questions about the relationship between democracy and development and the extent to which the two coexist to re-launch the nation on a course of sustainable socio-economic transformation occupied the minds of Nigerians (Jega, 2003: 4). In his analysis of the causes of authoritarian reversals, Svolik (2007: 5) argues that there is a close nexus between the level of economic development in a country and its susceptibility to democratic reversals. If the economy is essentially directed towards "liberalization" of democracy the success of the distribution of economic wealth is likely to become a mirage; only the interest of a few politicians and neo-liberal institutions would stand at advantage, while the majority of the people would be disempowered (Hippler, 1995: 15). Hippler's concept of "market democracy" thus becomes actualised in Nigeria with the unveiling of the economic reform policies of the civilian regime. A key element of the reforms is privatization (see Okonjo-Iweala, 2006), a policy which has created a renewed concern about whether the Nigerian government is really interested in amending the already debilitating conditions of the public enterprises in the country.

The whole idea of privatization in Nigeria is antithetical to democracy and the rule of law. It is being pursued with little or no regard for the laws that governing public corporations and enterprises. Besides, being a neo-liberal product, the law which introduces privatization and commercialization, Decree No. 28 of 1999, and even the Bureau of Public Enterprises (BPE) are a military creation and it was design to accommodate the whims and caprices of the political elites. The law gives power to the National Council on Privatization (NCP) and the BPE unconstitutionally, and the process of transferring state ownership of enterprises to the private sector does not account for constitutionality. For example, the privatization of NEPA, now Power Holding Company of Nigeria (PHCN), is diametrically opposed to the law that set it up, because Section 16 of the 1999 constitution prevents the concentration of wealth or the means of production and its exchange in the hands of few individuals or groups. The section also supports state ownership of major sectors of the economy to which many of the privatized enterprises belong. Nigeria's privatization as implemented simply raises more questions than it answers. Hers is a political economy that principally favours friendly local bourgeoisies in the government privatization of enterprises of public utilities.

Here, a reference is very good. Bangura's (1986) apt understanding of the intricate class alliance in the process of capitalist accumulation and in anchoring of the structural crisis of development process in Nigeria would help to see the government's privatization business in proper light. Bangura argues that the pattern of class relationship in Nigeria is not regime-bound; it passes from one government to another, military or civilian. This coalition of interests has warranted the continuation of class alliance specially anchored by the state in the process of democratization under civilian rule (1999-2007).

It has become very conspicuous that in the privatization programme of the civilian regime politics, class alliance and reforms are at work and are meant to either frustrate the democratization process or provide a secure private accommodation in the democratization process. Government's pretext for privatization is a necessity and an obligation of scaling down public spending on what the IMF considers "unproductive" social services (Mohammed, 2008). As the result, Nigeria's public sector service delivery has been collapsed by the neo-liberal privatization agenda.

Civilian Rule and Contradictions between the Democratic Process and Democratic Consolidation

When state institutions are not firmly rooted on the principles of democracy and the way the political class steers democratic system is antithetical to the development of a vibrant political culture, the expectations and hopes of civil society are usually doomed. A positive political culture endures when political socialization is purposeful and goal-oriented. Citizens of any democratic society learn over time, and the quickest means of imbibing democracy is by understanding it as an instrument of good governance, respect for the rule of law and provision of peoples' developmental needs. In developed democracies of the West the means of changing an unpopular government is through massive participation in election, which is seen as a discharge of fundamental civic responsibility of all citizens eligible to vote. That democracy has come to stay in Nigeria is no mere assertion, given the global dynamics of the art of governance now favouring representation and people's participation. Democracy must be so allowed to thrive that it will direct our social, economic and political compass for sustainable peace and development.

For instance, the situation in which the constitution provides immunity to executive chiefs of states not only promotes executive lawlessness and political corruption but also makes nonsense the democratic principle of accountability to the people. This explains why at the end of the first four years of civilian rule thirty-one state governors, out of Nigeria's 36 governors, were under federal investigation mostly on allegation of executive corruption, and five have been impeached (Lyndia, 2006). Anti-graft laws and institutions such as the Economic and Financial Crimes Commission (EFCC) have been overly politicized. As a result, some of the state governors arraigned before the court of law after their tenures has not been brought to book. Needless to mention that some of those state governors still have risen in the national politics and become members of the Senate, 'representatives' of their individual constituencies.

In a functional democracy the observance of the laws of the land as embodied in the constitution and the principle of constitutionalism defines the parameters of state actions. *Where the executive arm of government overreaches its constitutional functions, the independent and impartial judiciary is ready to engage and interrogate it on the legal ground.* However, since the return to civil rule in 1999 the judicial arm of government had operated without independence from the executive, not until much later when the

Yar'adua government put emphases on the importance of the rule of law in the country's democratization process. The recent court verdicts which cancelled the victory of state governors in the 2007 election illustrate the judiciary's redemptive role in Nigeria's democracy. In one of these landmark judgments, the Election Petition Tribunal nullified the election of Prof. Osunbor of the PDP and swore in as Governor of the state (Edo) former labour union leader, Adam Oshiomhole.

Dilemma of Civilian Rule in Nigeria: What is Needed?

Learning the Ropes of Democracy

Democracy is learned and the process has no ending, because it is a process of acculturation of the minds of the political actors, the system and the society at large. At different stages of its development, democracy presupposes that adjustments are made and past mistakes are corrected for future benefits. Maturity is only attainable in the democratization process when this mode of culture is cultivated in the minds of the political actors. However, when mistakes emanate from recurring omissions or commissions without deliberate rational efforts at providing them solutions, the end result is the adoption of the trial and error approach without frontally addressing the actual problems. Nigeria is one of the newest democracies today, and all hopes are not lost in her continuing quest for sustainable democracy. It is most important that the state realize the importance of the creating an enabling environment of justice and equity, a system where the rule of law is the catchword of the political actors. By these means, the negative political culture simmering in Nigerian politics that is called 'godfatherism', 'sit tight' executive monopoly of power and 'garrison democracy' could be checked.

Again, the culture of democracy is built and becomes rooted when relevant sectors of the society, particularly the civil society and its organizations are well empowered. Democratic consolidation is the function of a synergy of commitment on the part of the state and civil society. The empowerment of the 'third sector', i.e. civil society, through active participation in policy decisions, constructive input in the policy making process and meaningful political education help in consolidating democracy. The large arrays of organizations of civil society in Nigeria are potent agents of political transformation through promotion of human rights, gender equality, constitutionalism, and mediation for peace in the country.

Positive Dividends for the Greatest Number of Nigerians

Where unemployment and poverty ironically prevails amidst plentiful resources, a culture of peaceful coexistence among the different nationalities would be hard to cultivate. One of the paradoxes of oil wealth in Nigeria is that some 80 percent of the oil monies are accrued to 1 percent of the population with 70 percent of private wealth held abroad (World Bank, quoted. in Lubeck et al., 2005: 7). The existence of a wide gap between the rich and the poor in Nigeria results in the high degree of social tension in our society. For example, the proportion of population in poverty rose from 28 per cent in 1980 to 65.7 per cent in 1996, to 70 per cent in 2000 (Ajaike, in Jega: 2002). Today, more than half of the Nigerian population is living below one dollar per day. Thus, poverty provides the main catalyst for heightened conflicts and communal feuds in the country. Nigeria is among the 20 poorest countries in the world, and in 2002, the Human Development Index (HDI) ranking placed Nigeria 148th out of 173 countries, making the country as having the third largest number of poor people, after China and India (Igbuzor, 2003: 8). In 2006, the HDI report placed Nigeria 159th out of 177 countries, which is to say that the policy of privatization is pursued in the face of excruciating poverty in the country. The 'proceeds' of the policy is not utilized to service either the country's debt, create employment opportunities or improve the supply of public utilities. Diamond (1993: 96) notes that "[d]emocracy will not be valued by the people unless it deals with social and economic problems and achieves a modicum of order and justice.". What Nigeria need is not privatization as such, but leadership with the much needed transparency and accountability that would aid the transformation of the public sector/machineries for effective service delivery.

Good Democratic Governance

Good governance is dependent on a responsive and responsible, transparent and accountable leadership, and the flourishing of the rule of law. When a government is founded on some sort of electoral misconduct it is no more representative of the electorate, and it will endanger the flourishing of the rule of law; the government actually loses its social empowerment credentials. Political legitimacy in a democratic society is a function of credible, transparent and violence-free election. Citizens in democratic societies legitimize their government, because it governs according to the constitution. Political legitimacy is therefore associated with popular civic obedience from citizens, as belief in legitimacy of the authority commands the loyalty, respect and good will of the people and their compliance with the laws of their country. Government's attempt to reform the electoral system by setting up of the National Electoral Reform Committee is one of the most important steps taken by the Yar'adua's government. If well utilized, the recommendations of the committee which come mainly from the input of various stakeholders in the country will support the process of democratization.

Democracy and Peace Making

Governments at all levels in the federation should embrace tolerance dialogue and consultation with different communities in the resolution of communal and sectarian conflicts. The state should also address the fundamental problems of the aggrieved communities by means of dialogue and consultation. The November 2008 Jos religious crisis was precipitated by problems of election and politicization of religion in the multicultural setting. Thus, a culture of tolerance, transparency in governance as well as the practice of responsive and responsible leadership is required for system balance and sustenance. The point is that when leaders negate the interest of their citizens in favor of their inordinate political ambitions they overlook the rule of law. Wherever the latter is relegated to the background, animosity and acrimony break into the relationship between the state and society.

Conclusion

Civilian rule in Nigeria has a lot of promises, but for these to be realized the political class needs to redefine their objectives within the context of proper dividends of democracy. Although mistakes and misdeeds are made at an alarming rate, the lessons of the country's nasty political experiences since 1999 can be used to hasten the process of democracy through constructive reforms in the constitution, electoral system and respect for the democratic verdicts of the electorate at any election. The institutions of democracy must represent the yearnings and aspirations of Nigerians. As a toddling democracy, the process of re-engineering of the institutions of governance for democratic consolidation may not be easy. However, what stands clear is the fact that areas of gains such as the gradual reclaim of the independence of the judiciary and the continuing participation of civil society in political reforms as in the case of the recently concluded public hearing conducted by the National Electoral Reform Committee should be encouraged. Democracy prospers when there are democrats possessing deeply rooted political values. Civil society's input in public policy-making process adds legitimacy to government, while peace and stability are the ingredients of advanced modern democracies. Nigeria has a lot of lessons to learn from the recent American elections, because they were devoid of intolerable acrimony among the contestants as well as among their followers. Nigeria is bound to move faster than the present process of democratization so that horizontal and vertical gains of democratization will be attained and consolidated for the good of the present and future generations.

References

Adejumobi, S. (1999). Demilitarization and the Search for Democratic Stability in Nigeria. Mimeo.

Apam, J. (2007). Political Parties and the Furtherance of Democratic Ideals in Nigeria: What Hope. Paper Presented at the International Conference on "Nigeria's

Democratic Development, 1999-2007): Trends, Problems, Challenges and Prospects", CDRT, Mambayya House, Kano, February 13-14, 2007.

Asobie, H.S. (2007). Presidential Address at the 25th Annual Conference of the Nigerian Political Science Association (NPSA) held at the University of Port Harcourt, on August 28-30, 2006.

Aiyede, R.E. (2008). The Role of INEC, ICPC and EFCC in Combating Political Corruption. In Adetula, V.A.O. (ed.), *Money and Politics in Nigeria*. Abuja: International Foundation for Electoral System, IFES-Nigeria.

Ayoade, J.A.A. (2008). Godfather Politics in Nigeria. In Adetula, V.A.O. (ed.), *Money and Politics in Nigeria*. Abuja: International Foundation for Electoral System, IFES-Nigeria.

BBC News, Monday 23, April, 2007.

Bangura, Y. (1986). The Nigerian Economic Crisis. In Peter Lawrence (ed.), *World Recession and the Food Crisis in Africa*. London: James Curry.

Bako, S. (2002). The Crisis of Transition to Democracy under Obasanjo Presidency. In Jega, A.M. et. al. (eds.), *Democracy and Democratization in Nigeria* (1999-2001). Kano: CDRT.

Bako, S. (2007). The Rise and Consolidation of Garrison Democracy in Nigeria, 1999-2007. Paper presented at the 2-Day Conference on the theme: *Nigeria's Democratic Development: 1999-2007*. Organized by the Centre for Democratic Research and Training, Mambayya House, Kano.

CDP/CDRT Report (2008). *Financing Political Parties in Nigeria, 1999-2007*. Kano: CDRT.

Diamond, L. (1993). Three Paradoxes of Democracy. In Diamond and Marc F. Plattner (eds.), *The Global Resurgence of Democracy*. Baltimore, London: The John Hopkins University Press.

Diamond, L. (2004). The Imperative of Good Governance. Centre for International Private Enterprise, CIPE, May 2004.

Hippler, J. (1995). Democratization of the Third World after the End of the Cold war. In Jochen Hippler (ed.), *The Democratization of Disempowerment: The Problems of Democracy in the Third World*. London: Pluto Press.

Igbuzor, O. (2003). Privatization in Nigeria: Critical Issues of Concern to Civil Society. Paper presented at a *Power Mapping Roundtable Discussion on Privatization Programme in Nigeria*, organized by Socio-Economic Rights Initiative (SERI), held at Niger Links Hotel, Abuja, September.

Johnson, J.K. (2001). An Overview of the Three Functions of Legislative Trends in the Field of Legislative Development. *International Development Group*. Belgium, October 22.

Jega, A.M. (2002). Challenges to the Achievement of Nigeria's Security Objectives. Paper presented at the conference on the theme: *Building Peace and Security in Nigeria*, organized jointly by the Centre for Democracy and Development (CDD), the Centre for Global, International and Regional Studies (CGIRS), and the Centre for International Policy (CIP), September 16-18, in Washington DC, USA.

__________ (2003, Sunday 19). Economic Crisis and Democratization? *New Nigerian.*

__________ (2007). *Democracy, Good Governance and Development in Nigeria.* Ibadan: Spectrum Books Limited.

Leadership Newspaper, 2009, March 2.

Lydia, P. (2006). Money and Violence Hobble Democracy in Nigeria. *The New York Times* (Online). Retrieved from http://www.nytimes.com/2006/11/24/world/africa/24 nigeria.html?

Lubeck, M.J. et al. (2007). Convergent Interests: U.S. Energy Security and the "Securing" of Nigerian Democracy". *International Policy Report.* Washington, DC: Centre for International Policy.

Mohammed, H. (2005). Human Rights and The Rule of Law: Challenges for National Security Under a Civilian Regime in Nigeria, 1999-2004. In Ikonne C. et. al (eds.), *Security Social Services and Sustainable Development in Nigeria.* Port Harcourt: University of Port Harcourt Press.

Mohammed, H. (2008). The IMF/World Bank Structural Adjustment Programme (SAP) and Poverty Generation: The Experience of Public Sector Workers in Nigeria. In Mustapha D. Duze et al. (eds.), *Poverty in Nigeria, Causes, Manifestations and Alleviation Strategies.* London: Adonis and Abbey Publishers Ltd.

Momoh, A. (2007). Provisional Notes on Authoritarian Democracy in Nigeria. Paper Presented at the International Conference on the theme: *Nigeria's Democratic Development, 1999-2007: Trends, Problems, Challenges and Prospects*, organized CDRT, Mambayya House, Kano, February, 13-14, 2007.

Obiyan, A.S. (1999). Political Parties under the Abubakar Transition Programme and Democracy in Nigeria. *A Journal of Opinion*, Vol. 27, No. 1.

Okonji-Iweala, N. (2006). Nigeria's Economic Reforms: Progress and Challenges. *Brookings Global Economy and Development Working Paper* 6, March.

Omotola, J.S. (2007). Democratization, Good Governance and Development in Africa: The Nigerian Experience. *Journal of Sustainable Development in Africa*, Vol. 9, No. 4.

Sani, S. (2008). *Civilian Dictators of Africa.* Lagos: Prestige Publishers.

Smah, O. (2008). Money Politics and Electoral Violence in Nigeria. In Adetula, V.A.O. (ed.), *Money and Politics in Nigeria.* Abuja: International Foundation for Electoral System (IFES), Nigeria.

Svolik, M. (2007). Authoritarian Reversals and Democratic Consolidation. Paper Presented at IPES Inaugural Conference, USA.

Tamuno, T.N. (1997). Nigerian Federalism in Historical Perspective: Overarching Issues. In Amuwo, K., Suberu, R., Agbaje, A., and Herault, G. (eds.), *Federalism and political Restructuring in Nigeria.* Ibadan: Spectrum Books Limited.

Wiard, H.J. (2002). Introduction: Democracy and Democratization – Product of the Western Tradition or a Universal Phenomenon? In Howard J. Wiarda (ed.),

Comparative Democracy and Democratization. Orlando: Harcourt College Publishers.

Weingast, R.B. (1997, February). The Political Foundation of Democracy and the Rule of law. *American Political Science Review*. Vol. 91.

Yaqub, N. (2006). The Academic Community and the 2007 General Elections. Paper presented at a 1-day seminar organized by the Independent National Electoral Commission (INEC) at the Hamdala Hotel, Kaduna on 29th November.

2

Political Participation and Accountability: An Appraisal of Some Salient Democratic Tenets in Oyo State Nigeria

Lanre Olutayo and Tunde Abisoye

Introduction

The turnout of voters at elections is often perceived as a sufficient demonstration of peoples' participation in democracy. However, literatures have established that participation transcends voting if development is to be achieved. Limited participation by the people in democratic and development process has therefore been a major concern. The study examined the extent of participation of citizens beyond voting at the community levels in the democratic process and its implication for development as perceived at community level. Results showed that highly influentlal party patrons wield overriding influence on political parties' machineries and even government functionaries. The findings imply that contrary to democratic ideals, active involvement of the people in the democratic process at community level is weak, thereby leading to non-accountability of elected officials. Governments' development projects hardly improved people's lives as public input was lacking. The paper recommends mass political education of the electorates and politicians as a means of deepening the democratic process.

Conceptualizing Democracy

The concept 'democracy' is bitterly contested to this day. Although an almost inexhaustible literature exists on it, there is a glaring absence of consensus by scholars on the appropriate delineation of the nature and contours of the term. It is rather difficult to argue for a specific conceptualization of the term as the proper meaning. (Olowu, 1995; Olaitan, 1992; Oluokun, 2000).

There is, however, a modicum of consensus on the building blocks of democratic rule. These are free and fair elections through which the people may hold their representatives accountable for their actions or inactions; the rule of law which acts as a protective shield for the citizens and guarantees their access to the judiciary and their human rights, which at the very least entails the freedoms of expression, peaceful assembly and association; separation of powers among the three arms of government, namely, the executive, the legislature and the judiciary; majority rule which protects the rights of minorities; entrenchment of democratic political culture which is critical to the long-term consolidation of democratic rule and institutionalization of democracy as a sustainable system of governance; and discussion and compromise as means of conflict resolution. It is felt that where these pillars of democracy are firmly in place, they should, other things being equal, lead to the institutionalization of good government. A good government according to Obadan (1998) should be attentive, listen to the civil society, work in partnership with it (i.e. encourage citizens' participation in governance) and effectively carry out the following tasks:

(i) establish a foundation of law and order
(ii) maintain a non-distortionary policy environment
(iii) invest in basic social services and infrastructure
(iv) protect the vulnerable groups in the society
(v) protect the environment.

Democracies had been argued to have a great advantage of providing for moderate change, hence, it provides a better political framework for national development, the freedom of association and of expression, and participation inherent in democracies are values in themselves, independent of their values as means of attainment of other goals.

Democracy can be deduced to mean the free expression and determination by the people of a polity of how their society should be governed. The translation of this expression into action through appropriate policies and programmes is the function and, indeed, the purpose of government. Thus, democracy is the essence of the social contract between the people and the government. Once there is loss of faith in the social contract, and the feedback mechanism between government and the people breaks down, democracy becomes only a process of meaningless rituals. It (democracy), therefore, encourages the development of the feedback process of information dissemination. In such a system, the participatory role of the civil society is very crucial as it receives and digests political messages from the government with variable outcomes. Where the outcomes are the expected ones, the legitimacy and popular acceptance of the government is enhanced. However, where the outcomes are conflictual, there are usually feedbacks to government through the media, grapevines, protest and/or increased pressure-group activities. These feedbacks, which form part of fallouts from people's participatory role, are necessary to make government adjust particular policies (like in the case of fixing prices of petroleum products) to meet the expectations of the people. Democracy can, therefore, only make sense to the ordinary people if they are active participants in its processes, and if eventually they become better off through the implementation of concrete policies and programmes of a genuinely democratic government.

Authoritarianism has manifested itself in Nigeria through years of military rule marked by absence of debate on issues of public interest, through intimidation, disregard of civil rights and non-chalant attitudes towards due process and the rule of law. This has left an intolerant environment in which "the language of politicians is still militaristic and people resort to violence to settle issues" (IDEA, 2000). This is a marked contrast to a democratic culture where the people freely debate issues and help to build their own future, free from unwarranted interference by the state and its collaborators. In essence, a democratic system is such that dispenses with the military culture of arbitrariness, command-and-obey syndrome, and intemperate language, total absence of debate, intimidation of civil society, disregard for civil rights, absence of the rule of law and due process, and the emasculation of the judiciary.

The outcome of a research conducted by IDEA (2000: 5) listed the following indicators as prerequisites for having a consolidated constitutional democracy: a successful and transparent fight against corruption; poverty reduction for economic performance; security; provision of physical infrastructure; gender equality; ethnic, religious and regional harmony; strategy to facilitate citizens' participation in governance processes and to encourage strategic thinking, a national outlook, patience and tolerance among the elites; innovative management of civil-military relations to foster military subordination to civil authority.

Furthermore, the report proposed an electoral reform which would entail the following issues: independence and autonomy of the electoral commission; public and open process of nominating electoral commissioner; public hearings on nominees before selection; early registration of voters; free formation and organization of political parties.

Formal rules which together provide a minimal definition of democracy have been expressed by Bobbio (as cited in Akanji 2002) in a number of variously overlapping formulations. They may, however, be presented under the following five headings:

(i) Political elections should take place with equal and universal (or at least "very broad") suffrage and recur within a reasonable degree of periodicity;

(ii) Individuals should be free to vote according to their own judgement, formed as freely as possible in the context of open competition between rival political groupings;

(iii) "Real alternatives" should be put before the voters in order to give them a choice between genuinely different political solutions;

(iv) The principle of majority decision should be followed in the resolutions of elective assemblies (or. of compromise decision in the case of the "consociational or neo-corporatist" democracies);

(v) Some limits should be set to the legal extent of majority decisions, in the sense that no decision should violate the political rights of minority nor prevent it from itself becoming, given equal opportunity, a majority.

At the minimum, according to Diamond and Leornardo (2004), democracy requires (i) universal adult suffrage; (ii) recurring, free, competitive and fair elections; (iii) more than one serious political party; (iv) and alternative source of information. The broad conditions for achieving democracy-induced growth and development, in the opinion of Okpanachi (2005) include: minimal corruption, fair electoral process, a well-mobilized political class, favourable external environment, harmonious intergovernmental relations, effective conflict management mechanism, the will to develop and good governance based on power separation. Some scholars and philosophers had endeavoured to explain the essence and basis for formation of governments. Governance, as observed by Schmitter (2003), is a method or mechanism for dealing with a broad range of problems and conflicts in which actors regularly arrive at mutually satisfactory and binding decisions by negotiating and deliberating together and cooperating in the implementation of the decisions.

Democracy as a way of organizing the state has come to be narrowly identified with territorially based competitive elections of political leadership for legislative and executive offices. Yet, increasingly, this mechanism of political representation seems ineffective in accomplishing the central ideals of democratic politics, which is facilitating active political involvement of the citizenry, forging political consensus through dialogue, devising and implementing public policies that ground a productive economy and healthy society in a more radical egalitarian version of the democratic ideal, assuring that all citizens benefit from the nation's wealth.

Rather than seeking to deepen the democratic character of politics, the much political energy thrust in recent years has been to reduce the role of politics altogether. Deregulation, privatization, reduction of social services and curtailments of state spending have been the preoccupation of the government rather than engaged public participation, greater responsiveness, more creative and effective forms of democratic state intervention. The task of instituting democratic values and elements into a society that had been "militarized" is surely enormous.

Okpanachi (2005) and Akande (2003) observe that after almost four years into democratic experiment, Nigeria is still saddled with myriad of problems and true democracy remains elusive. What exists, according to him, is a government with a semblance of military rule.

Since it is impracticable for everybody to take part directly in the running of public affairs, the device by which few people required are chosen to perform these tasks has become a crucial test of how democratic a political system is so also is the extent to which those who are entrusted with the exercise of power are accountable to the people, and the disposition as well as the ability of the latter to ensure that their elected representatives act in their interest (Akinola, 1992). Many scholars, such as Joseph (2003), contend that democracy must be considered within the larger context of the social, political and economic problems. Democratization should, therefore, facilitate economic development, and economic development should be conducted democratically.

The pertinent questions that immediately come to mind are: what manner of relationship exists between the government and the people? Are the people part of decision-making process, and are their elected representatives accountable to them? Is the political system really democratic or merely civil?

Research Questions

Following are the definitive questions that this research seeks to answer:

1. What relationship exists between the politicians and the electorates pre/post elections.
2. Are the elected officials accountable to the electorates or not?
3. Are the elected representatives accessible and how much consideration do they give to electorates' views in the formulation of government policies?

Objectives of the Study

The general objective of this study is to sociologically investigate the relationship between politicians and electorates with a view to examining the extent to which the people are involved in the democratic structures in Oyo State (the nature of relationship) and its effect on development. Specifically, the study attempted to:

1. critically appraise the nature of interaction/relationship between electorates and politicians since the advent of the fourth republic.
2. assess people's perception of the extent of accountability of the elected representatives.
3. find out the extent to which the people are consulted by the people in government before the formulation of government policies.

According to Olaitan (1992), "A basic presupposition of democracy is that every member of 'the people' (electorates) has the opportunity of taking part in societal decision-making". The central theme of any democracy, therefore, is the people's popular participation. Contrarily however, Mabogunje (1995) reported that there is pervasive feeling of alienation among Nigerians. The need to further investigate this contradiction forms the major concern of this study.

Oyo State was chosen for the study in view of its socio-political history. The state has Ibadan as its capital and it can be described as the political nerve of Western Nigeria considering the fact that its capital city is the largest populated city in the country Nigeria (Adetunji, 1999). The state could be highly volatile politically bearing in mind the political upheavals of the First and Second Republics.

The populations of this study are the residents with suffrage right in 10 local governments in Oyo State. These are adults that have attained voting age of eighteen years. However, for its vastness such a population cannot be listed for sampling purposes. Hence, the study adopts a multi-stage sampling approach for the study. One thousand samples were initially targeted for the study but only the 949 (nine hundred and forty-nine) samples that responded formed the basis of the study. The focus of this study was mainly to investigate the nature of interaction/interrelationship between the people and their elected representatives in the local and state governments.

Firstly, in line with the three geo-political senatorial districts constitutional stipulation, Oyo State was clustered into three. The 10 LGAs studied were then randomly selected in the proportion of 4:3:3 from Oyo South, Oyo North and Oyo Central senatorial districts respectively, based on the 1991 population census result which reflected the population proportion as such.

Table 2.1: List of LGAs Studied/Pattern of Selection of Total No of Households

Senatorial District	*L/G Studied*	*Total No of Households*	*No of Households Selected*
Oyo South	Ibadan North	68464	254
	Ibadan South East	52278	194
	Ibarapa Central	13212	49
	Iddo	12085	45
Oyo North	Saki East	10041	31
	Ogbomosho North	23752	88
	Iseyin	26984	100
Oyo Central	Oyo West	17631	65
	Lagelu	14963	56
	Akinyele	30257	112
Total		269667	1000

Source: 2006 Field Survey.

Data Collection Instrument

Qualitative Data:

To obtain qualitative in-depth information and insight from the study population, combinations of two techniques were used, namely, In-depth Interviews (IDIs) and Focus Group Discussions (FGDs). The use of these techniques was meant to provide a deeper insight into some issues raised in quantitative data that might need further and/or wider explanation or clarification.

Focus Group Discussions (FGDs): A total sum of twelve FGD sessions were held at an average of four in each of the senatorial district. Each of the sessions comprised 6-10 volunteers who are registered voters among the age groups. The grouping of the participants was based on age and gender as follows:

Groups:

(i) Youths, 18 to 39 years (male);

(ii) Youths, 18 to 39 years (female);

(iii) Old males Group, 40 years and above;

(iv) Old females Group, 40 years and above.

It is presumed that members of the same age bracket and gender have the tendency of relating more cordially than otherwise.

FGDs were held at different locations in each of the senatorial districts as follows:

Table 2.2: List of Locations where FGDs were Held

	Oyo North Senatorial District	*Oyo Central Senatorial District*	*Oyo South Senatorial District*
FGD sessions	Locations	Locations	Locations
FGD with Youths Male 18-39 yrs	Ago Amodu in Saki East Local Govt.	Ikereku in Akinyele Local Govt.	Iddo in Iddo Local Govt.
FGD with Youth Female 18-39 yrs	Arowomole Area in Ogbomosho North Local Govt.	Lalupon in Lagelu Local Govt.	Bodija in Ibadan North Local Govt.
FGD with Adult Male 40 yrs & above	Koso Area in Iseyin Local Govt.	Ojongbodu in Oyo West Local Govt.	Lasogbon Area in Igboora in Ibarapa Central Local Govt.
FGD with Adult Female 40 yrs & above	Ori Oke Area in Ogbomosho North Local Govt.	Moniya in Akinyele Local Govt.	Eleta Area in Ibadan South-East Local Govt.

Source: 2006 Field Survey.

In-depth Interview (IDI) with Key Informants

Certain categories of opinion moulders in each of the three senatorial districts were purposively selected and interviewed. After clustering various interest groups together, eight randomly-selected individuals were interviewed

Table 2.3 : Pattern of Selection of No of Households per L/G

Senatorial District	*No of L/Gs in the District*	*Population Size*	*Percentage of population*	*Noof L/Gs Studied*	*Total No of House-holds*	*Total No of Households sampled*	*List of LGs Randomly selected*
Oyo Central	11	997.030	29	3	62,851	233	Oyo West L/G Akinyele L/G Lagelu L/G
Oyo North	13	1,005,793	29	3	60,777	225	Saki East L/G Iseyin LG Ogbomoso North L/G Isevin L/G
Oyo South	9	1,449,897	42	4	146,039	542	Ibadan North L/G Ibadan South East L/G Ibarapa Central & Iddo L/G
Total	33	3,452,720	100%	10	269,667	1,000	

Source: 2006 Field Survey.

in each senatorial division as follows: one elected local government chairman; chairman of the ruling party in a local government within the district; one religious leader; a youth leader in a political party; chairman of an opposition party; chairman of local government traditional council (i.e. a prominent traditional ruler); chairman of a Community Development Association; and a leader of Market Women Association.

Thus, a total number of 24 key informants were interviewed altogether using well-prepared guide to elicit far-reaching responses and in-depth information from respondents.

Quantitative Data

Quantitative data were generated through the use of carefully-packaged data questionnaire. Indeed, the survey questionnaire was structured in such a manner that it captured the nature of relationship between the politicians and the electorates vis-à-vis the nature of the people's participation in the democratic and development process. A total of 1000 questionnaires were administered in 10 selected local government areas. The samples were proportionally distributed among the 10 selected local governments based on the number of households in each local government. However, only 949 (nine hundred and forty-nine) questionnaires were retrieved for analysis.

The total number of households in the ten selected Local Governments based on 1991 census is 269,667. When the total number of households is divided by the total number of samples to be drawn (i.e. 269,667 ÷ 1000) we got 269.66, approximately 270.

In order to ensure evenness in the selection of households, the total number of households in each local government selected was divided by 270 to determine the number of households to be selected in each local government. One sample was drawn in each of the selected household in the ten local governments.

The systematic random sampling technique was adopted to select the sample population. This technique foreclosed the problems that are often associated with survey research, namely, distribution, representativeness and variation in LGA sizes.

Objective I: Relationship between the Politicians and the Electorate

In spite of the various avenues which the electorate can explore to interact with their elected representatives and vice-versa as shown in the table below, it is discovered that about 58% of the respondents claimed not to have had any contact in whatever form with any of their elected representatives. This discovery portrays a sort of lack of desired contact between the people and their representatives in government. In a situation where there is no effective interaction between the elected representatives and the electorates one wonders the extent to which the people's representatives really represent them, because communication gap may make adequate representation impossible.The mechanism that sets the game (democracy) in motion is the mix of wills, wishes, desires and fears found among the members of society. Some seek to realize their goals through the representative they favour and from whom they hope to gain favour, or patronage or advantage. But their aspirations can hardly be fulfilled where the person to defend their cause is so 'detached' from them. This type of poor and weak link could be frustrating and breed disaffection in the system. This might have led to the declining attitude of the electorates towards democracy as reported by Afro-Barometer (2001), which states thus: "Nigerians are less content with current political circumstances than they were eighteen months ago, and less enthusiastic about the system of democracy."

Table 2.4: Relationship between Electorate and Politicians

	Frequency	*Per cent*
No contact at all	550	58.0
Holding community consultative meeting	129	13.6
Individual persons visit to politician	66	7.0
Holding meetings at the instance of politician	99	10.4
Meeting politicians at social functions	47	5.0
Sending delegations to politician by the community	54	5.7
Others	4	0.4
Total	**949**	**100.0**
Perception of the Nature of Relationship between Politicians and Electorate		
	Frequency	Per cent
Very cordial	299	31.5
Fairly cordial	496	52.3
Not cordial	91	9.6
Suspicious	34	3.6
No response	29	3.1
Total	**949**	**100.0**
Can the Relationship Enhance Democracy?		
	Frequency	Per cent
Yes	333	35.1
No	616	64.9
Total	949	100.0
How to Enhance Cordial Relationship between Politicians and Electorates		
By sending money to electorates	105	11.0
By effecting developmental projects	294	31.0
By sending delegates to politicians	69	7.3
By holding regular meetings with them	441	46.5
Others	40	4.2
Total	**949**	**100.0**

Source: 2006 Field Survey.

The number of respondents who described the relationship as very cordial according to table 4 above is only 31.5%, while those who view the relationship as 'Fairly cordial' are 52.3%; 9.6% describe it as not cordial at all and 3.6% are of the opinion that the relationship is suspicious. As many as 64.9% felt that the nature of the relationship as it obtains presently is not good enough for enhancement of democracy. On the respondents' recommendations on how to promote cordial relationship between the people and their elected representatives, 46.5% felt that holding regular meetings with the elected representatives would do the 'trick'; 11% believed that sharing money with the electorates should be the way out; and 31% are of the view that the relationship can be enhanced if the elected representatives would fulfill their electioneering promises by effecting developmental projects in their various localities.

Juxtaposing the various findings during the field survey with the outcomes of both IDIs and FGDs, it was discovered that the general perception of the interviewees and focus group discussants on the nature of relationships between the electorates and their representatives is that the relationship leaves much to be desired. A participant at a FGD session stated:

> "...there is hardly any form of relationship between us from time. I don't know any one of them (elected representatives) and they don't know me. Then what relationship are we talking about?" (Male FGD, Oyo South Senatorial District, 40 years and above, 2006).

Another person at the same forum cut in:

> "...even those of us who have relatives among them, do we see them again? When one gets to their office they are either busy holding official meetings or away to attend a seminar. And when you go home they are either not around or sleeping".

The various outcomes as analysed above showed that the nature of relationship between the electorate and politicians especially after the general elections needs a sort of reappraisal, because the relationship as it obtains presently is far from being healthy for the enhancement of an enduring democracy.

Objective II: Level of Accountability of People in Government

The general opinion as regards the table 2.5 below is that the elected representatives are not doing enough in terms of accountability. Only 25% scored their elected representatives in the local government high, while 29.1% did the same thing with the state. It is indeed an irony that the local government which is expected to be the nearest to the people at the grassroots scores a lower rating even than the state; although a high segment of the respondents (61.1%) perceived the local government representatives as being fairly accountable, while 59% of the same sample rated the state as such.

This finding may have a bearing on the role of mass media in dissemination of information on government activities to the people. The State Government seems to be at an advantage at the use of mass media especially electronic media in reaching out to the people; whereas, the local governments often depend on interpersonal contact of its functionaries (who hardly go back to their constituencies after having being elected) with the people. This implies a stoppage of networking process after having election.

Table 2.5: Accountability of the Elected Representatives in L/G & State Government

	Frequency	*Percent*
Degree of accountability by representatives in Local Government		
Very accountable	237	25.0
Fairly accountable	580	61.1
Poorly accountable	89	9.4
Accountable at all	43	4.5
Total	**949**	**100.0%**
Degree of accountability by representatives in State Government		
Very accountable	276	29.1
Fairly accountable	560	59.0
Poorly accountable	72	7.6
Accountable at all	41	4.3
Total	**949**	**100.0%**

Source: 2006 Field Survey

Similar views expressed in the table above characterized the various opinions expressed during the Focus Group Discussion as captured by the following extracts:

> ...the people (referring to the elected representatives) have run away with our mandate. (Male FGD, 40 years & above, Oyo South Senatorial District)

Another discussant cuts in:

> ...we don't know what is going on in government, except the little information that we can gather through the radio. (Male FGD, Oyo North Senatorial District)

At another FGD session the opinion expressed includes:

> ...don't they suppose to be coming back to give us a report from time to time. "Bi irun agbon alagbase ba gun to apa, eniti o gbe oko fun saa ni oga re", meaning that "a labourer may be heftier than the owner of the work, yet his employer is the boss". (Male FGD, Adult group, Oyo South Senatorial District).

A participant in another FGD session, while speaking on accountability of their elected representatives stated:

...they are only accountable to their immediate families. They are rogues. Before we voted them, they promised that they shall count on our inputs from time to time. One of them was even nick-named "Ogun a jo bo, Ogun a jo je" meaning that "when we sacrifice together to god of iron, we shall reap the benefit together". But where are they today? (Female FGD, Oyo Central Senatorial District, 2006).

At another FGD, one of the participants stated :

...they are not accountable to us. They may be accountable to those who put them there. (Male FGD, Youth group, Oyo Central Senatorial District)

This statement was considered to be of particular significance, hence the participant was asked to explain those who he referred to as 'us', 'those' and 'them' in the statement. His explanation indicated 'us' as the electorates, 'those' as political godfathers and 'them' as elected representatives.

This contribution brings us back to the issue of overbearing roles of some opinion leaders who had, according to Manent (2003) and Omobowale (2006) assumed the status of political oligarchy. They serve as political power brokers or middlemen. They, in the spirit of networking, serve as link between the teeming electorates and their 'favoured' or 'anointed' candidates. The candidates in a bid to secure the people's mandate pledge his loyalty to the oligarchy and the electorates in order to have access to government largesse (patronage) also look up to the tiny but highly powerful oligarchy who constitute the political patrons.

Meanwhile, during the same FGD session another participant says:

...we put them there through our vote to serve us, but where are they now? You hear of them building houses, and marrying more wives. All the roads had gone bad, no social amenity to show that we have any government. Yet when we invited them to meetings they would not come. Even our councilLor [he mentioned his name] who used to be a very active member of our Community Youths Association is no longer accessible. Youths FGD, Oyo Central Senatorial District.

The various views expressed above are in congruent with the opinion of Joseph (2003) that whatever the rhetoric, the reality is that those who win government offices concentrate on serving themselves and their narrow circles of supporters.

The common denominator to all the analysis above is that there is a low rating of the level of accountability of the elected representatives. Contrary to the findings during FGDs, the general trend in the various IDIs conducted reflected that the elected representatives are accountable. In the words of one of the interviewee:

...a large majority of them (the elected representatives) are doing their best in the area of accountability. They often call on me to discuss what goes on in government with me. (Political Leader, Male IDI, Oyo North Senatorial District)

This finding further buttresses the research report by Afro Barometer (2001) that very few Nigerians have had direct contact with elected officials in the past year, preferring to turn to religious leaders or other influential persons for help with their problems.

Robertson et al. (2006: 1, 15) (qtd. in Aziken E.) also scores the Nigerian elected representatives very low in the area of accountability as follows:

> ...The one thing that we've spotted on the negative side and it was something that we picked up on the visit last year and that there is still lack of accountability by elected representatives. We visited villages and we talked to people and those that have been served with pumps have broken pipes and the pumps themselves only worked for two hours. Now, this is unacceptable, and yet when the people complained nobody does anything about it and the elected representatives have never been to their villages in the whole time they've been elected. And the only time they hear from them as representatives is when they send money or they have a party to celebrate their elections. These people want their pumps to work and they want their water to run and they want their elected representatives to go and talk to them and be accountable.

These findings are in accord with the position of some scholars like Manet (2003) who argues that delegate democracies are characterized by low level of horizontal accountability (checks and balances) and therefore exhibit powerful, plebiscitarian and occasionally abusive executive.

The various arguments above have shown that one of the negative impact of the overbearing influence of political patrons is that they, most of the time, block the free link or contact that is supposed to exist between the people and their representatives.

Objective III: Extent to which the People are Consulted by Their Elected Representatives

A large majority of the people (76.8%) with reference to the table below wish to be consulted on matters pertaining to formulation of government policies. Ironically, only 24.6% of them claimed to have been consulted on matters pertaining to their welfare. This shows how much detached the policies' formulators are from the eventual beneficiaries. Those who claimed to have been consulted either 'Very often' (6.8%) or 'Often' (8.2%) totalling 15% are in the minority, as against the 66.7% who claimed never to have been consulted. 9.1% claimed to be rarely consulted. Lack of consultation would, no doubt, have its effect and this might have been in the form of public passivity or no participation at all, thereby brewing political apathy. For example, except for 5.8% who claimed to be actively involved and 9.1% who are active, as high as 38.6% claimed not to participate at all. 37.8% regarded their involvement as very passive, while 4.4% are passive totalling 80.8%.

On the question of how projects are initiated as pertaining to identification of problems to be solved, it was discovered that only 24.3% claimed to have ever been involved in identification of problems to be solved. It means that this minority group determines the fate of the larger majority (75.7%) who claimed not to be involved.

Furthermore, 60.6% claimed that they did not participate at all in conception, execution and not even monitoring of government project 13.9% and 1.5% regarded their involvement to be passive and very passive respectively. This finding further affirms the earlier findings that democracy operates at the whims and caprices of a minority that are highly influential.

Consequent upon the foregoing analyses which indicate that the large majority of the people are not involved in solving problems facing their communities, it is therefore not surprising to discover that about 70% of the respondents claimed that government had not touched on their most pressing needs regardless of solving the problem.

On the question of accessibility of the elected representatives, 74.5% perceived them as not being accessible and only 25.5% regarded them as being accessible. This finding is further reinforced by the following discoveries. Only 7.3% and 8.2% described them as very accessible and fairly accessible respectively. Whereas an overwhelming majority, totalling 84.5%, claimed that they are either poorly accessible (38.6%) or not accessible at all (45.9%).This implies that a wide communication gap exists between the elected representatives and the people. This communication gap has a tendency of creating the feeling of being alienated in the people. The people's general ratings of the various tiers of government indicate that except for 10.8% who described the government as being 'highly democratic' and 18.1% who rated it to be 'democratic', the others scored the government low with 21.3% describing it as being 'fairly democratic', 40.6% described it as 'undemocratic' and 3.8% perceived it as 'highly undemocratic', totalling 65.1%.

These various findings, therefore, reveal that many of the developmental projects being executed by the government are being merely foisted on the people. This may, therefore, explain why there are many abandoned projects all around. The zeal to supplement government efforts would naturally be lacking in the people who do not count a project to be of relevance to their social life. These findings may also explain why the government projects get destroyed or damaged so soon. People are more likely to jealously guard any project which is of direct value to their daily living than a project which is foisted on them as a means of siphoning public funds or as a measure of satisfying selfish interest of infinitesimally small but highly powerful groups of people. Involving the people in the conception, execution and financing projects which touch their well-being would not only create a sense of belongingness in them but also ensure sustainability of such project Ake (2000).

The various findings under this section show that the present democratic structure deviates largely from the people's expectations. The various views gathered during the FGDs and IDIs largely buttress the various findings under the qualitative survey.

Table 2.6: People's Desire to be Consulted on Formulation of Government Policies?

	Frequency	*Per cent*
Want to be consulted		
Yes	749	76.8
No	220	23.2
Total	**949**	**100.0**
Been contacted before formulation of government policies		
	Frequency	Per cent
Yes	233	24.6
No	716	75.4
Total	**949**	**100.0**
How Often are the Consultation Made?		
	Frequency	Per cent
Very often	65	6.8
Often	78	8.2
Seldom/rarely	86	9.1
Never consulted	633	66.7
Don't know	32	3.4
No response	55	5.8
Total	**949**	**100.0**
Description of Participation		
	Frequency	Per cent
Very active	55	5.8
Active	86	9.1
Passive	42	4.4
Very passive	359	37.8
No participation at all	366	38.6
No response	41	4.3
Total	**949**	**100.0**
Whether the People had ever been Involved in Identifying Problems Facing their Communities		
	Frequency	Per cent
Yes	231	24.3
No	718	75.7
Total	**949**	**100.0**

Source: 2006 Field Survey.

Table 2.7: People's Ratings of their Involvement in Conception; Execution and Monitoring of Government Projects

	Frequency	*Per cent*
Very actively	71	7.5
Actively	84	8.8
Passively	132	13.9
Very passively	14	1.5
No participation	575	60.6
No response	73	7.7
Total	**949**	**100.0**
Has the most Pressing need of the Community been Met ?		
	Frequency	Per cent
Wholly	97	10.2
Partially	145	15.3
Not at all	664	70.0
Don't know	43	4.5
Total	**949**	**100.0**
Are the Elected Representatives Accessible?		
	Frequency	Per cent
Yes	242	25.5
No	707	74.5
Total	**949**	**100.0**
To what Extent are they Accessible?		
	Frequency	Per cent
Very accessible	69	7.3
Fairly accessible	78	8.2
Poorly accessible	366	38.6
Accessible at all	436	45.9
Total	**949**	**100.0**
General Ratings of the 4th Republic.		
	Frequency	Per cent
Highly Democratic	103	10.8
Democratic	172	18.1
Fairly democratic	202	21.3

(Contd.)

(Contd. Table 2.7)

	Frequency	*Per cent*
Undemocratic	385	40.6
Highly Undemocratic	32	3.8
Don't know	55	5.8
Total	**949**	**100.0**
Type of Government Favoured		
	Frequency	Per cent
Oligarchy (rule by the few)	-	-
Aristocracy (rule by the best)	-	-
Plutocracy (rule by the rich)	-	-
Ochlocracy (rule by mob)	-	-
Democracy (rule by the populace)	864	91
Militocracy (rule by the military)	85	9.0
Any other	-	-
Total	949	100.0

Source: 2006 Field Survey.

For instance, an interviewee responded:

"They are not democratic at all. They pretend to be democratic if the people's views are in agreement with their (elected representatives) opinions. But when it happens otherwise, they just apply force as if that is what they promised us. For example, who did they contact before price of petroleum products was increased beyond the limit of a common man?" (Male IDI, Oyo Central Senatorial District)

A male focus group discussant said:

"The old adage says, "He who wears the shoe knows where it pinches most". But in our own democratic setting, the reverse is the case. In this community our most pressing need is a borehole. Getting water is always a very serious problem during the dry season when the deep wells around got dried up. But instead of giving us a borehole, see what they brought (he pointed at an on-going construction work) – a television viewing centre. "Se iyen lo kan", meaning "Is that the next thing?" We have no electricity in this community to power the T.V. and they said generating set would accompany the T.V, but who will fuel it?" (Male FGD, Oyo Central Senatorial District.)

The view expressed above was further corroborated by a female discussant in Oyo North Senatorial District who stated:

> "If they had asked us, we would have asked them to repair our very bad road instead of the ongoing sinking of a new deep well. The well may not be really meant for us; otherwise it would not have been located so close to the one we have before." (Female FGD, Oyo North Senatorial District)

Most noteworthy is the answer of a traditional ruler in Oyo South District. He stated:

> "When I discovered that nothing in terms of developmental project was implemented I just called a meeting of my subjects. We identified our most pressing needs. I then went to visit our Local Government Chairman in company of some of my chiefs with a letter of request for the amenities. After a number of attempts we succeeded in meeting him. Although we had three items on the list, they had done one of it which is grading of our very bad road." (Male IDI, Oyo South Senatorial District)

The view of this interviewee is a pointer to the fact that contact or consultation could be initiated by the people. In other words, if the elected representatives would not come to seek the people's inputs into the way and manner they are governed, under the aegis of the various civil societies the people too can instead mobilize themselves to press their demands with the government with a view to enhancing their standard of living. In spite of the glaring shortcomings of the present democratic structure at enlisting the people's popular participation, it can still be gathered from the table above that a great proportion of the people (91%) still prefer democracy to any other form of government. This may not be unconnected with the harrowing experience of the people under despotic military regimes of the recent past.

The declaration of rights of man and the citizen affirms the classical meaning of democracy as a collective attribute, which immediately legitimized the mass as collective agents for self-determination. Democracy means popular power which entail peoples' participation in the act of governance. It also implies strict adherence to the principle of equality as well as the rule of law.

However, the study reflects a sort of contradiction between democratic ethos and the current governmental structure which is merely civil rather than being democratic. This finding is contrary to the widely-held view that democracy is strictly based on people's popular participation, which culminates in development. Basic to any democratic rule is the people's interaction with government with a view to effecting development. According to the most generic notion of democracy now popular in the international arena, we may assume that questions of legitimacy of a policy should always be addressed by those who seek its benefits and bear its cost. Anything otherwise would amount to a state that does not exist in the consciousness of the people which according to Ayoade (1988) is "a state without citizen".

Based on the outcome of this study, it has been established that there is a lack of effective communication flow (consultations) between the people and their representatives in government. In the opinion of Abudu (2003) as confrontation replaces consultation and accommodation, the government and the governed become adversaries of each other. Obviously, strategies of planning for the population without their active involvement create a lot of stress for the people. Such approach negates the most important element in the democratic process which stipulates consultation with the people in designing what is claimed to benefit them. The ideals of democracy still dictate that the choice of socio-economic objectives and related goals should be made voluntarily by the people. Once objectives have been identified, policy experts should then be invited to offer advice about the alternative strategies for meeting the objectives so that the citizenry may choose among affordable options. Whereas, this study has established that there is a defective communication link between the people and their representatives; it can be deduced from the various arguments that effective consultations between the electorate and their representatives form the fulcrum for development. The weak link between the government and the people as revealed in this study probably justifies the low rating of the development process under this political dispensation by the people.

Any democracy that therefore plays down people's participation may not be on the right path to development. Participation, when and if effective, has a particularly crucial relationship to all other social and political goals. Through participation the goals of the society are set in such a way as to maximize the allocation of benefits in the society to match the needs and desires of the populace.

It is, however, worrisome to note that it was discovered in the course of this study that hardly does any relationship exist between the electorate and their elected representatives after the general elections. This lack of effective interaction takes its toll in form of stultified development in the various communities.

The problem of democratization in Nigeria is not only the consequence of the absence of democratic norms and values, or of the preponderance of capitalist relations and the concomitant struggles, its components are the related problems of citizenship and statehood. This derives largely from the "father-figure" posture which the parties representatives assume soon after being elected. They assume the position without playing the roles expected of them. The various religious teachings also support the idea that "leaders are made by God". In other words, no leader could be without it being ordained by God. The leader, therefore, perceives themselves as symbol of the 'deity'. This socialization process makes the representatives assume the status of people with unfettered authority over the resources of the country. This reflects in the existing lopsided salary structure in favour of political office-holders, whereas an average graduate earns about seventeen thousand naira monthly, a councilor's monthly salary is over one hundred thousand naira. The resultant effect of which is the wide gap in the economic status of the electorate and the elected representatives. This culminates in non-existence or (at best) ineffective economic middle class which is one of the requirements for having an enduring democracy.

The wide communication gap between the people and their representatives may also have some bearing to the long period of military intervention in the nation's history. The fact that many of the key positions in government are now being occupied by retired military officers speaks volumes of the leadership styles as it may not be easy for someone who had been trained to believe in unitary authoritarianism to become a committed democrat overnight.

To build a truly democratic society and culture would naturally take a long time of determination and purposefulness. The democratic culture must manifest itself in all spheres and at all levels of society from the family to ancient traditional institutions, from age groups to social clubs and political parties. The socialization role of the family should be made to be in consonance with those of other agencies. This will constitute basis for the cultivation of a strong and united national character, which will create a fertile ground for true democratic culture.

Recommendations

To be sustainable, democracy must become internalized in the society. It must be a way of life manifesting itself at all levels of the social and political systems. This goal can be achieved through political education. The teaching of basic concepts of democracy and development may be included in the school curriculum at formal education level, while at informal level the campaign for the internalization of democratic ethos could be attained through mass media advertisement and participation of the people in politically-oriented seminars and workshops.

Finally, popular participation, being at the heart of a people-centered development paradigm, looks up to justice, empowerment, accountability, human rights and people's sovereignty as the defining principles of authentic development. Development in such circumstance becomes a people's movement and governments' primary role becomes an enabling one of providing people with the opportunity and environment for self-development.

References

Abudu, A.O. 2003. Imported development policies and why they don't work, *History and Philosophy of Science for African Undergraduates*, Helen Lauer Ed.; Hope Publications – Ibadan Nig. 165-169.

Afro, Barometer 2001. *Down to Earth: Change in Attitude toward Democracy and Markets in Nigeria*, SMS limited, Western House Lagos, p.1.

Akande, H.A. 2003. *Getting Nigeria to work again: A blue-print for poverty eradication and economic empowerment security to lives and property*, Economic Recovery and Socio-political Stability in Nigeria. Presented at the All Nigerian People's Party (ANPP) Convention, 2003.

Akanji, T.A (2002). Democracy rule of the law and development in Nigeria; *A public lecture* organized by Job Advocacy Foundation on 14th October, 2002.

Ake, C. 1993. "The unique case of African democracy". *International Affairs*, Vol. 62, No. 2, pp. 240-242.

Ake, C 2000. "Travail of democracy". *Council for the development of social science research in Africa*, Great Britain: Antony Rowe Ltd Clippenham, Wiltshire.

Akinola, G.A. 1992. "Factor in the development of a democratic ethos in Africa". *Democracy, Democratization and Africa*. L.A. Thompson, Ed. Africa-Links Books, pp. 17-19.

Alan, S. (ed) 1998. *What is Social Theory*? Black Publishers Inc.

Ayoade, J.A.A. 1988. The African Search for democracy: Hopes and Reality, *Democracy and Pluralism in Africa*. D. Romen Eds. Lyme Riencer Publishers, Colorado, 19-33.

Aziken, E. 2006. "British MPs Slam Nigerian Colleagues on Poor Accountability", *Vanguard*, Nov. 13:1 & 15.

Dalton, R.J. Scarrow, S. E. and Cain, B. E. 2004. "Advanced democracies and new politics. *Journal of Democracy*, Vol. 15 No. 1, January 2004.

Diamond 1990. "The illusion of liberal autocracy". *Journal of Democracy*, 14.4:169.

International Institute for Democracy and Electoral Assistance – IDEA 2000. *Democracy in Nigeria continuing dialogue(s) for nation-building*. Bulls Tryckeri, Halmstad: Sweden, 4.

Joseph, R. 2003. "African states in crisis". *Journal of Democracy*, 14.3:159-169.

Kanayo, E 2004- A new openin. *Journal of Democracy*, Vol. 15, No. 2, April 2004 pp. 125-132.

Manent, P. 2003. "Modern democracy as a system of separations", *Journal of Democracy*, 14.1:114-125.

Obadan, M.I. 1998 The Building Blocks of Democracy; Text of the welcome address delivered by the president, Nigerian Economic society at the public lecture delivered by Prof Adebayo Adedeji on Democracy, Growth and Development: Lessons of Experience.

Okpamachi, U.M. (2005) – Democratic Governance, Growth and development: The Nigeria experience; *International Review of Politics and Development*, Vol. 3 No 1 Jannuary 2005.

Olaitan, W.A. 1992. *Democracy and democratization in Africa: not yet the glorious dawn: Proceedings of the Symposium on democratic transition in Africa*, in B. Cargo, A. Gboyega and E. Osaghae, (eds) *Documents in Social Sciences and the Humanities*, CREDU, Ibadan, No.1, 434-435.

Olowu, D. 1995. *Transition to Democratic Government in Africa*. Ibadan Spectrum Books.

Oluokun, A. 2000. The transition and the media. *African Journal Political Science*, 5.2.33.

Omobowale, O.O. 2006. "Political Clientelism and Rural Development in Selected Communities in Ibadan, Nigeria", Ph.D. thesis, Department of Sociology, University of Ibadan, xii, 201.

Schmitter, C.P. 2003. Democracy in Europe and Europe's Democratization. *Journal of Democracy*, vol. 14, No.4, 72.

3

The Publics and Democratization in Nigeria

Olutayo, A.O.

Introduction

Societies have always been preoccupied with the issue of how best to structure governance. This suggests that governance is by far one of the most important existential needs of mankind, no matter the level of organization or position in the development process. Right from the pristine and the so-called "simple/pre-historic" era to the contemporary complex societies, governance remains central to the survival of human groupings. The pivotal and esteemed position accorded governance and its associated activities depends on the crucial roles they play in allocation of values, rights, privileges, maintenance of groups' solidarity, security and prevention of disintegration. Hence, governance and its structures form the image of the group and they determine the level of wellness of all, both at private and public domains. These domains include individual/micro-processes and collective/aggregate outcomes. If fundamental problems exist at governance level, therefore, the consequences are bound to be far-reaching and disastrous to the group. This is particularly challenging in the globalised world of today where events in a society affect others even in thousands of kilometers away in a matter of split-second.

This is particularly the case during anthrax, HIV/AIDS and bird-flu outbreaks, refugees and asylum seekers epidemic which were due to unresponsive, reactive and irresponsible governments in some parts of the world, that exert overwhelming impacts on other parts of the world. Governance is therefore a sensitive environment that stakeholders currently pay attention to given its multiplier effects when things go wrong or right around the world. The debate today, therefore, has been what the best form of government that can deliver public goods, protect fundamental rights and engineer development is. Why are current arrangements not achieving these vital needs and indicators? While all over the world and periods in history, people have instituted varying forms of governance with differing degrees of popular participations (monarchy, military, clan and democracy amongst others) (Olutayo and Omobowale, 2005), increasingly global embrace of democracy suggests it is "the only game in town". This democratic hurricane has given rise to such notions and concepts as "democratized societies", "transition societies", "early and late democracies", and so on.

While military regimes are obviously out of fashion, as often demonstrated through global negative reactions to their emergence, and monarchical systems are being dismantled and challenged, democratic governments are being strengthened, encouraged and reinforced, especially as closed Islamic regions and nations now express widespread support for democracy (Inglehart, nd). Inglehart's (nd) discovery is against hitherto speculations that basic values of Islamic publics may be incompatible with ideals of liberal democracy. Present happenings and projections, therefore, suggest favourable democratic course of events in a manner that makes one feels "There is No Alternative" (TINA) (see Olutayo, Olutayo and Omobowole, 2008 for detail exposition of TINA framework in international political economy) to democracy as practised in the United States of America and Western Europe. As Nigeria wholeheartedly embraces the 'TINA' framework of democratization and governance, observable events and measurable indicators reveal the need to engage in further interrogation of ideal democracy, 'Nigerian democracy' and noticed disjuncture as interface and causes of failed development trajectories codified in the popular 'dividends of democracy' as national governance conscientization instruments.

Democracy as Ideal Type

To put the foregoing discourse in appropriate perspectives, it is necessary to characterize the nature of democracy itself. Noteworthy is the fact that the objective reference to democracy and measurements of its performances are against the ideal constructs. Just like the Max Weber constructions of bureaucracy in the wake of Industrial Revolution in the 19th century to solve management crises, democracy is generally an ideal construct to solve governance crises especially in contemporary societies. Democracy, against this background, is a measuring framework which democratic states must aspire to meet as acceptable standard. This becomes obvious when considered in relation to the most popular definition of democracy ever adopted, that is, "the government of the people, by the people and for the people". According to Olutayo and Omobowale (2005), this universally, accepted definition potentially has the tendency to mislead people to vague and confusing ends.

The definition presupposes that every member of the society participates in government and that the government is constituted on mutual understanding with 100 per cent accountability in the provision and protection of the people. Popular participation at elections and governance, therefore, become fundamental backbone of democratic structures and institutions. Traceable to the origin of liberal democracy and the universal definition, the Euro-American model of democracy has become the mirror of what democracies should look like. This is bound to be further reinforced and legitimized with globally-applauded and uncontroversial emergence of Barrack Obama as the first black American president. Popular comments like "It is only in America that a thing like that can happen", "American has shown the world once again how to choose leaders", "This is a lesson to Nigerian leaders" and the controversial defence of Nigerian electoral process by Professor Maurice Iwu (Independent Electoral Commission [INEC] Chairman).

Embedded in these comments is the allusion that America is the torchlight in the jungle of the search for "acceptable model" of governance that this model of democracy allows for popular sovereignty, consent, equality and representative government (Joseph, 1991). These elements can be further restructured to be popular consent, political equality, majority rule and popular consultation in the process of instituting governance. These are the basic scaffolding of the Euro-American democracy and an inch deviation in origin, practice and outcomes from the "accepted" model is not considered democracy. Two points to note in rapid succession is that ideal democracy is heavily predicated on election and heavily sacrosanct in giving what is acceptable as democracy irrespective of socio-cultural compatibility or incompatibility. Democracy is, however, more than elections and should be allowed to evolve within the cultural frameworks and expectations of the people while democratic outcomes should be reflected in its transformation of people's lives.

This becomes necessary because even 'matured' democracies do not always have perfect elections/democracy but only resolve discrepancies within established democratic norms. This position was clearly shown in the case of Al-Gore-Bush elections, while the election of Obama is, in a way, a conscious socio-economic, cultural and political shift to legitimize the 'American model' of democracy. Africans should therefore be allowed to demand for their desired type of democracy and to express themselves whether are being provided it within their mental and socio-cultural expectations. This is a challenge that African intellectuals must rise up to and not always take the backseat while foreign experts dictate democratic model to be used to access local processes that can hardly be comprehended through outside spectrum no matter how standard it is.

Local and micro-studies are needed to bring hidden potent political dynamics to the fore. Professional insights and experience in Nigeria show that Nigerians, like other Africans, collectivise their cultural values, norms, social structural placements, experiences, rewards and non-rewards of political institutions in forming their attitudes about governance and its processes. This has been the case since the three fundamental system of government in Nigeria (the Hausa-Fulani centralised system, the Yoruba kingship system and Igbo acephalous system). Although the three systems were divergent in structure and compositions, they were evolved and practised to the popular support of the people and the admiration of outsiders. Hence, the level of political and institutional efficacy of such systems was never in doubt even till date. This is why even with the ascendancy of liberal democracy as mobilized by international sentiments they subsist.

Since it has been established that people draw lessons from their countries national political heritage and legacies about democracy (Mattes and Bratton, 2003), it then follows that national history will mix with democracy as 'given', and this must be appreciated as potent element that will fundamentally alter the ideal democracy construct. Measures of demand for democracy (legitimation) and its supply of democracy (institutionalization) (Mattes and Bratton, 2003) that do not prioritize local dynamics and refuse to pay attention to multi-causal elements of observable democratic outcomes will certainly achieve little. This is why even with heavy investments in democracy and its apparatuses in Nigeria, it is failing. Although research findings show that as much as 70 per cent of Nigerians prefer democracy to other forms of government (Mattes and Bratton, 2003) is encouraging, this should not be taken for granted. Nigerians' preference for democracy is bound to be traceable to the immediate past political torture this generation experienced from the earlier military administrations.

Time and events, therefore, have the capacity to generate a relapse in preference if democratic institutions are not strengthened in a manner that justifies the preference in real terms that could ensure sustainability. This can be assisted by locally mapping (through research) the demand and supply expectations of the public to enable to match actions and expectations and achieve results that have the capacity to strengthen democracy as seen by the people. "As seen by the people" is an operational clause for democracy in societies as ultimate assessment, sovereignty and sustainability rest with the people. The people are the doors to the society and windows to the future. Also, the people have the capacity to evolve their variant of democracy as understood and deemed appropriate. Since the ancient Greek experiment and experience, democracy has passed through processes of evolution to reach the ideal type today based on society and developmental challenges.

For example, while the Greeks all gathered at a centre to take decisions beneficial to all in a manner akin to African village square decision-making process, or the *Eke* market day meetings in the Igbo land precisely, social complexities necessitate representatives' voting and technology has introduced the new dimensions with electronic voting machines and digital voters' data capturing. This level of success is, however, still shrewd in controversy depending on political analysts' and actors' positions in the political equation. Democracy, therefore, is work in progress and bound to transit. Its process of evolution, adaptability and transition should be accommodated and not thwarted with uncritical indoctrinations that reify the ideal type. As already shown, early and subsisting societies have evolved democratic structures that allowed popular participation for universal survival (Olutayo and Omobowale, 2005). It then means that it is not that there has never been an alternative or there can never be one.

If contemporary global and regional happenings now tilt towards democracy and Nigeria is democratizing for various reasons, local and peculiar realities must be paid attention. Moreover, political actors and analysts must be aware that democracy as given is the ideal constructs and its practice may vary while outcomes, necessarily, only need to satisfy universal survival as determined by the people within. Thus, when people embrace democracy as it was the case since 1999 in Nigeria, it should not be confused as zenith of political development. Rather it should be conceived as the beginning of a long journey that must be threaded with care. This is because countries that fails to understand and appreciate the fact that embracing democracy is only the first step in contemporary public governance, and not the last and most important step towards democratization of citizenry (Shin and Tusalem, 2007) will certainly experience a 'post honeymoon' phase disillusionment with a democracy in which political actions declined (Ingelhart, 2002).

In fact, the post-honeymoon phase decline is already here as witnessed in the 2007 Nigerian General Elections and in other parts of Africa, where there were poor voters turn out, poor party participations, non-participation of credible candidates, stage managed primaries and general hijacking of political process by political godfathers. A piteous scenario in Nigerian democratization is that in a decade of re-democratisation there has not been commendable results observable in the quality of lives of Nigerians. In addition, it is saddening that just in a decade of re-democratization; the country is already experiencing the "post honeymoon" effect as there is regrettable decline in direct political actions. This is what Mulikita (2003) terms "Afro pessimism" as one government after another has sought to discard the democratic content of constitutions which were enthusiastically adopted and pledged to a decade ago.

The democratic reversals are clearly reflections of misconceptions and wrong practice of democracy as a form of government. In this orthodoxy, there is rapid decline in the rates at which elites challenge political behaviour while there is a growing popular elite-directed political mobilization and manipulation in the political system (see Inglehart, 2002 for details, characterisation and constructions of 'post honeymoon' decline in new democracies). How best then do we explain democratic failures in Nigeria, especially given the rising economic, social and political challenges facing the country in a magnitude that has forced some analysts to begin comparisons between current civil rule and past military regimes?

The Publics as a Theoretical Statement

Ekeh's (1975) *Colonization and the Two Publics in Africa: A Theoretical Statement* is one of the most cogent attempts to explain fundamental social dynamics in Africa which underlie and bedevil the political process (Joseph, 1991: 193). In fact, the work remains one of the most cited articles on African politics. The wide appeal of the Ekeh's (1975) work is due to its insightful analysis of the inter-penetrativeness of given cultural ethos of colonialism and local socio-cultural ethics of colonialism and local socio-cultural elements, behaviours and psychology that determine governance outcomes. Hence, Ekeh (1975) was right on time and in target in its contribution at a time in Nigeria's history and existence when African scholars and literature were relatively and comparatively immature enough to prioritize the determining influence of indigenous processes in modern public life.

The primary remit of Ekeh (1975: 91) is to argue that "The experiences of colonialism in Africa have led to the emergence of a unique historical configuration in modern post-colonial Africa; the existence of two publics instead of one public, as in the west". He further opines that "Many of Africa's political problems are due to the dialectical relationships between the two publics" (Ekeh 1975: 91). The essence of adopting Ekeh (1975) theoretical statements of the two publics is to illuminate the fundamental theoretical and empirical underpinnings of Nigerian democratization. Although Ekeh (1975) purposed to theorize on two publics, he came up with three eventually: one private and two publics. He was, however, still right on the two publics because his overall characterizations were within the two publics and his attempts to explain Africa's political dilemma were essentially within the matrix of the two publics.

In classifying his two publics, Ekeh (1975) names them the *primordial* and the *civic*. The primordial is the "sectional", "communal", and generally it has to do with ethnic sentimentalism. The civic public, according to the Ekeh (1975) classification is modern creation of colonialism with sharp expression in the military and civil service, police institutions, legal institutions, popular politics and generalized institutional structural arrangements of no original local evolution but largely based on enculturation through colonial socio-psychology and superior gun power. Another important element in *the publics* thesis is morality. The primordial public is moral, while the civic is mostly amoral. The primordial public is moral because it reflects the base and elemental priority pledged to community membership and a strong sense of citizenship, loyalty and participation. It gives a sense of home and the root. The civic from this perspective is superficial and largely baseless. It is only a space of survival for people to tailor their activities within its amoral state towards fulfilling their expected moral obligations and benefiting/sustaining the primordial public which must not falter.

According to Joseph (1991: 194) people's attitude towards the civic realm is purely materialistic and exploitative. The individual experiences absence of moral urge to give back to the civic public for any benefit. Indeed, people are constantly motivated to exploit the civic public for the development of the primordial networks. Generally, primordial groupings, ties and sentiments influence and determine the individual civic behaviour (Ekeh, 1975). The overall theoretical essence, succinctly, of Ekeh's (1975) thesis is to explain the unending and crippling corruption prevalent in the civic public of post-colonial African countries maintaining that civic public in Africa is amoral and lacks the generalized moral imperatives operative in the private and the primordial publics (Joseph, 1991; Ekeh, 1995). Hence, the destructive result of African politics in the post colonial era owes something to the amorality in the civic culture (public) (Ekeh, 1975). The "dialectical relationship between the two publics foments the unique political issues that has come to characterize African politics" (Ekeh, 1995).

According to Ekeh (1975: 93) the challenges of unique political issues are best x-rayed within historical, political and sociological instruments and occurrences. The political issues are manifested in corruption, while political actors combined their traditional and modern make-ups to traverse political landscapes within primordial and civic framework to meet expectations. While Ekeh deliberately terms his writing theoretical statement, it has enjoyed wide appeal and lots of practical usefulness. Although the writing was couched in elaborate abstractions that are expected of theories at that level, embedded terms and concepts are reducible for explanations of observable national occurrences. This quality has contributed to successes of known theoretical expositions like marxism, dependency theory and, more recently, McDonaldisation thesis. *The publics* are not abstractions with little or no pragmatic usefulness. The Publics are practically dynamic depending on the purpose and level of analysis. They have the capacity to take different forms at any time and space of analysis and scholarly examinations.

The publics are at once groups, institutions and locations, and they include organizational features (national, racial, ethnic), typologies (crowd, audiences, masses, citizens) normative attributes (topic, denegerate, progressive, retrogressive, dangerous), philosophical concerns (public, private) (Shin and Tusalem, 2007). These constructs are fundamental categories that have pigeonholed societal realities at different levels of existence, existences that face history, economy, philosophy, socio-psychology and governance. The formations classify liberalism basically in contemporary sociological and political constructions. They also seek to understand liberalism as political and economic dynamic that expresses itself in democracy and capitalism in contemporary time (Shin and Tusalem, 2007: Olutayo and Omobowale, 2005). Capitalism and democracy interface is a phenomenon that ensures and sustains organized contests and tensions in aspirations to the machineries of value allocation down the ages. Capitalism and democracy and thus holds the prospect of promise and peril, performance and non-performance, legitimacy and illegitimacy, and development and underdevelopment depending on which side of the publics the observer leans. *The publics* constructs, therefore give a solid base upon which the totality of happenings in Nigerian system can be viewed.

Nigerian Demoralization Process: *The Publics* as a Window

The major criticism against Ekeh's publics is a categorization of socio-cultural and political spaces that is too rigid, that is, sharp dichotomization of traversals as public and civic relations as if they do not overlap or interpenetrate. Social reality obviously does not operate through rigid vertical separations but in webs. However, Ekeh's categorisation is only a theoretical mapping of the spaces. He did not intend to argue that they do not overlap. At best, he has given a framework and an ideal format in the order of Max Weber's *Bureaucracy*, Ferdinand Tonnies' *Gelleschaft* and *Gemeinschaft* as well as Emile Durkheim's *Organic Solidarity* and *Mechanical Solidity*. Thus, excessive rigidity does not pose a major problem to the adoption of Ekeh's publics as a veritable theoretical constructs.

The only challenge to Ekeh's thesis today are time and reconfigurations, since about 34 years have passed after which Ekeh's article first appeared in *Comparative Studies in Society and History* and it is fair to say that about $3^1/_2$ decades is long enough in a fast moving globalized world for lots to have changed. Nigeria was under the military when Ekeh theorized the publics. He, however, stood on the shoulder of institutional events to see far into democratic prospects. This pragmatic projection and rich understating of political dynamics of Nigerian system make the thesis still relevant till date. While this chapter takes appeal from *the two publics*, events suggest that corruptions in Nigeria today have returned mostly to the private domain. Unlike Ekeh's theorization that people plunder the civic corridor to enrich their kinfolk, this is no longer the case. Nigerians today have three publics: private (self), primordial (this chapter finds the concept 'primordial' still very appropriate, even though Joseph (1991: 194) finds the term 'communal realm' more appropriate) and civic public.

Political actors in contemporary Nigeria plunder both the primordial and civic publics to enrich themselves or, at best, including their nuclear families. The primordial is nothing but machines to get to power; 'returns' no longer go to the 'villages'. As at the time of Ekeh's writing, pre-colonial institutions were still holding sway and people had to pledge their loyalty to traditional networks of relationship to be relevant in the political calculations of the First and Second Republics when people voted and aligned along ethnic lines (see Joseph, 1991 for a detail and classical presentation on this). People at that period galvanized political supports from the grassroots and saw themselves as representing local communities' interests. It is against these consciences that public players take chieftaincy titles to show alliance and acceptance of primordial level permutations so they could get support when operating at civic space. Current events contradict that situation.

Indeed, ethnically-packaged office seekers will not succeed in Nigeria today, at least at the macro national level, as Nigerians are struggling to jettison ethnic inclinations in politics (at least, so it appears). Although there is still zoning of offices and positions, it is to accommodate minority groups and there are usually national endorsements. Parochial ethnic sentimentalism and disaggregated arousal of one hundred per cent support for local development is taking the back seat in modern Nigeria political system. Political actors today even hijack primordial entitlements for personal enrichments. For instance, how many assembly members today have successfully executed worthwhile and sustainable community projects? What have they done with the money? How many roads and other infrastructures have been awarded to local contractors without executions, local contractors who are even "sons of the soil"? The time of civic for primordial political activities are over, or may be on the fast lane out, if not already out.

From 1999-2009, political patrons have been holding the process to ransom for selfish interests and not primordial. The emergence of General Olusegun Obasanjo (the immediate past Nigerian president [1999-2007]) in 1999 was obviously stage-managed by those who wanted a president with oligarchic loyalty. The same trend is being witnessed in the current government of President Umaru Yar'Adua. From ministers down to local councilors, politics is for the pocket and not for the primordial groups. Another point is popular realisation that primordial allocation of value leads to marginalization and underdevelopment. Even when political office holders attempt to engage in such activities, at least on large scale project, they are met with resistance. That was the case in Ekiti and Ondo when the states' universities and colleges of education were to be relocated to and established in the governors' town neighbourhood.

The point being made mainly is that while the notion of the three publics, private, primordial and civic, of Ekeh is still valid, the manifestation has shifted from primordial preferences to private in a form that is still amoral. Rather than corrupting the civic in favour of the primordial, both the primordial and civic are looted for private gains. This is why poverty is still high in the country irrespective of sections or ethnic groups. Poverty rate in Nigeria today is over 70 per cent (Federal Ministry of Women affairs and Social Development, 2007; Nigerian Bureau of Statistics, 2006) while infrastructures have decayed and development has become stunted. This is particularly observable in Niger Delta, the real treasure base of the nation with more than their fair share of poverty largely owing to corrupt representatives who corner the little given for community development for personal and private use mostly in Abuja, Lagos, United Kingdom and United States of America where they never benefit the primordial network.

This is part of the reasons why Nigeria is experiencing the post honeymoon phase this early in its democratic process. People do not wish to really participate in politics as they see the benefits only in the flamboyant lifestyles of politicians and not public improvement of livelihood. A poor man/woman yesterday in Nigeria is a billionaire today in politics, courtesy of rooms for looting security votes, amongst other funds and resources that do not need accountability. This is definitely inimical to democratisation in the country. Assessing the psychology of participatory democracy and the personality profiles of Nigerian politicians, Adebayo and Ogunleye (2008) maintain that the dispositions and profiles of the Nigeria politicians are antithetical to the enthronement of participatory democracy in Nigeria. Politicians are role models and determine public attitude to governance as they exert major influence on political will and direction necessary to drive development.

Achieving democratic gains, development and democratic disposition needs sterling personality traits in politicians (Adebayo and Ogunleye, 2008). Contrarily, however, Nigerian politicians mostly exhibit anti-democratic and corruptive behaviours hinged on lack of sterling personality traits expected of leaders (Adebayo and Ogunleye, 2008). Rather than engineering development selflessly, Nigerian civic public operators receive public goods, hoard public goods and market public goods for selfish purposes in ways that make them self-dependent and disempower others (Adebayo and Ogunleye, 2008).

Below is a theoretical model of patriotism allegiance and loyalty of a typical Nigerian:

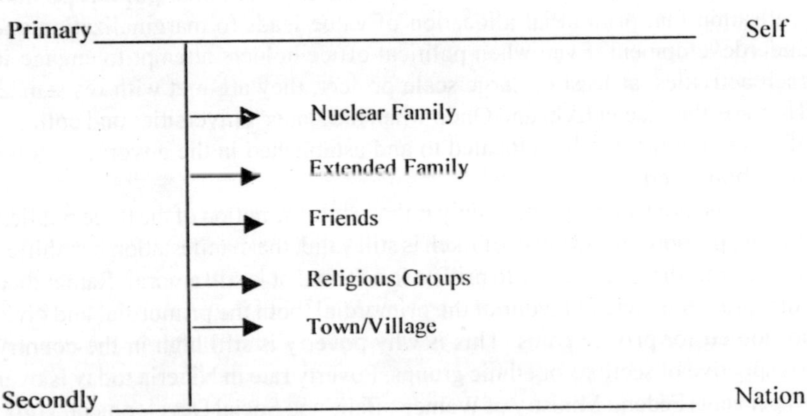

Adapted from Aluko, 2003

In the original Aluko (2003) theoretical schema, others come second, (un-disaggregated) town/village come third, ethnic group fourth, religious group fifth, nation last and secondary. This chapter has engaged this adapted format, as against the original model, to suite current democratization realities. Self is the primary motivating element in Nigerian democracy as against popular participation and goods as ideal concerns in democracy. The focus of Nigerian civic life is 'me', 'myself' and 'I' alone. This goes directly to benefit the nuclear family, followed by extended family (still personal) and friends. Nigerians are religious people at varying degree of adherence to doctrines, tenets and commandment.

People lift holy hands and bow heads regardless of civic atrocities. It is explainable especially as religion forms the basis of most activities in traditional Africa from which the modern is created. People give primacy to their religious lives even before primordial towns and villages. The nation is very secondary as seen at the bottom of the matrix. People have little or no attention to it and its development even when their occupation of the civic sphere is only relevant within that point of reference. People answer their names and think of themselves before nationhood and public governance. This kind of selfish and general sentimentalism is obviously a threat to successful democratization. It will only drive the process backwards and never forward.

Conclusion: The Necessary Reflections

This chapter has attempted, fundamentally, a theorization of democracy and democratization in Nigeria by first establishing that the popular notion of democracy is nothing but ideal type; in practical terms it must be appreciated in assessment. Adopting *the publics* frameworks is to be able to scholarly marry theory and practice in comprehending contemporary democratic dynamics in the country particularly as corruption and anti-democratic inter-penetrativeness. The place of colonialism and infusion of capitalism in the foregoing analysis cannot be overemphasized. It is an accepted axiom that although colonialism might not have replaced traditional pre-colonial norms, values, behaviours and institutions, it, however, reduced their influence and reconstructed them in a manner that make them nearly irrelevant as guiding principles in contemporary socio-economic and political environments.

Infusion of colonialism and associated capitalistic tendencies already established in western cultures gives primacy to capital accumulation and individual welfare and good in Nigeria in a manner that fair socio-economic arrangement becomes less valued (Olutayo and Omobowale, 2005). Such cultural and economic reconstructions are only manifesting in political domain which is the official terrain for power constellations and value allocations. The all-inclusive communal system that ensured universal economic rights, political rights and political participations of all and sundry and ensure survival of the kin-group, the sick, the elderly, the young, the handicapped and others in particular (Olutayo and Omobowale, 2005) has been replaced with ill-comprehended and ill-prepared for ideal type democracy. The time is ripe, therefore, to re-awaken potent native African democracy that enables all to participate and hold their leaders accountable.

This allows for mutual respect and accountability between the rulers and the ruled as both categories could be called to question. If Nigeria must democratize within the liberal democracy model, there is a need for public enlightenment to educate both politicians and electorates about public roles and expectations. Everybody's role must be well spelt out and defended in the electoral acts and Nigeria constitution. Again, a need exists to scrutinize the Electoral Acts and the Constitution to make them more than mere papers and toothless bulldogs especially now that Independent Electoral Commission (INEC) has boldly declared that it can only give the regulations but cannot enforce it. This chapter will not go into detail on INEC, electoral acts and other legal and para-legal issues because they are primary subjects of other chapters in this book and they have been well treated.

As it stands, the first decade of Nigeria's re-democratisation has not achieved much and it is gradually but steadily nose-diving due to public dynamics that violates basic elements of democracy. There is, therefore, a need for all to pause and have a rethink as explicated in this chapter to salvage the situation. Let all hands be on deck as democracy is played out in Nigeria. A vital note however is that a strong nexus exists among the past, present and future, and this nexus determines behaviours, political practices and eventual outcomes of democracy within the present framework of analysis.

References

Adebayo, S.O., & Ogunleye, A.J. (2008, January). The psychology of participatory democracy and the personality profile of the Nigerian politicians. *Bangladesh E-journal of Sociology. Vol. 5, No. 1,* pp.1-17.

Aisabor, I.S. (2005). *Nigerian State and Elite Corruption.* Tokyo: Mekiro.

Aluko, M.A.O. (2003). Ethnic nationalism and the Nigerian democratic experience in the fourth republic. *Anthropologist, Vol. 5, No. 4,* pp. 253-259. Kamlaraj.

Diamond, L. (2001, January 11). *How people view democracy: Findings from public opinion survey in four regions.* Presentation to the Sanford seminar on democratization.

Ekeh, P.P. (1975). Colonialism and the two publics in Africa: A theoretical Statement. *Comparative Studies in Society and History, Vol. 17, No. 1.* January. pp. 91-117.

Federal Ministry of Women Affairs and Women Development (FMWA & SD), 2007. *National Gender Policy.* FRN.

Inglehart, n.d. *How Solid is Mass Support for Democracy 5 and How can We Measure It*? Unpublished manuscript.

Inglehart, R. (2002). Trends in political action: The developmental trend and the post- honeymoon decline. *International Journal of Comparative Sociology.*

Joseph, R.A. (1991). *Democracy and prebendal politics in Nigeria: The rise and fall of the second republic.* UK: Cambridge University Press.

Joseph, R.A. (2003, July). Africa: States ın crisis. *Journal of Democracy, Vol. 14, No. 3,* pp. 159-170.

Mattes, R., & Bratton, M. (2003, October). Learning about democracy in Africa. Awareness, Performance, and experience: A comparative series of national public attitude surveys on democracy, markets and civil society in Africa. *Afrobarometer Paper, No. 31.*

Mulikita, N.M. (2003). A false dawn? Africa's post-1990 democratisation waves. *African Security Reviews, Vol. 12, No. 4.*

National Bureau of Statistics (2006). *The Nigerian Statistical Fact Sheets on Economic and Social Development.* Federal Republic of Nigeria.

Olutayo, A.O., & Omobowale, A.O. (2005). Globalisation, Democracy and the New Partnership for Africa's Development (NEPAD). *African Journal for the Psychological Study of Social Issues, Vol. 8, No. 2,* pp. 228-242.

Olutayo, A.O, Olutayo, M.A.O., & Omobowale, A.O. (2008, April/June). 'TINA', aids, and the underdevelopment problem in Africa. *Brazillian Journal of Political Economy. Vol. 28, No. 2.* pp. 238-248.

Ramsdal, K. (2006). *Nigerian Democratisation: A Text Analysis of Democracy Theory.* Universitet for Sammenliknende Politikk. December.

Shin, D.C., & Tusalam, R.F. (2007). The cultural and institutional dynamics of global democratization: A synthesis of mass experience and congruence theory. *Taiwan Journal of Democracy, Vol. 3, No. 1,* pp. 1-28.

Smith, D.J. (2001, November 1). Kinship and Corruption in Contemporary Nigeria. *Ethnos, Vol. 66, No. 3,* pp. 344-364.

Williams, A. (1998). Intellectuals and the crisis of democratization in Nigeria: Towards a theory of postcolonial anomie. *Theory and Society, Vol. 27,* pp. 287-307.

4

Inter and Intra-party Squabbles in Nigeria

Azeez O. Olaniyan

Introduction

Political party has adorned the toga of notoriety in Nigeria to the extent that its defining characteristics have been intrigues, bickering, backbiting, schisms and violence. Right from the colonial period to the current dispensation, party politics has been bedevilled by crises in varying proportions. This has left in its wake wanton destruction of party culture, democracy, lives and properties. Why is this so? Why is party politics concomitant with violence and intrigues in Nigeria? Why is political party rife with squabbling, both at inter- and intra-party levels? This chapter seeks to answer these problematic questions. It is divided into four parts. The first presents a conceptual analysis; the second discusses forms and patterns of squabbling in Nigerian political parties, the third accounts for the squabbling and the last concludes.

Political Party, Intra- and Inter-party Squabbling: A Conceptual Linkage

Political party has enjoyed robust scholarly interrogations. According to Edmund Burke, "Political party is a group of men who have agreed upon a principle by which the national interest might be served" (qtd. in Rodee et al., 1983, p. 195). Wilson defines political party as a group of persons that seeks to elect candidates to public office by supplying them with a label - a party identification - by which they are known to the electorate (qtd. in Agbaje,

1999:195). Leon Epstein (ibid) sees it as basically "Any group, however loosely organised, seeking to elect governmental office-holders under a given label", and Samuel Eldersveld (1964: 1-23) believes that political party is nothing but a social group engaging in a patterned activity within the social matrix. Philip Shively (1997:199) conceptualises political party as a group of officials or would-be officials who are linked with a sizable group of citizens into an organisation; a chief object of this organisation is to ensure that its officials attain or are maintained in power. Using Wilson as a reference, Agbaje (1999: 195) sums up the three aspects political party assumes: a label, an organisation and a set of leaders. The first relates to its psychological connotation in the minds of the public as something with which to identify people with. The second relates to its being a platform for mobilisation at the behest of vote canvassers, and the last represents the actual ruling of the people, the ultimate goal of any serious political party.

Specifically, the common thread binding the foregoing definitions is the existence of commonalities, i.e. of ideology, goals and expectations, of mission statement and, perhaps, of strategies, which Abubakar (2005: 249) describes as interest aggregation and articulation within the framework of the political system. However, if political party is built on commonality, then it does two things that are paradoxical: the foreclosure of the idea of intra-party squabbles and the establishment of inter-party rivalry. The foreclosure of intra-party squabbles, in the pristine meaning of political party, is contingent on the underlining commonality, which, in all material particular, presupposes congruence of interests, desires and aspirations, a semblance of birds of same plumage flying together. This means that members of the same political party ought not to have the basis for squabbling. But in reality, intra-party squabbles are common features in any society. This, again, raises a fundamental question: If people are so united by such commonalities, what could have been responsible for squabbling from within? This shall be examined in the due course.

Meanwhile, and as argued heretofore, the definition of political party establishes the basis for inter-party squabbles. This can be analysed from two levels: the essence and the practice of political party. At the first level, the hallmark of commonalities, on which political party is premised, is exclusivity. This presumes the assemblage of people of common ideology in what could be described as a 'political cubicle', separate from the others in a political system. The implication of this is the existence of different 'cubicles of ideology' and association in any given society. In a way, the existence of various 'ideological cubicles' is a recipe for inter-party rivalry. In other words, any society with more than one political party is bound to experience inter-party rivalries. At the level of practice, political party has, as its primary objective, the edging out of others in a political contest - what Schumpeter (1961, p. 279) describes as the overall ambition to prevail over the others in order to get to power or stay in it. Naturally, a political contest is bound to result in squabbles between or among political parties in any society; the art of politicking is soaked in rivalry and competition.

In a way, the foregoing deductions lead us towards two conclusions. One is that there is an inherent linkage between political party and squabbling. Two and flowing from the first, there is inevitability of political squabbling in any given system that operates party system. The degree of these squabbling, however, differs from one clime to the other. This is why Johari makes the case for environmental study of poiitical party, in the sense that political party is not an isolated institution. It operates in an environment. As such, a study of party politics requires its study in the context of all those forces, institutions and agencies that interact with each other. In other words, an empirical study of party politics requires that we must look into the interactions in which political parties are very much involved and, as a result of that, not only political but other dimensions of our collective life as well – say economic, social and cultural – are naturally affected (Johari, 2003: 300).

The need to be cognisance of the environment of political party becomes imperative in the reality that every society operates within a given environment, which invariably influences its party behaviour. It is from this background that both intra- and inter-party squabbles in Nigeria shall be analysed.

Forms and Patterns of Intra and Inter-Party Squabbles in Nigeria

Nigeria's experience with political party dates back to the colonial time, and the contemporary incidences of intra- and inter-party squabbles associated with party politics in Nigeria is nothing but a throwback to the past which is replete with schisms, bickering, backbiting, intrigues violence, packing and sacking. The present is, therefore, a reflection of the past, showing that the present may not be totally different from the past, and the future not likely to be clearly demarcated from the present (Agbaje, 2003, p. 1). What obtains, therefore, is a manifestation of practice that pre-dated the attainment of political independence in Nigeria. The major political parties during the colonial period include the Nigerian National Democratic Party (NNDP) formed by Herbert Macaulay in 1922, Action Group (AG) formed by Obafemi Awolowo in 1950 from the bowel of *Egbe Omo Oduduwa*; the Jam'iyyar Mutanen Arewa (Northern Peoples' Congress) formed by Dr. R. B. Dikko and Abubakar Imam in 1948, initially as a cultural association (Dudley, 1968: 69); the Northern Elements Progressive Union (NEPU) formed in 1950 through the alliance of *Taron Masu Zamunta* (KMZ) and the Kano Youth Association (KYA) (ibid); the United Middle Belt Congress (UMBC) formed by the union of the Middle Zone League (MZL) and Middle Belt Peoples' Party (UMPP) in 1955 (ibid); and the National Council of Nigerian Citizen (NCNC), which was under the leadership of Nnamdi Azikiwe. Although the pre-colonial political parties exhibited considerable harmony (Muhammad, 2008), yet, the political parties still witnessed internal strives as well as exhibited inter-party rivalries. The First Republic witnessed bitter internal wrangling within the parties as well as bitter rivalries and conflict among the parties. The Third Republic paraded five major political parties, the National Party of Nigeria (NPN), the Unity Party of Nigeria (UPN), the Nigerian Peoples' Party (NPP), the Great Nigerian Peoples' Party (GNPP), the Peoples Redemption Party (PRP), and at the tail end of the Republic, the Nigerian Advanced Party (NAP) came on board. The parties were not spared internal intrigues and conflicts. In the third pseudo-Republic, two political parties, Social Democratic Party (SDP) and National Republican Convention (NRC), two rather creation of military fiat also exhibited internal schisms and rivalries. Perhaps no other Republic exhibited intra- and inter-party squabbles more than the current Fourth Republic. It has recorded bitter and acrimonious struggles within parties as well as violent inter-party relations.

In Nigeria, these squabbles assume different forms such as factionalisation and breakaway, verbal attack and physical violence. These shall be discussed one after the other.

Factionalisation/Breakaway

This has its roots in pre-independent political development. Parties have been breaking into different factions from the colonial period. The emergence of NEPU as a political party was essentially a product of internal disagreement in the NPC. Members of the breakaway NEPU had accused NPC of conservatism, pussyfooting and dilly-dallying (Dudley, 1968). Also, internal wrangling, occasioned by the romance of the top echelon of the party with the NPC, resulted in the breakup of the UMBC into two factions, each headed by Moses Rwang and David Lot, and each holding conferences simultaneously (ibid: 95). In the early period of independence, a combination of ambition, ego and personality clash within the AG resulted in factionalisation. This was to snowball into national crises that eventually consumed the republic (Osaghae, 1988).

In the Second Republic, the emergence of GNPP owed largely to internal disagreement in the NPP. Alhaji Ibrahim Waziri was instrumental to the formation of the NPP but when he felt short-changed, he left to found the GNPP (Omotosho, 1988). Mallam Aminu Kano was initially in the NPN but due to intra-party schism, he had to leave to form his own PRP. Also, Chief Abiola was forced to leave the NPN as a result of inability to realise his presidential ambition due to internal intrigues in the party (Muhammad, 2008). The splitting of PRP into Aminu Kano and Michael Imoudu factions also had to do with internal strife within the party (Tyoden, 2002). Of all the parties of the Second Republic, the UPN recorded the highest level of internal strife and ferment. This manifested in defection of high ranking party stalwarts to other parties, particularly NPN. Included in the decamped are prominent party financiers such as Olaiya Fagbamigbe and Ebun Ogunyimika in Ondo state, as well as Chief Akin Omoboriowo and Sunday Afolabi, the party's deputy governors in the then Ondo and Oyo states respectfully who all pitched their tents with their erstwhile political foe, the NPN (Babarinsa, 2003; Okoosi-Simbine, 2005; Muhammad, 2008).

If the philosophy behind the imposition of two political parties on the people in the third pseudo-Republic was to eradicate stiff competition and strife, it did not succeed, for the period also recorded intra- and inter-party problems. The SDP was divided into the Yar'Adua and Kingibe factions and generally characterised by struggle for ascendancy, control, general mistrust and absence of discipline, which was to manifest in the tepid reaction to the annulment of its victory in 1993. The NRC, as recorded by Muhammad (op. cit.), was factionalised into two camps - the Republican Action Committee, led by Chief Tom Ikimi, and the NRC Consultative Forum, led by Adamu Chiroma, Umaru Shinkafi and Bamanga Tukur. It was also recorded by Tyoden that at the time of the dissolution of the party in 1993, it had cases against eleven of its members (Tyoden, qtd. in Muhammad, ibid.).

The Fourth Republic started off with the registration of three political parties – Peoples Democratic Party (PDP), All Peoples Party (APP) and the Alliance for Democracy (AD). The number was to move to 30 in the 2003 general elections and eventually 50 in the 2007 general elections. As argued earlier, none of the republics witnessed more party crises than the fourth. Aina vividly captures:

> The PDP is a marriage of strange quarrelsome bedfellows who do not only misunderstood themselves but are regularly feuding. APP is virtually moribund while AD is split into two contentious camps. (Aina, 2002)

Verbal Warfare

The squabbles were not limited to factionalisation, they also include verbal warfare. Hence, diatribes were thrown and vitriolic attacks launched against each other at will. Ahmadu Bello, the leader of the NPC, once described the NEPU stalwarts as "prodigal children who have temporarily strayed away from the fold of NPC" (Dudley, ibid.: 165). In the same vein Abba Habib, erstwhile NPC General Secretary, once dismissed the UMBC as "only an ideology infused by the Christian missionaries against the expansion of the Moslems in Northern Nigeria" (ibid: 91). By far, the most direct attack came from Azikiwe against the *Egbe Omo Oduduwa*, the Yoruba cultural association that gave birth to the AG. In response to the formation of the association, Azikiwe wrote in his *West African Pilot*:

> "Henceforth, the cry must be one of battle against the Egbe Omo Oduduwa, its leaders at home and abroad, up hill and down dale, in

the streets of Nigeria and in the residence of its advocates...it is the enemy of Nigeria; it must be crushed to the earth... There is no going back until the fascist organization has been dismembered" (qtd. in Coleman, 1958: 346).

When in 1981, Chief Awolowo wrote a letter to Presidential Shehu Shagari on the state of the nation, he was given a scathing reply by Chief Adisa Akinloye, the National Chairman of NPN as follows:

"Chief Awolowo is the chief priest of the Unity Party of Nigeria, UPN. History has undoubtedly but with purposeful accuracy turned over to the everlasting archives for the state of invaluable memory the political suicide brazenly committed by Chief Awolowo and his party, the UPN, in the 1979 presidential elections in Nigeria. So marooned and obliterated were Chief Awolowo and his negligible sycophantic worshippers ..." (qtd. in Babarinsa, 2003: 171).

As the 1979 general elections were approaching, political parties were scheming and aligning to upstage the NPN-controlled government. An alliance called Progressive Peoples Alliance (PPA) was formed by the trio of Obafemi Awolowo of UPN, Ibrahim Waziri of GNPP and Nnamdi Azikiwe of NPP. In his reaction, President Shagari simply dismissed this arrangement as an alliance of "three blind men who were doomed to fail" (ibid). But a far more scathing remark was to come against Azikwe who described himself as the beautiful bride of Nigerian politics and contemplated an alliance with the NPN after the collapse of the PPA. In rejecting the Azikiwe's offer of friendship, President Shagari told a party crowd in Enugu thus:

"There is an 80-year old, a beautiful bride in Nigerian politics who has been the subject of funny cartoons in the country's newspaper. (But) have you ever seen a beautiful bride at age of 80? This beautiful bride has a long record of broken marriages – the bride had flirted several times since she was married at a young age NPC, AG, Biafra, National Youth Movement and NPN. On each occasion, the marriage was dissolved. Now, the same bride had gone to marry the UPN and the PPA. I think that, from today, nobody should talk of any bride. She should be called a prostitute." (qtd. in Babarinsa, ibid.: 182).

The preludes to the 2007 elections also recorded both intra- and inter-party tirades between politicians. After he was frustrated from assuming the position of chairmanship of the PDP, Chief Sunday Awoniyi described members of the party as "electoral fraudsters and party infidels who have no redeeming features" (qtd. in Gadegesin, 2005, p. 26). Also, voicing out his anger against his party and justifying his defection to another political platform, the Movement for the Defence of Democracy (MDD), Yahaya Kwande blurted out that "if the attempt to revive PDP fails, we shall remove the soul and the spirit of the party and plant it somewhere". But in a swift reaction to the threat from the Kwande group, Chief Tony Anenih, the then chairman of the Board of Trustees of the PDP told reporters asking him questions that "when you get home, look at the list again (MDD). Those are people who cannot win their wards. They run their party on the pages of newspapers." (qtd. in *Tell*, 2005: 10). Equally, when Chief Solomon Lar, the founding chairman of the PDP was suspended from the party, Danladi Wuyep, one of his aides described the action as "arrogant display of democratic rascality" (qtd. in *Tell*, ibid, p. 29).

The tirades were more pronounced at inter party levels. Shortly before the installation of Segun Oni as the governor of Ekiti State on the platform of PDP, Sikiru Lawal, the Deputy Governor-elect, in a press statement, accused the AC party of gunrunning. According to him:

> Information has it that the AC has concluded plans to import explosives into Ekiti State that will be used to scare away people at Oluyemi Kayode stadium and other strategic places on the day of inauguration. All these ungodly acts are being put together by the AC to create the impression that the state is not safe under the incoming PDP government. The plan to cause the havoc, we gathered, is being coordinated by a professor of Ekiti origin based in Washington DC (qtd. in *The Nation*, 2007, p. 10).

The AC reacted in the following words:

> This is an arrant nonsense coming from a demented mind of perverse group of mindless party. We believe in the rule of law, we shall not succumb to any blackmail. Forget them, they are products of fraud. They are jesters. They are afraid of their own shadows. Very soon, the law of karma will catch up with them (qtd. in *The Nation,* 2007:10).

In a reaction to the favourable verdict of the Abuja Court of Appeal judgement in a suit challenging the election of President Yar'Adua, members of the PDP in Ado Ekiti rolled out the drums for celebration. The reaction of the Ekiti State AC to this goes thus:

> We are at a loss while searching for the source of joy of Ekiti government in celebrating the Abuja Court of Appeal on the election of President Yar'Adua. The indolent Peoples Democratic Party regime rolled out the drums to twist their weak bones to shameful rhythms on the streets of Ado Ekiti. They gleefully adduced President Yar'Adua's victory as their reason for the unusual excitement. ... This confirms our repeated outcry that Ekiti is now asleep because her emergency caretakers are mere undertakers. We cannot find a nexus between a Court of Appeal judgement on the President and the myriad of poll fraud allegations hanging on their necks in Ekiti... It is obvious that they have, since all these days nothing to celebrate, so they would roar into clownish joy over such a tantalising mirage. Since the joy of the wicked is temporary, they would once again be woken up by the reality of their situation that Ekiti would soon take

> away from them the stolen mandate which provides them with the intoxicant that propelled them into such childish exuberance (qtd. in *The Nation*, 2008: 5).

In the thick of the contest over the gubernatorial elections of Ondo State, Femi Agagu, the then Chief of Staff to former Governor Segun Agagu of Ondo State dismissed the possibility of the Labour Party upstaging the PDP. According to him,

> "Everybody knows that AC is just an experiment, which used to be AD before it disintegrated into DPA, DPP and others. And Labour Party is just a formation of disgruntled people who wanted to seize power by force and they were not lucky" (qtd. in *The Nation,* 2007: 12).

When President Obasanjo described the Action Congress Party, which his Vice President had defected to, as "Alliance for Corruption" which should never be voted for, Governor Bola Tinubu of Lagos State replied by referring to the PDP, at various times as "people destroying people", "people deceiving people" and "poverty development party", with Atiku Abubakar telling his supporters: "you have no business voting the PDP. We should bury the PDP because it has betrayed us. You have to be vigilant and protect your votes because we are dealing with people who steal votes." (*The Nation,* 2007:2).

Perhaps, what could be regarded as the greatest verbal threat came via the outburst of President Obasanjo:

> "This election is a do-or-die affair to prevent those who might drag the nation backward from coming to power. If we are targeting 2020 as the year Nigeria will become one of the 20 leading economies in the world, we must not pray for spoilers and criminals as our leaders." (*Punch,* 2007: 1; *The Nation*, 2007: 2).

Physical Violence

Intra and inter-party violence have become the hallmark of party politics in Nigeria. In the First Republic, infighting within AG resulted in *Operation wet e*, which eventually became the conflagration that consumed the republic. In the Second Republic, there was widespread violence in Oyo and Ondo states between UPN and NPN and it led to wanton destruction of lives and properties (Babarinsa, ibid.). In the Fourth Republic, there are several cases of intra- and inter-party violence. This included the crisis in Anambra state that culminated in the abduction of Governor Chris Ngige and the arson on the Government House by people loyal to Chris Mba, the PDP godfather of the state (Muhammad, 2005, Ologbenla, 2004). Included also is the crisis that followed the impeachment of Governor Rashidi Ladoja of Oyo State, where Chief Lamidi Adedibu was the mastermind. Added also are several cases of political assassinations of which the major ones are the killings of Bola Ige, Harry Marshall, Funsho Williams, Aminasoari Dikibbo and several others.

Bola Ige was a serving Attorney General of the Federation, who though belonged to the Alliance for Democracy party, was then serving under the PDP-led government. Harry Marshall was once a strong member of the PDP and fondly known as the kingmaker of River State. He later fell out with the party and was suspended. He decamped to ANPP and was campaigning against the PDP when he was assassinated (Igbafe and Offiong, 2007). Funsho Williams was a PDP gubernatorial candidate in Lagos State when he was assassinated. Aminasoari Dikkibo was the Chairman of South-South of PDP when he was assassinated on his way to attend a meeting of the party's Board of Trustees (ibid). The rampancy of crises in the Fourth Republic made Anifowose observe thus:

> The political scene has witnessed frequent discords, unresolved political issues, recriminations, threats of impeachments of executives, treacheries, flagrant breach of party rules, carpet crossing and resurgence of factional cleavages within the parties which have continued to threatened democracy in Nigeria (qtd. in Muhammad, 2008: 46).

It is deducible from the foregoing analysis that intra- and inter-party squabbles have debilitating effect on party relations in the country. This makes it expedient to ask the question: why squabbling? The probable answer is in what follows.

Accounting for Party Squabbling in Nigeria

According to Bowerson, all causes of conflict identified by scholars can be grouped into five: goal incompatibility, domain-position-role incongruence, communication breakdown, differing perception of reality and ideological differences (Bowerson et al., 1990). Taking a leave from Worlu Rowland (2007: 9), these elements can be appropriated to explain intra- and inter-party skirmishes in Nigeria.

Goal Incompatibility

Members of political party are presumed to share common interests. The set-up of any party provides for commonality: a common constitution, a rule guiding behaviour and a set of guiding ideology which make the very idea of intra-party schisms unthinkable. But as argued heretofore, this has hardly been the case. History is replete with members of same party disagreeing openly, quitting and even working against the interest of the party. Why is this so? The answer lies in goal incompatibility, which can be analysed from two levels. At the first level, goal incompatibility could manifest in form of clash of ambition of members within a party. In this form, the fulfilment of ambitions may result in crises for the party. In the First Republic, clash of ambition between Chiefs Awolowo and Akintola resulted in serious crises for the party and the nation. In the Second Republic, it emerged in the clash between Chief MKO Abiola and the top echelon of the NPN. In the current Fourth Republic, it manifested in the feud between President Obasanjo and his deputy, Atiku Abubakar over the former's desire for tenure elongation and the latter's desire to become the President. It led to the expulsion of the latter from PDP. At the second level, disagreements could ensue over the choice of who represents the party in an election (Rowland, ibid.). If a party's primary election fails to meet the transparency and credibility tests, then it could lead to disagreement among members, which could affect the fortunes of the party. In Nigeria, primary elections are problematic and have resulted in internal squabbling. The conduct of the primary election of Action Congress party in Ekiti, which saw the emergence of Kayode Fayemi as the winner, led to massive defection of members of AC to the rival PDP. Also, disagreements over the emergence of Babatunde Fashola as the flag bearer of AC in Lagos State led to defection of some other contestants to different political parties.

Position, Role and Domain Incongruence

According to Rowland, position, role and domain refers to party structures and the roles assigned to each by the laid-down party rules and regulations. In any party, there is always a laid-down principle guiding the party. A breach of the due process may result in internal strife for the party. For instance, a party chairman that imposes a candidate on members of the party will likely cause internal crisis. There are several instances of this in Nigeria. The imposition of candidates by the leaders of AD, and the sidelining of major stakeholders in the party, resulted in internal disaffection that largely affected the fortunes of the party in the 2003 general elections in Nigeria.

Communication Breakdown and Differing Perceptions of Reality

Communication breakdown is said to occur in two ways: failure to pass vital information at the right time and the presence of noise, which is interpreted as usage of confused and ambiguous language in political communication (ibid). Also, differences in the method of realizing party's goal could result in disagreement among members. This has to do with differences in perception. The "do or die" approach of President Obasanjo to the 2007 general elections was his own perception of winning an election at all cost for his party.

Ideological Differences

Even though ideological congruence, described earlier as commonality, is the defining characteristic of political party, it is often the case that members seldom subscribe to the ideology of political party in the same degree. The variations in ideological congruence partly explain why disagreements occur among members of the same party. Also, as earlier argued, the allotment of people into specific ideological cubicle in party system symbolizes the presence of different ideological bends on the society. There is bound to be conflicts. This partly explains the inevitability of inter-party crises in the society. It is a known fact that ideological congruence is never the basis for party formation in Nigeria. This explains the spate of internal upheaval, carpet crossing and political prostitution in the country.

Conclusion

In this chapter, analyses of intra- and inter-party squabbles have been made. It is argued that party politics in Nigeria, right from the colonial to the present period, has been dogged by squabbling and that it has debilitating effects in the polity. Specifically, the effects can be summarized as stunted party growth, loss of lives and property, instability and stunted development. But the important point to note is that squabbling is an inevitable phenomenon in any society that operates party system. In other words, intra and inter-party differences is not peculiar to Nigeria. What makes it so bad in Nigeria is the extreme extent it always takes, such as killing, destruction, sacking and packing. One major way of reducing destructive intra and inter-party squabbles is the need for ideological conviction among the Nigerian politicians.

References

Abubakar, A (2008, November 30). "I was Chased Away from PDP". *The Nation.*

Abubakar, D (2005). Political Parties and Federalism in Nigeria. In Onwudinwe, E., & Suberu, R. (eds). *Nigerian Federalism in Crisis, Critical Perspectives and Political Options.* Ibadan: John Archers.

Agbaje, A.B. (1999). Political Parties and Pressure Groups. *Elements of Politics.* Lagos: Malthouse.

Agbaje, A.B. (2003). The Historical Antecedents of the Phenomenon of Ethnic Militias in Nigeria. In Tunde Babawale (ed.), *Urban Violence, Ethnic Militias and Challenges of Democratic Consolidation in Nigeria.* Lagos: Malthouse Press.

Babarinsa, D. (2003). *House of War, the Story of Awo's Followers and Collapse of Nigeria's Second Republic.* Ibadan: Spectrum Books.

Bowerson, Lambert, D. M. B., & Taylor, D. M. (1990). *Management in Marketing Channels.* New York. McGraw Hill.

Coleman, J.C. (1958). *Nigeria: Background to Nationalism.* Benin City: Broburg and Wistrom.

Dudley, B.J. (1968). *Parties and Politics in Northern Nigeria.* London: Frank Cass and Company.

Duverger, M. (1954). *Political Parties.* New York: John Wiley.

Eldersveld, J. (1964). *Political Parties: A Behavioural Analysis.* Chicago: Rand McNally and Company.

Epstein, L.P. (1967). *Political Parties in Western Democracies.* New York: Frederick A. Praeger Inc.

Gbadegesin, S. (2005, August 1). The Yoruba Infidel. *The News.*

Igbafe, A. A. & Offiong, O. J. (2007). Political Assassinations in Nigeria: An Exploratory Study, *African Journal of Political Science and International Relations, Vol. 1, No. 1. pp.* 1986-2005.

Johari, J.C. (2003). *Comparative Politics.* New Delhi: Sterling Publishers.

Muhammad, R. (2008). Intra-party Relations in Nigeria. *Pakistan Journal of Social Sciences, Vol. 5, No. 1,* pp. 42-50.

Ngou, C.M. (1989). The 1959 Elections and Formation of the Independence Government. In Ekeh, P. et al. (eds.). *Nigeria since Independence, the First 25 Years.* Ibadan: Heinemann Publishers

Osaghae, E. E. (1998). *Cippled Giant, Nigeria since Independence.* Ibadan: John Archers.

Rodee, A. et al. (1983). *Introduction to Political Science.* New York: McGraw Hill Companies.

Rowland, W. (2007). Conflict Management in Nigerian Party Politics: The Marketing Paradigm. Paper presented at the 26th Annual Conference of Nigerian Political Science Association (NPSA) at Bayero University, Kano.

Schumpeter, J. A. (1961). *Capitalism, Socialism and Democracy.* London.

Shively, P. W. (1997). *Power and Choice: An Introduction to Political Science.* New York: McGraw Hill Companies.

Tyoden, S. G. (2002). Intra- and Inter-party Relations: Towards a More Stable Party System in Nigeria. *African Journal of Constitutional Development in Nigeria, Vol. 3,* pp. 1-23.

Newspapers and Magazines

The News, August 1, 2005.

Tell, November 28, 2005.

Punch, February 13, 2007.

The Nation, February 18, 2007.

__________, May 25, 2007.

__________, May 28, 2007.

__________, February 28, 2008.

SECTION - II

DEMOCRATIC MACHINERIES

5

An Assessment of Legislative Inputs in Nigeria's Democratic Governance: 1999-2009

Yahaya T.K. Baba

Introduction

The return of Nigeria to democratic rule on the 29th May 1999 brought an end to active involvement of the military in governance and politics of the country. This transition to democracy, which is fourth in the series of attempts at democratization, is unique in some respects. For instance, unlike the previous experiments which collapsed midway (First and Second Republics) or at the threshold of its completion (aborted Third Republic), the current democratic transition, at least for the first time, uninterruptedly transited power to another democratically-elected government (civilian to civilian transition). This is, however, not to suggest that the challenges and crises that besieged the previous experiments are effectively managed. On the contrary, the reoccurrence of these crises seems to be more intense and severe in both magnitude and dimensions. However, what seemingly is responsible for the survival of the current democratic regime is partly attributed to the influence of external factors on the Nigeria's domestic environment and perhaps the resolve of the populace at particularly the elite level to nurture and uphold democracy as the preferable framework of governance. In spite of this, the sustainability of democracy in the country is still in shambles. This is not unconnected with the pattern of manipulation and abuse of democratic principles and procedures by the elites (election rigging, personalization and autocratization of political parties and other institutions, corruption, unhealthy competition for power, etc.) and the widespread anti-democratic culture among the mass of the people (militarization of conflicts, intolerance, apathy, ethnic nationalism, etc.).

It is in light of the foregoing that this chapter aims to contribute to the understanding of a decade of re-democratization in Nigeria from the perspective of legislative performance. In this chapter, therefore, attempt is made to evaluate the inputs of the legislature in Nigeria's governance from 1999 to 2009. As a core institution of governance in a democracy, the legislature supposedly plays prominent role in democratization. For instance, from the standpoint of its traditional roles of law making, representation and oversight activities, legislative institution is deemed as a pillar of democracy. This is because it provides a platform for political participation through representation, in addition to making laws for peaceful coexistence, order and good governance. The legislature, through its oversight functions also entrenches accountability in the management of public funds and in the general conduct of governmental agencies. Thus, what seems to be central to our analysis in this chapter is the performance of the legislature in the Fourth Republic. Accordingly, what are the constitutional roles of the Nigerian legislature in the Fourth Republic? What seems to be the capacity of the Nigerian legislature? How does it respond to the challenges of its mandate? And more importantly, what are the prospects of enhancing its performance in deepening of democratic governance? Answers to these and other related questions provide insights into the inputs of the legislature in democratic governance of Nigeria. The discourse will begin with a theoretical examination legislative performance.

Legislative Performance: A Theoretical Background

To understand the various theoretical perspectives to legislative performance, certain contextual questions need to be addressed. These questions include: What are the various activities outlined for legislatures in a democracy? What constitute the required legislative capacity necessary for effective legislative performance? And what are the constraints for effective legislative performance in a democracy? These issues constitute some of the major concerns raised and addressed by some theoretical discourses on legislative performance. However, in these discourses, there are various perspectives to understanding legislative performance. For instance, some perspectives are basically concerned with individual legislators (members of the legislature and/or their aides) while other perspectives shift focus to the institution itself. In addition to these dominant perspectives, some scholars based their analysis of legislative performance from the standpoint of environmental influence on the legislature. All these perspectives are essentially important in understanding the theoretical viewpoints of legislative performance.

Thus, some of the theoretical contributions in the analysis of legislative performance are here examined. One of the famous studies that provided a theoretical impetus on the phenomenon of legislative performance is the one by Mezey (1979). His analysis of legislative performance across legislatures of the world is considered as a landmark comparative study on legislatures. Legislatures are divided into active, vulnerable, reactive, marginal and minimal. This categorization was mainly based on the perceived contribution of various legislative institutions in governance and democratic process. Some of the benchmark for assessing the performance of legislatures which formed the basis for the above classification includes: (1) which of the actors (executive or legislators) initiate bills that eventually become laws; (2) the policy-making power of legislatures and; (3) the level of support for legislatures by the political elites and the public. [1]

However, probing legislative performance is largely anchored on how well the electorates are represented in governance by the legislature. Thus, legislator-constituent relations are one of the dimensions of understanding legislative performance. To this end, the development of Constituency Development Fund (CDF) provides another theoretical perspective to the understanding of legislative performance. There are studies that attempted a broad based analysis of legislators' efforts towards constituency services. In the literature, constituency services are more often linked to incumbency advantage. In other words, constituency services are used by incumbent legislators to mobilize votes (electoral incentive) (See Cain, Fere John & Fiorina, 1987; Fiorina and Rivers, 1989; King, 1991; Levitt and Synder, 1997). Constituency services, therefore, enhances the functionality of legislature as a representative institution. Legislatures, through constituency services, represent the people and link local needs to government. This function in a way underscores the centrality of legislature in democratic governance. In Nigeria, constituency services are prioritized as part of the functions of the legislature. The provision for constituency offices and constituency allowances for legislators confirm this assertion.

However, it is also argued that voter attachment to political parties, to some extent, determines the impact of constituency services on the legislators. For instance, in parliamentary regimes, where parties are stronger, constituency services are less pronounced. On the other hand, constituency services seem to be more important in presidential regimes, because parties are less strong and thus individual legislators operate with greater degree of liberty and discretion in the discharge of their legislative functions including the provision of benefits to their constituents.

Keefer and Khemani's (2008) study of the effect of party influence on decision of legislators in relation to constituency services, provides one of the systematic analysis of how voter attachment to political parties reduces commitment to constituency services by incumbent legislators. Their analysis was based on Constituency Development Fund (CDF), which was described as a specific type of public spending programme adopted in India, Kenya, Philippines and other developing countries. In this regards, CDFs provide budgetary allocations directly to individual legislators to spend on public projects in their respective constituencies. The use of CDFs is to provide a clear-cut measure of assessment of legislators' efforts, because previous measures failed to distinguish between beneficiaries of output and do not also capture the degree to which output is due to efforts rather than other factors.

However, Shiller and Wendy (1995) are concerned basically with the number and relevance of bills that American legislators sponsor as a measure of performance assessment. Stratmann and Baur (2002), on the other hand, study committee membership of legislators and categorized some committees as better platform that enables legislators to provide some targeted benefits to constituents. Padro'I Miguel and Snyder (2004) base their analysis on subjective assessments of legislators' performance by third parties (journalists, civil society organizations, etc.). In essence, however, the provision of constituency services by legislators is seen as a better measure for assessing the performance of legislators compared to other yardsticks.

Another theoretical perspective to understanding the performance of legislatures revolves around the quest for the professionalization of legislative institutions. Squire (1988) argues that legislative professionalization is contextualized into three major components: member remuneration level, staff support and facilities as well as service time-demand. Thus, legislative professionalization supposedly enhances the capacity of individual legislators in their drive for effective legislative performance. For example, legislators seek to professionalize the legislature and advance their career prospects by demanding for more legislative staff, which not only benefits legislative leaders in their quest for equal standing with the executive, but also works to the advantage of individual legislators by giving them resources to improve their re-election bids and to become more assertive in policy-making process.

Krutz, (2000) conceives legislative performance from the standpoint of party affiliation of members. He argues that fragmented legislatures along party lines are likely to be constrained in their quest for effective performance. Fragmented legislatures are, therefore, more prone to uncertainties in law making and policy deliberations at the legislative chambers. It is, thus, argued that party membership distribution in the legislature, to some extent, affects the productivity of the institution, especially in areas of policy making. Thus, party control of Congress and presidency is essential in the production of legislation. In other words, unified control of legislature by one party results in more policy innovations and less gridlock than those in divided governments.

Legislative oversight also provides another theoretical viewpoint to understanding legislative performance. The task of overseeing the activities of the executive and other institutions of government remain one of the fundamental functions of a legislature. Thus, the effectiveness or otherwise of legislative oversight provides a standard measure for assessing legislative performance. In both parliamentary and presidential democracies, the conduct of oversight responsibilities distinguishes legislatures from other branches of government. However, oversight tools vary from one system of government to another. The number of tools and the level of involvement of legislatures in oversight define the complex nature of the institution, which is the key to understanding its performance. Quite a number of studies on legislative oversight abound in the literature. (See Pillezo and Stonpenhurst, 2004; Oslon, 2004; Schneir, 2004; Deposto, 2004; Sheppard 2004).

However, John Uhr (2005) presents a broad-based analysis of legislative performance. His study was limited to the Australian Commonwealth Parliament; it, nonetheless, provides deeper insights as to what constitutes the measure of legislative performance. In his operationalization of democratic auditing, which represents the standard measure for performance assessment of Australian Parliament, he was quick to distinguish 'democratic' from 'auditing'. He contends that democracy means democratization, progress towards greater degrees of democracy. On the other hand, audit approach in this context refers to assessing the strengths and weaknesses of political institutions, threats and opportunities against specified democratic standards. In this study, he dismisses the assumption by Australian political scientists that political parties with majority parliamentary seats truly represents the 'majority' and that restricted standard of majority rule is the appropriate and uncontested standard against which to judge the performance of parliamentary institutions.

As a departure from the above theoretical assumptions by previous scholars, Uhr (2005) developed a model of parliamentary assessment, which he argues may not be absolutely scientific but is capable of generating further theoretical challenges in the study of legislative performance. This model is classified into four different standards against which the Australian parliament is to be assessed. These standards include: political equality - referring to the contribution parliaments make in the strengthening of democratic citizenship and promoting equal opportunities for political participation and representation; popular control of government - referring particularly to the contribution parliaments make to strengthening accountability of government by protecting the public interests against undue private interests dominating the process of government; civil liberties and human rights- referring particularly to the contributions parliaments make to strengthening civil liberties through effective scrutiny of legislative proposals and through timely review of threats to human rights by holders of executive power and; public deliberations – referring particularly to the contributions parliaments make to strengthening the process of public deliberations by promoting opportunities for balance and diversity in opinion formation in the public sphere.

The above set of performance standards provides the convenient framework upon which the Australian parliaments are assessed. Notwithstanding their shortcomings in terms of scope and the scientific validity of the data to be used, these standards are essentially relevant in understanding the level of performance of legislatures. The major argument is that parliaments are critical institutions of democracy. As such, they are established to ingrain the course of democratization. Thus, these standards, to some extent, cover the core areas of democratic governance which include popular participation, human rights, accountability and political equality. These benchmarks may provide some guide to assessing the performance of Nigerian legislature.

On this review note, it can be concluded that theoretical discourses on legislative performance are diverse and conceived from different perspectives. In spite of the diversity of approaches to the study of legislative performance, it can be argued that performance measurement of political institutions and particularly parliaments can be done using a variety of standards and/or yardsticks. The concern, therefore, is mainly to ascertain the strengths and weaknesses in its drive towards higher degrees of democracy. In this study, however, the four set of standards developed by Uhr (2005) may serve as a theoretical guide in the analysis of legislative performance in Nigeria. This does not suggest that other standards of measurement are completely rejected. Depending largely on the utility of various yardsticks and standards of measurement, consideration may be given to rationalize a variety of assessment framework. To this end, certain empirical data may be presented to substantiate the utility and scientific validity of some of these measurement standards. The next section provides the analysis of legislative performance in Nigeria from 1999-2009.

Performance of the Nigerian Legislature: 1999-2009

Political institutions are established to perform certain functions in order to facilitate the political process and development of a given society. In a democratic system, these institutions are structured and nurtured to enhance the sustainability of democratization project. Thus, to keep the pace of institutional growth and development, the performance of these institutions is constantly measured against some predetermined standards. This is with a view to appreciate their strength and weakness in order to develop appropriate mechanisms and strategies for improving their performance. Accordingly, performance measurement in social sciences and particularly in political science is a significant research endeavour. Hence, quite a number of techniques abound in the literature and are often used by scholars in assessing the performance of one political institution or another. The preceding section unveiled some of the yardsticks of performance measurement as it relate to the legislature. This section reviews the activities of the Nigerian National Assembly between 1999 and 2009 against certain standards of performance measurement, particularly the standards of measurement advocated by Uhr (2005). These include: political equality; popular control of government; civil liberties and human rights; and public deliberations.

Political Equality: The question of political equality is a central one in the discourses of democracy and democratization. To a very large extent, democratic regimes are evaluated on the basis of the degree of equality among citizens. Democracy as a framework of governance evolved within the context of the principle of human equality. This may include equality of all before the law as provided by the rule of law and, to a large extent also, the conduct of free, fair and periodic elections. Democratic elections, in this regard, give citizens the opportunity to participate actively in the choice of representatives and leaders who are also accountable to them through a number of control mechanisms. These control mechanisms include the existence of a vibrant and autonomous legislature that keep track of the activities of the executive to prevent abuse of power and ensure that popular policies are conceived and implemented for the general well-being of the citizens. In other words, political equality, in the context of parliaments, implies the ways that parliaments represent the people's voice in all political diversity, facilitating equal representation of all participating political viewpoints.[2]

In particular regard to Nigerian National Assembly, it can be evaluated from the perspective of its role in promoting equal political opportunities for the citizens, particularly in their quest to represent people or to be represented through the conduct of free, fair and periodic elections. Accordingly, parliaments in a democracy play central role in this regard. They contribute to ensure that elections are free and fair and that the electoral systems fairly represent the diversity of political opinions attracting electoral support. It is also the responsibility of parliaments through legislation to devise rules of representation such as proportional representation, simple representation etc. In Nigeria, however, the National Assembly after a decade of existence, one is right to argue, has not contributed in any significant way towards the evolution of a truly independent, representative and functional electoral body that can conduct free, fair and transparent elections. More often than not, the executive, as provided by the flawed constitution imposed by the military, are substantially in charge of the electoral institution. In spite of the constitutional powers given to the legislature by the 1999 constitution to make and amend existing laws, such powers are not exercised by the parliament in Nigeria.

Thus, a recap of events and circumstances that surrounded the conception and enactment of the 2002 Electoral Act is a clear testimony to the fact that the legislature in the Fourth Republic is a mere rubber stamp of the executive. This is so because the deliberations that culminated in the scrutiny of such executive bill and the subsequent production of the said Act suggest that the legislature is not in any significant way a true representative of the people. It is alleged that members of the National Assembly were bribed by the executive to facilitate the passage of the bill with various clauses that protect the interests of the executive in power. The former regime of president Obasanjo, which showed apparent disregard for the rule of law and masterminded electoral malpractices and manipulation of various kinds, was desperate to make sure that such abuses are institutionalized in the country's electoral system. This was demonstrated by the way the scrutinized Electoral Act was doctored at the presidency. This was done with the view to ensure that the then executive had it ways of limiting the rights of the people to vote and be voted for.

The inability of the National Assembly to enact and/or amend existing electoral laws has contributed to the crisis of elections and the fluidity of the country's electoral institution. As the highest law-making body in the country, the National Assembly is empowered by law to make and/or amend laws that guide the conduct of elections, including the formation and conduct of political parties. However, members of the National Assembly in Nigeria have not live up to expectation. They have failed to make laws that could facilitate the active participation of the citizens in the political process through the conduct of free and fair periodic elections. As a matter of fact, one can argue that members of the National Assembly are also beneficiaries of the country's flawed electoral system. To some extent, the conspiracy of the elites, which include both the executive and the legislators, explains the reluctance of the legislature to provide a more functional electoral system by way of amending the existing laws on elections and overseeing the conduct of all institutions and agencies that are concerned with the conduct of elections.[3]

The conduct of the 2003 and 2007 elections is a pointer to the fact that the Nigerian citizens are highly constrained in the exercise of their right to vote and be voted for. The nature of manipulation, rigging and violence that characterized elections in the Fourth Republic has disenfranchised substantial number of qualified voters in the country.[4] The activities of political parties have also darkened the prospects for political equality among the citizens who are members of various political parties. To say it all, internal democracy is not entrenched in both the ruling and opposition parties. And the legislature did little or at best nothing to reform political parties through law-making, to serve as veritable platform for enhanced political participation.

Popular Control of Government: This standard also provides a yardstick against which the performance of a parliament can be measured. Popular control of government suggests the extent to which government and governmental officials are held accountable for their actions and inactions. Popular control of government is synonymous with accountability. As a major element of democracy, accountability describes the level of *democraticness* of a particular regime. To this end, parliaments play a prominent role in the entrenchment of accountability as a principle of good governance. In Nigeria, the National Assembly as established by law represents the diversity of the people in government and ensures that government, especially the executive is properly checked to prevent abuse of power. Thus, the law empowers the National Assembly to conduct investigations into the activities of government agencies and institutions to ensure responsibility in the conduct of public affairs. Uhr (2005) argues:

> There are many numbers of steps on the ladder of accountability, from the low ones of collective ministerial responsibility to the high ones of sustained investigation into individual ministerial responsibility. I should, of course, mention the many mechanisms of public service accountability to parliament - such as scrutiny and oversight committees- flowing from the financial accountability of public bodies for their contribution to public management. (Uhr, 2005: 23)

However, in Nigeria, from 1999 to 2009, there has been growing concerns as to whether the National Assembly is truly a representative institution of governance that is structured to institutionalize accountability. The conduct of this institution from inception is a clear testimony to the fact that the legislature in Nigeria is in a crisis of relevance and efficiency. This is so, because as a watchdog institution, which is supposed to enhance the efficiency of other governmental agencies and ensure transparency, probity and prudence in the conduct of governmental affairs, it has also fallen short of performing these functions.

For instance, the leadership crisis within the legislature itself constitutes a major challenge to institutionalizing accountability in the democratic process and governance. Thus, to have the moral grounds to effectively check the excesses of the executive, the legislature must demonstrate high level discipline, transparency and accountability in the management of its internal affairs, especially resources allocated to it. Contrarily, from 1999 to 2009, the score card of the National Assembly has been very poor. Misappropriation of resources, contract scam, forgery and other sharp practices by the leadership of both the upper and lower chambers of the Nigerian legislature have raised fundamental questions on the integrity of the institution and its resolve to engender accountability in Nigeria's democratization.

There are also allegations that members of both chambers, either as committee chairmen or in their individual capacities as members, receive or insist on bribe from the executive and its agencies with the view to either promote unpopular executive agenda or cover up some of their misdeeds. The nature and pattern of changes in the leadership of both Houses of the legislature, through impeachments and/or resignation, is a pointer to the fact that corruption has become endemic in this vital institution of democracy. The prevalence of corruption in Nigeria's National Assembly has left no one in doubt that its members lack the integrity as moral requirement to exercise their constitutionally assigned responsibilities. Hence, they remain handicapped in exercising firm control of the executive.

The evidence of corruption in the legislature is also affecting its legitimacy and is fast weakening its support base from its stakeholders (the general public, civil society organizations, labour unions, non-governmental organizations, etc.). The recurrent nature of corruption in Nigeria's National Assembly which continued unabated has turned the hope of Nigerians to despair. It is clear from the conduct of the lawmakers that they are immensely vulnerable to financial shocks. Thus, it takes the executive only a little time to influence their actions on any policy issue or legislation, by either bribing the leadership or the entire membership of the legislature. Since the return of the country to democratic rule in 1999, series of allegations and evidence of corruption in the legislature are reported and brought to the knowledge of Nigerians. These include forgery scandals of the first Speaker of the House of Representatives and the Senate President's allegations of corruption through contract scams by subsequent leadership of both chambers, thereby leading to impeachments and protracted leadership tussle, collection of bribes by members from the executive and its agencies on policy issues, legislations, budget and even screening of nominees for various appointments.

Of recent is the scandal within the leadership of the lower House, in which the speaker and other principal officers conspired and siphoned huge amount of financial resources in a contract inflation scam for the renovation of the residences of the then Speaker and her Deputy. This recent crisis polarized the House into 'integrity group' (those insisting for the resignation of the speaker) and the 'due process group' (those insisting for the retention of the positions of the speaker and other principal officers) (Ogunmade, *This Day*, 28 Febuary 2008). However, it is alleged that the selfish interests of members were the driving force behind the agitations. For instance, members of the 'due process' groups are believed to be beneficiaries of the scam and/ or chairs strategic committees otherwise known as 'juicy committees'. On the other hand, members of the integrity group are believed to be those who lost out in the game of committee appointment. The leader of the group, Hon. Farouk Lawan, is alleged to be the major victim. His redeployment to the committee on education from the committee on appropriation, which is said to be the most strategic and money fetching, sparked off the crisis. This is in addition to ignoring his leading role in the emergence of Hon. Patricia Eteh as the Speaker. This and other grievances culminated into unveiling the Speaker's abuse of office and her subsequent resignation as the speaker. (See *Daily Trust*, 22 March 2008).

In the upper chamber also, several financial scandals are reported, both within the leadership and among senators, especially at committee levels (Adisa, *Nigerian Tribune*, 25 December 2008). The most widely-publicized is the case involving Senator Iyabo Obasanjo Bello (Chairperson, Senate Committee on Health). This scandal has caused for the resignation, arrest and trial of top officials of the Federal Ministry of Health, including the said senator by the Economic and Financial Crimes Commission (EFCC). The alleged sharing of unspent monies of the ministry among these officials generated the crisis. The case is still pending in court.

The apparent lack of transparency and accountability in the conduct of the legislature has to a large extent affected its performance. It thus fails to be an institution of countervailing power of horizontal accountability across governmental agencies. The nature of patron-client politics in Nigeria has also encouraged the sharp practices of the legislators to meet the financial needs of their patrons and accumulate resources for re-election bid. This has diverted the attention of the lawmakers from their primary responsibilities to unprincipled practices that are self-centered.[5] This major weakness of the National Assembly has called to question the instrumentality of the institution as the watchdog of Nigeria's fledgling democracy.

Rights and Liberties: Rights and liberties are undoubtedly crucial elements of democracy. In essence, democracy as a framework of governance is conceived within the context of human rights and liberties. To some extent, a regime is deemed democratic on the basis of its commitment to and protection of the fundamental human rights. Across the globe, human rights are increasingly becoming one of the major indicators of commitment to democracy, all things being equal. Thus, abuse of human rights is a negation of one of the fundamental principles of democracy. So, regardless of whether or not other elements of democracy are met, human rights is ranked foremost in the assessment of a democratic regime. In this respect, the legislature as an organ of government is structured in a democracy to facilitate the realization of human rights and liberties through a number of activities. As a law-making body, legislation and scrutiny of executive proposals as well as timely review of threats to human rights buttress the relevance and centrality of the legislature in the promotion and protection of human rights and liberties. Uhr (2005), in his analysis of legislature's role in the defense of human rights, opines:

> "At the lower end of positive performance are those parliaments keeping up to date the public law protecting individuals against undue trespass and interference by governments and other power holders. Of course, every piece of legislation has the potential to impact adversely on individual rights and liberties. A democratic parliament would have safeguards in place so that the legislative process includes scrutiny of the civil liberties impacts of legislation, including of course regulations and other forms of subordinate legislation. Higher ranking would go to parliaments with more systematic protections against legislative and administrative intrusions against civil liberties. For instance, the power of the parliament to disallow rights-offending regulations is an increasingly important part of parliamentary armory. So too, scrutiny of bills committees with capacities to alert parliament to suspect legislative provisions and to

stall the passage of legislation until parliament is ready to supply its *informed* consent to government legislative proposals." (Uhr, 2005: 27).

In Nigeria, therefore, the legislature can be assessed on the basis of its contribution to the promotion and protection of people's fundamental rights. As the major institution empowered to make and/or amend existing laws, it is in a better position to evolve a better constitutional and legal framework that can facilitate the realization of human rights. Through legislation and particularly scrutiny of executive proposals, the legislature has the power to question and stall any attempt to institutionalize the infringement of the rights of the people. However, events in Nigeria since the inception of the current democratic regime in 1999 have shown that people's rights are under serious threat.

The return to democratic rule in 1999 after a long period of military rule has not significantly changed situations as regards the abuse of fundamental human rights. For instance, the right to freedom of speech and expressions which had been highly limited under military rule is also phenomenal under the current dispensation. There are quite a number of instances where the government, especially under the previous regime of President Obasanjo, maimed and/or killed individuals and groups who expressed their views concerning government policies and manifestoes.[6] The massacre of human lives in Odi and Zaki Biam by the said regime is a pointer to the fact that there is little or no commitment by the current democratic regime to protect the basic rights of the people, including the priceless right to life. However, the most disturbing and alarming setback that characterizes the rampant abuses of human rights, especially the infringement of the people's right to life is that the legislature has made little or no efforts within its powers to check this dangerous trend. More often than not, the response of the National Assembly to these and other similar abuses of human rights begin and end with the call on the executive to ensure respect for the rule of law. Concrete efforts are, therefore, not being made to address these issues in the most appropriate constitutional process. Thus, sanctions on culprits even when investigations show that they are guilty of the accused offences are not properly meted on them. They eventually escape legal sanction and the abuses continue unchecked.

Furthermore, where the legislature conceives the need for review and/ or initiates a new legislation that could facilitate the realization of some rights and liberties of the people, the process often becomes sluggish, thereby unnecessarily delaying or even jettisoning the attempt to broaden the scope of human rights and liberties in the country. The case of the bill on Freedom of Information, which has been long-standing with the National Assembly, is one among numerous examples. This bill, if passed into law, is expected to empower the citizens with some basic information about the activities of government which may serve as an instrument of control over elected representatives and other categories of public officials. However, the National Assembly, for political reasons arising from the conspiracy of both the executive and the legislature, the bill has been kept in view. This and other similar attitudes of the legislature in the Nigeria's Fourth Republic suggest that there is no clear commitment to the realization of basic human rights in the country.

In the context of the frequent and profuse infringement on the personal liberties of the Nigerian citizens under the current dispensation, one is perhaps correct to argue that the present dispensation is not quite different from what obtained under the military autocracy. For instance, the activities of the police with regards to unlawful arrest and detention of people without recourse to the provision of the law is still rampant in the country. The legislature is supposed to ensure that the police as an executive agency is properly checked through oversight functions to prevent their rampant abuses of human rights and liberties. The scenario in the Nigerian prisons is even worse than the conduct of the Nigerian police. The prison congestion and the inadequate welfare for the prisoners in Nigeria are suggestive of the fact that human liberties in the country are not issues of concern to the present democratic government. This is also in addition to the fact that significant number of people are in Nigerian prisons awaiting trials. Inadequate prison infrastructure and facilities have made life in prison traumatic and of course a major cause of recidivism in the society. In spite of this, the legislature did little or nothing to reverse this ugly trend.

This is also the case with other aspects of human rights and liberties that are constantly abused without the expected intervention of the legislature. There is the question of citizenship-indigene dichotomy. The right to freedom of thought, religion and conscience, right to freedom of movement and lawful assembly and procession is highly restricted in Nigeria. The wave of incessant ethno-religious violence that gulped a large number of human lives and properties worth billions of naira is an indication that some of these laws are outdated and needed to be repealed and replaced with new ones. Thus, under the current democratic dispensation, the country has witnessed the highest episodes of ethno-religious violence with human carnage that is comparable to a civil war.[7] The intensity of these violent conflicts, to a large extent, threatens the corporate existence of Nigeria as a nation. This in addition to the protracted agitations in the Niger Delta for resource control which have since transformed into an uprising or a secessionist movement. The inadequate legislative attention to these burning issues is questioning the integrity and relevance of the Nigerian legislature in democratic process.

Popular Deliberation: This is also an important standard for measuring the performance of a legislative institution in a democracy. The concept of popular deliberation shows the growing importance of deliberative democracy.

In relation to the parliaments, it shows how participatory the process of legislation and policy making is in a particular democratic dispensation. It is premised on the argument that people are sources of political power and that they ought to be carried along in the process of governance. Thus, since the legislature symbolizes the sovereignty of the people, members of the legislature are also supposed to be in constant touch with the people, at least to sample divergent opinions on various issues affecting their livelihood.

The legislature under the current dispensation is provided with the opportunity to interact with critical stakeholders on policy issues and legislation. To this end, as part of its procedures of information gathering, public hearings by various legislative committees are institutionalized in its procedures of operation. Civil society organizations, non-governmental organizations, labour unions, religious groups and other pressure groups are some of the targets of the legislature on issues that require the attention of the public. More so, the provision of constituency offices and allowances for the legislators suggest that a framework is institutionalized to facilitate public deliberations of issues before the legislature. More often, however, these provisions are negated by individual legislators. Investigations have shown that most of the constituency offices are not functional, as the necessary resources needed for their running are not provided for by the legislators. Thus, the resources collected for the purpose are diverted for personal benefits of the law makers. The legislators hardly frequent their constituencies let alone to interact with their constituents on pressing national or constituency issues. This act, indeed, has limited the participation of the people in public deliberation as a source of legislation or policy making.

The parliament as representative of the people is also expected to mediate between the state and civil society organizations. This endeavour is capable of facilitating active involvement of the general public whose views are promoted by a number of civil society organizations. To a very large extent, the civil society and other non- governmental organizations, depending largely on the vibrancy of such outfits, influences the activities of legislative institutions. In Nigeria, however, civil society organizations are more active and vibrant under military regimes. They were more vigorous in the struggle for the enthronement of a democratic order than in the drive towards sustaining it. In essence, they often appear to be lured into promoting parochial interests than the struggle for deepening of democratic governance. The legislature of the Fourth Republic does not also see the civil society as partners in the conduct of their legislative duties. Aside from the conventional participation of the CSOs in public hearings, they are hardly carried along in the deliberations of some major legislations and policy issues before the National Assembly. In some instances, however, one can argue that the corrupt nature of the CSOs to a large extent affects their active involvement in legislation and policy making process. Thus, the general public remains isolated from government and their views are often ignored.

Another dimension to understanding the instrumentality of the parliaments in public deliberations is the development of parliament's own bureaucracy.[8] The central role of parliamentary staff in information gathering and, of course, facilitating the engagement of the citizens in public deliberations cannot be overemphasized. They conduct research and investigations on behalf of the lawmakers, prepare and coordinate public hearings and series of activities that help the legislators reach out to the people. Kefee (1964: 68) opines:

> "The central reason for creating professional staff was to prevent committees from excessive reliance on research studies produced by executive agencies. For congress to function as co-equal partner with the executive in the legislative process, the congress should empower itself to obtain its own independent staff services and that it pay adequately for them."

In Nigeria, the parliamentary staff is not only inadequate and poorly remunerated but they are inefficient and lack the requisite capacity to enhance the efficiency of the legislature. The poor quality of legislative staff in the National Assembly is as a result of poor or non-existence of comprehensive training programmes. Training programmes are meant to build the capacity of personnel to support the legislators with information and quality services for effective legislation and particularly in facilitating public deliberations.[9] Although, funds are said to be voted for training and capacity-building, these funds are most often siphoned by the leadership of the legislature in collaboration with the management. There are also little efforts to attract funding for capacity building from donor agencies. [10]

Thus, the four standards of performance measurement advocated by Uhr (2005) in relation to parliamentary institutions are essentially relevant in the analysis of the performance of the National Assembly in Nigeria. In spite of the fact that empirical data is not presented to show performance level of the Nigerian legislature, these standards of measurement provide some insights as to what constitute the contribution and/or constraints of this institution to democracy and democratization in the country. This is because these standards cover a wider scope of democracy as a framework of governance.

Conclusion: From Hope to Despair

The return of Nigeria to democratic rule on the 29th May 1999 saw the establishment of some vital institutions of democracy among which the legislature is one. The legislature in Nigeria is one of the few institutions that suffered decay under the military. Thus, few self-appointed military personnel and others assumed the position of law making through the promulgation of Decrees. However, as part of the arrangement for smooth transition of power from the military to a democratically elected government, the legislature as a branch of government is constituted through electoral process. Conventionally, therefore, this institution is structured to perform the functions of law making, representation and conduct oversight activities. These functions are essentially central to the realization of democratic values of political equality, accountability, human rights and liberties and public deliberations. It is against these envisioned values of democracy that the national parliament in Nigeria is assessed.

From the foregoing analysis, it is evident that the national legislature in Nigeria has fall short of the standards of democratic rule. It is argued that the legislature has not done significantly well in enhancing the equality of the Nigerian citizens. This shortcoming has limited the level of participation of the people in the democratic process and governance. The constitution inherited from the military is not reviewed to ensure active and meaningful participation of the people, especially through the conduct of free, fair and transparent elections. In the area of public accountability, it is evident that the legislature itself is engulfed in series of corrupt practices that constitute a national embarrassment. The drive of the legislature towards accountable governance is greatly hampered by the enormous corruption that pervades the institution itself. The growing concern for the realization of wide range of human rights and liberties and the thirst for public deliberation of legislation and policy issues are equally in jeopardy. This development has turned democratic hopes into despair in Nigeria. Given these circumstances, therefore, are there prospects for improved legislative performance?

As an emerging democracy that is just a decade old, there are prospects nonetheless for strengthening and institutionalizing the Nigerian legislature for sustainable accountable governance. The development of vibrant civil society organizations and the media may serve as a check on the activities of the legislature, which will undoubtedly enhance its integrity for accountable governance. The current wave of legislative investigations in the various sectors of the economy and society (power, transport, FCT, agriculture, finance, Bakasi handover, etc.) with revealing facts on frauds and breach of procedures by various executive agencies is indicative of the fact that the Nigerian legislature is fast awakening from its deep slumber. As such, more of these endeavours will reposition the institution to engender accountability in Nigeria's democratization. [11]

However, whether or not these investigations are done with the view to entrench best practices in governance is also a function of the conclusion of these investigations, the objectivity of its findings and how appropriate sanctions are imposed on culprits, regardless of how highly placed they may be. This is because the fear of subjective judgment by these committees is confirmed by the intrigues that characterized their investigations. For instance, the investigations by the House committee on power, which appears to be the most alarming in terms of the gravity of scandals by both government officials and contractors/private companies, is alleged to be manipulated by certain quotas within and outside the legislature. These fears and allegations undermine the objectivity of the investigations and the commitment of not only the concerned committee but the entire legislature to foster accountability in governance. Some of these allegations are that members of committee collected ₦100 million as bribe from one of the contractors that abandoned project site after being paid. (See *Weekly Trust*, July 26, 2008).

References

Andrich, John H. (1995). Why Parties? The Origin and Transformation of Political Parties in America. In B. I. Page (ed.), *American Politics and Political Economy Series.* Chicago: University of Chicago Press.

Ashworth, Scott & Ethan, Bueno de Mesquita (2006). Delivering the Goods: Legislative Particularism in Different Electoral and Institutional Settings. *The Journal of Politics, Vol. 68, No. 1,* pp. 168-179.

Baba T.K.Y. (2008). The Legislature and Democratization in Nigeria: Towards Understanding the Prospects and Challenges of Accountability in the Democratic Process. Paper Delivered the International Conference on the theme: *Is Nigeria Democratizing*, organized by the Faculty of Arts, Obafemi Awolowo University, Ile Ife, 12-16 August 2008.

Caillaud, B., & Jean T. (2002, November). Parties as Political Intermediaries. *The Quarterly Journal of Economics,* pp. 1453-1489.

Cain, Bruce, E. et al. (1987). *The Personal Vote: Constituency Service and Electoral Independence*. Cambridge: Harvard University Press.

Daily Trust Newspaper, 22 March, 2008.

Davidson, R., & Parkar G.R. (1979). Positive Support for Political Institutions: The Case of Congress. *Western Political Science Quarterly, Vol. 25,* pp. 600-612.

Desposato, S.W. (2004). Explaining Patterns of Oversight in Brazilian Subnational Governments. In Pellizo & Stapenhurst (eds.), *Issues on Contemporary Parliamentary Development.* Washington, D.C.: World Bank Institute.

Fenon, John (1996). *Midwest Politics*. New York: Holt, Rinehart and Wiston.

Figueiredo, A.C., & Limongi, F. (2000). Constitutional Change, Legislative Performance and Institutional Consolidation. *Brazilian Review of Social Sciences, Special Issue, No. 1,* pp. 74-94.

Fiorina, M., & Douglas Rivers (1989). Constituency Service, Reputation, and the Incumbency Advantage. In Fiorina, Morris & David Rhode (eds.), *Home Style and Washington Work.* Ann Arbor: University of Michigan Press.

Jewell, M.E., & Breaux, D. (1988). The Effect of Incumbency on State Legislative Elections. *Legislative Studies Quarterly, Vol.13,* pp. 495-514.

Jones, Mark P. (1995). *Electoral Laws and the Survival of Presidential Democracies.* Notre Dame IL: University of Notre Dame Press.

Keefer, P., and Khemani, S. (2008). When Do Legislators Pass Pork? The Role of Political Parties in Determining Legislator Effort. The World Bank Development Research Group, May, 21.

Kefee, W.J. (1997). *Congress and American People, Second Edition*. United States: Prentice Hall.

King, G. (1991). Constituency Service and Incumbent Advantage. *British Journal of Political Science, Vol. 21, No. 1*, pp. 119-125.

Krutz, S. G. (2000). Getting Around the Gridlok: The Effect of Omnibus Utilization on Legislative Productivity. *Legislative Studies Quarterly, Vol. 25, No. 4*, pp. 533-549.

Levitt, S., & Snyder, J. (1997). The Impact of Federal Spending on House Election Outcomes. *Journal of Political Economy, No. 105*, pp. 30-53.

Levy, G. (2004). A Model of Political Parties. *Journal of Economic Theory, No. 115*, pp. 225-277.

Mainwaring, S. (1993). Presidentialism, Multipartism and Democracy: The Difficult Combination. *Comparative Political Studies, Vol. 26*, pp: 198-228.

Mainwaring, S., Shugart, & Mathew, S. (eds.) (1997). *Presidentialism and Democracy in Latin America.* New York: Cambridge University Press.

Morelli, Massimo (2004). Party Formation and Policy Outcomes under Different Electoral System. *Review of Economic Studies, No. 71*, pp. 829-853.

Odolofin, A.P. (2005). Electoral Politics, Elite Conspiracy and the Future of Nigeria. In Onu G., and Momoh (eds.), *Elections and Democratic Consolidation in Nigeria.* Proceedings of the 23rd Annual of the Nigerian Political Science Association.

Ogundiya, I. S. & Baba, T.K. (2005). Electoral Violence and the Prospects of Democratic Consolidation in Nigeria. In Godwin O. & Abubakar M. (eds.), *Elections and Democratic Consolidation in Nigeria.* A Publication of the Nigerian Political Science Association (N.P.S.A.). Lagos: Traid Associates Publishers.

Ogunmade, O. *This Day*, 28 Febuary 2008.

Olson, D.M. (2004). Administrative Review and Oversight the Experiences of Post-communist Legislatures. In Pelizzo & Stapenhrst (2004), *Series on Contemporary Issues in Parliamentary Development.* Washington DC: World Bank Institute.

Otorofani, F. (2008, September 15). *Nigerian* Newspaper.

Padro' i Miguel, G., & Snyder, J. (2004). Legislative Effectiveness and Legislative Life. Mimeo, MIT.

Pelizzo, R., & Stapenhurst, D. (2004). Legislature and Oversights. *Series on Contemporary Issues in Parliamentary Development.* Washington DC: World Bank Institute.

Polsby, Nelson W. (1968). Institutionalisation of the U.S.: House of Representatives. *American Political Science Review, Vol. 62*, pp.144-168.

Schneier, Edward (2004). Emerging Patterns of Legislative Oversights in Indonesia. In Pelizzo & Stapenhrst (eds.) *Issues in Contemporary Parliamentary Development.*, Washington DC: World Bank Institute.

Shephard, M. (2004). Administrative Review and Oversight: The Experience of Westminster. In Pelizzo & Stapenhrst, *Issues in Contemporary Parliamentary Development*. Washington DC: World Bank Institute.

Shiller Wendy, J. (1995). Senators as Political Entrepreneurs: Using Bill Sponsorship to Shape Legislative Agenda. *American Journal of Political Science, No. 39.* pp. 123-135.

Snyder, J., & Ting, M. (2002). An Informational Rationale for Political Parties. *American Journal of Political Science, No.46,* pp. 90-110.

Squire, Peverill (1998). Career Opportunities and Membership Stability in Legislatures. *Legislative Studies Quarterly, Vol. 13,* No. 1, pp. 65-82.

Stratmann, T., & Baur, M. (2002). Plurality Rule, Proportional Representation and German Bundestag: How Incentives to Pork Barrel Differ Across Electoral Systems. *American Journal of Political Science, Vol. 46, No. 3,* pp. 506-514.

Suberu, R.T. (2002). Can the Nigerian Federation Survive? In Osaghe, E. E. et al. (eds.), *The Nigerian Civil War and its Aftermath.* Ibadan: John Archers Publishers.

Taylor-Robinson, M., & Diaz, C. (1999). Who Gets Legislation Passed in a Marginal Legislature and is the Label Marginal Legislature Still Appropriate. *Comparative Political Studies, Vol. 32, No. 5,* pp. 589-625.

The Tide (online), April 18, 2008.

Uhr, John (2005). How Democratic is Parliament? A Case Study in Auditing the Performance of Parliaments. Democratic Audit Australia, Political Science Program, Research School of Social Science, ANU.

Vanguard Newspaper, April 8, 2008.

Footnotes

1. See Mezey, M. (1979). *Comparative Legislatures*. Durham, NC: Duke University Press.
2. John Uhr (2005) "How Democratic is Parliament?: A Case Study in Auditing the Performance of Parliaments" p. 15
3. Odolofin, A.P (2005) Electoral Politics, Elite Conspiracy and the Future of Nigeria in Onu G. and Momoh Elections and Democratic Consolidation in Nigeria Proceedings of the 23rd Annual of the Nigerian Political Science Association.
4. Ogundiya I.S. and Baba T.K. (2005) Electoral Violence and the Prospects of Democratic Consolidation in Nigeria in Onu G. and Momoh Elections and Democratic Consolidation in Nigeria Proceedings of the 23rd Annual of the Nigerian Political Science Association.
5. Baba T.K.Y (2008) The legislature and Democratization in Nigeria: Towards Understanding the Prospects and Challenges of Accountability in the Democratic Process, Being a Paper Delivered the International Conference on

"Is Nigeria Democratizing" Organized by the Faculty of Arts Obafemi Awolowo University, Ile Ife 12th -16th August, 2008.

6. See documented facts by Ogundiya I.S. and Baba T.K. (2005) Electoral Violence and the Prospects of Democratic Consolidation in Nigeria in Onu G and Momoh Elections and Democratic Consolidation in Nigeria Proceedings of the 23rd Annual of the Nigerian Political Science Association.
7. Suberu, R.T. (2002) "Can the Nigerian Federation Survive" in Osaghe, E.E. *et. al* (eds) The Nigerian Civil War and its Aftermath, Ibadan, John Archers Publishers.
8. See Uhr, (2005) op.cit.
9. In addition to lacking training to develop the expertise of staff in the Nigerian legislature, most of the legislative staff, particularly, Aides, are sons, daughters and relations of the legislators. Thus, merit and qualifications are always ignored in the recruitment of legislative aides. In fact, most of them are not permanent staff of the National Assembly (NASS). It can, therefore, be argued that, the character of NASS reflects the broad character of the Nigerian state, all things being equal.
10. See Baba T. K.Y. op. cit. p. 19.
11. See Baba T. K.Y. ibid p. 23.

6

Legislative Inputs and Good Governance in Nigeria: 1999-2009

Akanle, Olayinka

Introduction

The legislature is arguably the most fundamental and the most critical organ out of the four organs[1] of government in the development and crystallisation of open and democratic societies. This is because the legislature plays the crucial role of aggregating collective interests of the people and galvanising them through laws that protect the peoples' interests and aspirations. The appreciation of mechanisms and dynamics of the legislative arm, therefore, become necessary and central to legitimisation of democracy as the government of the people, by the people and for the people, as the legislature identifies popular problems, negotiate consensus and set agenda for policy implementations through the process of law making. While a healthy relationship among the organs is a necessity, the legislature must not fail in the assertion of its independence and discharge of its duties without which there is bound to be dangerous compromise.

This background is sufficiently recognised as it is factored into the composition of legislature. The legislature is for instance the single organ of government with the largest elected officials. While there is only one elected president for instance, there are at least 109 elected senators and 360 representatives in the Nigerian bi-cameral legislature. Each of the 36 states also has elected state assembly having 24-40 seats, depending on population strength, on 4-year tenure. The judiciary as the third organ does not have elected officials but were appointed by the executive. This is why there is usually fusion of interests between the executive and judiciary in Nigeria[2]. The legislature is, therefore, a unique organ empowered to ultimately protect the people and influence their livelihood.

To be an effective organ, the legislature must appreciate the enormity of its tasks, imbibe a culture of service to the public, constantly evaluate governance processes within the frameworks of expected democratic criteria and make necessary contributions. In other words, conscientious international best practices in legislative activities must be embedded into the Nigerian 21st century legislature. This realization is important because democracy, governance and constructions of legislature are global. In other words, it is against global yardsticks that operations and efficiency of any legislature will be measured even when recourse is made to unique and real state of democratic institutionalisation of the society in question.

Today's citizens most often have access to the desirable practice of democracy and its relationship with the achievement of development at the other side of global divide especially with the present Obama phenomenon and the *change we can believe.* It is, therefore, only incumbent for the scale of responsive governance and legislative activities to be improved in attempts to deliver dividends of democracy in real terms. The point then is that the legislature is strategic especially with the growing popularity of legislative oversight functions and threats of impeachments as necessary tool for uprooting deep-rooted authoritarian legacies of colonial and military rule as well as contemporary obnoxious executive agendas.

There is, thus, no gainsaying the fact that the legislature is a potent and lethal force in the annexation of democracy for sustainable development and improved livelihood, because it is involved at the three most crucial stages of governance and development process. That is, right from design (effective law making), evaluation of results (oversight functions/probes) and appropriate sanctioning (impeachment or its threat, sometimes). It is against this backdrop that this chapter assesses the legislative inputs of contemporary Nigerian legislature to governance in the quest for democratic justification and national development. The key bases to focus include historicisation, roles performance and legislative effectiveness.

History of Modern Legislature in Nigeria

There are exceedingly many lessons to be learnt from history because there is nothing that subsists without existential roots in the past. The present is at best a manifestation of the past. Therefore, to present an examination of contemporary Nigerian legislature without sufficient historicisation is to present a dangerously incomplete account of a crucial phenomenon. Although Osuji (2008) observes that the origin of the legislature is difficult to ascertain just as the definition and processes, this is not the case with Nigeria's. There are sharp episodic processes in Nigerian legislative history that make historical excursions possible without much confusion or controversy.

It is possible to identify primordial or traditional legislature on the one hand and contemporary or modern[3]on the other hand in Nigerian legislative history. As was the case in the Early Summerian City dwellers around 3500 BC, Acropolis gatherings of ancient Greece, Penchaya system of Local Government in India in early 6th century BC and The Kouroukanfouga Charter adopted in 1236 under the Mali empire (Diop and Liautier, 2007; Klein, 2001; Muhlberger, n.d.), traditional Nigerian societies had their own indigenous legislative processes prior to the balkanization of Africa. Before the arrival of British colonialists, Nigerians lived as well-organised, autonomous kingdoms and empires with internal legislative mechanisms that efficiently regulated internal affairs and external relations with considerable efficacy (Olutayo and Akanle, 2007).

Examples of such autonomous groups include The Oyo Empire, Benin Kingdom, Sokoto Caliphate, Jukun Kingdom and Igbo Society. Although the systems of government of these groups differ substantially,[4] they all had effective legislative processes that were highly defined. In the Oyo Empire for instance, the legislative process was collective between the *Alaafin* (the king) and the *Oyo mesi's* (chiefs) in a legislative fashion that has come to be known as *Oba-in-Council.* The *Alaafin* consulted widely with the chiefs who must have received inputs from their constituents and families before laws are made. It is primarily for this reason that the Oyo Empire system is often described as constitutional monarchy.

The Sokoto Caliphate system was vertically sharp as laws were handed down by the Emir. The Emir was the paramount ruler who himself headed the Council of State down to the village level (Taiwo, 1982). Among the Igbos, legislative processes were the most decentralized and diffused. Laws were made through the representation of all clans and families as the basic units through which the entire males of over fifteen years old met at village squares such as Oha, Amala to vote on issues affecting the society (Osuji, 2008) and laws made to institutionalise such decisions. For this reason, the Igbo system is usually described as egalitarian as it gives equal opportunities to all citizens to make contributions to decision making. It is important to note that these societies were stable due to their proactive and popular legislative mechanisms and outcomes. They made laws and took affirmative decisions that had direct bearings with the issues at hand. Put differently, their legislations were not divorced from social realities (Aguda, 1986) as they were not given to ignorance, selfishness and other parochial and partisan considerations.

The contemporary Nigerian legislature is largely different from the traditional discussed above. The modern parliament is highly formalized with insightful history that enables comprehension of current legislative environments in Nigeria. The history of modern legislature in Nigeria is traceable to the establishment of Legislative Council in 1861/1862 after the colony of Lagos had already been ceded to the British (Karibi-Whyte, 1987; Bugaje, 2003). The Legislative Council was made up of the colonial governor, six officials, two Europeans and two unofficial Nigeria members. The Legislative Council was by and large advisory and devoid of any legislative power in real terms. With the amalgamation of the Southern and Northern Protectorates in 1914, the Nigerian Council was established to complement the Legislative Council. The Nigerian Council had six Nigerian traditional rulers, 7 European businessmen and 23 European officials. Like the Legislative Council, the Nigerian Council lacked any meaningful legislative power and was only advisory. Primarily, it was to demonstrate colonial administration's sensitiveness and willingness to liaise with local people.

This subtle diplomacy to cajole local acceptance of colonial rule continued with Hugh Clifford constitution of 1922, Sir Arthur Richard constitution of 1946, Macpherson constitution of 1952 and that of Sir Oliver Lyttleton of 1954. While they all established legislative councils with mix compositions in terms of race, titles and responsibilities, they mostly lacked legislative powers, as the governors, representing the Queen of England, still reserved the power over public finance, public service, foreign policy (Karibi-Whyte, 1987; Bugaje, 2003) and agriculture. Particularly, it is noteworthy that before 1951 legislation applying to the colony was through letters. Patent was issued under the great seal of the United Kingdom by Her Majesty with advice of the Privy Council (Karibi-Whyte, 1987).

Legislation for the protectorate was by Order-in-Council made under the Foreign Jurisdiction Act while legislation for both the Colony and Protectorate jointly was also made by Order-in-Council (Karibi-Whyte, 1987). Lyttleton constitution was the only one to move Nigeria closer to the independence and local constitutionalism with allowance for the House of Representatives to discuss financial matters and creation of exclusive list, concurrent list and residual list. Also, it was beginning from Sir Oliver Lyttleton constitution of 1954 that no separate legislation was made for Lagos or for the protectorate (Karibi-Whyte, 1987). The 1960 independence constitution still allowed the Queen of England as the head of Nigeria until 1963.

The military coup d'etat of January 15th, 1966 disrupted legislative developments of Nigeria until 1976 composition of Constitution Drafting Committee (CDC) by the military government in readiness for return to democracy in 1979. The resultant 1st October 1979 constitution established bicameral legislature at the centre. The constitution was, however, suspended in 31st December 1983, after only three years and three months of civil rule, through another military coup d' tat. With the intention to return to democracy, General Abdusalami Abubakar, who assumed office as the military president of Nigeria after the sudden death of Late General Sani Abacha, ensured the drafting of 1999 constitution which is the one still in use in the country.

An observable trend from the foregoing historical analysis is that there has been at least one hundred and two (102) years of colonial inputs into Nigerian legislative lifespan (1861-1963). By implication the colonial influences were more than a century. Beyond that, as already observed by Bugaje (2003), a common feature of Nigerian constitution has been consistent limited peoples' involvements and participation as the colonial masters, military and politicians select areas for public discourse and those classified as 'no go areas'. Another important concern is the place of legislative imperialism. A case in point was the 1979 constitution which incidentally is the background upon which the 1999 constitution is built.

An analysis of provisions of the constitutions (both 1979 and 1999) and the drafting processes suggest that while that of 1979 was a carbon copy of the American constitution at the time, that of 1999 significantly mirrors that of 1979. Indigenous patterns of livelihood, culture, norms, values and aspirations were/are lacking in their provisions. There is a nearly irreconcilable disconnect between the constitutions and the national realities, and this is why critical observers have termed the 1999 constitution grossly inadequate and issued the call for a new constitution through a sovereign national conference since the subsisting constitution is nearly irredeemable. Moreover, it is possible to ask if there is actually a constitution of the Federal Republic of Nigeria, that is, whether the opening section of the 1999 constitution of Nigeria which says 'we the people of Nigeria' is actually true against the background of questionable historical antecedents and foreign influences in the legislative instruments. This is partly the reason why although Nigeria has had 10 written constitutions (Bugaje, 2003), the evolutionary process of the legislature is yet to crystalise, the reason that there are huge gaps among the history of Nigerian constitutions, provisions of the constitutions and the people of Nigeria who the constitution is supposed to govern.

In a related fashion, current legislative activities receive significant inputs from the West in various guises such as foreign technical partnering, refresher courses/trainings and foreign direct inputs into bills that are advocated by bilateral and multilateral agencies through non-governmental organisations (NGOs) and civil society organisations (CSOs). These partnerships and foreign inputs are, however, not bad in their own right. In fact, they could be necessary legislative capitals from mature democracies to a democratising nation like Nigeria thus making legislative journey to maturity smoother and more rapid. The crux of the issue notwithstanding is that the contents and implications of such inputs must be critically explored and synthesized against local socio-cultural, existential and developmental realities before annexations, if they are to serve useful purposes.

Roles of the Legislature

The roles of the legislature today are pigeonholed into larger frameworks for global and national governance. Such frameworks are further domesticated into the state and local governments in federal systems of government for outcomes' optimization that connects with the grassroots. As such, legislators do not perform their roles in isolation of the larger picture because they are only important to the extent that they interconnect with other organs and levels of government for far-reaching results. The legislature then operates with the understanding of policies like the Millennium Development Goals (MDGs), New Partnerships for African Development (NEPAD), National Economic Empowerment and Development Strategy (NEEDS), State Economic Empowerment and Development Strategy (SEEDS) and Local Government Economic Empowerment and Development Strategy (LEEDS). These are the policies that are expected to drive governance across domains and levels.

Fundamentally, the role of the legislature is to make laws. Every other function the legislature performs is derivable from this fundamental role and only becomes relevant and not diversionary when the law-making role is performed. The legislature is, therefore, ultimately the primary mechanisms through which modern states make laws, regulations and grand norms that form the basis on which states are governed (Wekwete and Sesay, 2001). Although there may be instances of delegated legislation in which case the legislature allows specialized agencies or experts make laws on its behalf, such laws must be sanctioned and subjected to legislative procedures as enshrined in the constitution.

Laws and regulations made by the legislature are expected to reflect norms, values, needs, aspirations and future of the generality of citizens in the nation. They must not be arbitrary, short-sighted, sentimental or parochial. This position is necessary against the fundamental recognition that laws and legislations are not just technical inputs but important parts of socio-economic and political development of societies (Wekwete and Sesay, 2001). Meaningful national development that is efficient, equitable and sustainable, therefore, largely depend on the extent of existence and commitment to quality law-making and not just formal legislative existence. In other words, legislatures must make laws that prevent and meet national emergencies (i.e. legislative proactivity) and create enabling environments in which development can thrive. Through law-making the legislature defines the direction and gives mechanisms through which national goals and development can be achieved. It then follows that the legislature is involved in national agenda/aspiration setting and represents national vision through qualitative legislations without which the nation either retrogresses to the state of nature or heads for anarchy.

Oversight function is another important role of the legislature. The legislature ensures accountability and transparency and serves as watch dog for public funds and resources. It checks other organs of government from being overbearing or lethargic in the discharge of their duties. It is through the oversight functions that the legislature regularly exercises its checks and balances power on other organs of government especially in democracies where bureaucracies and institutions are relatively undeveloped and corrupt.

Against the background of this constitutional function, the legislature can launch investigations or probes into suspicious activities of any organ or establishment to salvage potentially dangerous occurrence or trend. Oversight functions are performed through technical committees and sub-committees of the legislature. Popular examples of such committees are House committee for finance, House committee for power, House committee for external affairs and House committee for ethics and priviledges. After every committee assignment, the committees are expected to submit reports to the house for deliberations after which appropriate actions are taken.

Legislators must also perform constituency responsibilities. This all legislators must do by summarily detaching themselves politically and mentally from the legislature to reflect on their constituencies' needs. This is because every legislator is fundamentally a representative of a constituency. It is only in recourse to constituencies that legislators become relevant and derive their powers. A legislator does not even exist without a constituency. The legislators are thus expected to tender the needs of their constituencies and lobby their colleagues towards incorporating such needs into national plans of action. It is to ensure performance of this function that all legislators are empowered to have functional constituency offices through which they can constantly consult with their constituents to feel their pulses and realise their aspirations for onward presentation to the legislature for appropriate actions and interventions.

Ecological and environmental problems, militancy, poverty, unemployment, sectional marginalisations, gender discrimination, harmful traditional and cultural practices and other peculiar challenges that affect constituencies are expected to be exposed and advocated for by the legislators representing affected constituencies. Constituency responsibilities and the previous roles discussed are all important and interconnected. The degree of their satisfaction will either justify or falsify the existence of any legislature and they form the best practices against which legislatures' efficiency and relevance are measured.

Legislative Inputs in Nigeria: Critical Considerations

The activities of legislature across all levels in the Nigerian society since the re-democratisation experience in 1999 have been a subject of public commentaries. This is due primarily to its level of efficiency vis-a-vis its potentials as viable instrument of change in the face of endemic poverty and state comatose. Recognising this, the Senate president, Senator David Mark promised a different senate, a vibrant legislature with high discipline, streamlined focus and one that will lift Nigerians' standard of living (Ajunwa, 2009). The same posture was maintained by the speakers of the House of Representatives (Honourable Patricia Etteh and later Honourable Dimeji Bankole) and those of State Houses of Assembly. It is then possible to ask: what has changed? To what extent has these promises been realized? Or better still, what is the prospect of realizing these promises given the prevailing legislative happenings in the country? What have been the inputs of the legislature in Nigeria that have the capacity to lift the standard of living of Nigerians? These questions could be answered within the frameworks of international best practices as interface of expected roles of legislature and actual performance.

Law Making

The performance of Nigerian legislatures can be best described as below average as bills with sufficient effects on the citizens are yet to be passed. This is particularly the case at the National Assembly which has enjoyed considerable public attention and goodwill from the people since 1999. The major law reform process that would have negated the above position was hurriedly and prematurely truncated with the obnoxious third term imbroglio which made the lawmakers jettison the whole process in a manner that has come to be known as *throwing the baby out with the bath water.* That is, instead of the legislators to have removed the 'tenure elongation clause' from the agenda, they quickly cancelled the constitutional amendment process.

Generally, there have been two unsuccessful attempts by the National Assembly to amend the fundamentally-flawed Nigerian constitution since 1999. The same unsuccessful pattern is being observed now as there are major disagreements between the Senate and House of Representatives on the collective law-making and constitutional amendment process. Although such disagreements are not entirely bad in their own rights as they can serve as internal control mechanisms for the bi-cameral legislature, the current disagreements are, however, centred on existence, relevance, scope, independence and superiority to the detriment of necessary legislative assignments.

Rather than making laws, legislators at the federal, state and even the local government levels concern themselves with partisan divisions, unnecessary hecklings, infightings, cross government interference and corruption allegations all originating from greed and selfishness that ultimately lead to distraction from primary assignments. Even when some members intended to or moved motions sometimes, sentiments and parochial/partisan interests rob them of necessary two-third supports, regardless of merits of such bills. This is why it can be observed that private bills have been, most often, unsuccessful since 1999. For example, some states like Kaduna have not passed a single private bill but executive bills. This sentiment against private bills accounts for the delay in the domestication of the Child Rights Acts in most of the states and local governments. The sentiment equally accounts for the delay in passage of Freedom of Information Bill into law at the National Assembly even after infusion of mutilating and toxic sections like section 2 which demands security clearance before a piece of information can be released under the proposed law.

Delay or refusal of such laws is atavistic and dangerous. It is nothing but pure abuse of privilege that the legislature have in making law and handling state information. Unfortunately, while the National Assembly has refused to pass the Freedom of Information bill into law in Nigeria, observable trend in the world suggests that more nations are embracing and optimizing the law. For instance, about 65 countries now have such laws while 53 of them passed their own in just a decade and a half (Open Society Justice Initiative, 2006). The attraction to institutionalizing public communication strategies is the realization that it fosters transparency and accountability builds confidence of citizens in government and chart the way to inclusive and sustainable development.

Moreover, activities of the legislature can be further appreciated in relation to law making in the 2008 legislative year. In the year, only 8 out of 120 bills in the National Assembly were passed into law (Okanlawon et al., 2008; Sydelle, 2009). Some legislators were, however, quick to observe that performance of the legislature should not be based on the quantity of laws made but the quality. They were also of the opinion that the quantity of bills passed was due to rigorous process they subjected the bills to which would make the laws stand a test of time. This chapter contends, regardless, that such excuses are not plausible and are abuse of common legislative intelligence in a nation on survival mode, anxiously waiting for the right laws to create enabling atmosphere where development can jumpstart.

Besides the unacceptable quantity of bills passed, it is an axiom that frequency and quality of deliberations will enhance the quantity and quality of laws made. Regrettably, many of the legislators are absentee lawmakers. In fact, absenteeism and procedural delay tactics were parts of the most alarming challenges the legislature across levels faced at inception. There were cases where scanty chambers unsuitable for tangible legislative processes and procedural shenanigans prevented meaningful deliberations. Specifically, for instance, while the section 63(1) of the 1999 constitution provided that legislators shall sit for not less than 181 days in any legislative year, the federal legislature only sat for 90 days in 2008.

Hence, since the inception of second session of this third national assembly, only 21 bills have been passed at the Federal House of Representatives, while only eight reports are available for considerations out of which the deputy speaker have considered only three (Ojo and Akinboyewa, 2009). These, and other related activities, led the speaker of Federal House of Representatives (Honourable Dimeji Bankole) to judge the house performance below expectations after which he read riot acts to the members of the house (Ojo and Akinboyewa, 2009). At states level, the case is not totally different only that a lot of them were, additionally, either too preoccupied with cases of impeachments of speakers and governors or excessive allegiance to the governors.

Oversight Functions

Against this parameter, the legislature stands promising. As already mentioned, this function is to curb overbearing and reckless organs of government and this has been achieved to some extent. At least government officials are now aware that they might be summoned to give account of their stewardship. Efficiency of the legislature can be largely seen in this respect in the successful abortion of the third term agenda against the doggedness of the president with the connivance of some legislators. Through oversight functions, sagas like that of the Petroleum Technology Development Fund (PTDF) and other corruption scandals like in the power sector and Federal Capital Territory (FCT) probes have been publicized and at different levels of resolution. It has also led to interventions and public hearings, although with questionable degrees of success in the absence of prosecution of culprits.

Consciousness of oversight functions now make ministries struggle to pay significant attention to their corrupt tendencies through refund of 'unspent funds', a new concept in Nigerian governance lexicon. Government functionaries are now kept on their toes in the face of threats of impeachments and call for sack as effective legislative control. Already, over N600 billion ($513 million) of 'unspent funds' has been recovered into the national treasury from 1999-2008 (Ajunwa, 2009). This is aside the N2.1 billion ($1.8 million) returned by the Speaker of the House of Assembly (Honourable Dimeji Bankole).

This is unconnected with the growing legislative functions' consciousness and improved budgetary capacities of the legislature as the lawmakers have taken important strides towards improving quality of oversight functions of public funds (United States Agency for International Development [USAID], 2006). Such growing legislative functions' consciousness accounts for the determination of the legislature to take control of the Auditor General's office or create a parallel one. It is also responsible for the regular invocation of the section 80-83 of 1999 constitution which empowers the legislature to control public funds and advice the Revenue Mobilisation, Allocation and Fiscal Commission (RMAFC) for appropriate allocation (Abubakar, 2008). There is also the case of revocation of Certificate of Occupancy (C of O) of 19 of 45 plots of land in Federal Capital Territory (FCT) belonging to Mallam Nasir El-Rufai (former minister of FCT) by the senate. The parcels of land are to be re-allocated to the original owners on which court orders subsist. There is also the case of revocation of 3 presidential guest houses that El-Rufai and two others sold to themselves. The ex-president Olusegun Obasanjo was also not excused as some of its parcels of land were revoked.

As promising as the legislative oversight functions may be, however, there is a note of caution. The legislators need to observe and purge themselves to avert permanent character damage and integrity problems. This is because some of its members have been accused and are still being accused of corruption especially those on power and FCT land probes. Some members of the land probe committee were accused of being beneficiaries of illegal allocations of land being investigated, while those on power probe were accused of bribery. Although these allegations were all denied, a need still exists for internal procedures' sanitation because a single 'successful' scandal is enough to erode the gains of oversight functions and needed legislative integrity. The necessity of internal mechanisms' sanitation is predicated upon the fact that legislative duties, particularly oversight functions, rest solely on integrity and purity of character.

Constituency Responsibilities

The legislature is found wanting in this function. A lot do not go to their constituency regularly. A popular excuse is that legislative duties are demanding as they had to be at their state capitals making laws for common good. Another reason though less-mentioned is unrealistic demands from constituents who besiege honourables for personal assistance whenever they are around. Legislators consequently operate their constituency offices through middle men/women who are mostly designated as Personal Assistants (PAs). The PAs are expected to relate with the constituents and give feedbacks to his/her "Excellency" when he/she returns from Abuja or the state capital as the case may. A lot of the legislators largely do not have functional constituency offices. Target trips/schedule visits, informal discussions and general observations in the course of preparing this chapter reveal clearly that constituency offices are mere shadow offices without any meaningful or positive political/consultative activity.

Some were very weather-beaten and unkempt while a lot were under locks most of the time. Some constituents could not even remember when last they saw or hear from their representatives, unlike before elections. The point then is that when legislators do not regularly consult and rub minds with their constituents how would they know their needs particularly as some lawmakers do not live in the constituencies they represent.[5] Definitely, the needs reported by a few political loyalists may not really represent the actual position of things, yet lots of legislators depend on loyalists' reports - loyalists that will never give uncomplimentary and objective reports of emergencies at the constituencies even when they are the truths.

This explains the huge disconnect among the legislature, the law and the people. We are faced with the dangerous situation where legislations or/ and lack of them are divorced from social expectations and reality. Put differently, contemporary legislature lack full appreciation of what is required to make any legislation have the full effect as contemplated by the lawgiver leading to a tragedy of divorcing legislative programmes from the social facts of the society in which they are expected to operate (Aguda, 1986). Although lawmakers are not expected, constitutionally, to construct roads and build infrastructures, they are expected to constantly visit their constituencies to consult with the people to know appropriate motions to move in the House. When they do not do this but rely on top-of-the-hour concerns from the media to make laws, such laws most often would not affect the people positively. This is why most of the laws in Nigeria today are mere words without effects. Of all the laws in the massive 160-page Nigerian constitution, very few are justiceable while significant proportions do not translate to the needs and aspirations of Nigerians. They are merely hanging and useless to most people.

Towards Positive Legislative Inputs in Nigeria: Obstacles and Solutions as Conclusions

This chapter has attempted an assessment of the inputs of Nigerian legislature to governance in the country since 1999 in an uncompromising, no-hold-back fashion. This approach is not to unnecessarily sound polemic or unduly critical but to serve as a call to duty. This is also very necessary given the fact that there has been lack of significant and engaging scholarly works on the subject. The chapter has proceeded from the introduction to historicisation and roles of legislature. These were followed by an assessment of contemporary Nigerian legislature in the context of legislatures' expected roles. From the foregoing, it is possible to generally submit that the performance of Nigerian legislature has been below average and has not lived up to expectations. While the legislature may be considered relatively encouraging on performance of oversight functions, it falls far below expectations on law making which is its primary function as well as in and constituency functions. A need thus exists for legislative renaissance in Nigeria, if dividends of democracy are to materialise.

Questions that should be asked at this juncture are: what are the obstacles to positive legislative inputs in Nigeria that has led to this below average performance? What are the possible solutions?

Obstacles

Pecuniary interests stand out among factors militating against satisfactory performance of the Nigerian legislature. As already observed above, most of the legislators are in the various assemblies for personal gains. This, partly, accounts for why they frequently increase their salaries and allowances without hassles while they find it excruciatingly difficult to do the same for law making and constituency responsibilities[6]. The point, therefore, is that if the relative ease, speed and commitments with which legislators settle personal benefits are extended into performance of other important roles, they would have made better impacts on the nation.

There is also the case of cross government influence. In this case, the other organs of government meddle in legislative activities (Oyelowo, 2007).

This is usually in terms of refusal of executive assent to bills, denial of funds to legislature (referred to as power of the purse) and executive divide and rule of the legislature. Against the background of military and colonial legislative evolutions in the country, the executive organ through the President and governors often become overbearing on the legislature, thus hampering its activities. This is usually the case particularly at the state assemblies where legislators are mere representatives of the governors. The National Assembly witnessed executive imposition clearly throughout the first eight years of re-democratisation (1999-2007). During that time, President Olusegun Obasanjo almost turned the legislature to a subordinate extension of the presidential villa and was only sometimes kept in check through the threats of impeachment.

Overbearing executive/cross government influences are obvious manifestations of executive disrespect for the legislature which can be strongly linked with authoritarian and clientelistic practice in political nomination. Most of the legislators and other government officials are from the same party and they have same godfathers who exert 'control' on the legislators and expect them to work toward the same parochial 'goals' and respect the executive governor/president who is often seen as the overall leader of all in government. No matter what the constitution provides, therefore, extra-constitutional considerations determine their dispositions to official duties. This was the case in 1999-2007 when all political office-holders, including the legislators and Peoples Democratic Party (PDP) members who formed the majority in all organs of government, addressed President Olusegun Obasanjo as *baba* (father) with corresponding high degree of respect/obedience befitting a 'father' in traditional African settings.

Legislators in Nigeria also face the challenge of internal frictions and corruption. These have been clearly manifested in the popular corruption scandals in the country. While some led to impeachments, others were tactfully swept under the carpets depending on the prevailing in-house power dynamics. Notwithstanding the in-house approach, however, they were not resolved without generating embarrassments and in-fighting in the legislatures. At the federal level, such infighting and corruption scandals unseated senate presidents like Senator Evans Enwerem, Senator Dr. Chuba Okadigbo, Senator Adolphus Wabara and Honourable Mrs. Patricia Etteh of the House of Representatives. Cases also abound at the state level but few recent cases include the impeachments of Honourable Titilayo Oseni as the Speaker of Ogun State House of Assembly. Other states that have witnessed impeachments of their speakers include Plateau and Ekiti[7].

The implication of these is that it destabilises the legislature and distract them from primary assignments. After the frictions and blackmails, there would be process of reconstitutions and reconciliations that will take considerable amount of time before resumption of legislative duties. Some factions will be irreconcilable causing permanent divisions in the house at the detriment of successful legislative activities.

Some constituents place unrealistic demands on their representatives at the legislature either because of poverty or misunderstanding of the roles of legislature. Given the level of illiteracy and political ignorance in the country, most people confuse the roles of the executive with that of the legislature. Some constituents are of the opinion that their representatives should build infrastructures and put food directly on their tables unaware that it is not the purpose for which legislators are elected. Unfortunately, it is against such erroneous yardsticks that most constituents judge the performance of their representatives. On the other hand, the level of political illiteracy often exhibited by the constituents in relation to legislators' duties is due to misinformation by the legislators. Legislators out of desperation to win elections promise what they could not give. Instead of emphasising their eventual legislative roles, they *ab initio* promise execution of tangible projects to exploit constituents' needs in the face of abject poverty and government irresponsibility. The dysfunctional dispositions of the constituents, therefore, could be partly traced to the legislators and other political actors in the final analysis.

Some legislators lack needed capacities to function as lawmakers. Legislating is a technical enterprise. It combines various aspects of professional activities which were not factored into election of officials. Performance of legislative duties is cumbersome, complicated and technical. Appreciable educational/professional backgrounds and experience are, therefore, needed. Regrettably, however, the minimum educational qualification specified by the constitution appears not to prioritise this. Also the structure of legislators' emergence does not allow people to spend sufficient time at the legislature to gather needed experience and technical know-how. Legislators must return to their constituencies for re-election after a 4-year tenure. This often leads to situations where legislators are not returned but replaced with fresh and inexperienced ones that the prevailing political permutations favour. This is bound to regularly be the case since constituents usually judge their representatives against faulty parameters as already pointed out previously.

Solutions

As solutions to the obstacles above, some suggestions are given heretofore. There is a need for elaborate capacity building for the legislators. Also, the legislators must defend their independence and focus and embark on aggressive enlightenment campaigns for their constituents. To do this, legislators must form new legislatures' forum or strengthen existing ones through which they can inform their constituents of their real constitutional duties as against erroneous impressions being held at the constituencies.

This will benefit the nation and the politicians themselves. Intending legislators and other politicians should stop misinforming the electorates out of desperation to win elections as the ripple effects will eventually be devastating. The misinformation must stop and debriefing must start urgently. Otherwise, no matter what any legislator may enjoy in the interim, the future is ultimately bleak.

Although legislators go on tours and retreats, they must take refresher courses seriously to be familiar with contemporary ways of legislating. Legislating is both an art and a science that must be learnt. It is not politics or time-passing. It is a technical enterprise and not an avenue to compensate failed aspirants or please godfathers. Regardless of dynamics of emergence, the legislators must brace up and improve themselves to cope with legislative challenges. Research/legislative assistants that are capable could be employed to help in the process. These are not political/conventional personal assistants (PAs) who are just being compensated for loyalty or patrimonialism but they are professionals who can research into issues needing legislations and related issues. This will definitely improve quality of inputs legislators make into governance in the country.

Although President Umaru Musa Yar'Adua has not exhibited much of obvious executive influences on the National Assembly like his predecessor, the legislature must be on guard and not slumber. The states are however perpetually under the shadows of their executive governors. In fact, the position is that peaceful relationships among legislators and executive governors in Nigeria are nothing but compromise and legislative subordination to the executive. Legislators must therefore exercise their principles of separation of power and check and balances to make meaningful contributions and to be relevant. Internal wrangling must however be minimized to maintain their focus and discharge of expected duties.

References

Abubakar, A. S. (2008, August 5). The challenges before the Nigerian legislators. *Daily Triumph* Newspaper.

Aguda, T. A. (1986). *Nigeria in Search of Social Justice through the Law*. Nigeria: Nigerian Institute of Advanced Legal Studies.

Ajunwa, C. (2009, January 5). *Sixth Senate and the Quest for Stability. This Day* Newspaper.

Bugaje, U. (2003). *The evolution of the legislature and the challenges for democracy in Nigeria: An overview.* Paper delivered at the seminar on "Strengthening democratic values through parliamentary cooperation", organised by the National Assembly in collaboration with Canadian Parliament on 23-26, August in Abuja, Nigeria.

Diop, A., & Leautier, F. (2007). Democracy: An adaptable system critical for development. *Development Outreach, Vol. 9, No. 3.*, pp. 2-5. Washington DC: World Bank Institute.

Karibi-Whyte, A.G. (1987). *The Relevance of the Judiciary in the Polity-In Historical Perspective.* Nigeria: Nigerian Institute of Advanced Legal Studies.

Klein, J. (2001, January/February). The Birth of Kingship: From Democracy to Monarchy in Sumer. *Archaeology Odissey 4*, pp. 17-25.

Muhlberger, S. (n.d.). Democracy in Ancient India. Retrieved from http://www.nipissingu.ca/department/history/muhlberger/histdem/indiadem.htm.

Okanlawon, S., Amokeodo, T., Aleche, J., & Affe, M. (2008, December 23). *Senate Passes Eight Out of !20 Bills in 2008. The Punch.*

Ojo, J., & Akinboyewa, O. (2009, February 20). *Bankole Reads Riot Act to Reps. Daily Sun*, p.13.

Olutayo, A.O., & Akanle O. (2007). Modernity, MacDonaldisation and Family Values in Nigeria. *The Nigerian Journal of Sociology and Anthropology, Vol. 5,* pp. 53-72.

Open Society Justice Initiative (2006, September). *Transparency and Silence.*

Osuji, O. (2008, September 16). The Legislative Process in Nigeria. *Julius Ihonvbere.*

Oyelowo, O (2007, April). *Constitutionalism and the Oversight Functions of the Legislature in Nigeria.* Draft paper presented at African Network of Constitutional Law Conference on Fostering Constitutionalism, Nairobi, Kenya.

Sydelle, S. (2009, January 14-21). Should Nigeria's Senate be shown the door? *The African Executive.*

Taiwo, B. (1981). *Government and Politics in West Africa: A Critical Approach 1.* Great Britain: A Wheaton & Co. Ltd.

United States Agency for International Development (USAID) (2006). *Democracy and Governance Assessment of Nigeria.* Nigeria.

Wekwete, K. H., & Sesay, S. M. (2001). *Legislative Challenges for Sustainable Urban Development in Sub-Saharan Africa.* U.S.A: United Nations Publications.

Footnotes

1. Four organs because contemporary democratic societies consider a combination of the media and the Civil Society Organisations (CSOs) as necessary fourth organ to enhance checks and balances through whistle blowing mechanisms, advocacy and programming. It is only through the entrenchment of the fourth organ that the public can be sufficiently protected and democracy institutionalized.
2. The Supreme Court and Court of Appeal are however struggling to free themselves from the executive influence. This has been demonstrated through removal of some governors after nullifications of their elections.
3. The choice of the terms *primordial, traditional, contemporary* and *modern* is

for analytical clarity and periodisation. It therefore does not depict preference or sophistication of one system/period over the other because the legislative trajectories of these periods were all sophisticated in their own realms and terms as they served expected functions as dictated by their societal needs.

4. Hierarchical/pyramidal political structure in the Sokoto Caliphate, centralized in Oyo Empire and acephalous in Igbo societies.
5. Some legislators represent rural areas but have always been living in the city while some migrated later due to their change of status. Even for those that were living in the constituency prior to election and still live in the constituency, they spend more time in the capital in the cause of political assignment which may make them lose touch with the prevailing situations at the constituency to some extent.
6. Recently, the National Assembly increased members' pay by 100 per cent. Their salaries now stand at N52.4 billion ($44.8 million) a year and another N15.02 billion ($12.8 million) a year as multi purpose allowance on quarterly basis (Okanlawon, et al, 2008). This is regardless of the fact that about 9 out of 10 Nigerians live on less than $2 a day (Sydelle, 2009).
7. Aside the problem of corruption at the headship of the legislature, committees also face the problem of corruption as was the case in Fabian Osuji and the then Minister of Education bribery scandal to the House Committee on Education.

7

The Judiciary and the Democratization Process in Nigeria

'Dele Ashiru

Introduction

Right from the time of Plato, the quest for justice and, in a more elaborate sense, a just society has been of great concern to philosophers and political thinkers. Whereas Plato viewed justice as acceding to the interest of the strongest, other political thinkers after him especially Jeremy Bentham (1748-1832) and others in the "Utilitarian" school are of the opinion that justice should be viewed in terms of ensuring the "greatest happiness of the greatest number" of people in a society. This view no doubt seems to agree with the words enshrined in the declaration of America's Independence that "all men are created equally and that they are endowed with certain inalienable rights [and] that among these are rights to life, liberty and the pursuit of happiness".

Thus, within these two broad extremes of the idea of justice, as either the interest of the strongest or the pursuit of happiness for the greatest number of people, what then is justice? How is it to be determined? What institution or organ of state is responsible for what is just or unjust?

To start with, the idea of justice is determined by time and space. The constitutive element of justice differs from one place to the other and from one generation to another, in fact, even in the same generation, what is just today may become unjust tomorrow.

Despite this complex nature of the conception of justice, Gauba (2003: 372) avers that justice implies the quality of being just, right or reasonable. It is opposed to what is unjust, wrong or unreasonable. It embodies an ideal which is akin to the absolute truth..." Justice therefore entails ideals such as liberty, equality, freedom, fraternity and solidarity.

It must be noted that the custom and tradition of a people play a very great role in determining what is just or unjust. More fundamentally, the body of laws, rules and regulations enacted for use in any society remain the standard yardsticks upon which behaviour, actions and sometimes inactions are to be based. Put succinctly, what is regarded as the law in any society remains the barometer upon which justice can be measured.

Thus, the kind of law that would be enacted in any society would be determined by the relations of production at the substructure of the society upon which the superstructure having constitutive elements as law, politics, ideology, religion and even the culture of such society would be based. In this regard, what is just in an open competitive political system with its attendant contradictions of scarcity and choice may obviously be unjust in a socialist democratic political system with emphasis on the redistribution of societal wealth. However, whatever the political system there must be an institution saddled with the responsibility of justice administration. Most often, this institution is known as the judiciary.

This chapter examines the role of the judiciary in the democratization process in Nigeria, given its strategic role in the resolution of conflicts and disputes among individuals, organs of government, governmental agencies and such other disputes that emanate from the political and electoral processes. In doing this, the tentative assumption is that the nature and character of a state will, to a very large extent, determine the ability of the judiciary to dispense justice without fear or favour.

Thus, the chapter is divided into six parts. The first is the introduction. The second deals with the Nigerian State and the judiciary in historical perspective and the third part IS concerned with the judiciary and the democratization process. The fourth section deals with the assessment of the role of the judiciary in the democratization process in Nigeria while the fifth section suggests some recommendations. The sixth section is the conclusion.

The Nigerian State and the Judiciary in Historical Perspective

Although, there is yet to be a universally acceptable definition of a state, some see it as essentially a class structure. Others view it as an organization that goes beyond class differentiation but attending to general needs across societal classes. What however seems incontrovertible is that the state remains the most important and distinctive institution in any society. It is that organization that gives colour and direction to society. Even though Omeje (2007: 22) cautions that "a clear-cut demarcation between the state and society can be analytically tricky", there are basically three distinctive ways through which the state can be understood. The first is at the institutional level, the second is at the functional level while the third is at the relational level. Ismail (2007) clearly captures these three conceptions of the state when he submits:

> ...on the institutional side, the state is a set of interrelated governmental institutions responsible for making rules, controlling and regulating social relations; functionally, the state is a set of public institutions established according to accomplish specific objectives such as the provision of security and welfare for people under its juridical domain; and relationally, the state is a set of relationship and interactions among social classes and groups that is maintained, organized and regulated by political power. (cf. Omeje 2007:21)

Of the three conceptions of the state, the relational aspect as enumerated above is of crucial importance to the understanding of the nature and character of any state since it is based on the relationship and interaction among social classes and groups which is maintained, organized and regulated by political power.

When political power is unorganized and unregulated it negates the very essence of state, especially when the state is understood from the perspective of the social contract theorists where the people consent to surrender their rights to a sovereign who exercises those rights on behalf of all in order to safeguard people from the type of life described by Hobbes as being "solitary, poor, nasty, brutish and short".

Meanwhile, for what purpose is the state established? Anifowose (2005: 98) citing Adams Smith identified three purposes for which the state is created and they are as follows:

- The duty of protecting society from violence and invasion of other independent societies;
- The duty of protecting subjects from injustice, that is, the duty of establishing a system of justice; and
- The duty of erecting and maintaining certain public works and public institutions.

From the foregoing, it is clear that one of the very purpose for which the state is created is for it to protect its citizens or subjects from injustice through the establishment of a justice system. The extent to which a state can do this depends on the history, nature and character of the state which produces the ruling elites. What then are the history, nature and character of the Nigerian state and its ruling elites?

That the Nigerian State is a colonial creation is incontrovertible (Ake, 1981, 1996, Osaghae, 1998). Although some scholars like Dudley (1982) have advanced what Osaghae (1998:4) has described as "counterfactual" argument, that is, the relationship of trade, conquest and familial ties based on the myths of common origin which existed among the empires and kingdoms in pre-colonial era could have facilitated the emergence of a political entity like

Nigeria. Osaghae (1998: 4) further cites a more weighty "counterfactual" argument which was articulated by the late Sardauna of Sokoto and the premier of the Northern Region, Sir Ahmadu Bello who avers that "if the colonizers had not intervened, the Southern extension of the Jihad could have brought into being a state with approximately the present shape of Nigeria". Despite these counterfactual arguments, the fact remains that Nigeria was a colonial creation with the forceful amalgamation of the Northern and Southern protectorates together with the colony of Lagos in 1914 to form what is now known as Nigeria.

Suffice to say that before the amalgamation of 1914 the geographical entity now known as Nigeria was populated by diverse ethnic groups such as the Oyo Empire, the Benin Kingdom, the Sokoto caliphate, and scores of minority ethnic groups in the Middle Belt and the Niger Delta including the Igbo sedimentary societies. While it is not sufficient to assert that Nigeria was a colonial creation, what is of analytical importance to this study is the nature of the colonial state which has continued to have far-reaching effects on the post-colonial state and the nature of politics played by the ruling elites since independence.

For the avoidance of doubt, the colonial state was a law and order state with absolute and arbitrary powers at the political and economic levels. At the political level, the arbitrary use of power deprived it of legitimacy as there was constant antagonism between the state and the people. This can be said to have been the basis of the legitimation crises which have trailed the state from independence (Ninalowo, 1999). At the economic level, the colonial state was essentially extractionist in conformity with the logic of colonial exploitation and pillage, which also resulted in the forceful incorporation of the country's economy into the world's capitalist system, albeit as a weak and junior partner.

It bears no emphasis that this had serious debilitating effects on the country's political economy since the forceful incorporation disarticulated the economy through the introduction of cash crop farming which relied heavily on the technology from the metropolis. This ensured the dominance of foreign capital in the economy since indigenous methods were no longer required in the agricultural production process. When independence was achieved, the state and its oppressive apparatuses were inherited without any desire to change or transform it. The state and its oppressive apparatuses combined together created a ruling elite at independence which lacked any productive base as well as entrepreneurial abilities. They therefore relied on the state as a means of production for their unbridled material acquisition and primitive accumulation; these activities thus became parasitic and predatory on the state. The consequence of all these was the very high premium placed on the capture of political power in order to have unfettered access to the state and the privileges it confers. Given this situation, the struggle for political power was conducted in a war-like manner. Politics then knows neither rationality nor compromise but only what was expedient. This situation is best captured in the words of Ake (1985 : 4):

> "In the absence of autonomizing mechanisms in the post-colonial state, the resources of physical coercion become the tools of particular groups, especially the hegemonic factions of the ruling class... So, we have essentially relations of raw power in which right tends to be co-extensive with power and security depends on the control of power. The struggle for power then is everything and is pursued by every means."

This unfortunately has remained the bane of Nigeria's politics since Independence. Virtually, all the elections conducted in the history of post colonial Nigeria have been characterized by electoral malpractices and violence of an unimaginable proportion. This perhaps explains why the Nigerian state has been described as "a prebendal state" (Joseph, 1987), "a rentier state" (Graf 1988) a "neo-patrimonial state" and a "Predatory state" (cf Omeje, 2007: 21).

The history of the Nigerian judiciary is similar to that of the state. Just like the Nigerian state, the judiciary as we know it today was a colonial heritage. This is not to say that there was no system of judicial administration before the advent of the colonial masters.

Indeed, long before colonialism, the various kingdoms, empires and minority groups inhabiting present day Nigeria as indicated earlier, had their respective traditional systems of law and machinery for the administration of justice which was informed by each society's history, the nature of the political organization and the dominant social-cultural values of these respective societies. Although, Asein (2005:150) indicated that the judicial system of administration in pre-colonial Nigeria, did not aim at doing justice in the modern sense of the word but that it was aimed "at the maintenance of peace and order, the promotion of social welfare and the sustenance of the social equilibrium in the society concerned." The question to ask Asein (2005) is that what then is "justice in the modern sense" if it is not aimed at achieving the lofty goals enumerated above by him, which is at the root of pre-colonial justice administration in Nigeria?

In fact, it was the forceful imposition of the European style judicial administration with its erosion of these core societal values "maintenance of peace and order, the promotion of social welfare and the sustenance of the social equilibrium" as enumerated by Asein (2005) above, that has remained the bane of Nigeria's post-independence politics and its justice system.

Prior to the advent of the European colonial masters, the monarchical kingdoms were organized in a hierarchical order in terms of political authority. In the Yoruba speaking areas and the Benin Kingdom, the Oba was the head of government but was usually assisted by a council of chiefs and some "Baales". It is noteworthy, that powers were often delegated to these subordinate authorities like the village head or chief which gave them the opportunity to settle minor disputes within their areas of authority. However, appeals sometimes went to the higher chief or ultimately to the Oba whose court was usually the last resort. The Oba himself constitutes his own court for the determination of more serious disputes and offences against the state (Asein 2005:151).

In the Northern part of the country, the situation was similar to that of the Oba. The Emir held courts in the Emirate. Indeed the Fulani Jihad of the nineteenth century introduced the Maliki school of Islamic jurisprudence along with the Islamic faith and culture and as Asein (2005:152) noted that "since this was an import from a relatively more advanced culture, Northern state inherited a more organized and developed administrative and judicial machinery". Like the situation in the South Western states, the Alkalis and other chiefs had adjudicatory powers over matters and disputes within their jurisdiction. The Emirs court remained the last court of resort as they heard appeals from the Alkalis and other subordinate district heads.

The situation was slightly different in the Igbo sedimentary societies of South Eastern Nigeria. In these societies, adjudicatory powers were vested in the council of elders composed of mainly male members of the village or clan. The gerontocratic system of government ensured the primacy of the oldest man in the justice system of the community whose wisdom and wide experience occasioned by age was often relied upon in the settlement of disputes and the entire justice administration.

It is instructive to note here, the role which traditional religious institutions and beliefs play in the justice and adjudicatory system. Indeed, the strong belief in deities and spirits of ancestors helped tremendously in the maintenance of law and order in these communities.

With the coming of the European colonial masters, new courts which approximate the ones in Europe began to emerge. Specifically, there were the courts of Equity, the Consular courts and the courts of the Royal Niger Company. Whereas the courts of equity were designed to resolve disputes among European merchants and between them and the natives, the consular courts assumed judicial powers over British and non-British Interest, while, the courts of the Royal Niger Company, only exercised jurisdiction in civil and criminal cases involving natives and foreigners, within the business and commercial areas of the company, formerly known as the United Africa Company.

As a consequence of this, the Consul was empowered to make rules for peace, order and good government of British subjects is his area and also to execute and enforce by fine, imprisonment or banishment the observance of any agreement between the British council and the local chiefs.

However, with the official occupation of Lagos, the first Governor of the colony Sir Henry S. Freeman established according to Asein (2005:156) the following courts :

1. The police magistrates courts to settle petty cases and conduct preliminary hearings in more serious ones;
2. The commercial court concerned primarily with debt, compensation, commercial contract cases and the likes. It was renamed the Petty Debt court in 1863 and replaced by a court of Request in 1878;
3. The Slave Commission Court to handle problems relating to the payment of compensation to former slave owners and cases of runaway slaves, apprenticeship and liberation. (Asein 2005:156).

The situation was slightly different in the Northern protectorate in line with the logic of the indirect rule system which was introduced to govern the people at that time. The system encouraged the use of the prevailing native authorities system whereby Emirs and their respective chiefs dispensed justice in accordance with the Islamic jurisprudence of the Maliki School, earlier mentioned.

However, by 1900, the High Commissioner, through the Protectorate courts proclamation, established a Supreme Court, Provincial Courts and the Cantonment Courts. Another proclamation, the same year established a system of Native Courts for the entire Northern protectorate. One important fact to note is the prevalence of new courts styled along the English Courts in the South, while these were less prevalent in the North.

This situation changed in 1954 when Nigeria became a federation following the promulgation of the 1954 Lyttleton constitution. The constitution created a federal and three regional governments. In line with this arrangement, a federal supreme court was created for Lagos, while the regions had their respective magistrates' and native courts. Regional High Courts were also established to hear appeals from the magistrates and native courts.

Meanwhile by 1956, the Northern region created the Islamic Court of Appeal to entertain appeals from decisions of the native courts in matters concerning Islamic law. This court was replaced by the Sharia Court of Appeal in 1960 when Nigeria became Independent.

Also in 1960, the Eastern and Western regions effected some reorganization in their native court system and named them customary courts. By 1963, the Nigerian courts shelved the last vestiges of colonialism by severing all affiliations and appeals which used to go to the Privy Council in England. The Republican constitution of 1963 gave exclusive powers to the Supreme Court of Nigeria as the final appellate authority on any matter civil or criminal in the country.

Today, the 1999 constitution of Nigeria recognizes the following courts; the Supreme Court of Nigeria, The Court of Appeal, The Federal High Court, High Court of the Federal Capital Territory, The Sharia Court of Appeal of the Federal Capital Territory, the Customary Court of Appeal of the Federal Capital Territory, High Court of Appeal of a state, Sharia Court of Appeal of a state as well as Election Tribunals. There are, however, other Courts like the magistrate Courts, the Juvenile Courts, etc. in Nigeria.

The Judiciary and the Democratization Process

The absence of enabling conditions for democratic participation at the grassroots is the greatest obstacle to democracy in Africa, just as the transformation of society for the empowerment of ordinary people is the greatest challenge to democratization. (Ake 1996:11)

> If democracy is to be understood as popular power, (Ake 2000:8) the centrality of election to the selection of the managers of the state cannot be overemphasized even though election is not all that there is to democracy. Unfortunately, the practice of democracy has now largely been reduced to multi-party electoral competitions. Dahl (1989:221) identified three essentials conditions for a multi-party democracy to thrive and these are (a) "extensive competition by contestants including individuals, groups or parties for government; (b) Political participation that provides the choice for the electorate to select candidates in free and fair elections; and (c) Civil and political liberties that enable the citizens to express themselves without fear of punishment".

By the very nature of competition there has to be winners and losers. The zero sum, winner takes all nature of the political competition in Nigeria has increased tremendously the premium placed on electoral competition. Electoral competition is therefore constituted as warfare of which all manner of dangerous tactics are deployed. The nature and character of the Nigerian state and its ruling elite as elucidated in the second section of this chapter also account for the desperate and violent nature of electoral competition. In this instance, Ake (1996:13) noted "where every leader wants absolute power, society is at war, war without end, because amidst the defeats and victories of particular battles, the underlying social dynamics remain the same."

Apart from the violent nature of our electoral competition, the contestants for state power also try to undo or outdo one another using all shades of electoral malpractices such as recruiting Juvenile to vote, detaching ballot booklets, duplicating ballot papers, vandalizing voter materials, stuffing of ballot boxes, and outright intimidation of opponents as well as falsification of electoral results. It is the belief in all these shades of electoral malpractices that have embolden some of political leaders especially the government of General Olusegun Obasanjo to describe the 2007 election as "do or die affair for the ruling Peoples Democratic Party (PDP)". Also another prominent politician in the first republic Chief Fani Kayode was reported to have said "whether you vote for us or not we will remain in power" (Dudley, 1973:42).

By what means would they capture power whether the people vote for them or not? The answer to this was provided by Yoroms, (2007: 107) when he argues that electoral rigging has become too sophisticated that various aspects of anti-democratic activities have been concretely built into it. These include among others :

(1) Providing counterfeits ballot box, ballot papers and voting cards;
(2) Vote buying: giving money to voters to vote for particular party and/or candidate;
(3) Buying off of the electoral officers and party agents to manipulate the results for a particular political party or candidate(s);
(4) Changing of the figures of result counted at polls or collection centres in favour of political parties or candidates;
(5) Replacing genuine ballot boxes with fake ballot boxes containing illegal voters cards;
(6) Stealing or mutilation of electoral materials to avoid the conduct of the election;
(7) Inciting or causing violence at the polling units and or in the course of the election so as to threaten voters from voting or for the election or the results of the election to be cancelled;
(8) Attempts by the electoral officers to share votes cast in election among political parties;
(9) Giving of wrong information to the voters on the dates of the election of voting procedures (so) as to misguide them to vote for a party which is not of their choice; and
(10) Creating fear, intimidation and threatening the voting atmosphere; (Yoroms; 2007: 110)

When either or all of the aforementioned anti-democratic behaviours are exhibited during any elections, it vitiates the sanctity of that election and truncates the democratization process.

The only option left for those who feel aggrieved and short changed in the electoral process is to seek redress through the judiciary, whose sacred responsibility is to ensure that choosing which is the very essence of democracy is not derailed.

Section 239 subsection (1) of the 1999 constitution empowers and gives original jurisdiction to the court of appeal to hear and determine any question as to whether (a) a person has been validly elected to the office of the president or vice president while section 285 sub-section (1) and (2) provide for the establishment of election tribunals for the National Assembly as well as the Governorship and Legislative Houses Election Tribunal in order to adjudicate in electoral matters.

Assessment of the Role of the Judiciary in the Democratization Process

This section is designed to assess the roles of the judiciary in the democratization process. Given the centrality of elections to the democratic enterprise in Nigeria, our assessment will focus on the judiciary's handling of disputes and cases arising from the electoral process with specific emphasis on the 2003 and 2007 general elections.

Opinions are sharply divided about the assessment of the judiciary in handing electoral matters, this is so because the Nigerian courts were once described by Mohammed Haruna "as a safe sanctuary for election riggers....Election rigging is essentially a political problem not a legal one, the solution to (election) rigging is to be found in politics and not in the courts" (cf. The Nation Dec. 17, 2008). While some believe that the judiciary has played very commendable roles in the democratization process, there are those who believe that a lot still need to be desired. For the former category, their view is that the judiciary has lived up to its bidding as the last hope of the common man.

However, whereas there are courageous Judges, who have dispensed justice without fear or favour, there are those who have subverted the democratic process by giving *exparte* motion, frivolous injunctions and orders to disrupt the democratic fervour in the country. Indeed competence of counsel through the use of legal technicalities and in fact the disposition and temperament of Judges have combined to inform the nature of judgement usually delivered at the election tribunals and during civil and criminal litigation in Nigeria. As Akinola Aguda (1992:6) once noted :

"It is of course a matter of common knowledge that the manner in which some of the judges especially at the high court level dealt with election petition was one of the causes of the demise of the Second Republic."

Similarly, just two days to the conduct of the June 12, 1993 presidential election, the Association for Better Nigeria (ABN) sought and got what has arguably remained the most controversial injunctions ever, when Justice Bassey Ita Ikpeme of an Abuja High Court sat at about 9:00 pm and gave injunction restraining the National Electoral Commission from conducting the election. That election which was eventually annulled by the military turned out to be the freest and fairest in the annals of Nigeria.

Whereas Justice Ikpeme was timid, corrupt and willing to be used in the subversion of the democratic aspirations of Nigerians, the case of Justice Dolapo Akinsanya of the Lagos High Court was different. She was courageous and willing to serve the course of justice. She was the judge who heard the case filled by Chief MKO Abiola and his Vice presidential candidate Babagana Kingibe, challenging the annulment of the June 12, 1993 election and seeking the nullification of the Interim National Government (ING) set up by the Babangida regime. In a show of rare judicial activism, Justice Dolapo Akinsanya declared the ING as illegal on the 10th of November 1993. As Osaghae (1998: 265) pointed out.

Justice Akinsanya ruled that the ING's empowering decree (No 61) was illegal since at the time when Babangida signed it, he no longer had the legislative authority to do so. She accordingly declared the ING null and void, and directed that steps be taken to restore the annulled presidential election and give effect to the 1989 constitution as the only valid law by which they could be governed after 26 August.

Rather than give effect to this historic judgment, the ING under the leadership of Chief Ernest Shonekan was shoved aside by the military led by General Sani Abacha.

> At the return of the country to civil rule in 1999, the election that ushered in the Fourth Republic under the leadership of General Olusegun Obasanjo had its own fair share of judicial litigation and the Electoral Tribunals were said to have "faired satisfactorily in the carrying out their assignmen." (Ugochukwu, 2004: 92).

Unfortunately, the same could not be said about the electoral tribunals who heard petitions arising from the 2003 general elections. The tribunals were accused of corruption and bias in handling disputes arising from the 2003 elections. In fact, most of the petitions were struck out on frivolous technical grounds. For example, on the corruption charges against the tribunal, the gubernatorial election petition in Akwa Ibom state between Ime Umanah of the All Nigerian People Party (ANPP) and Victor Attah, the incumbent Governor of the Peoples Democratic Party (PDP) presents an interesting example.

According to Umanah, the tribunal chairman Ntiem Adamu received the sum of 6.4 Million Naira on May 28, 2003 from the state chief Judge, Justice Effiong Idiong on behalf of Governor Attah. The money was said to have been paid into two bank accounts belonging to Justice Adamu's children. Hadiza and Michael Ochoga. While it was not clear how much was given to other members of the tribunal, one of them Justice D.T. Ahura of the Federal High Court, Makurdi was said to have gone on a shopping spree after collecting his share...Ugochukwu, (2004:69).

The fact that the National Judicial Council (NJC) after investigating Umanah's allegation suspended those indicted and recommended the removal of Justice Idiong as the Akwa Ibom Chief Judge, lend credence to the allegation of corruption in the handling of electoral disputes arising from the 2003 elections.

Another fall out of corruption and bias during the hearing of election petition, was frivolous nature in which election petitions were struck out on the flimsiest and sometimes ridiculous reasons.

For example in the case of J.K.N. Waku V Joshua Adagba for Benue Senatorial District, the petition was struck out because, according to the tribunal, the person who contested the election was chief J.K.N. Waku while the person who filed the petition was senator J.K.N. Waku "Chief and Senator" turned out to make the difference while the real complaints of the petitioner were ignored... (Also) in Delta State the petition filed by Great Ogboru, candidate of the Alliance for Democracy (AD) in the gubernatorial election against the return of incumbent Governor James Ibori was thrown out on technical point. According to the tribunal, instead of suing the Independent National Electoral Commission (INEC), the petitioner sued instead the Independent Electoral Commission (IEC). What made the difference was the "National" that was missing, (cf Ugochukwu; 2004:61).

The 2007 General Elections in Nigeria has been said to have the unenviable distinction of being the most poorly and fraudulently-organized elections in the annals of Nigeria. This is so because as Mohammed Haruna noted.

...for the first time in Nigeria's electoral history, the electoral commission conducted elections without proper voters register as stipulated in the electoral act. Second, the ballot papers used in the elections had no serial numbers again as stipulated by law. Third, in far too many cases results were announced even before the polls had closed. Four, in many cases results were unsigned, unstamped and undated. Five, there were no provisions for secret balloting, which is a universal and basic requirement of freedom of choice. Six, electoral violence characterized by ballot snatching and voter intimidation among other things were wide spread especially in the South-South and South East. Seven, the electoral commission did not provide indelible ink for thumb printing the ballot papers as stipulated by the law. One could go on... (cf The Nation, Dec. 17, 2008).

Flowing from this, it was not a surprise that after the election, according to Justice Umaru Abdullahi, the President of the Court of Appeal, claimed that a total of 1,475 petitions were received as against the 570 received in 2003. This shows that the Independent (National) Electoral Commission led by Maurice Iwu was obviously ill prepared for the election. Apart from this, the desire by the then incumbent President Chief Olusegun Obasanjo to prevent his Vice-President Alhaji Atiku Abubakar from contesting the presidential election under the platform of another party, the Action Congress (AC) created very serious tension preparatory to the election.

Indeed the President, in a reckless statement, shocked the Nigerian electorates when he declared that the 2007 election will be a "do or die" affair. That the election was therefore fraught with irregularities was an unedifying testimony to this presidential declaration. Little wonder that the Peoples Democratic Party (PDP) the president's party swept the polls in the most bizarre and controversial manner.

Consequently, the aggrieved politicians and indeed the generality of the people looked up to the judiciary to right the perceived wrongs of the 2007 elections. As at the time of writing this chapter, opinions are still divided about the judiciary's handling of the petitions arising from the conduct of the elections. Whereas some analysts have praised the judiciary for some courageous landmark decisions by some judges the conduct and pronouncement of others leave much to be desired.

For instance, in some states like Cross Rivers, Adamawa, Bayelsa, Sokoto and Kogi states where elections were found to fall below acceptable standards, fresh elections were ordered. Other election petitions from Oyo, Imo, Ekiti, Abia, Delta, Katsina, Nasarawa, Niger, Kaduna and Taraba states are still pending at the various divisions of the Appeal Courts.

By far the most important instances to note in this new judicial activism were the nullification of the victories of the People Democratic Party (PDP) Governors in Edo and Ondo states. While, Comrade Adams Oshiomole of the Action Congress has been sworn in as Governor in Edo State, that of Ondo state, is still awaiting determination at the Court of Appeal. Also, in this category were the nullification of the election in Anambra State and the reinstatement of the All Peoples Grand Alliance candidate Mr. Peter Obi as the Governor of the state. The case involving Mr. Rotimi Amechi and Chief Celestine Omeha in Rivers State, where the Supreme Court ruled that Mr. Rotimi Amechi was the bona-fide PDP candidate in the 2007 election and that the then sitting Governor Chief Celestine Omeha be removed, while Mr. Rotimi Amechi be sworn in as Governor.

However, the situation playing itself out in Osun State where the election tribunal members have been pointedly accused of corruption such as the reported underhand deals and secret voice calls and text message communication between the tribunal chairman Justice Thomas D. Naron, and the Governors lawyer Chief Kunle Kalejaiye (SAN) are indicative of the penchant by some judicial officers to subvert Justice in Nigeria. At the presidential level, the Supreme Court in delivering judgement on the consolidated petitions brought before it by the presidential candidates of the All Nigeria Peoples Party (ANPP) General Mohammadu Buhari and his Action Congress (AC) counter-part Alhaji Atiku Abubakar, declared that the ANPP candidate's case was dismissed for lack of evidence while that of the AC was struck out for lack of merit.

However, it is to be noted that the four justices of the Supreme Court led by the Chief Justice of the Federation who gave the lead judgement may have considered the social, political, and financial implications of cancelling the presidential election and ordering a new one. Thus, the lead justices may have scarified justice on the altar of political stability like it has always been the case since independence. This, without doubt, Is gratuitous and disservice to the cause of Justice. It is a brazen contradiction of the legal maxim: "Fiat Justita ruat caclum" meaning "Let justice be done though the heaven fall." (The Nation, Dec. 15, 2008.)

Recommendations

As it has been indicated in the second section of this chapter, the violence and electoral malpractices that have remained a recurring decimal of the electoral process are symptomatic of the origin and character of the Nigerian state began during Colonialism which produced the decadent and self-serving ruling elites who have been in the corridor of power since Independence.

To this extent, the inherited Nigerian state which has been variously described as a "mere geographical expression", the "mistake of 1914" and with other derogatory words must be renegotiated to shed all the features and characteristics inherited from colonialism. These inherited features and the lack of vision and the ability to transform domination into hegemony by the ruling elites have militated against the democratization process and also created most of the problems for which the judiciary is now been assessed.

One way to solve this problem is to renegotiate the state along democratic lines. There is the need to institute a dialogue of all the diverse Nigerian people through their genuine and competent representatives and not the old ruling elites that are always recycled during this kind of dialogue in order to determine the future of the Nigerian state. The decisions emanating from this dialogue must form the basis for a new constitution based on the consent of the people as a democratic state in line with the *raison detre* of a state as espoused by the social contract theorist; that the state can only be established through the consent of the people. When this is done, the state will have the will and the capacity to deal decisively with the electoral malpractices and other societal vices militating against the process of democratization in Nigeria.

In the same vein, the electoral machinery, in this case, the Independent National Electoral Commission (INEC), should be made "independent" in the true sense of the word. Most of the electoral problems the judiciary may have to deal with through the electoral tribunal can be prevented when elections are properly and conscientiously conducted. The 2007 elections have remained one of the worst in the annals of Nigeria. The recommendation of the Justice Mohammed Uwais electoral reform panel report that has just been submitted, could make elections in Nigeria fairer as well as serve as a blue print for making INEC truly Independent, if faithfully implemented.

For the judicial arm of government to dispense justice without fear or favour, the executive arm of government especially the President and Governors should not be the one to appoint Justices of the Federation and the Chief Judge of states respectively. These positions, when vacant should be filled by the two other arms of government viz the judiciary itself and the legislature. As Justice Anthony Aniagolu once declared.

> You can default in every arm of government, but you dare not default in the judiciary. That's where God himself sits on the throne. You are therefore representing Almighty God himself as you sit on that throne (cf The News, July 14, 2008)

The words of this eminent jurist underscore the important premium placed on the sanctity of the judiciary as an important aspect of the justice administration process. Thus, their salaries, allowances and other emoluments should be improved in line with their status and responsibility and charged to the consolidated fund. This will insulate them from corrupt politicians who may want to entice and bride them to pervert the course of Justice.

When this is done, any Judge found culpable in any corruption charge(s) should then be prosecuted and severe disciplinary actions should be taken against him. Mere dismissal as was done to Justices Wilson Egbo-Egbo. Stanley Nnaji, Chris Selong, M.M. Adamu, B.T Ahura, AM Eleleagwu, Okechukwu Opene and David Adeniji, are not enough, more serious punishment like jail terms should be included to serve as deterrent to other judges who may want to pervert justice. In the same vein, any politician found guilty of electoral malpractices should also be prosecuted apart from removing him/her from office.

As part of the judicial process, lawyers must be made to understand that as ministers in the temple of justice, they have the obligation to ensure that the integrity and independence of the judicial process is not in any way compromised. The use of legal technicalities, practice behaviour and other legal tactics to either delay, distort of pervert the course of justice is unacceptable and unbecoming of those who should serve as the conveyor belt of justice.

The legal instruments for the conduct of elections especially the 2006 electoral act should be reviewed. Whereas the 2002 electoral act stipulates a time frame for the determination and conclusion of electoral petitions, the 2006 act was silent on this. It is therefore being recommended that the 2006 act be reviewed and amended to give a stipulated time frame for the determination and conclusion of petitions. Election should also be organized early enough to give room for petitions and appeals arising there from. A situation where electoral petitions drag for about two years will not serve the course of justice. The recent episode in Edo state and that of Anambra where people with questionable and dubious mandates were in Government House as Impostors until they were removed by the courts will neither serve the Course of justice nor that of democracy; Justice delayed, they say is justice denied.

The influence of money in politics should be reduced to the barest minimum if not totally eliminated. The ceiling which every politician could spend on electoral campaign should be strictly enforced. Indeed as Justice Akinola Aguda once observed.

The level of income and wealth permissible to any individual must be controlled and must bear some relationship with the income available to the poorest members of society....deep and everlasting restructuring of our whole social and economic posture is imperative in order to remove the prevailing gross inequality. (Aguda 1984:9)

Similarly, the zero-sum, first past the post, winner takes all politics that is currently played in Nigeria is disincentive to democracy and the democratization process. In its stead, the proportional representation model of electoral system is hereby recommended.

Above all, the Nigerian people should realize that a people develop themselves or not at all. Similarly, a people democratize themselves or not. The electorates and entire people should avoid being used as canon fodders in electoral violence and malpractices. They should resist the temptation to rigging elections either for their own party or against the opponent. They should then be ready to defend their mandate freely given to the candidate and their party by ensuring that elections are held in line with extant democratic principles.

Conclusion

This chapter examines the role of the judiciary in the democratization process in Nigeria. The paper argues that democratization will remain elusive where justice is absent. Put differently, democracy can only thrive in a fair and just society since election remains the most universally acceptable means of choosing the managers of the state.

It was pointed out that although election is central to modern day democracy but election is not all that there is to democracy otherwise, the society suffers from what has been called "Electoralism". In order to prevent this, the nature and character of the Nigerian State was analyzed, with the conclusion that unless the state is transformed along democratic lines, most of the electoral and democratization problem afflicting the country would endure for a very longtime to come. It was noted that despite the intrinsic merits of democracy, it will not solve most of Nigeria's problems unless her (political) leaders are imbued with a sense of fair play in the competition for power, respect for the rules of the game and the rule of law and a sincere commitment to ensuring free and fair elections where the people truly choose.

The chapter also assessed the role of the judiciary in handling petitions arising from electoral process, it argued that the barrage of petitions which inundate the electoral tribunals are the manifestations of the crude nature of politics and the intolerant and anti-democratic posture of the ruling elites in Nigeria.

Flowing from this assessment, it is the opinion of the chapter that in recent time the judiciary has played an activist role in the democratization process with some courageous and landmark decisions both at the tribunals and indeed at the appellate courts by either voiding elections and ordering a re-run or outright removal of an impostor and re-instating those who have truly won the election, even though much still needs to be desired.

The chapter opines that the presence of a few "undesirable" justice administrators in the judicial system is quite unfortunate given the strategic role which they ought to play in the process of democratization. The split decision of the Justices of the Supreme Court in the final determination of the election petition between the incumbent President Alhaji, Musa Yar'Adua and Alhaji Atiku Abubakar and General Muhammadu Buhari is in consonance with democratic principles. Whereas the majority had their way the minorities also have their say by the dissenting judgment.

Above all what are however needed in the democratization process is the political will and the sincerity of purpose on the part of the ruling elites to act only in accordance with the laws of the land at all times and deal decisively with the violators of the laws appropriately. No individual or group of individuals should be allowed to be more powerful than the rest of the society. While, the electorate must remain vigilant at the polls, the people must realize that they are the guardian of their democratic mandates, they must therefore ensure that they defend it all the times. Until all these are achieved, democracy may remain elusive in Nigeria.

References

Aguda, Akinola (1984). Law versus Justice, Ado-Ekiti. Second Foundation Day Lecture. Obafemi Awolowo University, Ile-Ife.

Aguda, Akinola (1985). The Quintessence of Justice. 6th Convocation Lecture. University of Maiduguri, Maiduguri.

Ake, Claude (1996). *Democracy and Development*. Ibadan: Spectrum Books Limited.

-__________(1981). *A Political Economy of Africa*. England: Longman Group Ltd.

__________(2000). *The Feasibility of Democracy in Africa.* Dakar: Codesria.

Anifowose, Remi (1999). State, Society and Nation. In Remi Anifowose & Francis Enemuo (eds.), *Element of Politics*. Lagos: Malthouse Press Ltd.

Asein J. O. (2005). *Introduction to Nigerian Legal System*. Lagos: Ababa Press Ltd.

Babajide Kolade-Otitoju (2008, July 14). A Mega Scandal. *The News* Magazine.

Ball R., Allan (1971). *Modern Politics and Government*. Basingstoke, London: Macmillan Press Ltd.

Constitution of Federal Republic of Nigeria, 1999.

Dahl Robert (1989). *Democracy and its Critics.* New Haven: Yale University Press.

Gauba, O. P. (2003). *Introduction to Political Theory, 4th edition.* India: Macmillian India Ltd.

Hay, C., & Marsh, D. (2006). *The State: Theories and Issues.* New York: Pelgrave Macmillan.

Haruna Mohammed (2008, Dec 17). Supreme Court Verdict: a Judicial Dead End. *The Nation* Newspaper. Lagos: Vintage Press Ltd.

Jega M., Attahiru, Wakili Haruna et al. (eds.) (2002). *Democracy and Democratization in Nigeria (1999-2001)*. Kano: Centre for Democratic Research and Training.

Laski, J. Harold (1967). *A Grammar of Politics*. London: George Allen and Unwin Ltd.

Ninalowo, Adebayo (ed.) (1999). *Crisis of Legitimation: The State and Vested Interest.* Lagos: Obaroh and Ogbinaka Publishers Ltd.

Omeje Kenneth (2007). *Reappraising Contemporary Political Development in Nigeria.* Kenneth Omeje (ed.), *State Society Relations in Nigeria: Democratic Consolidation, Conflicts and Reforms*. London: Adonis and Abbey Publishers Ltd.

Osaghae, Eghosa (1998). *Crippled Giant. Nigeria since Independence.* Bloomington: Indiana University Press.

Owolabi, A. Kolawole (1999). *The Quest for Democracy in Africa: A Theoretical Exploration.* Lagos: Obaroh and Ogbinaka Publishers Ltd.

The Nation (2008) "Editorial", Lagos, Vintage Press Ltd.

Ugochukwu, Basil (2004). *Nigeria: Tribunals and the 2003 Elections*. Lagos: Legal Defence Centre.

Yoroms Gani (2007). Elections and Election Rigging in Nigeria: Implication for Democratic Growth. In Keneth Omeje (ed.), *State Society Relations in Nigeria: Democratic Consolidation, Conflicts and Reforms*. London: Adonis and Abbey Publishers Ltd.

8

Electoral Legitimacy in Nigeria: Controversies and Prospects

Akanle, Olayinka

Introduction

The notion of electoral legitimacy presupposes the centrality of democracy to the issues raised in this chapter. Focusing democracy becomes expedient given its pivotal position in the literature and global governance which reinforces its growing popularity as veritable machinery of governance in contemporary societies. Reference to *electoral* suggests election, at least in liberal democracy domains. Most often, discussion on democracy is based on its interface with development in a manner that establishes the possibility of democratic annexation in the quest for national development. It theoretically and pragmatically follows that if democracy is well practised in a manner that accommodates popular legitimacy, it has the capacity to jump start human development. The relationship between the duo has engendered discussions down the ages among scholars and policy makers. These discussions are predicated particularly upon the understanding that democracy and development are essentials of prosperous and equitable societies (Diop and Leautier, 2007). It is against this background that this chapter proceeds.

Largely central to the current discourse is the notion of *process*. Democracy is not only a practice or an act but an art and a science whose process must be sufficiently appreciated. It then means that associated activities of democracy must be respected even within national history and culture. This is democracy that can be enduring and suitable to peoples' socioe-conomic and physical environments and ensure universal rights of the citizens (Olutayo and Omobowale, 2005). Democracy is therefore only usetul if it is practiced within established, proven and sustainable procedures that guarantee legitimacy.

While democracy has popular definitions that have come to be acceptably linked with due process and majority rule, development is still shrewd in definitional controversies. A point of convergence in development constructs is however discernible. Development is generally taken to be popular good, human progress, quality livelihood, happiness and satisfaction of needs of the average majority of people as defined in the society but not necessarily as imposed form without. Development is the absence of wide gaps in the existential unmet needs of the average citizen. Legitimacy on its part is the level to which the process of peoples' emergence at different political realms is acceptable to the people to the extent that they are considered worthy of popular support and recognition (Soyombo, 2006). Legitimacy has strong procedural and outcomes dimensions. In terms of procedure, it has to do with how political office holders derive their power and authority while in terms of outcomes it is based on responsibility and accountability to the electorates (Rothstein, 2007; Odukoya, 2006).

That is to what extent they (political office holders) derive their authority from the people and guarantee to protect the people and ensure their desired livelihoods. Legitimacy from this dimension embodies equality, participation, good governance, rule of law, transparency (Odukoya, 2006; Langer, 2004), justice and popular perception. Although the outcome subset is important, once democratic process lacks legitimacy it is bound to run into troubled waters. This is why Rothstein (2007) in creating The Five Basic Models of State Legitimacy challenged the output (outcome) side to legitimacy and maintain that the real electoral legitimacy rests on peoples' contribution to elections. Once the important procedural angle is compromised it creates the scenario that has come to be known as "legitimacy crisis".

Legitimacy (whether in crisis or otherwise) is an evaluative and judgemental schemata (Odukoya, 2006). Lack of perceived political legitimacy is often expressed through political apathy as demonstrated in poor peoples' turn out at campaign rallies and polling stations in 2003 and 2007 Nigeria's general elections compared to the first republic and June 12, 1993 elections (see Akanle, forthcoming [a]). The procedure is therefore central to legitimizing democracy, eventual public office holders, popular democratic expectations, commitments and actual delivery of 'dividends of democracy' to the people. These factors are necessary for achieving objective development as defined in contemporary societies. This is because legitimacy means people are legally elected within the frameworks of popular participations. As such, politicians, especially rulers, supposedly represent the people who gave them their votes.

There is therefore expected be a to-fro relationships between the electorates and their representatives in defining development needs and best approaches to their achievements in a manner that enables democratic assessments and quality of governance within democratic institutionalization and legitimation parameters. This is the only way sustainable development and democratization can be guaranteed. However, where democratic processes are violated through kangaroo electoral processes that do not enable transparency and due process that could sustain public responsibility and accountability, 'elected' officials are certain to hold electorates in disrespect since they (electorates) do not count in their (political office holders) emergence. On the other hand, unfair electoral deals make the electorates and the general public lose respect for government in power which they see as not originating from their (electorates) votes. Constituted governments are thus seen as impostors who lack legitimacy and consequently do not deserve respect and support. These unfortunate scenarios have dangerous implications for democratic institutionalization and notion of democracy as popular liberation mechanism.

Prosperous times in history of mankind have established and justified the cry for enthronement of democratic ideals in modern societies. This is especially reinforced with wanton human and material waste in autocratic and repressive regimes especially in past and present Africa and Asia. Experiences and literature have shown that development mainly thrive in sustainable atmosphere of justice, peace and progressive conflict which democracy often embodies. Democracy from the foregoing is seen as the necessary harbinger of prosperity and the advancement of human rights (Diop and Leautier, 2007). Democracy and development thus go hand in hand when acceptable processes are followed in a manner that resonates public trust as espoused in legitimacy of emergent political machineries.

Historical facts thrown up by the activities of early Sumerian City dwellers about 3500 BC, Ancient Greece Cities 2000 years later, the Penchaya system of Indian Local government in the 6th century BC and the Kouroukanfouga Charter of 1236 under the Mali empire (Diop and Liautier, 2007; Klein, 2001; Muhlberger, n.d) that encouraged development, peaceful intercity and inter village relationships, human rights protection and generalized progress apparently sustains current democratic agitations particularly as the historical facts are intercontinental (Asia, Europe and Africa for example). There are consequently no racial or sentimental, historical and contemporary impediments to establishing the link between democracy and development. It is therefore not *whether* there is a development advantage in democratization but *how* to maximize developmental performance particularly in new democratisers (Siegle, 2007) like Nigeria.

This chapter is divided into six sections the introduction being the first. This is followed by a discussion of primary elections in Nigeria as the second section, electoral finance as the third, political violence as the fourth, and transparency and due process as the fifth. The necessity of electoral reforms is the sixth and it is at the same time the concluding section.

Primary Elections in Nigeria

The question to pose *ab initio* is why and how are primaries usually subverted in Nigeria? What are the socio-economic and political determinants of candidate selection at primaries in Nigeria? How do this impact on the quality of leadership to be produced from such primaries? What is the implication of this for legitimacy of the electoral system?

The Nigerian democratic experience has no doubt been fascinating to keen observers. A fair submission is clearly that the political and socio-economic environments before elections did not present desired optimism necessary to drive free and fair elections in Nigeria. While many challenge party formation, registration and finance at various levels including courts, such challenges take root at the level of primaries. This is because primaries are the final selection process before the general elections. Also, for some parties, it is constantly believed that whoever emerges the candidates automatically becomes the winner of the general elections. Good examples are Peoples Democratic Party (PDP) in many states and federal level, Action Congress (AC) in Lagos state and PPA in Abia. The level of inimical scheming in PDP was very high particularly given its feat as the largest political party in Africa, the ruling party in Nigeria, the party with over 67 per cent and about 60 per cent of Senate and House of Representative respectively and with the control of most of the gubernatorial seats and states Houses of Assembly consistently in 1999, 2003 and 2007 across the geo-political zones (Omobowale, 2008).

As already hinted above however, dangerous political manipulations was/is common to all Nigerian political parties in their 'election' of candidate in primaries. Party primaries in Nigeria can therefore be said to be nothing but hand picking and selection of loyal candidates that are to be rewarded for loyalty and 'hard work' to the party leadership. This is often met with rebellion from groups within the parties who perceive such selections detrimental to their political career and fight such perceived oppressions through what has come to be known as 'anti-party activities' in Nigerian political lexicon. There are numerous spoken and unspoken instances of such rewards to party loyalists.

A clear one is that of Asiwaju Bola Ahmed Tinubu (the past governor of Lagos state and foremost leader of Action Congress). He (Asiwaju) openly maintained at the party's pre-primary meetings that there were people in the party (Action Congress) who he would like to personally reward through automatic selections as Local Government chairpersons for their past and consistent contributions to the party. Although this utterance was met with intra-party, public and media outcry, Asiwaju did have his ways as he successfully put his own 'god sons and god daughters' in power in Lagos state. This is archetypical of primary elections in Nigeria without any reservation or possible exceptions to any political party or state.

Primaries are subverted primarily due to the popular but abnormal perception of power and governance by politicians in Nigeria. Governance in Nigeria is no longer public service to fatherland but service to self, family, ethnic group and geopolitical zone. Politicians regrettably see public offices as shortcuts to becoming billionaires and this is why there is alarming increase in the numbers of professionals in politics as against hitherto popular notion of professional politicians. This time is one where PhD holders, lawyers and medical doctors, for example, fall for the obnoxious demands of godfathers to contest councillorship elections. It is no longer for layabouts. Political offices are opportunities for economic mismanagement without measure. Being in power is an opportunity for officials to corner public treasury towards sentimental and primordial networks that are inimical to popular development. Political systems that are this porous and lucrative are bound to be attractive to most people given the fact that human beings are selfish and rational. It is then not surprising that the process to getting to such positions is hotly contested and subverted by the political gladiators with impunity.

A contest is naturally set in motion and the contestants are party leaders, incumbents who do not wish to relinquish power and the new aspirants who want to take power to have their own share of the national cake. The incumbents and their godfathers dominate the system while the aspirants contest for domination. This is why current and former members of the National Assembly have repeatedly argued that the existing party infrastructures in Nigeria are nothing but cartel organized to control candidates' selection and limit competition (Carl Le Van, 2006). It is particularly so because party executives committees nominates delegates from the local governments rather than having congress system or open primaries where candidates' popularities can be openly ascertained. Primaries today are organized for purpose rather than process (Carl Le Van, 2006). They are mechanisms for compensation of conformity and punishment of dissent. Even when there appear to be free interlock of competitions and political ideals they are regulated by standardized political norms, practices and other deviant trajectories. This is regardless of established knowledge that enthronement and sustenance of democracy only depend on political institutions and political actors that perceive the system as fair and worthwhile. (Akinyele, 2004)

Once there is disruption of primaries' ideals, it is an early warning sign that all is not well with the democracy and its processes. That is, disputes at that level suggests that there is no level playing field for all the political actors in the political system (Akinyele, 2004) and it portends danger for the country. With a slight and possible exception of 1999, contemporary primaries in Nigeria can be candidly adjudged unfair, shady and violent. As examples of myriads of reports on the elections, Amnesty International Report (2007) and International Republican Institute (IRI) (2005) concluded that primary elections took place amid heightened political violence, several candidates for political offices were attacked during primaries, and at least 4 were killed in different parties' primaries across the country. At least, 31 governors were haunted through the Economic and Financial Crimes Commission (EFCC), 4 governors were impeached for political reasons while there were political assassinations and violent clashes amongst supporters and candidates during primaries. There were cases but popular ones were the murders of Engineer Funso Williams (a sure Peoples Democratic Party governorship candidate in Lagos state) on 27th July 2006 and that of Dr. Ayo Daramola (another governorship aspirant in Ekiti state) on 14th August, 2006.

Moreover, there were cases of substitution of candidates even after primaries had been concluded. This attested to the unmistaken potency of the political barons. In Lagos, after Hilda Williams, the widow of Late Engineer Funso Williams, had emerged victorious at the primaries, she was later substituted by the party with Senator Musiliu Obanikoro. (Omobowale, 2008) In Imo and Rivers states cases of substitution after primaries were repeated. Senator Ifeanyi Ararume was replaced with Engineer Ugwu in Imo state while in Rivers state Mr. Rotimi Amaechi was replaced with Mr Celestine Omehia (Omobowale, 2008). Although less controversial, the emergence of Alhaji Atiku Abubakar as Vice Presidential candidate in 1999 and Alhaji Umaru Yar'adua as the PDP presidential flag bearer in 2007 were by no means different as they were both governors of Adamawa and Katsina states respectively before being imposed on the political system. While the court intervened successfully in very few cases, it does not remove the fact that primaries are largely teleguided by anti democratic forces in Nigeria.

A lesson to be learnt by all and political parties in particular is that primary elections are important procedures that must be respected objectively if democracy must thrive. Particularly, if parties must succeed in the final analysis, they must conduct primaries in fair manners. Peoples' opinions and interests start from the primaries. Against stooges, credible candidates that will protect the party, state and its people can only emerge from good primaries. It is better for parties to note that there is no quick fix to enduring political popularity. There are no short cuts to sustainability. Parties that will endure must follow established and proven process. Primary elections are important processes that must not be subverted in the democratic equation. Thus, it is noteworthy from contemporary political history of Nigeria and beyond that those parties that conducted primaries in objective and transparent manner and were able to mediate and acceptably reconcile internally conflicting interests of political aspirants had better opportunities of success in the future than those parties that either avoided primaries entirely or allowed the conduct of primaries to degenerate into avenues for parties' disintegration through intra-party bickering, dissensions and acrimonious court cases (Akinyele, 2004).

Ready examples and tests of the above 'theory' are Alliance for Democracy (AD) and All Nigerian Peoples Party (ANPP). AD avoided primaries in quite a number of situations particularly in gubernatorial elections (*to reward pro-democracy elements who suffered military brutality* [emphasis added]) while ANPP lost control of its process for primaries to the extent that both parties damaged their future chances (Akinyele, 2004). As a matter of fact, AD today is dead in practical political terms while ANPP is surviving at the margins compared to its prospect and fortunes in 1999. Is the PDP possible exception to this 'theory'? Well, the party is already sowing the seeds of its own destruction as events are suggesting in Kogi, state, Lagos state, Ogun state and other places across the country, but time will soon tell affirmatively.

Electoral Finance

From the perspective of those familiar with Nigerian political intricacies whether as electorates, contestants, political office holders, INEC, international observers or just as interested citizens, funding of democratic processes in the country is a major procedural problem is easy to comprehend. People, especially political actors have come to see spending in politics as short-term investment with sure and unrivalled returns on investment. In Nigeria, no business is as lucrative as holding political office. Occurrences attest to this position. No political actor is immune to this. There are so much financial gains in Nigeria's political arena and recent scandals in the Ministry of Health and House of Representative attest to this. Politicians talk in billions of Naira and US dollars of unaccountable monies. Examples are Constituency Development Allocations and security votes. That security votes are to be spent unaccountably is, for instance, the root cause of the then intractable Ladoja and Adedibu[1] crisis (see Omobowale and Olutayo, 2007 for detail on Adedibu system of political patronage in Oyo state).

Political offices in Nigeria enable people to get rich quickly either by budget gaps and lapses, frivolous award of contracts or outright stealing without punishment especially now that the only seeming potent anti-graft agencies have been purposefully emasculated. It is with this knowledge that political money bags and investors invest their money in politics and corner the process through imposition of candidates that are sure of bringing the coveted returns. This becomes easy for electoral sponsors since electioneering in Nigeria is expensive without legal and formal institution to regulate the cost. Take for example, in conducting the 2007 general election, there was a budget of N42 billion (approximately $ 330 million), 120,000 polling stations with an average capacity of 500 voters (International Republican Institute [IRI], 2005). To obtain party application forms, some parties' fees were as high as N50, 000 ($ 375) while Peoples Democratic Party's (PDP)[2] presidential election application form was obtained with millions of naira. There must be tours and campaigns across the wards, local governments, senatorial districts and states depending on the level of contest.

For INEC, the conduct of elections runs into billions of Naira (as high as $ 600 m for 2011 general elections) while for the political office seekers, it could also run into millions and billions depending on the level of contest. The fact is that the presidency allocation to INEC for the conduct of elections is not adequate compared to the enormity of the task. This is provided that the entire fund allocated will be judiciously spent not factoring mismanagement and outright embezzlement into the financial quadrant. Consider the issue of logistics, manpower and financial implications of screening the mammoth crowd applying to contest gubernatorial elections across the states and actual conduct of elections in 2007 for example. The number ranges between 8 and 23 per state (Ajayi, 2007). It was 8 in Gombe, 11 each in Kaduna and Ogun, 23 in Lagos, 19 in Kwara, 18 in Abia, Enugu and Rivers respectively, 16 each in Imo and Kano, 12 in Oyo, Bayelsa, Delta, Plateau and Taraba respectively, 11 in Akwa Ibom, Borno, Katsina, Nassarawa, Niger, Sokoto and Yobe respectively, 10 each in Bauchi and Cross River and 9 in Jigawa (Ajayi, 2004).

Hence, how do people finance their elections in a country where poverty is as high as 70 per cent and unemployment is as high 11.9 per cent? (Federal Ministry of Women Affairs and Social Development, 2007; National Bureau of Statistics, 2006). Once the political money bags who have embezzled enough from the system are too high for certain electoral posts, how do upcoming politicians who do not have enough to bank roll their campaigns and politicking foot their bills? Although INEC give allocations to parties, the allocations are stipends compared to the to parties' actual financial demands for elections. The incongruence between financial demands of Nigerian democracy and available funds has engendered quite a lot of process subversion. The gulf has given rise to INEC officials been financially induced especially as most of them during elections are ad hoc staff. Also, most of the vehicles and other facilities often used during elections are hired making them susceptible to dangerous influences. The funds are not enough for INEC and it is at the mercy of presidency just as political office-holders are at the mercy of godfathers subjecting the whole electoral process to abuse.

The case is particularly disheartening on the parts of contestants. The enormity of the financial needs make them pledge their loyalties to their godfathers who are willing to bankroll electoral invoices. Even when godfathers' demands are against their wills and principles, there are few alternatives left to the extent that they sell their hearts and consciences at shrines. Such is the pressure and need that exposed; educated and financially comfortable politicians subject themselves to unimaginable, dehumanizing bigotry and enslavement. To them, it is a do or die affair and every obstacle, including financial, must be surmounted regardless of the process. Electoral finance is so much a problem to Nigerian democratization process that Professor Maurice Iwu (the INEC Chairman) (2008) the "pervasive influence of money" both from local and international sources is a great challenge to democratic governance in Nigeria. People source for fund from various sources for different purposes that they make conduct of elections a nightmare. According to Professor Iwu, (2008) money was deployed excessively in 2007 both internally and externally to ensure imposition of *chosen* candidates.

Unfortunately, unlike in America and Canada where there is practical limit to the amount and sources of contributions to elections, such limits do not exist practically in Nigeria. An individual can bankroll a whole election in Nigeria thus turning him/herself to a godfather and political institution. A clear picture was painted during the just concluded American election. While a cohort of highly placed but ignorant Nigerians were busy organizing the "Africa for Obama" fund raising, little did they know that they were violating a long standing American law and jeopardizing Obama's chances. This is because non-Americans are not allowed to contribute in any financial way to the election of an American. Little wonder Obama's campaign team quickly disowned the over-zealous 'supporters'. Lack of sufficient institutional mechanisms to moderate electoral finance is therefore, to a large extent, a threat to credible elections, generalized democratization and national security of Nigeria. Rather than credible candidates emerging at party levels and beyond, godfathers that fund and consequently control the process ensure indirect primaries (Carl Le Van, 2006) to protect their interests and punish dissent in parties by refusing to bankroll candidates' elections fund while they also withdraw necessary social capital they maintain through their financial pool. It is then very easy, from the foregoing, to appreciate the strong link between electoral finance mechanisms and electoral outcomes as they interface quality, responsive and popular leadership.

Once electoral procedures are sacrificed on the altar of finance, the outcomes are pretty predictable. Succinctly and rhetorically, one may then ask, if funding is a constant and nearly most important in getting elected into political offices in a political system built on patrimonilism and godfatherism, to what extent will political office-holders be accountable to the people (electorates) who do not have any contribution to the electoral purse? Won't they rather continue their allegiance to their financiers for present survival and future relevance? A popular Yoruba adage *t'enu ba je oju a ti* (once you got help from somebody, you become obliged to respect and satisfy the wishes of the person) drives home the point. This becomes particularly appreciable as financing elections in Nigeria is purely about putting financiers' money where their mouths are. Money politics can then be seen as a major problem of Nigerian political arena (see Omobowale and Olutayo, 2008; Yaqub, 2001).

Political Violence

As an element of conflict, violence is ubiquitous. It is existent in one form or another in every society and every institution of societies. The concern of this section is to discuss political violence since lacunae is bound to be created without it. This is particularly so because political violence is a twin concept in Nigerian political terrain (Ekiran, 2006). This explains massive redeployment of police officers during elections, elections petitions and appeals. A recent example is that of massive redeployment of a significant cross-section of the Nigerian police to Edo State on 11th November 2008 during the court of appeal judgement on Oshiomole versus Osunbor case. The massive police presence was besides a public holiday already declared by the state government in anticipation of outbreak of violence.

Although there are as many definitions of political violence as there are authors interested in the problem, political violence within the current discourse is disorderly conducts targeted at frustrating, eliminating and humiliating political machineries and opponents to silence and get rid of unwanted others (Ekiran, 2006). Popular modes of perpetrating political violence in Nigeria include: arson, assassination, rioting, confusion, inducement, manipulation of votes, ballot box stuffing, threatening, blood-letting, assaults, insults, hooliganism, vandalism and rape amongst others too numerous to mention. Against this backdrop, it is obvious that political violence is a common occurrence in Nigerian political environment. In fact, Iwu (2008) describes electoral violence as "looming danger" in the conduct of elections in Nigeria and this has led observers to constantly express concern over the security environment during elections. The uncountable numbers of Nigerian politicians driving bullet proof cars and maximum security houses comparable to the Ikoyi Maximum Prison is a testimony to the prevalence of electoral violence during and after elections.

The important fact that must be taken is that political violence is a major tool and process through which democratic procedures are subverted. A lot of politicians intentionally resulted to it to scare opponents and electorates in a manner akin to *kaka k'eku ma je sese a fi s'awa danu* (a Yoruba adage popularly used to capture selfishness. It literally translates to: it is either me or nobody. If it will not be to my benefit, I would rather destroy the whole process and its benefits). Political violence is not spontaneous and uncoordinated activity by layabouts, illiterates, *yandaba boys* or *area boys* but orchestrated activity by political elites who are determined to get to power by all means regardless of consequences even when they know. It is often times based on intolerance by the political gladiators. It is pertinent to know however that intolerance and political violence are enemies of democratic culture just as looting of the treasury creates a feeling of disillusion and desperation which feeds violent crimes (Ogunsanwo, 1994).

It is regrettable that the concept of tolerance and peaceful changing of government has not been well internalized in Nigeria even when tolerance is the crux of democratic consolidation. The problem is largely based on parochial cultural and selfish tendencies as already mentioned elsewhere in this chapter. Main causes of political violence in Nigeria can thus be summed up to be selfish interest of political actors to get and maintain political power regardless of their popularity or unpopularity, political intolerance and flagrant electoral malpractices like election rigging especially when peoples' candidates are rigged out.

Electoral violence wastes lives and properties and violently disrupts democratic regimes as was the case in the abrupt termination of the first and second republics. Attempting 'democratic evolution' of Nigeria, Akinyele (2004) vividly demonstrates that after two decades of nationalist struggles that led to eventual independence, political violence of 1962 through to 1965 "Operation Wet E" led to military interference in January 15th 1966. Political history suggests that the Nigerian civil war of 1967-1970 had a bearing with degenerated political violence of 1962. Cases of political violence were repeated in 1979, 1983, 1993 (see Akanle Forthcoming [a] for detail account of 1993 political violence and its environments), 1999, 2003 and 2007. Generally, political history has shown in Nigeria that turbulent elections have plagued Nigerian democracy (Mamud, 2008). Due to its inimical consequences and recurrence in elections in the country, political violence is best described as the rule and norm rather than exception. Election violence is obscene (Ekiran, 2006) and second national political nature to the extent that military regimes often claimed that their coup d' tats were "corrective measures" (Piombo, 2003) to save lives, properties and their beloved fatherland from anarchy.

To paint a contextual picture, the following is a brief summary of political violence related murders and assassinations since 1999:

- September 9, 1999 - Sunday Ugwu, elder brother of Nwabueze Ugwu, a member of the Enugu state House of Assembly (Nkanu East) was killed. He was mistaken for the legislator.
- December 21, 2001 - Hon Odunayo Olagbaju, member of the Osun state House of Assembly was killed by unknown gun men in Ile-Ife.
- December 23, 2001 - Bola Ige was shot dead in his bedroom in Ibadan.
- August 15, 2002 - Ahmed Pategi, Chairman of Kwara State chapter of PDP and his police orderly were murdered on a highway near the state capital in Ilorin.
- August 29, 2002 - Dr. Victor Nwakwo, younger brother of the leader of the People Mandate Party (PMP), Chief Arthur Nwankwo was killed in Enugu.
- September 1, 2002 - The Chairman of the Nigerian Bar Association (NBA) in Anambra state, Barnabas Igwe and his wife, Abigail, were murdered in Onitsha.
- October 20, 2002 - Professor Chimere Ikoku, former Vice-Chancellor, University of Nigeria, Nsukka (UNN) was killed in his residence.

- February 10, 2003 - Chief Ogonnaya Uche, former Commissioner in Imo State, a senatorial candidate of the All Nigeria Peoples Party (ANPP) died a couple of days after he was attacked in Owerri.
- February 22, 2003-Theodore Agwatu, principal secretary to the Imo State Governor, was murdered in his home by unknown attackers.
- March 3, 2003 - Mrs Emily Omope, an AD member in Ekiti State died after an acid attack.
- March 5, 2003 - Chief Marshall Harry, national coordinator, south-south of the ANPP presidential campaign was murdered in Abuja.
- March 7, 2004 - Chairman of the Kogi State Independent electoral Commission, Chief Philip Olorunipa, was shot dead in his home by assassins.

Source: Ekiran, 2006, p. 294.

High profile political assassinations in the wake of the 2007 general elections not captured in the Ekiran (2006) list above include that of Engineer Funso Williams (a sure Peoples Democratic Party governorship candidate in Lagos state) on 27th July, 2006 as well as that of that of Dr. Ayo Daramola (another governorship aspirant in Ekiti state) on 14th August, 2006. All the above cases were separate from some low profile and pocket of cases of assassinations mentioned earlier in the chapter. Such is the disastrous consequence of political violence yet it is pervasive in the country. The apprehension and anxiety that greet the wake of elections are better imagined than experienced and they are traceable to nothing but violence. People consequently prefer to stay in safety and comfort of their homes rather than be exposed to risk of violence. This is partly the reason why people do not believe in the process of election and the candidates they impose. Popular confidence is generally eroded especially as people see politicians as same irrespective of party leanings and professional affiliations while the electoral process is seen as a charade.

In line with the above assertion, Afrobarometer (2006) empirically discovered in a nationally representative survey that although Nigerians still prefer democracy, they are broadly discouraged by the political system. According to the Afrobarometer (2006) survey, Nigerians have minimum trust in elections, one of the core institutions of democracy, and as much as two-third believed that elections do not represent peoples' choices and therefore not reliable mechanism. One cannot but agree with these findings especially with high level of complaints of corruption, protests, fraud, political domination, thuggery and violence that immediately follow elections results declarations in contradistinction to widespread jubilations that usually follow court verdicts that upturned election's results as was the case in Mimiko's Ondo state and Oshiomole's Edo states. It is particularly happy to note that such judgements have capacity to improve peoples' believe in the political system. Regrettably however, popular and legal reinstatements are still isolated cases and are shrewd in judicial technicalities and delay that disinterest people. It is submitted that electoral violence is common in Nigeria and it has the capacity to impinge on the electoral process, undermine legitimacy and threaten democratic stability.

An Advocacy for the Missing Ligaments: Transparency and Due Process

A consistent theme that must have been clear from the foregoing analysis is the absence of transparency and due process in the Nigerian electoral system. Right from the conduct of primaries, electoral financing and prevalence of electoral violence, the two crucial ligaments can be held constant in the political equation. The political processes are driven like secret cults in the hands of some priests that could not be challenged. If parties and other political actors appreciate the place of transparency and due process and right attention paid to them, the story would certainly be different. As outcome interface, cases of election results cancellations by election petitions tribunals and call for fresh elections due to electoral frauds would have been unnecessary. For instance, regardless of huge financial, material and human resources committed to the conduct of Nigerian 2007 general elections, so far, the election petition tribunals across the nation have nullified the election of seven governors (Ugborgu, 2008). At least five of these annulled governorship elections have already been re-conducted while others are either awaiting court of appeals' judgements or permanently overturned as was the case in Edo state. At the levels of State Houses of Assembly and National Assembly the pattern is identical across the country. In Ondo state alone, no fewer than 12 elections have been nullified by the tribunals sitting in Akure in what has come to be termed 'harvest of elections nullification' (Sowole, 2008).

The two factors are cornerstones of democracy. As a matter of fact, there can never be a workable democracy without the crucial but missing ligaments. Having made the point; brief conceptualizations of transparency and due process are in order.

Transparency

The notion of transparency connotes different meanings depending on the context of discussion. That is, its representation in photography is different form that in politics, philosophy, religion and finance. The notion however converges in all the spheres. Transparency simply means the need to be able to see through an object or operation. It is the ability to make something easily comprehensible. The meaning in democratic processes does not radically differ. Transparency in politics is the ability of a body, organization or individual to make its operations and others detailed, up to date, accurate and easily accessible to authorized bodies and individuals. This enables the determination of suitability, quality and fairness to all stakeholders and players.

This succinctly, is democratic transparency. As simple as it has been made to appear to allow for comprehension and pragmatism, transparency is a proven challenge to political parties and actors and general conduct of elections in Nigeria where democratic institutions are nascent but extraneous as well as primordial influences are deep rooted and more developed.

Introducing the concept and practice of transparency at this stage is to emphasize the need for considerable attention to it in all activities especially in primaries which has been described as 'mini elections' (Akinyele, 2004) that determines the eventual general elections, confidence in the system and the eventual leadership quality. Transparency is central to the electoral process and must never be compromised. Transparency is the first step in the electoral procedures as it serves as check against corruption and generalized undue influences over public space meant for all in seeking elective positions (Piccone, 2007).

Due Process

This is technically a relatively new concept in Nigerian democratic scope and governance. However, the notion it represents is as old as mankind. It means following laid down guidelines, principles, rules and laws in detail while performing duties and responsibilities. This involves not cutting corners, adopting short cuts or compromising standards for personal, familial and other parochial reasons to the detriment of democratic goals and objectives. This nevertheless takes into account the dangers of red-tapism, complexity and bureaucratic bottlenecks. That is, as people follow due process they must not undermine performance and quality output. Within this orthodoxy, political parties and other stakeholders must stick to due process in electing party flag bearers and other democratic activities to ensure international best practices and strengthen governance and public institutions.

Necessity of Electoral Reforms in Nigeria: Statements of Conclusion

Thus far, it is obvious that Nigeria must as a matter of sincerity and urgency reform its electoral machineries if democracy must endure. What this chapter has attempted to do is to synthesize the major challenges to electoral legitimacy to access its extent of presence or absence and give a road map out of the present quagmire. With this analysis, it is clear that legitimacy is largely lacking in contemporary Nigerian electoral set up. It is against this submission that a need exists for electoral reforms in the country. This tallies with the observation of stakeholders in the country since the nations' redemocratisation (Mamud, 2008; Utomi, 2008; Suberu, 2008; Balogun, 2008; Frazer, 2007; Innocent, 2007; Ajayi, 2006; Carl Le Van, 2006; Yaqub, 2001). As popular as the movement for electoral reform in Nigeria is however, its nature, scope and methodology remain subject of controversies (Mamud, 2008) given national peculiarities and extraneous forces traceable to unneglectable political aficionados in the country. Political juggernauts that are immovable and discretely as well as openly determine the course of political happenings. They are powerful and must be recognized if they are to be dismantled and the political future of Nigeria reshappened.

President Umaru Musa Yar'adua bought into the urgent call for electoral reforms when he honestly described the elections that brought him to power as far from been perfect and in August, 2007 inaugurated a 22 member Electoral Reforms Committees (ERC) headed by former Chief Justice of Nigeria Justice Muhammed Uwais with a one year mandate. The political will is commendable but it is hoped that the draft report and recommendations will be adopted practically. It is equally hoped that their provisions will be actionable and justiceable particularly when current Electoral Act has been popularly described as 'election rigging manual' that disempowers the electorates and discourages popular participations. It is therefore summarily expected that the government of the servant leader will walk the talk and not only talk the talk with respect to electoral reforms. This point is particularly necessary especially now that serious doubts are already been cast on the reliability of the electoral reform process and its outcomes by opposition parties and other objective stakeholders (Civil Society Organizations, scholars and international observers amongst others) in the electoral system.

Based on review of literature, observations, and informal discussions with stakeholders, commentaries' synthesis and professional insights, particular areas to be focused in the reforms are suggested heretofore. There must be sustained commitments to electoral reforms in a way that ensures free and fair elections. There is no gainsaying the fact that free and fair elections are primary ingredients of lasting and popular democracy that yields dividends to expectant public. Any reform that does not ensure independence and builds the capacity of electoral body is a waste. Although some people are already of the opinion that INEC is too powerful at the moment, this chapter takes an exception to such position. INEC, if anything, should be further strengthened but be made to be more transparent. As it stands, INEC is still not in charge of elections in Nigeria but is only a stooge and an arrow in the hands of the political cabal. It should therefore be strengthened in all ramifications to stand alone and perform its statutory roles without fear or sentiments.

Since conduct of credible elections need independent, non partisan, competent and professional body (Mamud, 2008), appointment of INEC officials must be objective and transparent in a manner that do not impose card carrying members of political parties as the electoral body's chairman. Further, funding of the body must be severed from the presidency and linked with the consolidated funds to ensure independence so that the electoral body will be independent of the presidency in terms of funding. Let all parties be fairly represented on the board of the electoral body. All officials and board members must be worthy in character and sound judgement and this can be guaranteed through independent conduct of search and due diligence on all current and prospective staff members. This may be demanding but it is very worthwhile given the sensitive and overarching nature of the electoral body. This also presupposes that the electoral body's members must be professionals who can hold their own against financial and political intimidations from desperate politicians.

In reforming the electoral process, there is also the need to strengthen Civil Society Organizations (CSOs) to be partners in progress since they are the third body in the process after the public and private sectors. This has a lot of advantages (see Akanle forthcoming for detail discussion on the role of CSOs in Nigerian democratization) especially since CSOs are often independent and socially and technically equipped. CSOs can be further empowered by including them in democratic decision making processes. This gives a lot of unclassified information to them that enable them to further disseminate the right information to the electorates who have come to trust them in a system with high level of government and generalized political irresponsibility. This has a strong relationship with citizenship education about electoral process. INEC has recognized this and their campaign of "your vote is your power, use it wisely" appeared to be striking the right cord in a way.

As already demonstrated in electoral finance section, there is need to limit the amount of money an individual can spend in any election. This should be emphasized and enforced. Rather than excessive electoral funding been disregarded, it should be criminalized with heavy penalty if possible jail term. It is that serious because political money bags exert unimaginable influence on the electoral system and militate against electoral legitimacy. They are a danger to democratic future of Nigeria because people have come to recognize their influence on the system and are losing interest believing their votes and time will not count once the money bags are still in control. A flipside to this is punishment of election criminals. The current arrangements where culpable INEC officials are allowed to sit unruffled in office even when elections they conducted and results they declared are being upturned are not acceptable. The election riggers and their INEC syndicate should be declared criminals and punished accordingly, if possible with criminal charges pressed against them.

Primaries should be more transparent. INEC should get more involved in party primaries. INEC should exercise some measure of control and not necessarily see primaries as party affairs even when they are abused. The Electoral Act gives this power to INEC it only needs to action it by paying more attention and perform its oversight functions that are statutory. To limit the level of abuse of electoral procedures especially at the level of primaries, independent candidates should be allowed and encouraged once they have the capacity and credibility to stand elections. Currently, political actors that are sincere are often held to ransom by political gladiators who blackmail office seekers to the extent that they cannot contest elections without registered party platforms. Even when the party harasses aspirants, they (the aspirants) are still punished for anti-party activities rather than the party been accused and punished for anti-aspirants activities, misdemeanours or crimes as the case may be. Allowing independent candidates at elections has the capacity to redress this ugly trend.

If the reforms sincerely scale through and enforced within the suggested frameworks, a sufficient level of legitimacy may return to Nigerian electoral process and the democratic political institutions sufficiently strengthened to the extent that they have the capacity to yield the coveted dividends of democracy and put sustainable development on course.

References

Afrobarometer, 2006 July. *Performance and Legitimacy in Nigeria's New Democracy.* Afrobarometer briefing paper, No. 46.

Ajayi, F. (2007). *Unemployment and Violence in the 2007 Nigerian Gubernatorial Elections*. Retrieved on 11th October 2008, from http://www.nigeriaworld.com.

Ajayi, K. (2006). Security Forces, Electoral Conduct and the 2003 General Elections in Nigeria. *Journal of Social Sciences, Vol. 13, No. 1*. pp. 57-66. Kamla-Raj.

Akanle, O. Forthcoming [a] Nigeria, 1993 Political and Electoral Violence. *The International Encyclopaedia of Revolution and Protest: 1500 to the Present.* UK: Blackwell Publishing.

____________ [b] Caught in the Morass: Road Map for Civil Society Organisations in "Democratic" Nigeria. Chapter contribution in *State and Civil Society Relations in Nigeria.*

Akinyele, T.A. (2004). The 2003 Nigerian Elections that broke the jinx. *West Africa Review, Issue 5*. Africa Resource Centre Incorporated.

Amnesty International Report, 2007. *Nigeria*. p. 15.

Balogun, A. (2008, January 15). *2007 Elections and Challenge of Electoral Reform. Nigerian Tribune*.

Carl Le Van, A. (2006, May). *Current and Future Challenges for Nigeria's Electoral Framework.* Presentation at Nigerian Peoples Forum Annual Conference. Washigton DC.

Diop, A., & Leautier, F. (2007, November). Democracy: An Adaptable System Critical for Development. *Development Outreach, 9.3.*, pp. 2-5. Washington DC: World Bank Institute.

Ekiran, M.A. (2006). Governance and Political Violence in Nigeria. In Oyekanme, F. A. D., & Soyombo, O. (eds.), *Society and Governance: The Quest for Legitimacy in Nigeria* (pp. 284-304). Lagos, Nigeria: Department of Sociology, University of Lagos.

Federal Ministry of Women Affairs and Women Development (FMWA &SD), 2007. *National Gender Policy.* FRN.

Frazer, J.E. 2007. *Nigeria at a cross roads: Elections, Legitimacy and a Way Forward.* Testimony before the House Foreign Affairs Subcommittee on Africa and

Global Health. Washington DC. June.

Innocent, C. 2007. *An election programmed to fail: Preliminary report on the presidential and National Assembly elections held on Saturday, April 21.* Unpublished manuscript.

International Republican Institute (IRI). 2005. *2007 Nigerian National Elections: Pre-election Assessment Final Report.* USA:Washington DC.

Iwu, M. 2008. *Reflections and lessons from the 2007 Nigerian elections.* Vanguard Newspaper. Saturday 15th November.

Klein, J. 2001.The Birth of Kingship: From Democracy to Monarchy in Sumer. *Archaeology Odissey.* 4. January- February. pp. 17-25.

Mamud, A.Y. 2008. *Electoral Reforms in Nigeria.* www.buzzle.com. Retrieved 11/10/2008.

Muhlberger, S. n.d. Democracy in Ancient India. www.nipissingu.ca/department/history/muhlberger/histdem/indiadem.htm.

National Bureau of Statistics. 2006. *The Nigerian Statistical Fact Sheets on Economic and Social Development.* Federal Republic of Nigeria.

Odukoya, A.O. 2006. Democracy, National question and Legitimacy Crisis in Nigeria: Agenda for national integration, in: *Society and Governance: The Quest for Legitimacy in Nigeria.* Oyekanme, F.A.D. and Soyombo, O.eds. Nigeria: Department of Sociology, University of Lagos, Lagos. pp. 234-264.

Ogunsanwo, A. 1994. Problems of Democratisation in Africa, in: *Democratisation in Africa: African Perspectives.* 2. Omo Omoruyi, Berg-Schlosser, D, Sambo, A and Okwuosa, A. eds. Nigeria: Centre for Democratic Studies. pp. 137-144.

Olutayo, A.O and Omobowale, A.O. 2005. Globalisation, Democracy and the New Partnership for Africa's Development (NEPAD). *African Journal for the Psychological Study of Social Issues.* 8.2. pp. 228-242.

Omobowale, A.O and Olutayo, A.O. 2007. Chief Lamidi Adedibu and patronage politics in Nigeria. *Journal of Modern African Studies.* 45.3. pp. 425-446.

Omobowale, A.O.2008. Flawed political party primaries in Nigeria's fourth republic: The case of the Peoples' Democratic Party. *African Journal for the Psychological Study of Social Issues.* 11.2. pp. 282-291.

Piccone, T.J. 2006. Building Institutional Capacity for Democratization. *Development Outreach.* 9.3. November. U.S.A. Washington DC: World Bank Institute. pp. 9-11.

Piombo, J. 2003. The import of Nigeria's April 2003 elections. *Strategic Insight.* June 2.

Rothstein, B. 2007. *Creating State Legitimacy-The Five Basic Models.* Paper presented at the annual meeting of the American Political Science Association, Chicago. August 28-29.

Siegle, J. 2006. Overcoming autocratic legacies. *Development Outreach.* 9.3. November. U.S.A. Washington DC: World Bank Institute. pp. 6-8.

Sowole, J. 2008. Nigeria, Ondo: Harvest of Election Nullifications. *This Day* July 7. http://www.allafrica.com/stories/200807080882.html. Retrieved 27/12/2008.

Soyombo, O. 2006. Leadership and the crisis of Legitimacy in Nigeria, in: *Society and Governance: The Quest for Legitimacy in Nigeria.* Oyekanme, F.A.D. and Soyombo, O.eds. Nigeria: Department of Sociology, University of Lagos, Lagos. pp. 265-283.

Suberu, R.T 2007. Nigeria's muddled elections. *Journal of Democracy.* 18.4. pp. 95-110. October.

Ugborgu, V. 2008. *Trials of Election Petition* Tribunals http://nigerianmuse.com/nigeriawatch/2007/trials_of_election_petition_tribunals by _victor _ugborgu_independent. Retrieved 27/12/2008.

Utomi, P. 2008. *How to Fix Nigeria: The Electoral Process.* www.findajobinafrica.com. Retrieved 26/10/2008. The Newswatch Communication Ltd.

Yaqub, N.O. 2001. 1993 Presidential elections in Nigeria and the alleged use of excessive Money: Implications for the country's political culture and future politics. *The Journal of Third World Studies.* Fall.

Yaqub, N.O. 2006. Society and Governance: The quest for Legitimacy in Nigeria, in: *Society and Governance: The Quest for Legitimacy in Nigeria.* Oyekanme, F.A.D. and Soyombo, O.eds. Nigeria: Department of Sociology, University of Lagos, Lagos. pp. 15-39.

Footnotes

Alhaji Rashidi Adewolu Ladoja was a governor of Oyo state while Alhaji Lamidi Ariyibi Adedibu was arguably the most formidable political godfather in the contemporary history Oyo state. The feud between the godson and godfather for political supremacy and economic aggrandizements led to one of the most consequential political tussles in the history of Nigerian democracy.

PDP was the party of choice during the 2007 general election. This was due to the fact that it was the ruling and biggest party in Africa. Hence, it was the only party with increasing influence and prospect in the political calculations of the country. This endeared the party to most aspirants who wanted 'sure way to power' regardless of the cost.

9

Presidential Democracy, Executives and Good Governance in Nigeria

Sulaiman Balarabe Kura

Introduction

Democracy ... can survive and prosper *only* if the public interest is upper most and the institutions which do the work of society stick to their *briefs* (Tahir, 2003: 10, emphasis added).

The survival of democracy in any society is conditioned by the breadth and degree to which public interests and values are addressed. Addressing public interests through the institutions of democracy are conditioned by the extent to which those institutions adhere strictly to their constitutional *briefs* (i.e. frameworks). The sum of these is what in contemporary development parlance called *good governance*. This arguably suggests that the survival of a democratic system is a function of (i) the constitutional framework(s) through which institutions evolved (ii) the actual performance of the institutions particularly premised on public interests as 'upper most' priority. Thus, there is a relationship between the functions of democratic institutions and constitutional frameworks. Constitutions are the catalysts for functional and responsive democratic institutions. This chapter aims to achieve two primary objectives: to analytically examine the relationship between presidential democracy and constitutional frameworks and empirically explain how presidential democracy operating under Nigerian constitution influences the governance functions of the executive institutions towards providing the 'public goods.' The capability of the institutions to provide the public goods is, according to Mudasiru (2005: 214) "... what gives credence to the power of the state in terms of autonomy, organisational unity and ruling capacity" vis-à-vis defines the popularity of existing political regime. Specifically, the chapter seeks to explain the constitutional nature of Nigeria's democracy in terms of the powers and limitations of the executives and how such constitutional prerogatives influence its governance performance.

It is important to caution that this chapter seeks to 'measure' the extent to which the executive institution or arm of governance deliver on the general expectations of the citizens, especially following the return of democracy in 1999 in Nigeria. The analysis is premised on the basis of its operation under presidential system and with the kind of constitutional framework guiding its activities. The paper is structured as follows: the next section reviews some fundamental theoretical debates concerning presidential democracy and its impetus in engendering responsive democratic governance in general and Nigeria in particular. This discussion is integrated with the contemporary passion of the idea of good governance. Section three assesses executive's performance on the basis of UNECA's good governance indicators. The last section identifies four salient points as the major conclusions of the paper.

The Essential Desirables: Presidentialism and Good Governance

The aims of this section it to critically review the concept of presidential democracy and good governance. This helps in disaggregating and appreciating the operation of presidentialism vis-à-vis its impetus in endangering good governance. This is because it appears that both presidentialism (perhaps in view of its importance) and good governance are essential desirables for democratic sustainability and participatory development. It is important to note, however, that the inauguration of presidentialism as a model of democracy is meant to precipitate good governance. This is, especially in countries that have recently been liberated from the shackles of military, monarchical or even one and multiparty parliamentary authoritarianism. Furthermore, the integrated theoretical discourse is also meant to serve as the analytical framework for measuring the performance of the Nigerian elected executives, particularly at central level after a decade of operation (1999-2009).

Presumed upon the importance of constitution (Oyediran, 2007), there are two popular models of modern representative democratic government: presidential and parliamentary. Presidential system is distinguished by its constitutional separation of powers among the three institutions of governance, easy to constitutionally limit the tenure of elected executives, its complimentary symbolic ceremonial importance (FRN, 1987), and the conduct of separate elections into the office of the president and parliament. This, as Axford *et al* (2002) argue saves the executives from relying on the confidence of the legislature.

Presidentialism is also distinguished by its differentiated enormous and perhaps unlimited powers of the president, a situation which many argued to have engendered presidential authoritarianism in Africa. An important feature of a presidential government is the essentiality of the constitution in defining and specifying the roles and functions of all institutions of a political system (Axford et al., 2002). Mainwaring and Shugart (1997a) maintain that by "providing the president with limited legislative power, encouraging the formation of parties that are reasonably discipline in the legislature, and preventing the extreme fragmentation of the party system" presidentialism enhances the viability of democratic governance (qtd. in Elgie, 2004). Similarly, Shugart and Carey (1992) argue that properly designed and crafted presidential regimes could overcome its major disadvantages. Yaqub (2005) further adds that presidentialism ensures regime's stability of tenure, integrativeness and the ability of regime to provide focus and relative direction in policy formulation and implementation.

Table 9.1: Characteristics of Presidential Government

Characteristics of Presidential Government :
The assembly remains an assembly only.
The executive is not divided but is a president elected by the people for a definite term.
The head of government is the head of state.
The president appoints heads of departments and agencies who are subordinates.
The president is sole executive Members of the assembly are not eligible for office in the administration or vice versa.
The executive is responsible to the constitution. The president cannot dissolve or coerce the assembly.
The assembly is ultimately supreme over the other branches of government and there is no fusion of the executive and legislative branches as in a parliament.
The executive is directly responsible to the electorate.
There is no focus of power in the political system.

Source: Verne (1959, qtd. in Axford et al., 2002: 349).

More fundamentally, that is in heterogeneous societies, such as Nigeria, presidentialism enables the leader to be a national figure, as he/she is directly elected by all citizens (the nation as the constituency), and it enhances efficiency because of differentiation and specialisation of functions among various governance institutions (Yaqub, 2005). This is only possible due to constitutional separation of powers among the three key institutions: the executive, the legislature and judiciary. From these theoretical values of presidentialism, it can be conveniently argued that the system could engender democratic good governance. And the extent to which democratic good governance is enshrined in the crafting and operation of a presidential regime essentially determines its sustainability.

On the contrary, a-not-well crafted and operated presidential democratic government can be described thus:

> [It] is considered to be a potentially dangerous regime type because it is associated with competing claims of democratic legitimacy by both the executive and the legislature. There is an essential rigidity to presidential regimes that may weaken the mechanism for dispute resolution. There is an inherent winner--takes-all logic to presidential elections. Finally, presidentialism [...] encourages populist leaders who may threaten the democratic process (Elgie, 2004: 314).

It encourages populist leaders because of the mammoth powers that are bestowed on the president. In fact, Yaqub (2005) argues that an average American president is imbued with powers that it is only the eternal vigilance and political consciousness of the American citizenry that saves them and perhaps the rest of the world from the abuse of such powers. Whereas, in Africa, because of the arguably non-vigilance of the citizenry and their economic and political powerlessness, presidential leaders not only abuse these enormous powers, they tend to arrogate more to themselves and easily metamorphosed into 'presidential monarchies' (Adejumokbi, 2005) and authoritarian leaders. In fact, Linz (1990) and Przeworski et al. (1997) studies have provided empirical evidence to show that presidential governments have shorter life-span than parliamentary regimes. In particular, Przeworski et al. (1997) using a cross country data of about one hundred and thirty countries for the period between 1950 and 1990 argue that the probability for parliamentary systems' survival is much higher than that of presidential governments. They note:

> The probability that a democracy would die under presidentialism during any year of our study was 0.049; the comparison under parliamentarism was 0.014. If this difference appears small, think in terms of expected lives: democracy's life expectancy under presidentialism is less than 20 years, while under parliamentarism is 71 years (Przeworski et al., 1997: 301, qtd. in Adejumobi, 2005).

Perhaps, in order to minimise the shortcomings of presidentialism and draw benefits from parliamentary system, some countries, such as France, India, Ireland and Iceland combine both system in the establishment of their political system. This system is popularly called semi-presidentialism (Axford et al., 2002; Elgie, 2004). The important issue in semi-presidentialism is the existence of both a president and a prime minister; however, the powers of each differ from one country to another. Only few countries adopt this system.

The *power* of presidential system prompted many countries to adopt it. The locus of executive power around the president engenders rapidity and promptness of actions and decisions. Ayeni (1994) for example argues that a "society is best run by a government that is effectively organised under a clear and definite authority. A plural authority situation often leads to confusion, unnecessary conflict and inability to locate responsibility." It is this impetus that arguably helps the system to be functional in many countries, especially the US. Where it fails, a combination of its theoretical limitation and socio-economic and political existentialities of societies could have been the contributory factors. Put differently, in societies where presidential government survives is because of the regime responsive and judicious utilisation of its values and political ethos. Where it fails, the regime does the contrary and did not sticks to its briefs. This suggests that presidential system could survive only in societies that emphasise good governance. Good governance should therefore, not be taken as only a product of presidential system. It is a defining element of the survivability and responsiveness of a regime, regardless of its type. It is a process that is inbuilt in the overall democratisation and governability of a political regime. It can also be conveniently (with specificity and methodological caution) employed as an instrument of measuring the responsiveness and performance of a political system. Thus, what is good governance? Why can it be used as a measuring instrument of regime performance and how?

Good Governance: A Framework of Analysis

Good governance can be used as a measuring instrument of regime performance because the existence of a government is a question of management of economic and political resources. Through this management, which is carried out on a contractual agreement between the existing government and the citizenry, the government is expected to provide all the mundane and temporal needs of the society. How good governance can be employed to make this measurement is a matter of methodological choice and the character and model of a political regime. What is also interesting about using good governance as instrument of measurement is that it can be employed to examine the performance of different institutions. The sum of their result would determine the overall performance of a political regime.

In conceptual terms, World Bank (1994) defines governance as the management of a country's socio-economic resources. Hence, the Bank identifies three main aspects of such management: (i) governance as a form of political regime; (ii) governance as a process through which authority is exercised in the management of a state's socio-economic resources for development and (iii) governance as the capacity, and capability of governments to formulate and implement policies and discharge all necessary functions. This triangular aspect of governance is basically designated as political governance, and which the state is the principal actor. By this, one can also assume that governance is a general term that involves the state and other political actors in the management of economic and social resources for societal development. This is why the adjective of 'good' is often used to distinguish between traditional governance and democratic governance. In other words, any exercise of power by the state or its agencies is governance, but not all governance is democratic unless it is 'good governance' (Kura, 2008: 234-235). Thus, UNDP (1997: 1-2) defines democratic good governance as the exercise of political, economic and administrative authority in the management of a country's affairs at all levels, and which comprises the complex mechanisms, processes and institutions through which citizens and groups articulate their interest, mediate their differences and exercise their legal rights and obligations (cited in Kura, 2008). Thus, UNDP identifies three principal actors of democratic good governance: the state, the private sector, and civil society. For this chapter, concern is given to the state, which greatly influences the activities of the two other actors.

Thus, the underlining importance of good governance was further emphasised by Kofi Annan observation that "without good governance the rule of law, predictable administration, legitimate power, and responsive regulation - no amount of funding, no amount of charity will set us on the path of prosperity" (cited in UNDP, 1997: 20). The World Bank (2000: 51) broadly argues that "without the foundations for good political and economic governance, Africa's development will be sluggish or stalled." This needs no further clarification. The symptoms of sluggish development or stalled development are quite visible in Africa. What is rather important to emphasise is that good governance is not only desirable but an essential component for the sustainability of a democratic presidential governments.

Good governance, therefore, logically flows from the concept of governance (Adejumobi, 2003). Hence, governance becomes good only if it is operated legally and ethically (Mohideen, 1997). This shows a clear linkage even if normative between good governance and the survivability and sustainability of democratic regimes. It also expresses the universality of good governance. While good governance is crucially amenable to democratic regimes and vice versa, its values and ethos could be well appropriated by authoritarian regimes as well. In this context, Huntington (1997: 12-13) aptly argues:

> [...] while authoritarian rule may provide good government for a decade, or even a generation, it cannot provide and throughout history never has it provided good government over a sustained period of time. It lacks the institutions for self-reform: public debate, a free press, protest movements, opposition political parties and competitive elections. Democracy [and all its models] in contrast is based on a much more realistic and complex view of the human nature and on

Table 9.2: UNECA Good Governance Indicators

Core Elements	*Indicators*
Political Representativeness: (Qualitative and Quantitative Dimensions of Representation)	Structure of representation. Depth of representation. Equity in representation. Rights of opposition. Civil and political rights.
Institutional Effectiveness: (Institutional Capacity & Efficacy)	Rule of Law. Independence of the judiciary. Efficacy of law enforcement agencies. Oversight mechanisms for the main branches of government: executive, legislature and judiciary. Levels of decentralization. Strengthen and involvement of civil society in policy process.
Economic Management (Efficiency and Credibility of the Economic System)	Role of private sector. Fiscal discipline. Efficient and equitable revenue system. Transparent and credible procurement system. Budgetary disaggregation. Regulatory oversight. Transparency/accountability in resource management.

> the recognition that (as James Madison put is) "ambition must be made to counteract ambition." [...] Experiences clearly show that only democracy produces good government over the long haul.

As this observation hold a lot of stream, the issue, therefore, is about the form of democratic government which could easily ensure good governance. By implication, it can be argued that good government and the form of democratic government that ensure it, is an issue of structure and outcome (i.e. institutions and their performance). This could logically suggest that Przeworski et al.'s (1997) findings regarding the higher probability of the survivability of parliamentary over presidential government could partly be informed by the former's strict adherence to the values and ethos of good governance. In fact, at face value, the operationalisation and structural -organisations and complexities of governance are more differentiated in parliamentary than presidential system.

To 'measure' or examine the performance of a particular democratic government means that certain methodological tools have to be employed. Thus, various tools have already been provided by international development donors. The tools were constructed in the course of their series of interactions with Africa. These development agencies include the World Bank, IMF, OECD, UNECA, UNDP, and ADB and so on. In its numerous examinations of Africa, the World Bank (1989) identifies the crises of governance as the main cause of its developmental problems, the way forward of which for Africa was to get its 'politics right.' In other words, good governance is a precondition for 'take off' (i.e. for getting the economies and the politics of Africa back on track).

For theoretical reasons, UNECA which was involved in the new governance reform in Africa provided a methodological framework of studying institutional performance. This is represented in Table 9.2.

The above UNECA's methodological operational parameters for measuring progress of governance in Africa have three core areas: political representativeness, institutional effectiveness and economic management. These core issues together with specific elements attached to each represent the broad areas of governance. Similarly, the OECD provided measuring parameters of good governance. The core elements here are: rule of law, corruption and military expenditure. Even though, it is a very good effort, however, the underlying problem with OECD's parameters is their quantitative inclination. Quantitative figures alone may not explain the extent of the performance of a particular political or economic institution. Beyond this limitation, Adejumobi (2003: 16) argues that these methodological tools/parameters face the problem of teleology. According to him:

> A unilinear process of political development is being recreated reminiscence of the modernisation theory. Virtually all the indicators developed for good governance are prototype of liberal democracy. [...] The second critique of the governance indicators is one of

Table 9.3: Checklist of Variables and Indicators of Quality of Governance

Variables	*Indicators*	*Checklist of Criteria for Ranking*
Executive Quality of Governance	CI - Consultation with opposition and other political stakeholders in major policy matters	(i) Open debate on major policy issues (ii) Arrangements made for a suitable body to obtain public opinion on matters of public interests. (iii) Findings of such bodies made known to the public
	C2 - Civil participation in executive functions.	(i) Civilians as chief executive of federal, regional, state and local governments and governmental agencies. (ii) Civilians as chief executive officers of strategic enterprises.
Legislative Quality of Governance	D I-Legislative Independence	(i) Legislature elected and legally and technically (ii) separate from the executive. (iii) Legislature elected but not legally separated from the executive (iv) Legislature not elected and not separate from the executive
	D2- Legislative Function	(i) One-party legislature (ii) Two-party legislature (iii) Multi-party legislature

(Contd.)

(Contd. Table 9.3)

Variables	*Indicators*	*Checklist of Criteria for Ranking*
Quality of Judicial Governance	E l-Constitutional support	(i) Constitution fully in operation. (ii) Constitution partly suspended. (iii) Existence of legal provisions that prohibit courts from entertaining some cases.
	E2- Independence of the executive intervention	(i) The likelihood of political stakeholders or individuals critical of federal governance policies getting fair justice outside their areas of political influence. (ii) Executive obedience to court orders and unfavourable judgements. (iii) Career prospects of judges who pass unfavourable judgements likelihood of them being fired (by executive fiat) without due process of the law.

> reductionism. The attempt to reduce governance, a complex and variegated process, to quantitative and mathematical analysis is quite problematic. [...] The third critique of the good governance measurement project is the problem of data gathering. Africa does not present a well-organised social milieu in which reliable data can be easily generated for statistical purposes (Adejumobi, 2003: 16).

These criticisms do not really dismiss the importance of this framework in measuring regime governance performance. They are perhaps, meant to caution whoever is interested in employing it for such an exercise. In any case, a framework is always a framework. It should be moulded to suit socio-economic and political character of any government under review. However, no matter the extent of attempt to reconstruct and adjust it to capture regime specificities, the framework, arguably cannot be used for monarchies and totalitarian regimes. This is because it contains some elements that are characteristics of only democratic polities.

At this juncture, it is imperative to search for a localised framework of measuring the performance of presidential executives in Nigeria. Dinneya (2006) has provided a somewhat broad methodological thermometer for measuring the quality of governance in Nigeria. The thermometer was constructed on the basis of the characteristic of presidential regime, especially its constitutional separation of powers.

The above framework could be used cautiously to examine the operation and performance of executives in Nigeria. The problem with the above framework is methodological and empirical. It is not clear whether it is possible to study the performance of the executives separate from other arms of government. Moreover, even if the discussion is forcibly limited to executives, there is still the problem of boundaries. Where to start and where to end? This means that the discussion would directly and/or indirectly involve other institutions, all things being equal. It is also not clear how such study could be carried out (i.e. not clear whether to limit such studies to the political elites only or to involve ordinary citizens). Methodologically, it is also not clear of which instruments of data collection to be used. Perhaps, because of the focus of this paper, discourse method would be much relevant, as it would allow one to manoeuvre. As the analysis is limited, there is need to disaggregate any adopted framework vis-à-vis the executive institutions in order to bring out and incorporate other fundamental issues not visible in the framework.

Presidential Democracy in Nigeria: Operations and Governance Performance

Although the focus of this assessment is Nigeria's Fourth Republic, however, it is important to examine the historical and constitutional evolution of presidential system in Nigeria. This would help in appreciating the performance of the Fourth Republic. To start with, Nigeria is a product of colonialism. Needless therefore to say, Britain, which colonised the country exported its parliamentary system to Nigeria. Before independence in 1960, Nigeria, like other British colonial appendages were administratively regarded as her Majesty, the Queen of England's subjects. Colonial administration and especially during the years preceding independence, the country was politically and administratively moulded towards parliamentarism. The idea was that parliamentary system would endanger political interactions and bargaining at the centre among the three dominant regions and their respective dominant political parties. However, despite its worldwide higher probability of durability and survival, parliamentary democracy did not last long in Nigeria. It was abruptly and violently terminated by military on 15th January, 1966. That military coup in itself was to turn the country upside down. It precipitated the structural and institutional rearrangement of Nigeria, accentuated and redefined ethno-religious character of the state, remotely contributed to 1967-1970 civil war and laid the foundation for a long period of military authoritarianism in the country, among others. Thus, it suffices to say that parliamentary model of democracy "could not be a safeguard against systemic breakdown" (Adejumobi, 2005: 102). The system could not endanger sustainable democracy and curtail the major problems of ethno-nationalism, corruption and zero-sum game associated with party politics.

The violent termination of the parliamentary system and the consequent political turmoil vis-à-vis the long military rule provided the need for a reconstruction and restructuring of the Nigerian political system. Parts of these restructuring and political reconstructions include the creation of states and local governments and of course the crafting of new constitution. The new constitution (1979 Constitution) was a product of the quest for a stabilising formula (Suberu, 1988) for addressing the shortcomings of the parliamentary system on the bases of the socio-cultural contextualities of Nigeria. The process of the formulation of the 1979 Constitution started with the formation of Constitution Drafting Committee (CDC) in October 1975 and charged with among other things the responsibility of recommending a constitutional framework that would guarantee the development of a sustainable democracy as well as stable governance. Furthermore, the Committee was particularly tasked to recommend a system that would prevent the issue of "winner-take-all" practice, perhaps as a way of addressing the zero-sum game associated with Nigerian party politics. Accordingly, the CDC was also charged with recommending a governmental system that would ensure a national leadership, which would withstand the taste of ethnic chauvinism, sectionalism and religious influence. These parochial issues have remained the bane of Nigerian politics. Consequently, at the end of its assignment, the CDC recommended the adoption of a presidential system of government patterned after that of the United States. The implementation of the presidential democracy was further supported by the formulation of the

1979 presidential Constitution. Thus, this sets the stage for the operationalisation of presidentialism in Nigeria. From 1979-1983, the country operationalised this system, but such experiment was marred by serious problems of corruption, ethnic politics, religious chauvinism (Dudley, 1982; Oyediran, 1979; Ayeni, 1988, among others).

The collapse of the Second Republic presidential system arguably shows the incapability of the model in addressing all shortcomings associated with parliamentary system. In particular, the winner-take-all syndrome (Yaqub, 2005) under presidentialism has generated serious socio-ethnic and religious acrimony and rivalry among the political parties. It also shows that the "putative advantage that would have been enjoyed by its adoption has evaporated by this inherent contradiction" (Yaqub, 2005: 116). In terms of assessment, one can conveniently argue that the first experiment with presidential model has woefully failed. The failure was evident not only from the structural fluidity of the system, but from its operation as well, as the democratic government of the time could not deliver the much needed services to the public. As a matter of fact, the costly nature of the operation of presidentialism, coupled with excessive constitutional powers bestowed on the president in Nigeria influence its failure (see 1999 Constitution). For example, the costly nature could be linked with the powers of the president to approve anything and anytime and consequently affect the way government finances are managed. The way and manner the finances are managed contributed largely to high rate of corruption in the country.

Accordingly, it is categorical that the symptoms of the failure of the presidential system, especially in relation to governance are hardly disputable. These symptoms are palpable in the areas of erratic power supply, poor telecommunication services, lack of adequate portable drinking water, corruption, poor health services, excessive poverty, and many others. These symptoms are exhibited in the character of the Nigerian society, and contributed largely to political instability, electoral violence, persistence of ethno-religious conflicts. In other words, the democratic institutions, which are the catalysts for the provisions of these services, are in shambles. One is aware that this is a direct and dangerous assessment of the presidential democracy in Nigeria. Nevertheless, it is important to also note that presidential democracy works successfully in other parts of the world. At least, it is working successfully in the United States. Thus, for a relatively adequate appreciation of the performance of the presidential executives in relation to good governance, it may not be out of point to make such assessment employing the good governance framework identified earlier in this chapter.

In this context, the UNECA Good Governance Indicator is employed. It is the best approach to be used within a limited period of time. It is easy to understand. It can be used for comparative analysis. It can also be used to make internal comparison of institutions and sectors. However, its limitation is that it is very difficult to cover all the indicators in this paper. It is also not clear which methodological approach would be more appropriate to assess each indicator. In any case, capitalising on these major strengths and given the time constraint, it can still be useful in making broader analysis, devoid of getting to the specificities of the indicators. The broader analysis serves as a good pointer to the nature of various indicators (see table 9.2). Following is the analysis.

(a) Political Representativeness

This is concerned with the qualitative and quantitative dimensions of representation. Hence its indicators are: structure of representation, depth of representation, equity in representation, rights of opposition and civil and political rights. On a general note, representative democracy itself has been seriously challenged for its failure to actually form an acceptable government that represents all and sundry. Indeed, representative democracy has been criticised for institutionalising minority rule over the majority. For the sake of this analysis, it is better to narrow the analysis to rights of opposition and civil and political rights. Regarding the rights of opposition, democracy as commonly known, is a political system built on opposition. Opposition parties strengthen the quality of governance in any state. Dolo (2006: 5) argues that "an authentic democracy is one where the ruling party has an effective opposition." For Schmitz (1988: 2) "[genuine political opposition is a necessary attribute of democracy, tolerance, and trust in the ability of citizens to resolve differences by peaceful means. The existence of an opposition, without which politics ceases and administration takes over, is indispensable to the functioning of parliamentary political systems." As Schmitz (1988: 2) argues "the division between government and opposition is as old as political democracy itself." LeBas (2003: 2) similarly argues that "a strong opposition may be the most effective means of creating checks and accountability in hybrid regimes and, therefore, the most important prerequisite for democratic deepening."

However, in Nigeria, as the case since 1999, opposition parties were initially denied registration, until the Supreme Court ruling. Similarly, when the opposition parties were allowed to be registered by INEC, the ruling party (PDP) continued to employ all manner of strategies of not only suffocating members of the opposition, in some instances, they were harassed, intimidated, or even assassinated. It has never been an irony that most of the high profile killings and assassinations involved strong members of opposition parties. This is not to talk of subtle ways of eliminating opposition in Nigeria. These include tactful exclusion in election, rigging out opposition candidates[1] and the manipulation of INEC to act according to the briefs of the ruling parties. In terms of assassinations of seemingly strong members of opposition parties, examples can be cited of Chief Bola of AD, Marshall Harry, Chuba Okadibo,

Adamu Waziri, and so on of ANPP, Jesse Aniku of ACD and several others that could not easily be mentioned here (Kura, 2007; Ogundiya and Baba, 2005). For example, CDHR (2003: 31) observes that "the spectre of political violence and assassinations in the country had become so intense that... one can still not really see the remarkable difference between it [civilian regime] and the days of the military" (emphasis added).

Regarding the manipulation of INEC, Ogunsanyo (2003) observes that INEC has never been in absolute control of its activities before, during or even after election. This means that INEC "is a partial arbiter that exists at the mercy of [PDP] government and which can be directly or indirectly susceptible to manipulations with the consequent subversion of wishes of the people" (Akinboye, 2005: 307). Subversion of the people's wishes, which in itself represents a disgusting violation of their freedom to contest and elect candidates of their choice takes place when by:

> [...] mere subterfuge of manipulating the party lists submitted to INEC in Abuja and replacing the names on the original list, victory was declared for some individuals. This was well after the deadline has passed for submitting new names to replace disqualifies one (Ogunsano, 2003: 16).

The performance of Nigeria's presidential executives is arguably even worse when it comes to the issue of civil and political rights. Provision of and respect for civil and political rights is a fundamental element of representative governments. In fact, scholars of democratic theory often defined democracy in terms of freedom (Diamond, 2003; Powell, 1982; Schimitter and Karl, 1991) disaggregated as civil and political rights. The US Human Rights Reports on Nigeria stated:

> The [Nigerian] government's human rights record remained poor, and government officials at all levels continued to commit serious abuses. The most significant human rights problems included the abridgement of citizens' right to change their government; extrajudicial killings by security forces; the use of lethal and excessive force by security forces; vigilante killings; impunity for abuses by security forces, torture, rape, and other cruel, inhuman or degrading treatment of prisoners, detainees, and criminal suspects; harsh and life threatening prison and detention centre conditions; arbitrary arrest and prolonged pre-trial detention; executive influence on the judiciary and political corruption; infringement on private rights; restrictions on freedom of speech, press, assembly, religion, and movement; domestic violence and discrimination against women; female genital mutilation (FGM); child abuse and child sexual exploitation; societal violence; ethnic, regional, and religious discrimination; trafficking in persons for the purpose of prostitution and forced labour, and child labour (*Leadership*, 15th March 2009: 10).

This report sums up the ugly situation of civil and political rights in Nigeria. By extension, it also sums up the assessment of executives in terms of the provisions of civil and human rights and other areas, such as curtailment of people's rights to chose or change their governments and suffocations of the judiciary to perform its duties diligently and independently.

This further raises the question of the 'representativeness' of the legislature. Evidently, the Nigerian legislature not only remains a rubber stamp, but is simply incapable of performing its duties. Its failure is always linked to the executive indiscipline and high-handedness. The executive-legislative relation is often marred by acrimony and suspicion. This is even despite dominance of the PDP in both Chambers of the National Assembly (see Baba, 2009; Maimako, 2007). It is apparent that the National Assembly could not even be allowed by the executive to perform all its major functions of oversight, law making and adequate representation. The consequence is that the failure of the executive affects the performance of the legislature and other institutions of the political system.

(b) Institutional Effectiveness

Institutional effectiveness involves rule of law, independence of the judiciary, efficacy of law enforcement agencies, oversight mechanism of the main arms of government, levels of decentralisation, strengthening and involvement of civil society in policy process. Though institutional effectiveness could be examined from their nature and functions, however, this could also be appreciated from their relationships and interactions with the executive. Because of the linkages that exist between the activities of these institutions and in view of the centrality of the executive in performing these activities, it is not out of point to limit the assessment to rule of law and the efficacy of the law enforcement agencies. Not only because the executive is responsible for the appointment of their chief executives, but indeed because it is responsible for providing their finances. Similarly, the degree and the extent of the exercise of rule of law and the efficacy of law enforcement agencies are a function of the executive. This to say that rule of law and the activities of law enforcement agencies are central to the performance of the executives. The rule of law is a defining element of a democratic government, it is the means and ends of social justice by serving as a catalyst to realising civil, political, social, economic and cultural rights of the citizens, protects the vulnerable, ensure the absence of arbitrariness, provides equality and protect the dignity of human person (Ladan, 2004; Muhammad, 2005).

The practicality of rule of law is intertwined with the provisions of human rights and other basic and substantive elements of justice and justness. The idea of justness is a philosophical issue and which is obviously beyond the boundaries of this paper. However, it is imperative to note that adequate provision of human rights can be easily equated with the degree of the rule of law practice in a particular political system. It can be assumed therefore that

Nigeria's poor human rights record is a consequence of the failure of its rule of law. At a more general albeit broader perspective, there are ample evidence suggesting executive high-handedness and negation of rule of law. Examples could be cited of how persistently the executive intervenes in the activities of the legislature. The intervention was not on principle but intervention that jeopardised the functions and independence of the legislature. For instance, the executive has been fingered in the impeachment of several leadership of the National Assembly, particularly the Senate. In this respect, mention can be made of Chief Enwerem, Chuba Okadibo, Adolphus Wabara and several others. In the Lower House too, the executive has been meddling in their affairs to the extent that the House under the leadership of Gali Vmar Na-Abba was at loggerheads with the executive. All these had not only affected the development of democracy in the country, it has also presented the country in bad light.

The crisis that engulfed the ruling party was a crisis of the executive. The crisis reached its peak when President Obasanjo attempted to unconstitutionally sacked his VP. The process of such episode was a total violation of rule of law. In fact, the situation was further compounded when at the eve of 2007 general elections many aspirants were arbitrarily excluded or forced to decline their electoral candidacies. This is not to even mention the unconstitutional impeachments of several state governors who refused to submit to the dictate of executive high-handedness. Some of these impeachments were later to be reversed by courts. The implication of this has been very clear. The country was thrown into what many observers perceived as 'crises of democracy'; It also shows that virtually all the institutions of governance were not effective and arguably dysfunctional. The failure of EFCC/ICPC to check and control corruption is a case in point. Given the wider spread and deepening nature of corruption in Nigeria, the Obasanjo regime introduced these institutions with a view to control corruption. However, executive excessiveness did not allow the institutions to conduct their activities constitutionally and successfully. The consequence was that they become mere toothless bulldogs and witch-hunting tools for vendetta and political arbitrariness (Kura, 2008; Omotola, 2006).

Executive-cum-institutional ineffectiveness has also been demonstrated in the failure of INEC to conduct a successful election in Nigeria. For instance, Academic Staff Union of Universities (ASUU) (2007: 9) observes that INEC was an "umpire in whom the majority of the players and spectators have no confidence." The electoral commission *ab initio* was ill prepared to conduct credible elections. It could not conduct a successful voter registration exercise, which is a prerequisite for hitch-free and credible general elections. The failure of INEC to conduct a credible election was amounted to disallowance of citizens to elect the government of their choice and to change it periodically, which is a gross violation of their fundamental right. Similar verdict can be conveniently said of other institutions, such as security apparatuses and other development agencies such as Niger Delta Development Commission (NDDC), poverty alleviation programmes and many others. By this assessment, Nigerian institutions are in a state of what Huntington (1968) describes as prectoranism. The ultimate consequence of this would be institutional decay, unprecedented corruption and general economic quagmire.

(c) Economic Management

Economic management involves the role of private sector, fiscal discipline, efficient and equitable revenue system, transparent and credible procurement system, budgetary disaggregation, regulatory oversight and transparency/accountability in resource management. Perhaps due to the technical limitations of this paper, broad analysis of the economic management vis-à-vis performance of the executive is made. In the light of this, it is pertinent to note that the economic history of Nigeria is a history reforms and counter reforms. Reforms and counter-reforms are expressions of policy inconsistencies, confusion and dilemmas on the part of those managing the economy, contradicting interactions between international and domestic interests and the deepening *problematiques* of a mono-cultural economy. Mono-culturality of the Nigerian economy, at face value, may appear not be a problem. However, the crisis accentuated by Nigeria's dominance on oil and its revenues at the expense of other sectors is demonstrated by the crisis in the oil sector itself. The situation is different with other oil rich countries. Lack of diversification of economic activities contributed to over dependence on oil wealth and suggests ineffectiveness in the management of Nigerian economy.

It is a common knowledge that Nigeria has generated more oil revenues between 1999 and 2007 than any other period in her political existence. However, the continuous increase in the oil revenue has not corresponded whatsoever with improvement in the living standard of ordinary citizenry. For example, the 2005 UN Report rated Nigeria as the 158th country out of 177 nations studied in the report. Accordingly, Nigeria was among the bottom 20 countries by HDI ranking, with a value of 0.453 in 2003, Life Expectancy Index of 0.31, Education Index of 0.66, GDP Index of 0.39 and GDP per Capita stood at just 1,050 (PPP US$). Table 9.4 below presents a comparative human development index of selected countries. The figures show that Nigeria is highly lagged behind even among her African counterparts, such as Sudan, Togo, and Zimbabwe. This is not to even mention Botswana, Mauritius and Ghana, which are the models of African democracy. History indicates that apart from Asian Tigers, whose economic development were achieve without democracy, all the developed countries are democratic and are the ones reaping the benefits of globalisation. In fact, the Asian Tigers were able to record such remarkable achievement perhaps because to some extent they observe some elements of modern good governance. Suffice to say that the long period of military

Table 9.4 Human Development Index Trends of Selected Countries

Year	*Botswana*	*Ghana*	*Malaysia*	***Nigeria***	*South Africa*	*Sudan*	*Togo*	*Zimbabwe*
1975	0.503	0.439	0.615	0.318	0.655	0.349	0.423	0.546
1980	0.577	0.468	0.659	0.376	0.674	0.376	0.475	0.574
1985	0.638	0.482	0.695	0.386	0.702	0.396	0.474	0.640
1990	0.681	0.511	0.721	0.406	0.735	0.428	0.500	0.637
1995	0.659	0.531	0.760	0.418	0.742	0.465	0.510	0.589
2000	0.596	0.556	0.790	N.A	0.696	0.500	0.519	0.527
2003	0.565	0.520	0.796	0.453	0.658	0.512	0.512	0.505

Source: United Nations Development Programme (2005) *Human Development Report: International Cooperation at a Crossroad: Aid, Trade and Security in an Unequal World (New York: UNDP).*

leadership in Nigeria was a curse on the political and economic histories of the country.

It is gruesome to note that despite the relative increase in the exploration of oil and revenue generated by the government, Nigeria is still wallowing in chronic underdevelopment and its citizens are suffering from abject poverty. For example, more than 70% of the population are living below income poverty line, spending only and/or less than $1 a day (UNDP, 2005). The environmental pollution and degraded living conditions of people in the Niger Delta not only suggests mismanagement but a strong factor in the upsurge of terrorism in the area. It is also noteworthy that despite this domestic economic underdevelopment, Nigerian economy has been open. This is measured by the country's share of import in the gross domestic product (Orubu and Awopegba, 2004: 167). For instance, between 1979 and 1989 the share of the import in the GDP was 24.3% and between 1990 and 2000 the figure increased to 26%. The export further shows that the economy is highly dependent on oil. During the same period the total export value from petroleum accounts for 97%. The manufacturing sector contributes very low to the GDP (Umar and Kura, 2007). In this context, Okonjo-Iweala and Osafo-Kwaako (2007: 7) argue:

> Nigeria's economic performance in the two decades prior to economic reforms was generally poor. [...] With an estimated population growth of 2.80 per cent per annum, this implied a contraction in per capita GDP over the years that had resulted in a deterioration of living standards for most citizens. The major challenge [...] was its macroeconomic volatility driven largely by external terms of trade and the country's large reliance on oil export earnings. Public expenditures also closely followed current revenues, implying that fluctuations in oil earnings were transferred directly into the domestic economy. Fluctuations in public expenditure reflected both the over-reliance on oil earnings and weak fiscal discipline [...]

The poor economic situation was even against multifarious reforms and counter reforms and the huge sum of oil monies that were dolled for their execution. Nevertheless, some microeconomic reforms at face values appeared to generate changes in the economics of Nigeria. The reforms introduced between 1999 and 2009 cut across all the areas of the Nigerian political economy include: privatisation; civil service; banking sector, telecommunication; and trade policy reforms (Okonjo- Iweala and Osafo-Kwaako, (2007). These reforms have generated hopes in the citizenry but seemingly failed to radically change the social living standard of Nigerians. It is obvious to state that most of these reforms were tied to the struggle for debt relief and cancellation and as good governance conditionalities. In order words, they were not home-grown reforms. They were rather an imposition by the International Financial Institutions.

The reforms have further reintegrated the Nigerian economy with the forces of globalisation (Kura, 2005). The reforms, in particular, had liberalised the Nigerian economy and consequently exposed it to the tentacles of imperialism. This is evident in the manner in which Nigeria has continued to be a net importer of foreign goods. The presence of China, India, Korea and other Asian Tigers is never in doubt. Against this background, it must be stated that the reforms, particularly in the ICT has led to the development of GSM to the extent that Nigeria has the fastest growing mobile (phone) telecommunications market in the world after China. For instance, this has resulted in an increase in the number of telephone lines in the country from about 500,000 landlines in 2001 to over 32 million GSM today. Investment in the sector is estimated to be over US $l billion. Through this, thousands of citizens have gain employment. Studies have shown that over 2000 individuals are directly employed by GSM operators and an estimated number of 40,000 Nigerians are benefiting from indirect employment generated by GSM operators (Ndukwe, 2003, qtd. in Omar, 2009).

At the institutional level, the reforms include, public procurement, which is now popularly known as Due Process mechanism. The due process mechanism has encouraged open tender process vis-à-vis competitive bidding for government's contracts. By Due Process mechanism, it means any project exceeding N50 million (US $400,000) requires approval. Government, similarly, publishes a public tender's journal periodically as means of reducing patronage and the award and management of contracts. Other institutional reforms are public expenditure management, the oil and gas sector and the N-EITT initiative, and prosecuting corrupt practices through the establishment of EFCC and ICPC (Iweala and Osafo-Kwaako, 2007). The case of ICPC and EFCC and the politics that influence their operation is a case of how laudable initiatives are rubbished in Nigeria (Kura, 2007). On the basis of the little success at both economic and institutional level generated by these reforms Iweala and Osafo-Kwaako (2007: 19) argue that "despite existing challenges, recent governance reforms appear to have yielded some concrete results." However, the result is contestable, especially, against the backdrop of the living conditions of an average Nigerian. Take all the seven crucial areas (7-point agenda) identified by Yar' Adua government as example. None of these areas has made any serious and remarkable achievement that would radically change economic status of average Nigerians. The seven-point agenda represents the extent of the deceptiveness of Nigerian governments. This is because, as the government maintains, the 7-point agenda would be the basis for transforming Nigeria into the twentieth most developed economics in the world by 2020. This is a sheer mockery and an attempt to deceive Nigerians and to psychologically coerce them into believing and accepting this fraudulent government.

Concluding Notes: Four Salient Issues

Four conclusions could easily be made from these discussions: the first is that economic and institutional reforms have been introduced from

1999-2009. One decade is enough periods for such reform to radically change the living conditions of average Nigerians. The current poor state of power supply, the bad conditions of roads, the inability of the country to feed itself, the dying state of manufacturing industries (Ojediran, 2009), the disappointing situation in the Niger Delta, poor health services and many more examples are evidence of the failure of these reforms. The reforms have virtually been translated into nothing, especially against the background of the large amount of oil revenue expended in their implementation. The second conclusion is a result of the first: the failure of the reforms has led to the development of a presidential system of government that was interested in continual accumulation of power and act even beyond its constitutional prerogatives. Today, Nigerians are comfortably talking about 'civilian dictatorship' or what Adejumobi (2005) aptly describes as the development of "presidential monarchy". Presidential monarchy and its logic have been played out by the executive in at least two cases: (i) the nature of the legislative-executive relationship and the control of the relationship by the executive through impeachment of several leadership of the National Assembly, and (ii) the attempt by the executive to smuggle some clauses into the 2001 Electoral Act. The third conclusion is drawn from the sum of the results of the first two and that is the higher rate of corruption in the country. Corruption is here been seen as a consequence of the failure of good governance and the development of civilian dictatorship in Nigeria. The fourth conclusion is drawn from a more general and theoretical problem associated with the assessment of a regime with the use of good governance framework. The problem is that because of obvious limitation associated with writing a chapter or a journal article, it is not possible to do justice to all the elements of good governance. The theoretical problem is even more compounding when a single institution/arm of government is to be singled for analysis. This problem is duly acknowledged here. Thus, given the first three salient conclusions and the consequent failure of the executive to provide good governance that would change the conditions of living of Nigerians and nurture a sustainable democracy in the country, the question is what are the impending challenges?

The challenges are summed up as follows: the need for extending the reforms to the sub-national levels, focusing on non-oil growth and employment generation, need for improvement in the domestic business climate, expanding and maintaining investments in infrastructure, strengthening domestic institutions, tackling the unrest in the Niger Delta, and increasing the quality of social sector spending (Iweala and Osafo-Kwaako, 2007). But these are only possible through prioritisation of reforms or prioritisation of some key elements of good governance agenda. Perhaps, because of the expediency and resilience of political institutions and as shock absorbers, emphasis should be given to them. There is need for urgent reform of the electoral system of the country in order to establish a legitimate and acceptable government. Once this is done, and Nigerians are able to elect the government of their choice and change it accordingly, the stage is set for success in other structural and institutional reforms.

References

Ayeni, V. (1994). The Executive Presidency as a Concomitant of Multipartyism in Africa: An Assessment. In Omo Omoruyi (eds.), *Democratisation in Africa: African Perspectives*, Vol. 1. Abuja: Centre for Democratic Studies.

Academic Staff Union of Universities (2007). *State of the Nation's Freedom.*

Adejumobi, S. (2003). Democracy and Governance in Africa: Theoretical and Methodological Issues. In Abdalla Bujra & Said Adejumobi (eds.), *Breaking Barriers, Creating New Hopes: Democracy, Civil Society and Good Governance in Africa.* Addis Ababa, Ethiopia: DPMF.

Axford, Browning, G. K., Huggings, R., Rosamond, Grant, A. & Turner, J. (2002). *Politics: An Introduction.* Second Edition. London and New York: Routledge.

Baba, YTK (2009). On the Question of Legislative Productivity in Nigeria: Beyond the Chambers. Paper presented at the National Conference on Work and Productivity on *The Era of Globalisation: The Nigerian Experience*, organized by the Faculty of Social Sciences, Usmanu Danfodiyo University, Sokoto, 2nd - 27th February.

Diamond, L. (2003). Consolidating Democracies. In Lawrence, LeDuc, Richard,G. Niemi & Pippa, Norris (eds.), *Comparing Democracies 2: New Challenges in the Study of Elections and Voting.* London: SAGE Publications Limited.

Dinneya, D. (2006). *Political Economy of Democratisation in Nigeria.* Lagos: Concept Publication Limited.

Dolo, E. (2006). Opposition parties: Benefits and Challenges in Building Democracy. *The Perspective*, pp. 1-8, 20 October 2006. Retrueved on September 17, 20087: http://www.theperspective.org/articles/l 020200602.html.

Elgie, R. (2004). Semi-Presidentialism: Concepts, Consequences and Contesting Explanations. *Political Studies Review*, Vol. 2, pp. 314-330.

Federal Republic of Nigeria (1987). *Report of the Political Bureau.* Lagos: Government Printers.

Huntington, S. (1997). Democracy for the Long Haul. In L. Diamond, M. Plattner, Y. Chu and H. Tien (eds.), *Consolidating the Third Wave Democracies: Themes and Perspectives.* Baltimore: John Hopkins University Press.

Huntington, S. P. (1968). *Political Order in Changing Societies.* New Haven: Yale University Press.

Kura, S. Y. B. (2005). Globalisation and Democracy: A Dialectical Framework for Understanding Democratisation in Nigeria. *Globalization*, Vol. 5, Issue 1.

Kura, S. Y. B (2007). African Ruling Political Parties and the Making of Authoritarian Democracies: Extending the Frontiers of Social Justice in Nigeria. Paper was presented at the Global Social Justice in Theory and Practice Conference, organised by Centre for the Study of Global Ethics and Department of Political

Science and International Studies, University of Birmingham, Edgbaston B15 2TT, 3-5 September.

Kura, SYB (2007). Snagging the Wheel of Progress: Corruption, New Anti-corruption Drive and Nigeria's Quest for Development. *NESG: Economic Indicators*, Vol. 13, No. 3, July-September.

Ladan, M. T. (2004). Legal Pluralism and the Development of the Rule of Law of Nigeria: Issues and Challenges in the Development and Application of the Sharia. In Jibrin Ibrahim (ed.) *Sharia Penal and Family Laws in Nigeria and in the Muslim World, Rights-based Approach*. Zaria: Ahmadu Bello University Press.

Leadership (2009). US Human Rights Report on Nigeria, 1st March.

LeBas, A. (2003). The Contributions of Contention: Political Change in the Hybrid Regimes of Southern Africa. Paper prepared for delivery at the 2003 Annual Meeting of the American Political Science Association, Philadelphia, P. A. August 28-31.

Linz, J. (1990). "The Perils of Presidentialism". *Journal of Democracy*, Vol. 1, No. 1.

Maimako, S. S. (2007). Evidence of Legislative Participation in Public Budget Process. *Nigerian Journal of Legislative Affairs*, Vol. 1. No. 2, pp. 36-58.

Mainwaring, S. & Shugart, M. S. (1997a). Juan Linz, Presidentialism and Democracy. *Comparative Politics*, Vol. 29, No. 4, pp. 449-471.

Mohideen, A. (1997). Stock Taking and Assessment of Democracy and Good Governance. *The Proceedings of the Development Policy Management Forum (DPMF) Conference on Democracy, Civil Society and Governance in Africa*, December 1-4, Addis Ababa, Ethiopia.

Mudasiru, S. O. (2005). National Conference, Federalism and the Project of Statehood in Nigeria. In Warisu O. Ali (ed.) *Political Reform Conference, Federalism and the National Question in Nigeria*. Abuja: NPSA.

Muhammad, H. (2005). Human Rights and the Rule of Law: challenges for national security under a civilian regime in Nigeria (1999-2004). In Chidi Ikonne, Ima O. Williams & Eucharia N. Nwagbara (eds.), *Security, Social Services and Sustainable Development in Nigeria*. Port Harcourt, Nigeria: University of Port Harcourt Press.

Ogundiya, I. S. and Baba, T. K. (2005). Electoral Violence and the Prospects of Democratic Consolidation in Nigeria. In Godwin & A. Momoh (eds.), *Elections and Democratic Consolidation in Nigeria*. Lagos: Traid Associates Publishers.

Okonjo-Iweala, N. and Osafo-Kwaako, P. (2007). *Nigeria's Economic Reforms: Progress and Challenges*. Washington, DC: The Booking Institution.

Omar, A. (2009). Work, Workers and Productivity in the Era of Globalisation: The Nigerian Experience. A Keynote address paper presented at the a National Conference on *Work and Productivity in the Era of Globalisation: The Nigerian Experience*, organised by the Faculty of Social Sciences, Usmanu Danfodiyo University, Sokoto, 25th-26th February.

Ojediran, B. (2009). Is Manufacturing Dying? *This day*, March 10.

Omotola, J. S. (2006). 'Through a Glass Darkly': Assessing the New War against Corruption in Nigeria. *Africa Insight*, Vol. 36, No. 3-4, pp. 214-227.

Orubu, C.O. & Awopegba, P.O. (2004). Market Economies, Globalisation and the Role of Good Governance in the Development Process: Challenges for the Nigerian Economy. *Journal of Social Sciences*, Vol. 9, No. 3.

Oyediran, O. (2007). *Nigerian Constitutional Development* (Ibadan: Oyediran Consults International).

Powell, G. Jr. (1982). *Contemporary Democracies: Participation, Stability, and Violence.* London: Harvard University Press.

Przeworski, A., Alvarez, M. & Limongi, F. (1997). What makes Democracies Endure? In Larry Diamond, Marc Plattner, Yun-han Chu & Hun-mao Tien (eds.), *Consolidating the Third Wave of Democracies: Themes and Perspectives.* Baltimore and London: John Hopkins University Press.

Schmitter, P. C. & Karl, T. I (1991). What Democracy is ... And What is not. In Geoffrey Pridhan (ed.) (1995), *Transition to Democracy.* England & USA: Darthmouth Publishing Company Ltd.

Schmitz, G. (1988). The Opposition in a Parliamentary System. *Political and Social Affairs Division*, BP-47E, December, 1988.

Shugart, M. S. & Carey, J. M. (1992). *Presidents and Assemblies: Constitutional Designs and Electoral Dynamics*. Cambridge: Cambridge University Press.

Suberu, R. (1988). Background and Principles of Nigeria's Presidential System. In Victor Ayeni and Kayode Soremekun (eds.), *Nigeria's Second Republic*. Lagos: Daily Times.

Tahir, I. (2003). The Challenge of Democracy: The Role of Traditional Rulers. 22nd Convocation Lecture for Usmanu Danfodiyo University, Sokoto. 11th December.

Umar, M. Z. & Kura, S.Y.B. (2007). Globalization and Sustainable Democratic Development in Nigeria: Perspectives, Prospects and Challenges. *Maiduguri Journal of Peace and Development Studies*, Vol. 1, No. 1.

United Nations Development Programme (1997). *Governance for Sustainable Growth and Equity*. New York: UNDP.

United Nations Development Programme (2005). *Human Development Report: International Cooperation at a Crossroad: Aid, Trade and Security in an Unequal World.* New York: UNDP.

Verney, D. (1959). *The Analysis of Political Systems*. Glencoe, IL: Free Press.

World Bank (2000). *Can Africa Claim the 21st Century*? Washington, DC: World Bank.

Footnotes

1. In fact, even within the ruling parties, candidates that do not belong to a favourable camp are excluded from primaries. And those, who scale manipulations at the primaries, could be excluded by INEC or the EFCC. If eventually a candidate successfully sails through all the initial huddles, the obvious will be to rig him/her out during the election.

SECTION - III

IMPEDIMENTS TO DEMOCRACY

10

Anti-corruption Reforms in Nigeria: Challenges and Failures

Ilufoye Sarafa Ogundiya

Introduction

There is little doubt that Nigerians have reaped more deficits than dividends of democracy since the country's return to democratic rule in 1999. Nigeria, like ever before remains grossly politically unstable and economically undeveloped. Political instability in this sense is conceived as the endemic, persistent and seemingly insoluble socio-economic crisis embedded in the political system. Political assassinations, extreme poverty, high unemployment rate, general insecurity and other negative indicators of development remained the core features of Nigerian political life. The euphoria, hopes and expectations which accompanied the re-democratisation of the country in 1999 have been frustrated by bad governance characterised by lack of performance, policy failures and above all, pandemic systemic corruption. Unarguably, one of the single most important reasons for the crass instability and development tragedy in Nigeria is widespread bureaucratic and political corruption. Perhaps, what Myrdal (cf. Amuwo 2005: 127) called "folklore of corruption" (which explains that most government officials are corrupt) has assumed eccentric and ludicrous proportion in Nigeria.

The problem of bureaucratic and political corruption have been a long drawn issue in Nigerian politics and has been acknowledged by several observers of Nigerian politics as the hidden disease of democracy and blight of development in the country (Ekeh, 1985; Diamond, 1991; Gboyega, 1996; Amuwo, 2005; Obayelu, 2007; Falana, 2007; Oyelowo 2009). Political and bureaucratic corruptions have been responsible for acute crisis of legitimacy and intermittent military coups that the nation experienced between 1960 and 1999. Cognisant of this problem and its devastating effect on the legitimacy of government, successive Nigerian leaders have embarked on various reforms measures to combat corruption in the country. Despite all the anti-graft measures, corruptions remain persistent and endemic.

It is worthy of note therefore that the fight against corruption in Nigeria has been fraught with frustrations and failures. This chapter examines the problem of bureaucratic and political corruption in Nigeria and the reform measures that have been taken to tackle the problem. Though the focus of the chapter is on the past nine years of democratic rule, a brief analysis of the pre-1999 attempts to short-circuit the cycle of corruption is reviewed as a take-off point. The chapter also identifies the setbacks to anti-graft reform measures in Nigeria and examines the implications of political and bureaucratic corruption for democratic consolidation. It is argued that the "reformers" must be reformed or rather "transformed" for the anti-graft reforms to be able to achieve its vision. Nigeria suffers from double jeopardy in that the reformers apart from being the beneficiaries are also the epitome of political and bureaucratic corruption. In other words, the problem with Nigeria is how to reform the reformers.

Corruption: Conceptual Clarifications, Forms and Dimensions

Despite an abundance of research on corruption, there is no real consensus on what corruption is. This is so because corruption is a multifaceted and multidimensional socio-economic and political problem. Put differently, corruption is a broad term subsuming a wide variety of illegal, illicit, dishonest, irregular, and/or unprincipled activities and behaviours (Brinkerhoff 2000: 241). Nonetheless, most definitions of corruption share an emphasis on the exploitation of public position, resources, and power for private gain (Nye, 1967; Dobel, 1978; Amuwo, 2005; Obayelu, 2007; Fjeldstad and Isaksen, 2008). For instance, Nye (1967: 419) conceives corruption to mean an act which "deviates from the formal duties of a public role because of private regarding (personal, close family, private clique) pecuniary or status gains; or violates rules against the exercise of certain types of private role-regarding influence". Similarly, Dobel (1978: 958) defines corruption as "the betrayal of public trust for individual or group gain". In the same vein, Amuwo (2005: 127) sees corruption as "actual and unauthorised diversion of government largesse to private hands". It is worth noting that corruption can also take place among private sector parties. Hence, an alternative definition of corruption used by Transparency International (TI) is "the misuse of entrusted power for private gain".

It is important to note however that though there is a problem of definitional consensus, analysts and activists agree on several points. First, corruption is a complex issue with intricate linkages to other political and economic factors, both within a country and internationally. Second, tackling corruption is not a one-shot endeavour, but a challenging long-term undertaking. Third, successful anti-corruption efforts depend upon political will. This includes both political will to initiate the fight against corruption in the first place, and subsequently the will to sustain the battle over time until results are achieved (Brinkerhoff 2000: 240). Fourth, there is a consensus that when corruption becomes entrenched, its negative effects multiply: it creates negative national image and loss of much needed revenue; it devalues the quality of human life; it discourages foreign investments leading to decrease in Direct Investment; it exacerbates inequality, desecrates the rule of law and undermines the legitimacy and stability of democratic regimes; it limits economic growth; it slows down administrative processes thereby making the implementation of government reforms policies ineffective (Brinkerhoff, 2000; Gboyega 1996, Obayelu, 2007; Lawal, 2007).

Corruption is simply conceived in this work as misuse or improper use of power and influence, deliberately and consciously for personal aggrandizement or group advantage. Therefore, for the purposes of this discussion, the basic definition of corruption as the misuse of public position for private, group or sectional gain is maintained. This may take four important interrelated forms and dimensions: bribery and grease payments, petty and grand corruption, political and bureaucratic corruption.

The first form is bribery and grease payments. Bribery is the payments sought by public officials – or offered by private agents – in return for favours such as government contract while Grease payment is money paid to public officials to do work that they are already being paid to do, such as issuing a license. Second is petty and grand corruption. Petty corruption is the collision of a public official with a member of the public to subvert the system over relatively small transactions. It therefore mostly involves lower level public officials. Grand corruption is the subversion of the system by senior government officials, ministers and heads of state. In a broad term, grand, petty, bribery and grease payments are all forms or dimension of political and bureaucratic corruption. Though political and bureaucratic corruption may overlap, a thin line of demarcation can be drawn between the two. Mookherjee (2001: 3) provides a distinction between political and bureaucratic corruption thus:

> Political corruption in a democratic context refers to the problem of agency between citizen and elected official, and the way it is affected by institutions that define the electoral process, such as division of powers between different branches of and levels of government, the role of the legal system media and civil society in influencing public

policy and its implementation. In short, it deals with the policy formulation process and high level corruption of politicians". In contrast bureaucratic corruption is concerned with problems of policy implementation, and how it can be stymied by poor information and coordination system, corruption among government bureaucrats and employees. This is otherwise known as petty corruption. A form of corruption that is common and more visible to citizens in their everyday lives manifested by bribes that citizen must pay government officials to receive services to which they are entitled.

Bureaucratic corruption therefore is the abuse of discretion by public officials to bend or circumvent rules and regulations in exchange for certain benefits. It occurs mostly where there are considerable rewards and punishment discretion under an official's control. Bureaucratic corruption arises when bureaucrats pursue personal interest at the expense and to the detriment of the public interest. This corresponds then to the consequences of a decline in ethical norms of bureaucrats. According to Isaksen and Fjeldstad (2008: 6):

> Most bureaucratic corruption takes place at the implementation end of public policies, although it may in some cases have its roots in the planning and budgeting stages that precede implementation. It involves appointed bureaucrats and public administration staff at the central or sub-national levels. In simple terms, it comprises corrupt acts among those who implement the rules made by top officials. This includes interaction with private agents, such as demanding extra payment for providing government services, speed money to expedite bureaucratic procedures, or bribes to allow private actions that violate rules and regulations. It also includes interaction within the public bureaucracy, such as bribes or kickbacks to obtain posts or secure promotion, or mutual exchanges of favours.

Political corruption on the other hand is evident when governmental power is abused for illegitimate private, group, or sectional advantage. This is the trading of influence and authority by political leaders and may extend to granting favours, irregularities in campaign financing and electoral fraud. It is an effort to secure wealth for private benefit at public expense (Lipset and Lenz, 2000: 112). Forms of political and bureaucratic corruption include but not limited to bribery, extortion, influence peddling, fraud, embezzlement and nepotism. The problem is worst in Nigeria because bureaucratic corruption is complemented by political corruption. This makes the problem of combating corruption substantially more difficult. These two forms of corruption have taken a debilitating dimension in Nigeria since independence. It has had a ruinous consequence on the socio-economic and political wellbeing of the nation. In view of this, various socio-economic and institutional reforms have been employed to arrest the problem of political and bureaucratic corruption. These shall be discussed later.

Effects of Political and Bureaucratic Corruption

The effect of corruption, on any nation, is socially, economically and politically damaging. In Nigeria, corruption has been responsible for gross social and political instability which had bedevilled the country since her independent nationhood in 1960. Indeed, corruption is no longer the hidden, but open disease of democracy in Nigeria. In fact, anti-corruption crusades have been used to justify military coups that undermined, weakened and toppled democratic governments in the country. Paradoxically, the same has been used to justify counter-coups in the country. Gross poverty, seemingly unsolvable politically motivated ethno-religious crises are both symptoms and consequences of crass bureaucratic and political corruption. The sudden turn-around or transformation of the economic well-being and enhanced social status of the "insider elite" has made politics a do-or-die affair. In Nigeria, politics is money and money is politics. The "outsider elite" are always determined to force the insider elite out of the corridor of power, while the latter are also obstinate in retaining power by force. For this reason, contract killings or political assassinations have become part and parcel of Nigeria's political culture. Above all, corruption has been used by many scholars as a potent explanation for Nigeria's development tragedy. Infrastructural decay, widespread poverty, preventable waterborne and airborne epidemics and diseases, slums, rural and urban violence, acute low standard of living are consequences of corruption.

Furthermore, it is a herculean task to convince an average Nigerian that the state or the incumbent political head is worthy of his/her loyalty, allegiance and political support due to apathy and cynicism which corruption has engendered. In one word, the cyclical crisis of legitimacy in Nigeria today is a resultant effect of corruption. The worst scenario is that the Nigerian democracy is built on and sustained by corruption in the form of election rigging and manipulation, vote-buying to mention a few. The political and bureaucratic elite who survive on corruption use it as instrument of manipulation, oppression and domination. Corruption is a potent instrument not only to perpetuate the grip of the elite on the society, but also to sustain their social, economic and political relevance. Therefore, to uproot corruption is tantamount to deracinating the political and bureaucratic elite in the Nigerian society. The attempt here is not to present a hopeless situation but to demonstrate the challenges and the enormity of huddles that a determined effort to confront corruption head-on in Nigeria must prepare to face. Corruption is already a thorn in the flesh of Nigerian politics, planted and nurtured by the Nigerian political and bureaucratic elite. This explains why the fight against corruption has become a fragile endeavour in a fragile nation. The military regime of General Murtala Muhammad which strongly condemned corruption did not last long. The General was assassinated in the aborted coup of February 13, 1975. Generals Muhammad Buhari and Idiagbon, whose War Against Indiscipline (WAI) was devoid of rhetoric was also removed after 18 months of successful war against corruption in a palace coup by General Ibrahim Babangida on August 27, 1985. It has been a fact of history in Nigeria that regimes that harbour corruption tends to last longer than regimes that abhorred corruption. The longevity of Babangida regime for instance is a function of its over-permissiveness of corruption. Gboyega (1996) concludes that it was as if Babangida regime lives for corruption to thrive. As shall be discussed in the subsequent section, Nuhu Ribadu, the police officer who headed the anti-corruption crusade under Obasanjo administration has also had a taste of the fragility of the fight against corruption in Nigeria. The officer was ignominiously frustrated out of his job by the succeeding Umar Musa Yar'Adua's administration.

Anti-corruption Measures in Nigeria: Pre-obasanjo Civilian Era

Anti-corruption campaigns have a long tradition in Nigeria. From 1960 to date several measures and approaches to eradicate corruption have been employed. These include institutional approach, constitutional engineering or legal approach, the use of propaganda and political education and aggressive pursuit of economic and political cum institutional reforms.

Political education or propaganda designed to change the attitude of Nigerians and re-orientate them have been embarked upon by successive administrations. These includes: Ethical Revolution between 1979-83, War against Indiscipline (WAI) introduced by the duo of Generals Muhammad Buhari and Tunde Idiagbon (1983-85), War against Indiscipline and Corruption (WAIC) implemented by General Sani Abacha (1993-1998) and National Orientation Agency (NOA), among others. Some administrative reforms were also carried out. These were done through the various civil service reforms formally designed to improve efficiency, professionalism and improve productivity of the public service. The point here is that whether stated or otherwise, one of the primary motives of the various public service reforms was to reduce corruption and the level of wastage in the public service. Such reforms embraced salary reforms, privatisation and commercialisation of public enterprises, structural organisational reforms, judicial reforms, to mention a few.

The legal or constitutional engineering approach includes the use of decrees during the military era and the entrenchment of certain provisions, guiding the conduct of public officials in certain sections of the constitution. For instance, upon assumption of office every public officer is required to abide by the code of conduct for public officers outlined in the constitution. Nigeria's 1979 constitution (and even subsequent constitutions) for instance, contains several provisions geared towards good governance, supported by the enactment and judicial validation of accountability and transparency augmented anti-corruption legislations. For example, Section 15 sub-sections 5 of the 1999 Constitution provides that, "Government must eradicate all corrupt practices and abuse of power", thereby making the fight against corruption the political objective of the state. Others are the provision for Judicial Commissions of Enquiry, the Code of Conduct Bureau and Public Complaints Commission.

The inadequacies of the constitutional provisions have necessitated the promulgation of decrees and enactment of anticorruption laws. A mention of few will suffice: The Public Officers (Investigation of Assets) Decree of 1966; Investigation of Assets (Public Officers) Validation Decree No. 45 of 1968; Forfeiture of Assets (Public Officers) Validation Decree; Corrupt Practices Decree of 1975; The Public Officer (Investigation of Assets Decree No. 5 of 1976); Recovery of Public Property Act of 1984, Miscellaneous offences Act of 1984, Bank and other Financial Institutions Act of 1991, Failed Banks (Recovery of Debts) Act of 1994, Advance Fee Fraud Act of 1995, Nigeria Drug and Law Enforcement Agency Act of 1998, Nigerian Deposit Insurance Corporation Act of 1998, Forfeiture of Assets, etc. (Certain Persons) Decree No. 53 of 1999. All dealt with the investigation and forfeiture of assets of corrupt officers and politicians. Remarkably, one fundamental lesson from all these laws is that corruption eradication cannot only be constitutionally engineered. Therefore, in spite of the penal provisions of these laws, corruption seems to be on the ascendancy in Nigeria (Falana, 2007). The failure of constitutional engineering calls for certain institutional, administrative, economic and political reforms.

Eradicating Corruption Through Reforms: 1999 to 2009

To fight corruption, it is vital to appreciate its variations, forms, causes and consequences. Corruption has taken various forms and dimensions in Nigeria. It is also multi-causal and multifaceted. For instance, corruption in Nigeria is rooted in the country's political and legal development, its social history, bureaucratic traditions, economic conditions and policies. This actually informed the holistic approach employed by the civilian administration of Olusegun Obasanjo to tackle the problem of corruption head-on.

Olusegun Obasanjo (1999-2007) laid the foundation of his civilian administration on the vociferous campaign and determination to eliminate corruption in the public life. In his inauguration speech on May 29, 1999, the President stated that "corruption the bane of our society today, will be tackled head-on at all levels". He further emphasized that "no society can achieve anything near its full potentials if it allows corruption to become the full-blown cancer it has become in Nigeria". Obasanjo stressed his determination to combat corruption in all its ramifications and assured Nigerians that "there shall be no sacred cows. Nobody, no matter who and where, will be allowed to get away with the breach of the law or perpetration of corruption and evil". The administration demonstrated this by taking a number of steps:

- Promulgation of laws against graft-Independent Corrupt Practices and (Other Related Offences) Commission (ICPC Act, Economic and Financial Crimes Commission (EFCC) Act, Money Laundering (Prohibition) Act 2004;
- Strengthening of anti-corruption and other economic crimes institutions for effective law enforcement;
- Prosecution and conviction of high-ranking administration officials and tracing, seizing and confiscation of all proceeds of crime;
- Institution of Due Process Mechanism in public sector procurements;
- Deregulation/Privatisation of failing public institutions and creating an enabling environment for effective private-public partnerships;
- Monthly publication of distributable revenue from the Federation Account to the different tiers of government;
- Institutions of transparencies in the oil and gas sector through the work of the Extractive Industries Transparency Initiative (NEITI); and
- Monetisation policies and other administrative reforms in the Civil Service.

Indeed, the period between 1999 and 2007 could be aptly described as the era of reform. Indeed, one important thing to note is that the stated and unstated objective of the major reforms as demonstrated in the speeches of President Obasanjo is the amelioration of corruption and the acceleration of development. The question is whether the reforms have been effective in reducing corruption and generate socioeconomic development. A proper answer to this question requires a brief discussion of some of the reforms and their objectives.

The first approach to eradicate corruption by the government of Olusegun Obasanjo is the legal cum institutional approach. To demonstrate his commitment to the elimination of corruption in public life, Obasanjo proposed and signed Anticorruption bill into law. He established two anti-graft commissions, the Independent Corrupt Practices Commission (ICPC) and Economic and Financial Crime Commission (EFCC) in 2003 and 2004 respectively. These two anti-graft agencies were established as part of the national reform agenda to address corruption and money laundering. The mandate of the ICPC is "to prohibit and prescribe punishment for corrupt practices and other related offences". Section 6 of the ICPC Act confers three main responsibilities on the ICPC. They are:

- To receive and investigate reports of corruption and in appropriate cases prosecute the offender[s];
- To examine, review and enforce the correction of corruption prone systems and procedures of public bodies, with a view to eliminating corruption in public life;
- Educating and enlightening the public on and against corruption and

related offences with a view to enlisting and fostering public support for the fight against corruption;

The EFCC is also empowered to investigate, prevent and prosecute offenders, who indulge in money laundering, embezzlement, bribery, looting and any form of corrupt practices, illegal arms deal, smuggling, human trafficking, and child labour, illegal oil bunkering, illegal mining, tax evasion, foreign exchange malpractices including counterfeiting of currency, theft of intellectual property and piracy, open market abuse, dumping of toxic wastes, and prohibited goods (Section 46, EFCC Establishment Act, 2004).

The performance of EFCC and ICPC has remained a subject of controversy. While some see EFCC as a veritable instrument for promoting good governance, others view the anti-graft agency as instrument of oppression and intimidation in the hand of the Executive. However, the story of EFCC and ICPC is that of mixed successes and failures. While the agencies could be credited for the recovery of certain stolen funds, the agency could also be pronounced guilty of selective prosecution, because certain powerful individuals or political gladiators were spared. For instance, while Chief Evans Enwerem, Chuka Okadigbo (late), and Adolphus Wabara (all former Senate Leaders) who were impeached on account of mismanagement and corrupt enrichment escaped the wrath of the law, Governor Alamieyeseigba of Bayelsa state was impeached tried and convicted on corruption and money laundering. The former vice president under Olusegun Obasanjo was also pronounced guilty of diverting US $145million Petroleum Technology Development Fund. Earlier Salisu Buhari, the first speaker of the National House of Assembly who was guilty of certificate forgery was granted state pardon by President Olusegun Obasanjo. President Obasanjo himself was implicated in a number of scandals during his last years in power, including an alleged attempt by his aides to bribe members of the National Assembly to support Obasanjo's bid for a third term. Days before leaving office, Obasanjo controversially sold off two of Nigeria's three troubled oil refineries to a consortium of investors including Transcorp, a corporation that has purchased a number of high profile government and other assets since its formation in 2004.Transcorp has itself been a target of controversy since it became known that Obasanjo had acquired 200 million shares of its stock by unknown means (HRW, 2007: 44).

The first challenge to Yar'Adua's administration was the financial scandal in the House of Representatives involving the female Speaker, Madam Patricia Etteh. She was pronounced guilty over the misappropriation of public funds in multiple contracts of N628m (US$5 million) for the renovation of her official residence and the purchase of 12 official cars. The president washed off his hand under the pretext of non-interference in the affairs of the legislative house. The case was never heard in any court of law. These are few among many cases of political corruption at the higher level of governance. What is common to all these cases is that the culprits were beyond reproach and hence part of the political untouchables in the Nigerian society. And as noted by Okurounmu (2008) "in a climate of unpunished corruption, any laws enacted or any agencies created, for the benefit of the people can never serve their purposes. They only constitute avenues of corruption by those entrusted with their implementation or management". This is indeed the pitfall of the legal and institutional approach to corruption eradication under the present dispensation, where action contradicts intention.

Another anti-graft measure of Obasanjo administration is the privatisation and deregulation of the economy. The policy of deregulation is a recommendation of the World Bank for those states determined to combat corruption. Perhaps in the case of Nigeria and of many developing countries, anti-corruption reforms are means of bowing to external pressure from donors. Indeed a representative World Bank ((World Bank 2000: 21) policy formulation in 2000 prescribed that an effective anti-corruption strategy should:

(1) Encourage the reduction of rents by means of economic liberalisation, deregulation, tax simplification, de-monopolisation and macroeconomic stability;

(2) Reduce discretion through administrative and civil service reform, including meritocratic recruitment and decentralisation; and

(3) Increase accountability by building up institutions such as auditing and accountancy units and through legal reforms such as judicial strengthening.

Therefore, the policy of deregulation as an anti-corruption measure of Obasanjo administration could be said to be externally propelled. The rationale behind the programme of deregulation and privatisation is that state enterprise have failed to generate the expected amount of returns on investment due to mismanagement, corruption and stupendous wastage of resources (Ogundiya and Baba, 2005: 161). Rather than enhancing accountability, transparency and greater efficiency in Nigeria, privatisation and the policy of economic deregulation have been fraught with corrupt practices. Privatisation and deregulation processes, at the initial stage lacked openness, transparency and accountability. It was only the corrupt politicians and opportunistic bureaucrats who had benefited from earlier corrupt practices that took the advantage of the privatisation and deregulation exercise. Equally important, in many of the privatisation exercise, entire enterprises or equity shares in enterprises have been sold at bargain prices to those with the 'right connections' 5 members of the federal and state executives, legislative members, top echelon of the board of parastatals, privileged and opportunistic bureaucrats, political godfathers and their cronies.

The institution of Due Process Mechanism in public sector procurements is another major reform to curb political and bureaucratic corruption. Its instigation is informed by a dire need to correct what had over the years became recognized as the "Nigerian factor" in not only the conduct of government business but in virtually every sphere of the country's social and political live. In short, due process entails recourse to the laid-down rules and regulations, policies and guiding principles in whatever transactions one is engaged in. In the process, the all-encompassing circles which are driven by genuine consultations, realistic privatisation and steadfast funding of approved budget items are institutionalized. In this direction, the Budget Monitoring and Price Intelligence Unit, otherwise known as Due Process, was established. The revelations after Obasanjo had left office showed that nothing was really "due" in the "Due Process".

The anti-corruption reforms under the democratic administration in Nigeria since 1999 will be incomplete without the Service Delivery component of the reforms. It is pertinent to recall that the Federal Government initiated a comprehensive reform programme in order to make the agencies of government efficient, corruption-free, effective and procedurally relevant in the modern world (Okafor, 2009). While delivering a speech at the opening of the Special Presidential Retreat on Service Delivery Obasanjo stated that:

Under the popular caption of the 'Nigeria Way', many Nigerians have grown accustomed to regarding public service as something you battle for, and you cannot succeed unless you know someone inside the system. Few Nigerians expect to get routine acknowledgement of letters written to public offices, let alone getting attention for telephone enquiries. Few Nigerians apply for service without budgeting time and money to follow their applications from desk to desk, while bracing themselves for the phenomenon of the 'missing' file that would re-appear after settling someone.

It is worth noting that Servicom as it is known has suffered the same fate that befell the previous policies. Another reform measure designed to curb corruption under Obasanjo civilian rule is the monetisation policies.

Government introduced the monetization programmes, on the conviction that the policy will reduce to the barest minimum such negative fiscal tendencies as waste and abuse of public facilities. For instance, it cost Government lots of funds to construct, purchase or rent residential accommodation for public servants. Large amounts of resources were occasionally spent on renovation, maintenance and furnishing of such accommodation, as well as on the purchase, fuelling and maintenance of official vehicles for public servants. Government argued that the reforms were necessary due to lethargy in official action, insensitivity to the value of time, irregular attendance at work, wastefulness in the use of government resources, corruption and nepotism. Many able-body civil servants were laid off and were not accommodated in the palliative measures outlined by the governments. Expectedly, this created a sense of job insecurity among those that escaped the wrath of the policy. Above all, the effect of the policy has not been very significant considering the media report on corruption each passing day.

Other institutional reforms aimed at curbing bureaucratic corruption includes: Police Reforms, Custom Reforms, Immigration Reforms, Banking

Reforms, and Prison Reforms. One important thing to note is that despite all these reforms and the energies and resources that went into it, corruption remain persistent, endemic and even more pronounced in the country. In her critical assessment of the police reforms in Nigeria, Hills (2008: 215) caustically concludes her essay in the following words: "Despite decades of police assistance and the recent introduction of reform plans, Nigeria's public police remain notoriously brutal and corrupt". Recent increase in the salary of the police has worsened the situation. What account for the failure of anticorruption reforms? Answers to this question shall be provided in the next section.

Road Blocks to Anti-corruption Reforms

Despite all the policies and anti-corruption reform measures, corruption remains one of the major problems of governance in Nigeria. The persistence of corruption at the various levels of governance is an indication that all the reform measures have failed. To understand the failure of the anti-graft measures, one needs to understand the nature and character of the Nigerian state, the nature and character of the elite and the forms and nature of corruption itself. All these, perhaps constitute the socio-cultural, economic and political environment of corruption.

The question of the nature of the state that is supposed to implement the anti-corruption policies is depicted in such theories like prebendalism, patrimonialism, neo-patrimonialism, clientelism, soft state thesis and theory of two publics (Ogundiya, 2009, forthcoming). These theoretical analytical frameworks explain the menace and persistence of corruption in the developing countries from different perspectives but with similar conclusions. The analytical framework of neo-patrimonialism developed by French political scientists working on Africa provides a pessimistic view on the issue of political will to implementing reforms (Blundo and Olivier de Sardan, 2006; Bayart et al. 1999; Chabal and Daloz, 1999). Within this analytical framework corruption is understood as an integrated part of the dominant elites' extraction and rent seeking practices. Because neo-patrimonial elites are the main profiteers of widespread corruption, they have limited will for reform and its implementation. Thus, any lasting effects of institutional and administrative reforms may be doubtful. In this context, such reforms may even be aimed at securing the political and economic power of the ruling elites (Fjeldstad and Isaken, 2008). This is indeed the tragedy of anti-corruption reforms in Nigeria.

Bardhan (1997) in consonance with Gunnar Myrdal soft state thesis argues that some African states in recent history have become predatory in their rent extraction not because they are strong but because they are weak. The state cannot enforce the laws and property rights that provide the minimum underpinnings of a market economy, leading to disloyalty and theft among public officials. In a climate of unpunished corruption, any institutional reform or any laws enacted or any agencies created for the benefit of the people cannot be effective or serve their purposes. Some cases of unpunished corruption under the eight years rule include the following:

Christopher Alao-Akala, then the PDP nominee for governor in Oyo State, was reportedly put on the EFCC list of candidates deemed "unfit" to run in the 2007 elections but then taken off in response to political pressure. The same allegations were made regarding current Nigerian Vice President Goodluck Jonathan, then serving as governor of Bayelsa State. An investigation into allegations of corruption by PDP chieftain Olabode George during his time as head of the Ports Authority was allowed to die without any convincing explanation on the part of the EFCC during Obasanjo administration. The case was later revived during Yaradua/Goodluck administration and the old man was sentenced. The EFCC refused to investigate widespread allegations of corruption against Andy Uba, a powerful aide to President Obasanjo and ultimately the PDP candidate for Governor of Anambra State, even after he was caught by US customs officials attempting to smuggle $170,000 in cash into the United States on board Nigeria's presidential jet. The EFCC made no real attempt to investigate credible allegations that officials in the presidency attempted to bribe members of the National Assembly into voting in favour of Obasanjo's abortive attempt at changing the constitution to allow himself a third term in office.

Reforms in the climate of unpunished corruption only constitute another avenue or opportunity for further corrupt enrichment. Importantly, the cost of corruption is low in Nigeria. The most obvious cost is the risk of getting caught and punished. The probability of getting caught depends in part on the effectiveness of the country's legal system. The Nigerian legal system is to say the least ineffective in fighting corruption. The situation is even worse with limited access to information by the press and the generality of the people. Most official businesses in Nigeria are still shrouded in secrecy. It is common to see official files with the tag or inscription "official secret" or labelled "highly confidential". The Information Bill which would have helped to create access by individual to the so-callèd official secrete has suffered considerable set-back in the hand of President Obasanjo and his successor, Umar Musa Yar'adua.

Moreover, anticorruption reforms of the Federal government and certain agencies like ICPC and EFCC were seen as tools in the hands of the executive to witch hunt certain real or perceived political opponents especially after the aborted third term agenda. While the president quickly pronounced state pardon for Salisu Buhari, the same president fervently sought the prosecution of Governor Alamaesiagha.

One critical factor that could help in explaining the predatory nature of African states and persistent corruption, particularly in Nigeria, is party funding/financing. To Vifredo Pareto, there are three important reasons/motives for providing political/party funds. The first is idealistic or ideological, and second is social, that is aiming at social honours or access and third, financial striving for material benefits (cf Babawale and Ashiru 2006: 72). In Nigeria, the major reason for party financing is for personal aggrandizements and material benefits. This is the reason, as it has been pointed out earlier, why bureaucratic corruption is complemented by political corruption. Wealthy individual members have constituted themselves into kingmakers in all the political parties. Godfather syndrome has made the fight against corruption in Nigeria an exercise in futility. These godfathers have hijacked virtually all the political parties through bogus donations. Expectedly, the godfather expects the godson to pay back as quickly as possible when he/she gets into office. The process of paying back takes different dimension: award of undeserving and un-implementable (unrealistic) contracts; monthly cash reward from the state treasury; indirect control of the state pause through allocation of certain sensitive political posts to the godfather's loyalists who in turn are directly responsible to the godfather but not to the state governor or the president as the case may be. In its apt description, Human Rights Watch (2007: 34) contends:

> These godfathers are not mere financiers of political campaigns. Rather they are individuals whose power stems not just from wealth but from their ability to deploy violence and corruption to manipulate national, state or local political systems in support of the politicians they sponsor. In return, they demand a substantial degree of control over the governments they help bring into being - not in order to shape government policy, but to exact direct financial "returns" in the form of government resources stolen by their protégés or lucrative government contracts awarded to them as further opportunities for graft. Godfathers also require their sponsored politicians to use government institutions to generate patronage for other protégés

Therefore, the anti-corruption posture of a governor or the president often times makes government unpopular among the political kingmakers. The Anambra and Oyo states saga were typical examples. In Anambra state, Chris Uba boasted that he single-handedly installed all elected officers in that state and hence had the power to remove them should they refuse to dance to his tune. Indeed, the refusal by the governor, Ngige, to "adequately" reward Chris Uba led to his removal. In Oyo state, Adedibu fell apart with Rasheed Ladoja because the latter refused to release one quarter of the monthly security vote of Oyo state to the erstwhile godfather. For that singular reason, Ladoja did not succeed to secure a return ticket under the Peoples Democratic Party.

Still, these godfathers or party kingmakers are politically untouchable and beyond legal reproach. Hence, they serve as protective umbrellas to their political boys. They are so dreadful because of their abilities to kill or assassinate both real and perceived opponents with impunity. Even, when they are confronted or any of their boys suffers humiliation for engaging in corrupt practices in the hands of state security agents or any political leaders, the prosecutor may pay with his work or with his/her life. In one word, the fight against corruption is a fragile one in Nigeria and a case of 'look before you leap'. For instance, Nuhu Ribadu, the agile police officer, who headed the EFCC, the anti-corruption agency under Obasanjo administration in Nigeria was humiliated out of office against the general public opinion.

Furthermore, many of the anti-corruption reforms failed because they are "non- political" in nature, while most of the corruption in the country is inherently political. Few anti-corruption campaigns dare to attack the roots of corruption because the roots lie in the distribution of power itself. Many Nigerian politicians are 'vote buyers' and many Nigerian voters are 'vote sellers'. In certain instances political offices and higher echelon in the civil service are for the highest bidder. Therefore, in most occasions, anti-corruption strategies are adopted and implemented in cooperation with the very predators that control the government and, in some cases also, the anti-corruption instruments. In certain cases, the institutions that are established to enforce the rules and check corrupt practices are implicated in political corruption. With reference to political corruption, there is ample evidence that Independent National Electoral Commission (INEC) officials colluded, sometimes under the influence of money, to perpetrate violence, rigging or doctoring of election results. The same applies to the police, the State Security Service (SSS) and the National Intelligence Agency (NIA) (Aiyede, 2006).

Another factor that has made the anti-corruption crusade a fragile endeavour in Nigeria is the interconnection between the citizenship question, nature of ethnicity and character of the Nigerian state. As argued elsewhere by (Ogundiya 2009):

> The privileged elite have successfully disillusioned the psyche of the masses with the virus of ethnicity, even to the extent that when corrupt acts are unveiled and the perpetrator(s) are under probe, it is customary in Nigeria to associate such probe with ethnic politics. And question such as – How many Hausa, Ibo or Yoruba are under probe or how many have been punished are not uncommon. The question would not be how many Yoruba/Hausas/Ibos as the case may be are involved in corrupt acts. Virtually anything in Nigeria can be ethnicized.

Factors that account for the failure of the anti-corruption reforms in Nigeria are indeed multifarious. In summary, the following factors are preponderant: lack of commitment to a national agenda even when it is formulated; ineffective legal system and low cost of corruption; the pursuit of short-term personal interest as opposed to the long term interest of the nation; obsession with ethnic considerations as the basis of politics, lack of leadership with vision, that is, an absence of leaders whose word is their bond, who possess principles and will, and who put integrity and character above wealth; the politics of godfatherism and the complementary nature of bureaucratic and political corruption among others.

Conclusion and Prescriptions

Arguably, corruption has become a thorn in the flesh of Nigerian politics. It is undoubtedly Nigeria's economic, social and political tsunamis. Therefore, rather than abating, corruption has continue to spread like flame of fire. Every-day new revelations emerge of the extent to which the evil indulgence has permeated the ruling and the bureaucratic class. As at the time of writing this chapter, Officials of the National Electricity Regulatory Commission (NERC) have been indicted by the EFCC over their shares of N100million naira each, and other acquisitions made by them from the funds of the commission, including a N500million bank lodgement into a private account by its chairman. So, while the nation suffer in darkness, day in and day out, the officials of the commission have all become multi-millionaires simply by the fortune of their appointments to that commission. The implication is that anticorruption reforms in Nigeria have not been a successful endeavour.

The greatest challenge to anticorruption reform, oddly enough, is the purported reformers. In a situation of prevalent corruption among the state managers and the top echelon of nation's bureaucrats, the fight against corruption would be far from being realised. The Nigerian situation presented a difficult scenario in that the initiators and implementers of the anti-corruption reforms are archetype of corruption. To compound the problem, the agencies and institutions empowered to prosecute corrupt individuals are corruptly constituted, hence individuals in such organisations are not immune from corrupt practices. Therefore, where sound laws are put in place sound enforcement which is an essential precondition to fighting corruption is patently weak.

To avert these problems, the legal provisions should be enforced by adequately and transparently resourced executive, judicial and independent institutions. At the political level, anti-corruption crusades have to have genuine commitment from leaders, be protected from being politicized, and be inclusive of and participatory for all stakeholders of a society. This is also currently lacking in Nigeria. Economically, a system of incentives that rewards good conduct and penalizes corrupt or unethical behaviour will contribute to reducing petty bureaucratic corruption. Therefore, the cost of corruption must be all-time high and unbearable. Finally, government employees should be adequately rewarded to stem the tide of corruption. It must be noted that even at the society level, unless people can attain a minimum living standard through their employment, corruption will continue to take place. Above all, the problem with the war against corruption in Nigeria was and is how to reform the reformers.

References

Aka, P. C (1999). Corruption and the Crisis of Institutional Reforms in Africa. Retrieved on 12th November 2008: <http://findarticle.com/p/articles/mi_qa3821/is_19910/ai_n8871406/prin?tag=artBody>

Aiyede, R. E. (2006). The Role of INEC, ICPC and EFCC in Combating Political Corruption. *Money, Politics and Corruption in Nigeria*, pp. 37-54. A Publication of IFES.

Akivaga, S.K. (2001). Fighting Corruption: Challenges to the Civil Society and Political Parties. In K. Kibwana, S.K. Akivaga, L.M. Mute, & M.O Odhiambo (eds.), *Initiatives Against Corruption in Kenya: Legal and Policy Interventions 1995-2001*, pp. 83-107. Nairobi: Claripress.

Amuwo, Kunle (2005). The Peripheral State: Critical Perspectives on the Structure and Role of the Public Bureaucracy. *Journal of Development Alternatives and Area Studies*, Vol. 24, No. 3 & 4, pp. 119-130.

Bardhan, P. (1997). Corruption and development: A review of issues. *Journal of Economic Literature*, pp. 1320-1346.

Bayart, J.-F., S. Ellis & Hibou, B. (1999). *The Criminalization of the State in Africa.* Oxford: James Currey Press for the International African Institute.

Blundo, G. & Olivier de Sardan, J.-P. (2006). *Everyday Corruption and the State. Citizens and Public Officials in Africa.* London and New York: Zed Books.

Brinkerhoff, Derick W. (2000). Assessing Political Will for Anti-corruption Efforts: Analytic Framework. *Public Administration and Development, 20*, pp. 239-252.

Chabal, P. & Daloz, J.-P. (1999). *Africa Works : Disorder as Political Instrument.* Oxford: James Currey for the International African Institute.

Diamond, L. (1991). Nigeria's Perennial Struggle. *Journal of Democracy*, Vol. 2, No. 4, Fall, pp. 73-85.

Dobel, Patrick J. (1978). The Corruption of a State. *The American Political Science Review, Vol. 72, No. 3, September*, pp. 958-973.

Ejiogu, Aloy (2000). Morality and National Development: A case for National Rebirth. *Occassional Publication of the National Orientation Agency, No. 2.*

Ekeh P. P. (1985). The African State and the African Crisis. Paper presented at the First Symposium of the Special Committee on Africa of the United Nations University. Nairobi, Kenya March 4 -7, 1985.

Falana, Femi (2007). Ethics and governance, the Rule of law and Anti-Corruption: A Nigerian Dilemma. Retrieved from http://www.saharareporters.com/www/interview/detail/?id=69

Federal Republic of Nigeria. Constitution of the Federal Republic of Nigeria, 1999.

Fjeldstad Odd-Helge, & Isaksen Jan (2008). Anti-corruption Reforms: Challenges, Effects and Limits of World Bank Support. *Public Sector Reform: What Works and Why?* An IEG Evaluation of World Bank Support.

Gboyega, Alex (1996). Corruption and Democratisation in Nigeria, 1983-1993: An Overview. In Gboyega Alex (ed.), *Corruption and Democratisation in* Nigeria, pp. 3-12. Ibadan: Agbo Areo Publishers.

Hills, Alice (2008). The Dialectic of Police Reform in Nigeria. *Journal of Modern African Studies*, Vol. 46, No. 2, pp. 215-234.

Johnston, M. (1991). Political Corruption: Historical Conflict and the Rise of Standards. *Journal of Democracy,* Vol. 2, No. 4, *Fall*, pp. 48-60.

Johnston, M. (1996). Public Officials, Private Interests and Sustainable Democracy: Connections between Politics and Corruption.

Lawal Gbenga (2007). Corruption and Development in Africa: Challenges for Political and Economic Change. *Humanity and Social Sciences Journal,* Vol. 1, No. 1, pp. 1-7.

Lipset, S.M & Gabriel, S. Lenz (2000). Corruption, Culture and Markets. In Lawrence E. Harrison & Samuel P. Huntington (eds.), *Culture Matters*. New York: Basic Books.

Maduabum, Chuks (2006). *Reforming Government Bureaucracies in Nigeria: The Journey so Far*. Topo-Badagry: The Administrative Staff College of Nigeria.

Mookkherjee, Dilip (2001). Combating the Crisis in Government Accountability: A Review of Recent International Experience. R.C Dutt Memorial Lectures, Centre for Studies in Social Science, Calcuta, December 27-28.

Mushtaq, Husain Khan (2008). Governance and Anti-Corruption Reforms in Developing Countries: Policies, Evidence and Ways Forward. Retrieved on January 29, 2009: <http://www.google.ca/search?hl=en&q= anti corruption+reforms&btng=search&mega=.

Obasanjo, O. (2004). Speech Presented at the Opening of the Special Presidential Retreat on Service Delivery, Abuja, March 19-20.

Obayelu, Abiodun Elijah (2007). Effects of Corruption and Economic Reforms on Economic Growth and Development: Lessons from Nigeria. Paper Prepared for 2007 African Economic Conference.

Ogundiya, I.S., & Baba T.K. (2005). Deregulation, Poverty and Sustainable Democracy in Nigeria. In Akpotor A.S. et al. (eds.), *Deregulation and Globalisation in Nigeria: Issues and Perspectives*, pp. 152-169. Ekpoma: Ambrose Alli University Publishing House.

Ogundiya, I.S. (2006). Minimizing the Cost of Governance in Nigeria through the Civil Service Reforms: Rightsizing, Downsizing or Retrenchment. In Akpotor et ál. (eds.). *Cost of Governance in Nigeria: An Evaluative Analysis*. Ekpoma: Ambrose Alli Publishing House.

Ogundiya, I.S. (2009). Political Corruption in Nigeria: Theoretical Perspectives and Some Explanations. *Anthropology* (Forthcoming).

Okafor, E. E. (2009). Public Service Reforms in Nigeria: A Critical Assessment. In Ogundiya I. S., Olutayo L. & Amzat J. (eds). *State and Civil Society Relations in Nigeria* (Forthcoming).

Okurounmu, Femi (2009). Successive governments have diminished our nation. *Nigerian Tribune*, Tuesday 17th February.

Olofsgard, A., & Zaharan, Z. (2007). Corruption and Political and Economic Reforms: A Structural Breaks Approach. Retrieved from <http://ssrn.com/absract=1008147>.

Oyelowo Oyewo (2009). Constitutions, Good Governance and Corruption: Challenges and Prospects for Nigeria. Retrieved on November 12, 2008: <http://www.enelsyn.gr/papers/N16/paper%20by%20prof%20O yelowo%20Oyelowo.pdf.>.

Ribadu, Nuhu (2006). Nigeria's Struggle with Corruption (Abridged and Edited Version). Presentation to US Congressional House Committee on International Development, Washington DC on May 18. Retrieved on May 5, 2009: <http:www.google.ca/search?hl=en&9= corruption+in+ Nigeria&btng=google+search&meta=>.

Treisman, Daniel (2000).The causes of corruption: A Cross-National Study. *Journal of Public Economics,* Vol. 76, pp. 399-457.

World Bank (2000). Reforming Public Institutions and Strengthening Governance: A World Bank Strategy. Washington, DC.

11

Political Agitation and Terror Potentialities in Niger Delta Area of Nigeria

Amzat, Jimoh and Ogundiya, I. Sarafa

Introduction

A common theme in much recent writings among the social scientists in Nigeria today has been the daunting list of problems with which the political system must come to grips. These problems are multi-causal and multifaceted. It ranges from the problem of ethnicity, identity, citizenship, morality, corruption, etc. to the problem of resource allocation. More pernicious and exigent is the glaring imbalance in resource allocation among the different geo-political zones in the country. The case of the Niger Delta area is undoubtedly and unequivocally critical. The inherent marginalization, perceived neglect, economic peripheralisation and political domination coupled with reckless environmental degradation culminates in the deep seated and seemingly non-solvent political agitation, which has transformed over the years to violent political confrontations directed at the Nigerian state on the one hand and the multinational oil companies operating in the region on the other hand.

Despite all measures by the Nigerian state to address the situation, the desperation is improving in bounds in the Niger Delta which has been the flashpoint of resource-conflict for more than four decades. For instance, Ibiyemi (2006) reports that Nigerian National Petroleum Corporation (NNPC) recorded 1306 cases of line breaks of petroleum in 2005 which represents an increase of 40.5% over the 929 cases reported in 2004. More worrisome is the fact that the confrontation is assuming alarming dimension with the emerging terror potentialities. The destructive capacity of the militancy and the reoccurring pandemonium has not attracted the desired attention. Terrorism, a socio-political infraction on security system and socio-economic stability is therefore becoming feasible and indeed has been utilized in political agitations which have resulted in unimaginable lost of lives and properties in Niger Delta area of Nigeria. The economic loss on the part of the Nigerian state is enormous. For example, it is estimated that Nigeria lost a huge sum of 12 billion US dollars, arising from production disruptions, within 7 months between February and September 2006 (*Business Day*, September 4, 2006).

Although there is apparent difficulties on what actually constitute terrorism (Robert, 2002, Henry, 2002), common in most of the definitive meanings of terrorism (Jenkins 1978, Crenshaw, 1981, Mooney et al, 2002, CFR, 2005) is the element of extra normal force towards achieving a set of goals (be it sociopolitical or economic). For instance the America's States Department defines terrorism as "premeditated, politically motivated violence perpetrated against non-combatant targets by sub-national groups or clandestine agents, usually intended to influence an audience. Shultz (1978) in a similar manner conceives terrorism as the threat and/or use of extra normal forms of political violence in varying degree, with the objective of achieving certain political goals. Conceived this way, it is not superfluous to assert that the militants in the region are gradually utilizing terror tactics in advancing their political demands. In this light, this paper examines factors necessitating rising waves of terror in political agitation, foundation of political agitation and terror potentialities in the Niger Delta region of Nigeria.

Rising Trends of Terror in Political Agitation

Fighting for socio-political rights is not uncommon among heterogeneous groups in the society where there is real or perceived deprivation. It is in this light that equity is central in resource allocation among groups within the state. Without relative equity, there is bound to be agitations. The agitation in the Niger Delta is premised on the efforts to ensure equitable distribution of resources to the region. But over the years the agitation has been extremely confrontational with the utilization of terror tactics, e.g. kidnap, pipeline vandalization, hostage taking, etc.

Terror in recent times has been a major socio-political problem and one of the dimensions of global risk. At the global realm, terror attacks have brought states closer together and have sharpened the understanding of what globalization actually is: a worldwide community of destiny confronted with violent, destructive obsession (Beck, 2003). The concept 'terrorism' is in the end also misleading with respect to the novelty of the threat it represents, since it pretends a familiarity with the motives of national liberation movements that does not at all hold true for the perpetrators of suicide and mass murder attacks (Beck, 2003). With the horror images of New York terror groups who established themselves as new global actors in competition with states, economics and civil societies (Beck, 2003), it is disheartening to view this risk with impunity.

The risk is spreading across the globe. In Nigeria there is the emergence of violent confrontation in political agitation with gradual sophistication in the perpetration of the upsurge. Hence, the risk is becoming pervasive. Militants' networks have become 'NGOs of violence'. This is premised on the fact that most of those involved are not usually part of any definite governments. So the militants in the region are becoming stakeholders in commanding the attention of the government. They are acclaimed liberationist fighters and they operate within and outside the country posing great threats to civil societies.

The formation of the militant groups is usually accorded with large gathering with ceremonies over the years. The upshot of these 'NGOs' became community frontline in the acquisition of power to fight for political rights. All this tends to 'individualization of war'- a war of acclaimed 'liberationists' who organize themselves under different covers, seek wide enrolments, acquire capacity for militancy, demonstrate (profound) threat to the civil societies and form 'associations' fighting for the 'emancipation' of the people of the region. This is indeed war of individuals against the state. Such individuals do not need to order for weapons but could make their own weapons with little expenses and the networks of communication facilitate linkages and links that enhance the penetration of terror. With the porous border of the Nigerian state, a proliferation of weapons is facilitated. Terror act is thus becoming a vital tool in political agitation. As in the case in the Niger Delta several factors account for the increasing terror potentialities.

1. **Terrorism and Heroism**: This has to do with the problem of conflicting perception. Though seen as militias by the Nigerian state, terrorists by the outside world, the communities perceived the agitators as heroes and they are treated with utmost respect. In view of this, they enjoy absolute and maximum cooperation from their community. In this regard, to the communities, they are champions, deliverers, liberators, freedom fighters and indeed God-sent messiah with the task of unfettering their people from the morass of economic stagnation, environmental degradation, oppression and perhaps political domination and other forms of social injustices emanating from the activities of the multinational oil companies and the structural imbalance of the Nigerian federation. Therefore, in the eyes of the community, the militias are fighting a just course and the bravery of the militants is applauded either

openly or secretly. This is not surprising as there is apparent disagreement about who is a terrorist: What actually makes a terrorist is not really the issue or the grievance at stake but the approach or strategy utilized to realize its ambition. For instance, despite the allegations levelled against Bin Ladin as a terrorist, he still receives applause by some groups. Hence, the argument that 'One man's terrorist is another man's freedom fighter is to a reasonable extent authentic. This explains why, even as the confrontation is taking terror dimension, there is still popular support for the divergent groups.

2. **Multifaceted and Causal Complexities of the Agitation**: There are also interwoven factors responsible for violent uprising in the region. The proceeding section examines the apparent etiologic basis and demands of the militant groups. There are other internal and other external explanations, some ethnic, and other varying socio-cultural and economic factors. For instance, with the 13% derivation to the region, it is assumed that there should be adequate improvement in the welfare and infrastructural development in the region. This is lacking. Perhaps this is the only oil region in the world that suffers acute youth unemployment, crash poverty environmental degradation and infrastructural neglect. Corruption may be an explanatory factor. And the lack of corporate responsibility of oil companies in the region could also be a vital point in the violent upsurge in the region.

3. **Community Allegiance and Support**: That the militants enjoy unflinching support is not a hiding fact. This is related to the problem of perception discussed above. No wonder, access to bombs and other weapons by the militants is facilitated by well-to-do individuals in the community. The porosity of Nigeria border also compounds the problem.

4. **International Reference Points**: Globally, terror is becoming fashionable among political agitators as a potent means of enforcing their demand. This is because it is cheaper than the conventional wars and the numerical strength of the agitators also support the use of terror as a political weapon. Not only have these terrorist groups enjoyed the attention of national, regional and international organizations, they have commanded respect among some nations of the world. Terrorism is found in most parts of the world and is networked and united in its violent upsurge and consensual goals. There is no doubt that there is increasing emulation of this network by the militant groups in Nigeria and elsewhere in the world. Such network provides a reference point for the militants in the development of terror potentialities in agitation for their political rights.

5. **Mass Amplification of Information**: The media helps in the amplification of deviance transferring the signal of threats transnationally as desired by the militants. Media is the critical communications instrument that modern technology provides for terror groups which willingly or unwillingly serve their specific or general propaganda and psychological warfare needs (Alexander, 1978). It is further observed that terrorists operations require

extensive coverage: television, radio and press for the maximum amount of propagandizing and publicizing to reach their audience by transmitting fear. Everyday militant leaders are seen in the front pages of Nigerian dailies justifying that their grievances are communicated not only to the government and the public but also to the international community. Sometimes, media examinations of all 'sides of the story' provide some justifications for terror acts.

6. **Weakness of the State**: The problems generated by weak and failed states are among the most relevant issues in the world today (Eizenstat et al, 2005). Weak states include a broad range of states that are inherently weak because of geographical, physical or fundamental economic constraints or basically strong, but for the moment weak because of internal antagonisms, bad management, despotism or external conflicts (Rotberg, 2003). Rising ethnic-, religious-, linguistic- and cultural hostilities are common feature of weak state. Nigeria undoubtedly exhibits all the characteristics of a weak state. This is demonstrated in the manner with which the country is handling the militants. All this provides fertile haven for terror potentialities in the Niger Delta region. In the region, government often exchange hands with the hostage takers in order to free hostages. This further encourages hostage taking and the attendant fear that it might spread to other cities like Lagos and Abuja. This demonstrates weak resolve on the part of the government to impose sanction on the militants and address the needs of the region.

7. **Inequality and Inequity**: Relative deprivation also accounts for grievances. As some section of the community feel deprived, they organize into groups for various form of agitation. In Nigeria for instance, there is unequal socio-economic and political development among the geopolitical zones. This accounts for violent agitations by different zones in the country.

All these without doubt, not explained in terms of the etymology of terrorism, significantly contribute to the rising wave of terror potentialities in the region. However, commenting on the increasing trends on a global scale, Jenkins (1978) argues:

> ...the current wave of terrorism is seen as a result, not only of unique political circumstances, but also of recent technological developments-international travels giving terrorists worldwide mobility, improved communication providing them with almost instant access to a worldwide audience, the increasing availability of weapon and explosive; and new vulnerabilities in a society increasingly dependent on fragile technology-or if terrorism is seen as a new set of tactics whose use inspires other groups-then terrorism is likely to continue.

The continuity of terrorism could only be sustained by access to different means utilized. The proliferation of weapons around the world seems to have been out of control. Terrorists have utilized different techniques which include kidnapping, barricade, hostage, bombing, armed assault or ambush, hijacking, skyjacking, rail-derailment, hostage taking, threats, incendiary attack or arson, assassination, chemical, radiological or bacteriological pollutions. Out of all, bombing has been a major tactics of terrorists' techniques. The use of bombs is also featuring in the Niger Delta crisis. Jenkins further observes:

> Bombing probably will remain the most common terrorist tactic. Explosives can be easily purchased, stolen, or manufactured from commercially available materials. Knowledge of at least primitive explosives is widespread. Bombings require little organization; it can easily be a one-man operation.

It is further observed that seizing hostages whether by kidnapping individuals, will also continue to be a popular terrorist tactic. In dealing with hostage incidents, government appears to be increasingly willing to respond with force (Jeckins, 1978). As it will later be shown in the case of Nigeria, hostage taking is becoming rampant in the agitation for political rights.

Foundation of the Political Agitations

Since colonial days, the Niger Delta has played a crucial role in the Nigerian economy. The Niger Delta of Nigeria is among the richest deltas in the world. The Niger Delta is believed to hold at least twenty billion barrels of oil reserves. Nigeria pumps 2 million barrels of oil daily from the Niger Delta. The region has huge oil and gas reserves and ranks as the world's sixth largest exporter of crude oil. Due to prolonged dependence on the natural resources of the region, land resource degradation, renewable resource depletion and oil pollution are now the irreversible consequences. There is extreme poverty arising from total dependence of the rural population on unsustainable agriculture, fishing, forestry and wildlife exploitation, which have depreciated. The nature of the Nigerian federal structure, which not only makes the central government the major distributor of the national revenue but also renders other levels of government subservient and over dependent, does not help the situation. Environmental conservation and economic development in the Niger Delta depend, to a large extent if not solely on the flow of federal funding into the region. This has been considered to be grossly inadequate considering the level of devastation in the region. This has led to the whole question of resource control and the demand for a reversal of the resource allocation formula in favour of the oil producing states. This demand has taken a violent dimension because of the reluctance of the Nigerian state to respond to the demand and the radical approach of some of the agitating groups.

Violent political agitation by the people of the Niger Delta for improved and equitable resources allocation and involvement in the petroleum industry is a most serious threat to the economy and national security. These protests involve loss of human life, damage and seizure of oil installations and hostage-taking. Attempts to suppress them have not restored peace. There is increasing emerging violent trends in the historical dimension of the youth restiveness in the region. Ile and Akukwe (2001) asserts that Nigeria's current political experiment will continue to be hounded by the environmental, health and economic morass of Niger Delta. The Niger Delta issue is a complex web of political betrayal at all levels of government (local, state, and federal), endless economic marginalization and massive environmental insensitivity and neglect. Ile and Akukwe (2001) identify the following critical and foundational issues in the political agitation in the region:

Oil spillage: Spillage kills plants, de-fertilizes the earth, harms animals, fouls farmlands, and destroys aquatic life.

Gas flaring: For the host communities, gas flaring is a cause of acid rains that corrode metal roofing sheets atop houses, increase soil temperatures and visibly damage vegetation near the flares.

Environmental degradation: this is a major plague in the Niger Delta.

Poor health status Apart from other forms of diverse diseases, Oil has also become, to the people of the Niger Delta region a doom that has contributed in no small measure to the AIDS boom in the region (Udonwa, et al 2004). The affluent lives of the oil workers lured the poor young girls into prostitution and other related vices.

Poverty: Oil spillage and other forms of environmental degradation prevent the major economic activities of the area which are farming and fishing. Hence the host communities live in inhuman condition of extreme deprivation.

Pipeline explosions over the years there have been series of explosion which have claimed hundreds of lives and properties.

Limited government/public sector presence: the region is not a fertile land for government amenities as the region is grossly untouched by different developmental process.

Distrust of the government/petrol-business alliance: Nigerian government as always collided with the oil companies in the exploitation of the region and perpetration of the inhuman acts against the host community. There have not been any major public policies that will enhance development in the region.

Lack of basic infrastructure: the region that fill the purse of the government suffer most from lack of basic infrastructural facilities such as road network, schools, health facilities and so on.

From the discussion so far, it can be observed that the terror potentials in the region are as a result of the various problems facing the region. It seems the government has not been responding adequately to the trends in the political agitation. The weak response of the government denotes the lack of knowledge of the potentials and the threats posed by militant groups to the economy and national stability.

Table 11.1: Some Terror Incidents in Recent Years

March 1997	Youths captured a barge delivering goods to a Chevron installation: the crew of seventy Nigerians and twenty expatriates were held hostage for three days.
December 13-17, 1997	13 employees of Western Geophysical were held hostage by youths in a barge off the coast of Ondo State.
On October 14, 1998	Militant seized control of two Chevron flow stations, at Abiteye and Olero Creek, near Escravos on the Atlantic coast, taking some thirty workers hostage for two days.
November, 1999	Odi-South-East, 12 Policemen were held hostages and murdered by the youth.
October 10, 2001	19 sosldiers on a peace mission in the conflict area were abducted and killed by the Tiv militia in Zaki-Biam.
On March 12, 2003	Government forces Vs Ijaw militia (Some soildiers and militants were killed)
On June 5, 2004	The Nigerian military killed 17 bandits in the oil-rich Delta State as part of an effort to combat oil theft, piracy and kidnappings of oil workers.
January, 2006	Four hostages seized.
February, 2006	Nine hostages seized.
April, 2006	Militant claimed responsibility of bomb explosion 2 people died, six others injured.
May, 2006	Five military personnel killed in surprise raid by the militants.
May 2006	Seven hostages: 4 Briton, 2 Canadian, 1 American.
31st May, 2006	Five Koreans were held hostage by joint militant action.
July 13, 2006	4 military personnel including a naval chief killed.
July, 2006	2 explosions rocked pipelines convening crude oil to Nigeria Agip oil, Twon Brass, Bayelsa State.
October 1, 2006	Militants killed 13 soldiers while escorting two oil vessels along the Cowthorn Channel and sank their vessel.
October 3, 2006	Seven expatriate oil workers held hostage from their residence at Essan Akpan estate in Eket.
October 10, 2006	Sixty oil workers taken hostage by militant youth in Balyesa.

Terror Potentialities in Niger Delta Region of Nigeria

Studies (Crenshaw, 1981; Roberts, 2002; Ulfstein, 2003; Walker, 2004) trace the history of terrorism to the revolutionary years. It is now common in most countries in recent time. In Nigeria however, there are certain instances of domestic or intra-state terrorism. The letter-bombing of Dele Giwa, editor-in-chief of *Newswatch* in 1986, the crash of Nigerian Air Force Plane in September, 1992 and other series of assassinations during past military regimes are described as acts of terror. The bomb explosion in Kwara Stadium on May 30th, 1995 and series of bombing during Abacha regime are also suspected acts of Terrorism (Saliu, 1999; Adeoye, 2005). The struggles in the Niger Delta region manifest some potentialities for insurgent terrorism.

Petrol-politics enhances conflict especially in the Niger Delta. This has taken several dimensions and employing some crude violent means in their agitations. Obi (2003) commented that the extreme of wealth and poverty, energy (power) and disempowerment, profit and expropriations, global extractions and local existence which lie in the heart of the production and reproduction of violent dynamics of petrol-politics are responsible for the bunch of violent outburst in the region. Crude marginalization is responsible for the cold and violent agitations in the region. Hence, the Niger Delta is a flashpoint defined by varied degree of violence and aggressive behaviour (Omuku, 2000). The struggle has started long ago and has been carried on from generation to generation despite the maiming and killing of the front liners in the struggle (for instance the murder of 8 Ogoni activists in 1995). Crisis is inevitable due to the undesirable consequences of oil exploration and the incapability of the state to yield to the demands of the oil producing communities to ameliorate their plight. It has also been argued that wherever there are natural resources, there could be crisis. Such confrontation has also been described as resource war (klare, 2001).

Crenshaw (1981) posits the formation of groups whenever grievances exist. In times of struggle against injustice, efflorescence of associations is usually prominent to channel the course of the struggle (Olukoshi, 1996). Such was the situation in Nigeria during military rule for the pursuit of democratic governance. The case of the Niger-Delta has also accounted for the formation of several militant groups which have championed both the cold and violent confrontations. There are more than a hundred groups in the region. Some of the militant groups include: Niger Delta Volunteer Force (NDVF) led by Asari Dokubo; Movement for the Sovereign State of Biafra (MASSOB); the Chicoco Movement formed in August 1997 on a joint rally at Aleibiri; Egbesu Boys of Africa (EBA) formed in 1998 which consists of Ijaw/warri ethnic groups; Ijaw Youth Council (IYC) formed on January 1, 1999; Isoko National Youth Movement (INYM); Itsekiri Nationality Patriots; Movement for the Survival of the Ogoni People (MOSOP) formerly headed by Late Ken Saro-Wiwa ; Movement for the Survival of Ijaw Ethnic Nationality (MOSIEN); Movement for the Emancipation of the Niger Delta (MEND); Movement for

Reparation to Ogbia (Oloibiri) (MORETO); Egi Women's Movement; Niger Delta Vigilante (NDV), led by Ateke Tom; Federated Niger Delta Ijaw communities led by Oboko Bello.

The major demands of the region include clean up of oil spills, reduction of gas flaring, fair compensation for lost land, income, resources, life, equitable allocation from oil revenue and human empowerment.

Table 11.1 shows that series of bombing and hostage taken are the major means of agitation. The table shows some of the cases recorded in recent times. Balogun (2006) observes:

> Kidnap and hostage taking particularly of foreign oil workers, by militants in the oil-rich Niger Delta region of Nigeria is assuming an alarming rate. Before youths militants became daring in 2006, they had limited their exuberance to just disrupting operations of oil-producing companies, blowing up oil pipelines and invading oil fields with the aim of collecting ransom.

There have been terror dimension to the struggle in the Niger Delta. This explains the terror potentials in the region. The militants have vowed that hostage taking would continue until the environmental degradation as a results of oil spillage is curtailed; there is improved social welfare or corporate responsibilities by the oil companies; and improved resource allocation to the region. Balogun further observes a that opinion is divided on that an all-military attack on the militant may result in a civil war that may lead to the balkanization of the country since the militants have access to international arms market.

However, this does aim to brand the militant groups as terrorist networks but to demonstrate their potentialities in such realm and to ignite concern towards curtailing such graduation as most of them are already employing terror tactics in their agitations. This could graduate to what Madunagu (2005) describes as civil society terrorism or what Barkan and Snowden (2001) calls Domestic or insurgent terrorism. The trend may continue as a mainstay of the tactic for political rights in the region as government exchange hands with the militant all the time for the release of the hostages.

Conclusion and Recommendation

The paper submits that political agitation is intense in Nigeria and the agitation is now manifesting some forms of terror potentialities with series of bombing and hostage taking. The trends may continue if the government does not yield to the collective aspiration of the Niger Delta region. Government's response of exchanging hands with the militant group for the release of hostages will further enhance the use of terror acts in political agitation in the region. It should be acknowledged that government has utilized some measures in the past. The Oil Mineral Producing Area Development Commission (OMPADEC) was established in 1993 to address the disaffection of the region. Due to certain setbacks of the commission, which include lack of a master plan that would define its developmental objectives and strategies and inadequate funding (Akpan and Akpabio, 2003), the Niger Delta Development Commission (NDDC) was set up in 1999 to replace OMPADEC. Despite this specialized agency, the problem is taking more violent dimension. The federal government has also been utilizing direct military measures which seem to be aggravating the crisis. The creation of Ministry of Niger-Delta by Yar'dua administration has not yielded the desired results and hostage-taking and kidnapping has increased.

Other measure that is being proposed to address the terror dimension is constitutional engineering. Recently, the legislative arm of the government has received two bills entitled (1) "An Act o Prohibit Terrorism" and (2) "Prevention of terrorism Act". The first bill sponsored by one of the Senators prescribes life imprisonment for those involved in hostage-taking, kidnapping and related activities while the second bill sponsored by the president prescribes a maximum of 20 years jail term for offenders of such terror actions. The bills also recommend the establishment of anti-terrorism agency in the country. These efforts are both responding to the international affairs and local problems. While all these are in the right direction, the major preventive measure is for the government to respond to the aspirations of the region through appropriate developmental policies focused on employment generation, infrastructural development and meaningful representation in government.

References

Adeoye, M. N. (2005). Terrorism: An Appraisal in the Nigerian Context. In Alanamu, A. S. (ed.), *Issues in Political Violence in Nigeria.* Ilorin: Hamson printing Communications.

Akpan, N. S. & Akpabio, E. M. (2003). Youth Restiveness and Violence in the Niger Delta of Nigeria: Implications and Suggested Solutions. *International Journal of Deelopment Issues,* Vol. 2, No. 2, pp. 37-58.

Alexander, Y. (1978). Terrorism, the Media and the Police. *Journal of International Affairs,* Vol. 32, No. 1, pp. 101-114.

Balogun, S. (2006). Hostage Taking to Continue: those Behind Renewed Wave. *National Mirror* Newspaper, June 4.

Barkan, S. & Snowden, L. (2001). *Collective Violence.* Boston: Ally and Bacon.

Beck, U. (2003). The Silence of Words: on Terror and War. *Security Dialogue,* Vol. 34, No. 3, pp. 255-267.

Bussinessday, (2006). Nigerian Loses $12bn to Niger Delta Crisis in 7 Months.

CFR (Council on Foreign Relation), (2005). Terrorism: Question and Answers. Retrieved on January 7, 2006: <http://cfrterrorism.org/terrorism/introduction.html>.

Crenshew, M. (1981) The Causes of Terrorism. *Comparative Politics* Vol. 13, No. 4, pp. 379-399.

Eizenstat, Stuart E., John Edwards Porter & Jeremy M. Weinstein (2005). Rebuilding Weak States. *Foreign Affairs,* Vol. 84, pp. 134-146.

Heng, Y. (2002). Unravelling the 'War' on Terrorism: A Risk Management Exercise in War Clothing? *Security and Dialogue*, Vol. 33, No. 2, pp. 227- 242.

Ibiyemi, S. (2006). NNPC Pipeline Vandalisation Rises by 40%. *Financial Standard* January 30, p. 3.

Ile, C. & Akukwe, C. (2001). Issues, Challenges and Opportunities for Equitable Development. Retrieved from http://nigeriaworld.com/feature/article/niger-delta.html.

Jenkins, B.M. (1978). International Terrorism: Trends and Potentialities. *Journal of International Affairs*, Vol. 32, No. 1, pp. 115-123.

Klare, M. T. (2001). *Resource War: The New Landscape of Global Conflict.* NY: Metropolitan Press.

Madunagu, E. (2005). Aspect of our Own Terrorism. Retrieved on August 5, 2005:<http://www.nigerdeltacongress.com/articles/aspects_of_our_own_terrorism.htm>.

Mooney, L. A., Knox, D. & Schacht, C. (2002). *Understanding Social Problems.* Third Edition. US: Wadworth/Thompson Learning.

Mullen, R.K. (1978). Mass Destruction and Terrorism. *Journal of International Affairs*, Vol. 32, No. 1, pp. 63-89.

Obi, C.I. (2003). The Oil Paradox: Reflection on the Violent Dynamics of Retro-Politics and (Miss) Governance in Nigeria's Niger Delta. Paper Delivered at the Institute of African Studies, University of Seizing Winter school on *Structural Instability and Government in Sub-saharan Africa. Perspectives to Conflict and Conflict Prevention,* November 1-3.

Olukoshi, B. (1996). Associational Life. In Diamond, L., kirk-Greene, A and Oyediran, O. (eds.) (1996), *Transition without End.* Ibadan: Vantage Publishers.

Omuku, P. (2000). The Crisis in the Oil Producing Commontier: A Representative Perspective of oil Corporation. In Ayodele W.R. & Akinwola, E. (eds.), Boiling point: A CDHR Publication on the Crisis in the Oil Producing Committees in Nigeria Lagos: Committees for the Defence of Human Rights, pp. 197-205.

Roberts, A. (2002). The Changing Faces of Terrorism. Retrieved on January 7, 2006:<http://www.bbc.co.uk/history/war/sept_11/changing_faces_01.shtml>.

Rotberg, R. I. (2003). Failed States, Collapsed States, Weak States: Causes and Indicators. In Rotberg, R. I. (ed.), *State Failure and State Weakness in a Time of Terror*. Washington D.C.: Brookings Institution, 2003.

Rotberg, R.I. (2002). Failed States in a World of Terror. *Foreign Affairs*, Vol. 81, No. 4, pp. 127–140.

Saliu, H. A. (1999). Nigeria, UN and Contemporary Realities Under Abacha. In Saliu, H. A. (ed.), *Selected Themes in Nigerian Foreign Policy and International Relation*. Ilorin: Sally and Associates.

Shultz, R. (1978). Conceptualising Political Terrorism: A Typology. *Journal of International Affairs*, Vol. 32, No. 1, pp. 7- 15.

Udonwa N.E., Ekpo M., Ekanem I.A., Inem V.A., & Etokidem A. (2004). Oil Doom and AIDS Boom in the Niger Delta Region of Nigeria. *Rural Remote Health*, Vol. 4, No. 2, pp. 273-289.

Ulfstein, G. (2003). Terrorism and the Use of Force. *Security and Dialogue*, Vol. 34, No. 2, pp. 153-167.

Walker, M. (2004.) A Brief History of Terrorism. Retrieved on February 25, 2004: <http://www.eurunion.org/magazine/0110/p26.htm.>.

12

Yet Unanswered! The Youth and Gender Questions in a Decade of Democratic Governance in Nigeria

Freedom C. Onuoha

Introduction

The end of the Cold War provided the much needed momentum for the third wave of democratization that swept across most countries in Asia, Africa and Latin America in the 1990's. The wave which surged across the African continent, caught-up with Nigeria on 29 May 1999, following the inauguration of the civilian administration of President Olusegun Obasanjo. The transition ended sixteen years of authoritarian rule under various military Heads of States that have variously organized "transition [to civilian rule] without end" (Diamond et al., 1997). Nigeria's return to democracy in 1999 rekindled new hopes and expectations among the populace about the possibility of the new political arrangement providing the institutional context for the resolution of many and varied challenges that have stunted the process of national development. Such challenges include (but are not limited to it) endemic corruption, widespread incidences of violent crimes, the lingering crisis in the Niger Delta, high rate of poverty and unemployment, gender inequality, infrastructural decay, ethno-religious crisis, and the high prevalence of diseases such as Malaria and HIV/AIDS.

Without doubt, the attainment of a decade of uninterrupted democratic politics in Nigeria is unprecedented in the annals of the country's political history, and it is worth celebrating. However, after about ten years of democratic rule, which has witnessed three civilian-to-civilian administrations, the challenges that confronted the country during the height of military rule are as worrisome as they were before the advent of democracy in 1999 as they are today. This has generated debates on whether Nigeria is truly practising democracy or just a civilian rule. One of such engaging challenges is the issue of youth and gender questions in Nigeria. A concern many view as constituting one of the many paradoxes of democratic politics, not only in Nigeria but also in other countries of the world. This entails a situation where the demographic majority (youth and women) constitutes both the least represented politically and the worst marginalised socially, economically and materially. The marginalization of women and youth in politics and governance is not unique to Nigeria. However, it is widely believed that democracy, which is predicated on the principle of majority rule, offers a window of opportunity for the marginalised groups to participate in shaping policies and decisions that affect their lives (Walby, 2008). Embedded in this understanding is the conviction that democratic governance should aim at providing equal opportunities and improving the socio-economic conditions of the people irrespective of ethnicity, religion, age or gender.

The subsisting argument is that there can be no democracy if women are not full political participants both in the process and institutions of governance (Azuike, 2005). Similarly, it is argued that youth participation and incorporation into decision-making processes is critical to building a sustainable democracy in Nigeria. The understanding therefore is that the issue of women and youth marginalization in institutions of political governance and decision-making structures of the state constitutes a critical challenge to democratic inclusiveness in Nigeria.

Therefore, a decade of democratic rule in Nigeria provides a background to and the context for assessing the extent to which the issue of youth and gender questions has been tackled in the last few years of civilian rule in Nigeria. It is in the light of the foregoing that this chapter addresses the following questions. How do we understand or frame the youth and gender questions in the context of Nigeria? Has the decade of democratic rule in Nigeria substantially expanded opportunities for youth and women to participate in governance and development in Nigeria? What factors could be advanced to explain the seeming disconnect between youth and women demographic strength and their marginal participation/representation in democratic governance in Nigeria? And what measures could be adopted to enhance youth and women participation in governance and development in Nigeria? These and other related questions are what this chapter seeks to address.

Conceptual Discourse

Given the tendency, especially in the field of social sciences, for concepts to elicit varying interpretations, matters of conceptual clarification are apposite not peripheral in a discourse like this. Accordingly, the concepts of 'youth' and 'gender' are central to this chapter and as such deserve a clarification of their meanings as used here.

Youth

The term 'youth' has been a subject of intense polemics in academic writing. At least four major definitional interpretations of the term are identifiable in extant literature, namely: youth as an age category; as transitional stage between childhood and adulthood; a social construct; and as a 'social shifter'. Without prejudice to other definitions by member states, the United Nations defines 'youth' as those persons between the ages of 15 and 24 years. Social constructionists like Manni and Truzzi (1982) see youth as 'mere social creation', explaining that the way society organizes its labour, values and symbol influences how the youth is defined (qtd. in Bomoi, 2007). For transitionists, youth refers to a period of life between childhood or adolescent and adulthood (see for instance Kenniston, 1972; Manning, 1973). Yet, others view the youth from the perspective of a social shifter – a relational term incorporating identity, time and space (Balle, 2007; Soares, 2000). However, scholars like Richter and Panday (2007: 293) has questioned these classifications, insisting that "young people are not fixed category, neither historically, politically, culturally, socially and personally".

Essentially for policy purposes, most African countries adopt the age-category definition. For instance, Kenya and Malawi define youth as 15-39 years of age; Sierra Leone, Ghana, Madagascar and Senegal as 15-35, and South Africa 14-35 years (Richter and Panday 2007: 294). In Nigeria, the youth are defined as "all young persons of ages 18-35 who are citizen of the Federal Republic of Nigeria" (*National Youth Policy*, 2001:3).

Though varied in their interpretations, these definitions are useful in that they call for caution in dealing with youth matters and the necessity to put in place effective policy and programmes to mobilize, empower and channel the energies of youths to positive end in society (Bomoi, 2007). This is crucial given that the youth is the critical bridge that connects the incoming (younger) generation with the outgoing (older) generation in every society. Therefore, the way and manner the youth is treated in any society has grave consequences for the three generations, that is, the young, youth and old. This underlies why most advanced countries implement policies and programmes consciously targeted at empowering and developing the youth. Given that our paper focuses on Nigeria, we shall adopt the definition of youth as offered by the National Youth Policy (2001), Nigerians who are between the ages of 18 and 35 years.

Gender

Like the concept of youth, the term *gender* has been subjected to varying interpretations. In fact, there are as many definitions of gender as there are people, scholars, analysts and institutions grappling with the subject. According to the United Nations Development Programme (UNDP), the term gender denotes:

> The qualities associated with men and women that are socially and culturally, than biologically determined. Gender includes the way in which society differentiates appropriate behaviour and access to power for women and men. Although the details vary from society to society and change over time, gender relations tend to include a strong element of inequality between women and men and are strongly influenced by ideology (UNDP, 1986: 258).

Amali (2003: 385) defines gender as socially constructed and culturally variable roles that men and women play in their homes. It is a structural relation of inequality between men and women, manifested in labour markets, in political structures as well as in the household. It is reinforced by customs, law and specific development policies. In other words, gender is a "social construct that establishes and differentiates statutes and roles between men and women particularly in the way they contribute to, participate in, and are rewarded by the economy and the prevailing social systems" (National Population Commission, 2001: 3). Gender concerns involve women as well as men. Hence, understanding gender means understanding opportunities, expectations, responsibilities and constraints as they affect both men and women in any given society.

More often, people confuse sex with gender. While sex differences are biologically determined, gender differences, which refer to ideals, rights, traits, and expectations on the basis of masculinity and femininity, are socially and culturally constructed. Nevertheless, it is important to point out that though the two concepts (sex and gender) mean different things, an understanding of one enhances the comprehension of the other. Logically therefore, our understanding of the binary biological division of humans into male and female, as determined by their sex, is the irreducible minimum in understanding the social and cultural construction of roles in a society (defined in terms of gender) which derives essentially from the biological division of human beings. Although it is important to make a distinction between *sex* and *gender*, it is equally important to understand that the former lays the foundation for the latter, since it provides the main criterion for the assignment of roles in a society through role socialization. Gender role socialization is instrumental in encouraging or discouraging males and females from undertaking certain activities or acquiring certain attributes or skills. Gender roles are therefore "prescribed expectations and obligations, responsibilities and behaviours, of the masculine and feminine genders" (Ezumah, 2003:82). Thus, in identifying gender, there are socio-economic attributions and roles, which characterize the status and life performance of women/girls as a distinct social category from men/boys. A unique feature of the gender system in any society is that it is characterised by inequality. This is usually expressed in terms of asymmetry in the access to societal resources, structures and values.

It is important to note that discourses on gender in Nigeria usually slide into an analysis of the disadvantaged position of Nigerian women as they struggle to realize their full potentials in the society. The reason for greater focus on women rather than men is primarily because of the patriarchal nature of the Nigerian society. By patriarchy, we mean a "universal, trans-historical power system whereby men as a *sex-class* dominate women as a *sex class*" (Lawson and Heaton, 1999: 195). It should not be surprising therefore that the gender question in this article would focus on the Nigerian women given that they are the marginalised gender.

Framework of Analysis

The argument of this paper is anchored on the Marxian political economy. The original theoretical formulation is traceable to the works of Karl Mark (see Stenning, 1926), however this paper adopts and adapts its simplified version by Ake (1981) which uses dialectical materialism as its methodological approach. Its fundamentally theoretical postulates thus:

> Once we understand what the material assets and constraints of a society are, how the society produces goods to meet its material needs, how the goods are distributed, and what types of social [including gender] relations arise from the organisation of production, we have come a long way to understanding the culture of that society, its laws, its religious system, its political system and even its modes of thought (Ake, 1981: 1).

The theory of dialectical materialism is anchored on four methodological assumptions. First, is that it gives *primacy to material conditions*, particularly economic factors, in the explanation of social life. Hence, it advocates for particular attention to be paid to the economic substructure of society, and indeed use it as the point of departure for studying other aspects of society. Second, it emphasizes the *dynamic character of reality*. This requires that the analyst views society as something which is full of movement and dynamism, being provided by the contradictions which pervade existence. Third, it focuses on the *relatedness of different elements of society*, especially economic structure, social structure, political structure, and the belief system. According to this theory, it is the economic factor which is the most decisive of all the elements of society and which largely determine the character of the others. That is not to say that the economic structure is autonomous and strictly determines the others. All the social structures are interdependent and interact in complex ways. Each one of them affects the character of every other and is in turn affected by it. Fourth, by adopting a developmental perspective, it treats problems concretely rather than abstractly. By putting social phenomenon in the context of their development, this theory enables an analyst to understand not only how social phenomenon come to be what they are, but also to make reasonable conjecture as to what they might become (Ake, 1981: 1-8).

In the context of the youth and gender questions in Nigeria, a proper understanding and application of this framework would lead the analyst to arrive at the following conclusions. First, those from the economically privileged groups (men) tend to be better educated, to have higher social status and to be more 'successful' professionally and politically. This suggests that economic inequality tends to reproduce itself endlessly in a series of other inequalities evident in the society. Second, those who are economically privileged (men) tend to be interested in preserving the existing social order. And those who are disadvantaged (women and the youth) by the social order, particularly its distribution of wealth (including power and other valuable resources), have a strong interest in changing the social order. In this sense, the economic structure sets the general trend of political interests and political alignments. Third, in so far as there is wide economic inequality in a society, such society cannot have political democracy because political power will tend to polarise around economic power, further creating room for exclusion of certain groups (like women and youth). And finally, the moral and societal values tend to support the preservation of the existing division of labour and the distribution of resources in that society.

From the foregoing, it is evident that this theory is analytically fecund to capture, if not explain, the complex contradictions that shape and define the youth and gender questions in Nigeria. Its fundamental assumption that a focus on the economic substructure is crucial for understanding other superstructures (politics, ideology and religion) of a society is quite apt, much as its postulation that political structure in turn affects the economic substructure is logical. Given the patriarchal nature of the Nigerian state, the theory suggests that the poor socio-economic conditions of women and youth account for their low representation in governance and politics in the country. Similarly, political power in Nigeria shapes the contours of social and economic development of the country. Consequently, women's and youth have restricted access to political and decision-making structures have repercussions for their access to other vital resources of society.

What is suggested therefore is that if politics were to be a game of numbers in Nigeria, women and youth would occupy a percentage of the political and decision-making positions commensurate with their demographic strength. However, the reality on ground shows that those (especially men) who control greater share of the economic resources of the state also control the politics. Therefore, those who control state power in Nigeria use it to divert all kinds of resources, including state funds (Ofong, 2002: 4). Although women have contributed significantly to economic productivity in the country, which are largely unaccounted or unpaid for in macro-economic calculations, they lack access to state resources and handicapped financially to engage in Nigerian brand of politics. The utility of this framework would become clearer as the discussion in this chapter unfolds.

Understanding and Contextualizing the Youth and Gender Questions in Nigeria

One useful way of appreciating the youth and gender questions in Nigeria is by understanding the paradoxical situation of women and youth in Nigeria. Indeed, Nigeria is a country caught in-between affluence and affliction. It is this contradiction that sets the context for what is commonly referred to in academic and political parlance in Nigeria as the *national question.* The core of the national question consists of political mobilization and struggles by dissatisfied and aggrieved groups to redress and exact more just and equitable accommodation in the Nigerian polity (Onimode, 2001). Thus, the youth and gender questions are integral part of the national question. Overall, the country has the potential to build a prosperous economy. With a population of over 140 million, Nigeria is not only Africa's most populous country but also one of the four largest economies in Africa, accounting for at least 41 per cent of West Africa's gross domestic product. It is the 6th largest oil-producer and has the 6th largest deposit of natural gas in the world. Coupled with the possession of over 100 tertiary institutions, producing more than 200,000 graduates per annum, the country is endowed with abundant natural resources and human capital critical for national development (Onuoha, 2008a).

Without doubt, Nigeria's huge population is one of its critical assets. Nigeria accounts for 47 per cent of West Africa's population, and in global terms, her population constitutes 2 per cent of the world population and the country is expected to be among the six most populated countries in the world by 2025 (APRM, 2008: 141). The provisional figures of the 2006 census put the population of Nigeria at 140,003,542 million. Of this figure, 71,709,859 million are men, representing about 51.22 per cent of the total. Women constitute 48.78 per cent of the population, numbering 68,293,683 million in actual figures.

In terms of the youth population, Nigeria is among the African countries experiencing youth bulge – that is rapid growth of large youthful population. It is estimated that Nigeria's youthful population is close to 70 to 80 million, about 55 to 60 per cent of the entire population. In addition to the youth population, 32.4 per cent of the total population is children below the age of 18 years. If these two groups are taken together, the population of Nigerians below the age of 35 comprises more than half of the population. In absolute numbers therefore there are more young people in Nigeria than ever before (Giwa, 2008; Youth Position Paper, 2007: 4).

Both women and the youth play key role in the Nigerian economy. The agricultural sector provides employment for a large proportion of Nigerians, and women accounts for about 70 per cent of agricultural labour, 50 per cent of animal husbandry related activities and 60 per cent of food processing activities (Pogoson, 2008: 13). They play a major role in the production, processing and marketing of food crops. However, they account for only 8 per cent of the labour force in the formal sector, occupying the lower cadre positions. Their access to agricultural inputs is only 10 per cent, with less than 5 per cent access to institutional credit. Although women contribute significantly to economic productivity in Nigeria, especially in the informal sectors of the economy, studies (Federal Ministry of Women Affairs, 2006: 73; IFAD, 2006: 2) have shown that they remain largely marginalised in terms of reward. It has been noted that female farmers had less access to farmland and credit. They also have lower social status than men and consequently less access to schooling and training. Women were found to be responsible for the sale of most farm produce but the control of proceeds from the sales was by men.

While it is easy to access data detailing the contributions of women to the various sectors of the Nigerian economy, there is a dearth of statistics quantifying the contributions of youth to the Nigerian economy. Undoubtedly, the youth accounts for much of the driving force in the financial sector, especially if we are to take the banking sector as the basis for our generalization. However, they still remain a segment of the Nigerian population that has been marginalised and disempowered. Unemployment, poverty and diseases (such as HIV/AIDS) have taken a greater chunk of the potential contributions and resourcefulness of the Nigerian youth.

Poverty and unemployment are pervasive in Nigeria, with disproportionate impact on women and the youth. Youth Unemployment and poverty in Nigeria have continued to worsen since the 1980's. Recently, the Minster of Youth Development, Mr Akinlabi Olasukanmi, lamented that "more than 80 per cent of Nigerian youths have no source of livelihood (employment) and 10 per cent are underemployed" (qtd. in *Leadership*, 2008). The remaining 10 per cent in employment are burdened and depressed with near total dependence of relative and family members. Youth unemployment in Nigeria which previously was limited to school-leavers has progressed steadily to catch up with graduates of tertiary institutions. Statistics released by the National Bureau of Statistics shows that just 10 per cent of graduates released annually by Nigerian universities and other tertiary institutions are able to secure paid employment. Worst still, those that are employed are underpaid. For instance, a graduate is paid a paltry sum of ₦14, 000 naira (approximately US $120) as monthly salary in some states of the federation (Nasir, 2008; APRM, 2008).

Consequent upon lack of any gainful employment, majority of the Nigerian youth are trapped in endemic poverty, running through generational lines. Overall poverty prevalence in Nigeria increased from 27.2 per cent in 1980 to 42.7 per cent in 1992. By 2004, the poverty level increased to 54.4 per cent (National Bureau of Statistics, 2006). It is currently estimated that over 70 per cent of the population are poor, with 35 per cent living in absolute poverty. The burden of poverty has fallen largely on women and the youth (Onuoha, 2008b: 1903). The United Nations (2007: 86) in its *World Youth Report*, observed that "over 90 per cent of the young people in Nigeria and Zambia live on less than US$ 2 per day". The deplorable situation of the Nigerian youth has made them very vulnerable to contacting diseases such as HIV/AIDS. Since the 1990's, HIV/AIDs prevalence rate in Nigeria has been a subject of public concern. For instance, its prevalence rate jumped from 1.8 per cent in 1991 to 3.8 per cent in 1993. It was 4.5 per cent in 1995/6 before increasing to 5.4 per cent in 1999. The prevalence rate peaked at 5.8 per cent in 2001, before declining to 5 per cent in 2003 and 4.4 per cent in 2005 (Federal Ministry of Health, 2005:29). The 2005 sentinel survey indicates that the youth, especially those between the ages of 15 – 34 are the worst hit by the scourge of HIV/AIDS. The statistics shows that young people between the ages of 15 – 19 had 3.6 per cent prevalence rate; 20 – 24 years had 4.7 per cent, while 4.9 per cent was for those between 25 – 29 years (Federal Ministry of Health, 2005: 24). Regrettably, the former Director-General of the National Agency for the Control of Aids (NACA), Prof. Babatunde Osotimehin has revealed that 61 per cent of Nigerians newly infected with HIV/AIDS were women, especially young girls (Sam, 2008).

One can therefore posit that the youth and gender *questions* in Nigeria generically capture the contradiction between demographic strength, economic rewards and political representation, and how the ramifications of this contradiction impinges on the dynamics of sustainable democratic governance and development in Nigeria. The youth and gender questions in Nigeria are simply twofold: first, why is it that those who constitute the numerical majority, who equally contribute significantly in economic productivity but rewarded only marginally, are underrepresented in decision-making and governance structures in Nigeria? And why is it that those whose energy and resourcefulness should serve as the locomotive for national development has been disempowered by the country's political leadership in the way they exercise authority and power and manage resources are exercised in the country? These contradictions are basic challenges that the return to democracy is expected to address.

The Youth and Women in Democratic Politics in Nigeria: How Far after a Decade?

Undoubtedly, women and the youth remains a segment of the population that have been disadvantaged for so long in Nigeria. However, the return to democracy in Nigeria in 1999 rekindled hopes on the prospects of greater women and youth participation in the process of governance, politics and national development. Suffice it to say at this juncture that it is beyond the scope of this chapter to provide details of the history and contributions of

Table 12.1: Comparison of Representation of Women in Elected Positions in Nigeria from 1999 - 2007

S/N	*Position*	*No of Available Seats*	*No of Women in 1999*	*No of Women in 2003*	*No of Women in 2007*
1.	Presidency	1	0	0	0
2.	Senate	109	3	4	9
3.	House of Reps	360	13	23	27
4.	Governorship	36	0	0	0
5.	Deputy Governorship	36	1	2	6
6.	36 States Houses of Assembly	990	12	38	54
Total		**1531**	**27**	**67**	**96**

Source: United Nations Fund for Women (UNIFEM), Gender and Election Unit, Abuja.

women and youth to democratic governance and national development in Nigeria since the independence. Their roles, no matter how insignificant, have been appreciated in other studies (see for instance Adereti, 2008, Karunwi, 2003; Awe, 1992). The chapter is concerned with how a decade of democratic rule (1999-2009) in Nigeria has addressed the marginalization of women and the youth in the development process, especially in democratic governance.

Nigeria has articulated and even signed various laws, policy frameworks, conventions, and protocols that seek to guarantee the rights and participation of women and youth in political and decision-making structures. These include, but are not limited to, Section 40 of the 1999 Constitution, Convention on the Elimination of all forms of Discrimination against Women (CEDAW) 1987, the African Union's Protocol on the Rights of Women 2003, the National Policy on Women 2000, and the National Gender Policy 2006. Yet the plethoras of legislative provisions and conventions have not translated into concrete empowerment for the youth and women to effectively participate in governance and politics in Nigeria.

After prolong years of military rule, Nigeria has had three elected democratic government from 1999 to 2008 and hopefully, the fourth one in 2011. However, a thorough analysis of the Nigerian landscape in the last few years would undoubtedly reveal that a decade of democratic rule has not substantially expanded the space for women and youth to insert and assert themselves meaningfully in governance and development. At best, a decade of democracy has only symbolically broadened the scope of women's representation in politics at the three levels of government (local, state and federal). Despite constituting almost half of the population in Nigeria, in addition to a constitutional guarantee for gender equality, women constitute less than 5% of those in political and governance institutions in the country. Figures in table 1 below, for instance, still show gross under-representation of women in elective offices in spite of ten years of democratic politics in Nigeria.

Observably, there were only 3 women Senators out of 109 (a meagre 2.8 per cent) in 1999. Their number increased to 4 and 9 in 2003 and 2007 respectively, representing only 3.9 per cent for 2003 figures and 7.3 per cent for 2007. Similarly, there were 13 female members of the House of Representatives out of 360, representing only 3.6 per cent during the inauguration of President Obasanjo's administration in 29 May 1999. In 2007, it increased to 27 female members, compared to 23 in 2003.

In 1999, there were only 12 female members out of the 990 members of the 36 State Houses of Assembly, representing a negligible 1.2 per cent. In 2003, the number of women in the 36 State Houses of Assembly increased to 38, representing 3.9 per cent of the total. Also, there was an increase in the number of women in the 36 State Houses of Assembly, from 38 in 2003 to 54 in 2007. It is important to note that Nigeria is yet to witness the first-ever female Governor or President even though some female governorship and presidential candidates have contested in the past general elections.

Nonetheless, history was made on 5 June 2007, when Mrs. Patricia Olubunmi Etteh, a three-time member of the House of Representatives, was elected Nigeria's first female Speaker of the House of Representatives. Her emergence as the country's number four citizen represents a symbolic elevation of women's political representation in key elective offices in Nigeria. However, her speakership was short-lived, having been forced to resign on 30 October 2007 on account of corruption scandal involving ₦628 million (naira) spent on the renovation of the Speaker's (Etteh) and Deputy Speaker's official residence. Part of the money was also used to purchase plush cars and a body massaging machine for the Speaker. For certain, the emergence of Mrs. Patricia Etteh was a thing of jubilation for the womenfolk in Nigeria. However, the circumstances surrounding her rise and fall may well corroborate the argument of some scholars that the political inclusion of women as elected representatives by itself is not a sufficient condition for reducing corruption and engendering accountability in managing public resources (see for instance, Vijayalakshmi, 2008; Swamy et al., 2001).

Under President Obasanjo's tenure (1999-2007), Nigeria made notable progress in terms of political appointment of women in key public offices. In relation to appointment of women as Ministers and Special advisers, the percentage representation increased from 20.5 per cent in 1999 to 27.3 per cent in 2003. Among the numerous outstanding federal appointments of women to

Fig. 12.2: Percentage Increase in Women's Representation in Nigeria since 1999

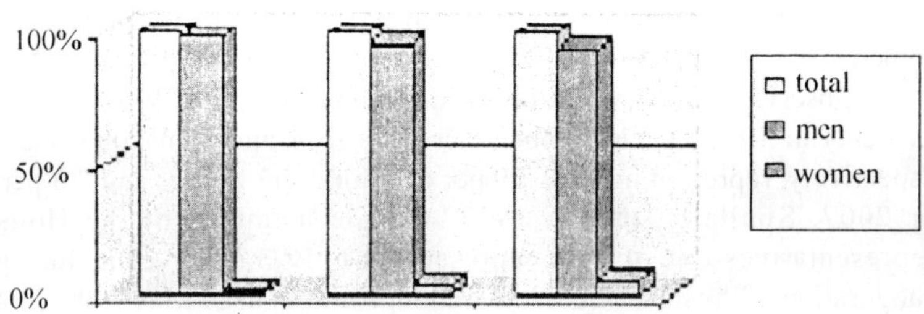

	1999	2003	2007
total	100%	100%	100%
men	98%	96%	94%
women	2%	4%	6%

Source: United Nations Fund for Women (UNIFEM), Gender and Election Unit, Abuja, 2008

high-profile positions was the appointment of Honourable Justice Aloma M. Muktar who became the first woman in Nigeria's judicial history to be appointed to the Supreme Court of Nigeria. Others include, among others, Mrs. Nenadi Esther Usman (Minister of state for Finance), Mrs. Oby Ezekwesili (Minister for Solid Minerals), Ms. Ifueko Omoigui (Director General, Federal Inland Revenue Service), and Professor Joy Ugwu (Minister for Foreign Affairs). The administration of President Umaru Musa Yar'Adua's has also appointed few women into ministerial and advisory positions.

Although there are indications of marginal increase in the number of women in public offices in all branches of government in the federal and state levels, however with only about 6 per cent of women holding elective offices in the federal legislature, Nigeria has one of the lowest rates of female representation in Parliament on the continent (APRM, 2008: 68). Statistical evidence from figure 1 shows that there is still huge gender gap between women and men representation in political leadership as in other important aspects of public life.

The past three General Elections have allowed for a steady increase of only 2 per cent in the numbers of women occupying key elective positions in a decade of democratic governance in Nigeria. These increases, no matter how marginal, attest to the fact that women are determined to overcome entrenched gender barriers in order to participate and contribute to democratic governance in Nigeria.

The experiences of the youth are not different from those of women. In fact, if there is anything that binds the Nigerian youth and women together, it is the burden of domination and marginalization sustained by *gerontocratic* patriarchal structures in Nigeria. As Richter and Panday (2007: 299) have noted: "the voices of young people in Africa [including in Nigeria] have not been silent in efforts to bring about social and political change, often at high costs to themselves through death, disability, and lost education and livelihood opportunities". Yet mechanisms and resources to involve the youth in meaningful ways in democratic decision-making processes remains a challenge.

Although young people below the age of 35 constitute more than half of Nigeria's population, this social category finds it very difficult to participate meaningfully in policy and decision-making as well as in nation building. This has made them passive recipients of socio-economic and political policies rather than stakeholders with interests and roles in the process of governance at all levels of society. Despite that the demographic structure of Nigeria is skewed in favour of young people, there exist a seeming disconnect between their demographic strength and political representation as it relates to strategic national political institutions in Nigeria. As shown in table 12.3 below, Nigeria's key political institutions provide little or no opportunity for effective youth representation or participation, thereby making it difficult for them to contribute maximally to development process and democratic governance.

Table 12.3: Constitutional Age Qualifications for Voting and being Voted-for in Key Political Positions in Nigeria

S/No.	*Political Positions*	*No. of Available Positions*	*Constitutional Age Qualification for Voting*	*Constitutional Age Qualification to be Voted-For*
1.	President	1	18	40
2.	Vice President	1	18	40
3.	Governor	36	18	35
4.	Deputy Governor	36	18	35
5.	Senate	109	18	35
6.	Nat. House of Representative	360	18	30
7.	State House of Assembly	990	18	30

Source: Onuoha (2008:18).

Although youth participation and incorporation into decision-making processes is a key step to engaging them as active members and citizens of their local environment, and thus towards strengthening of democracy (Merkle, 2003: 205), regrettably most existing political structures such as party youth wings do not actually function as entry points for youths to party leadership and elective positions. Ample evidence during the last three general elections in Nigeria shows that the so-called youth wings of political parties serve more as reservoirs of political thugs than institutional leverages for political empowerment of youths. Going by this reality, the participation of the Nigerian youths are limited to voting, but not to be voted for during elections or serving as political thugs during elections and electioneering campaigns.

More so, as rightly noted by Garvin (2008), almost all the 'Ministries of Youth' across Africa are at best a marginal and marginalizing institution. Over the years, the Ministry for Youth Development in Nigeria has equally proven to be ill-equipped to function as sustainable mechanisms for accommodating and responding to the size and potential strength of youth political activism. This partly contributes to the absence of constructive youth participation in Nigeria's democratic politics.

Hence, provisionally and even structurally, the nature and character of Nigerian politics marginalizes the youth and women, and only engages them when politically expedient. Therefore, the challenge for genuine democratic inclusiveness is the pivot on which the youth and gender questions revolve in Nigeria, and it is evident from the above that a decade of democratic rule has not enlarged the political space for women and the youth to meaningfully engage with the political process.

Some Obstacles to Women and Youth Participation in Governance in Nigeria

It has been noted the youth and women are deprived and marginalised in different ways in Nigeria. Their marginalization in the processes of national development, including democratic governance does not suggest that they do not participate at all in the overall process. However, their exclusion in democratic politics and governance is multidimensional and derives from the interplay of some political, economic, socio-cultural, and institutional factors. This section briefly highlights these factors from the point of view of there interrelatedness.

In fact, any discourse on the marginalization of women and the youth in democratic governance and politics in Nigeria must necessary begin with the specific feature of Nigerian politics. Nigerian politics has been variously charactersised. However, the specific features of Nigerian politics which have greatly undermined women participation is the increasing *monetisation* of political contest and the resort to *violence* involving the use of specialist of violence (thugs, cults, and militias) of which the youth are paradoxically the vanguard and the main victim. Indeed, the use of money and violence in

Nigerian politics is mutually reinforcing, and greatly disempowers women and the youth in the political terrain.

There is no doubt that over the years the stakes of partisan politics in Nigeria have become higher and the battles tougher for women. This is basically because of the huge amount of money needed to make any meaningful inroad into the political (elective and appointive) sphere in Nigeria. The highly corrupt and monetized nature of electoral process from the party formation, party primaries, intra-party and general public campaigns to the election proper, all put women and the youth at a greater disadvantage than the men. The high cost of electoral finance in Nigeria goes beyond registration fees. A lot of money is required for a vibrant electioneering campaign and mobilization. Much more is even needed for security purposes in the course of the campaign given the violent brand of Nigerian politics (Omotola, 2008: 218). Such amount of money is usually not readily available to female candidates due to their marginalisation in economic undertakings, resulting in the *feminisation* of poverty in Nigeria (Eboiyehi, Bankole, and Eromonsele, 2006).

The situation is compounded by the emergence of powerful political godfathers who are not averse to sponsoring youth or women candidates owing to the fear of losing in an election. As aptly captured by *Human Right Watch* (2007), these godfathers are not mere financiers of political campaigns. Rather they are individuals whose power derives not just from wealth but from their ability to use violence and corruption to manipulate national, state or local political systems in support of the politicians they sponsor. The excessive monetisation of Nigerian politics has meant that politics is a serious commercial enterprise in the country, requiring huge initial capital. And it is only those who have access to state resources that can provide the enormous fund required. Hence, the godfathers who finance or invest heavily in this enterprise want their candidates to win at all cost in order to make returns. Only those (usually men) who are ready to win at all cost get party tickets at all cost too. Herein lies not only the real challenge for women and youths, but also the mutually reinforcing connection between *monetisation* and *violence* as key defining features of contemporary Nigerian politics.

Logically therefore, political contest in the last few years of democratic politics in Nigeria is dialectically linked to the process of primitive accumulation which is reminiscent of colonial politics in Nigeria. As Ake (2003:3) rightly noted:

> In struggling to advance their interests,...politics was thus reduced to the crude mechanics of opposing forces driven by the calculus of power. For everyone in this political arena, security lay in the accumulation of power. The result was an unprecedented drive for power; power was made the top priority in all circumstances and sought by all means. As the rulers and subordinates extend their rights to their powers, the idea of lawful political competition became impossible.

This violent brand of politics seldom accommodates the participation of women. It is therefore not surprising that prior to the last general election, former President Olusegun Obasanjo admonished his fellow Peoples Democratic Party (PDP) members to view "the 2007 General election in Nigeria as a do-or-die affairs" (see Adebayo, 2007). Hence, given that *godmothers* in the mould of *godfathers* are yet to emerge in Nigerian politics, women and youths tend to be marginalised and manipulated in the process of political contests since they can neither provide the amount of money needed nor suite the violent brand of Nigerian politics. Therefore, what the godfathers do is to co-opt and compensate women with few appointive positions in Nigeria. This serves the ideological purpose of legitimising the government in power as being 'gender sensitive', while masking the real unresolved gender question: that is the extent to which the marginal numerical increase in political representation of women creates the condition for improved autonomy and capacity of women to act as agents of positive social transformation for the advancement of women's interest in particular and national development in general.

Another factor that helps to explain gender inequality in governance and politics in Nigeria is the problem of unfounded societal prejudices which tend to marginalize women and youth. In relation to women, two interrelated prejudices prevalent in Nigeria and worthy of attention are (i) the idea of politics as a 'dirty' game, and (ii) a female politician as a 'prostitute'. These prejudices derive partly from the violent nature of Nigerian politics, including its predominant nocturnal underpinnings. Given this situation, women who venture into politics are usually derided as dirty, or at best prostitutes by the society. This pejorative interpretation has been acknowledged by an Oyo State-based female politician, Mrs Mosunmola Adeniran, when she asserted:

"We face lots of challenges; our men won't allow us to spread our wings and we really want to fly.... if you are a married woman, the marital problem is there where they tag you a prostitute. People believe that any woman in politics is a prostitute, but it is not so. They give us bad names and there is the financial constraint." (qtd. in Ligali, 2008: 19)

As a result of these misconceptions, some women of proven integrity who could contribute positively to national development in general and women empowerment in particular have deliberately avoided Nigerian politics in order to save their 'reputation' or 'homes'.

Beyond the womenfolk, certain entrenched cultural values have equally consigned youths to the margins of politics and governance in Nigeria. Young women are particularly disadvantaged amongst the youth, as they grow up in a traditional and patriarchal society. Many African cultures place an extremely high premium on respect for elders. Young people are expected to know their place and to abide by the wisdom of the elders – believed to be rich in life experience. Yet, if youth are trapped – indefinitely – in some sort of preparatory state, awaiting the time when they are accorded the respect, position and responsibility associated with being full-fledged adults (Gavin, 2008: 26), their society forecloses the opportunity for youth to gradually master the democratic rudiments as well as participate effectively in decision-making that affects their lives. This has made it impossible for the Nigerian youths to contribute positively to national development, including in the deepening and consolidation of democracy (Onuoha, 2008: 18).

In Nigeria, the youth are rhetorically, if not blasphemously prided as the 'leaders of tomorrow'. Hence, "entrenched cultural norms that value the political leadership of elders in the community and in politics reinforce this expectation of young people as future societal resources rather than as both current and future participants" (Okpanachi, 2008: 8). Suggesting, as the Nigerian reality has proven that they will wait patiently for a day that is nowhere in sight. This judgmental prejudice has "made it possible for governing elders to refuse appointing certain personalities to public office on the basis of their being 'too young'". Ironically, many of them [elders] had their first shot at public offices in their 20's and 30's (Bolaji, 2008: 8). By being excessively caught up in the rhetoric of *leaders of tomorrow*, coupled with the entrenched cultural value that emphasizes respect and obedience to the elders, Nigerian youth has consequently been manipulated to sustain a brand of violent politics that disempowers them, while making it almost impossible for women (their mothers) to venture into the political arena.

Given the high rate of youth unemployment and poverty in the country, politicians easily employ the services of the teeming idle and hungry youth to violently gain political power, and political power is used to criminally mismanage national resources. This in turn creates an expansive pool of unemployed and poverty-ridden youths; from where the political elites recruit the specialist of violence to attain and retain political power. This creates a vicious cycle of poverty, unemployment and underdevelopment in Nigeria, with disproportionate impact on the youth (Onuoha, 2008a). Interestingly, studies have documented both the criminalization and exploitation of the youth and youthfulness in the new democracy (see for instance Gore and Pratten, 2003; Onuoha, 2001). This is a basic contradiction that inheres in the nature of Nigerian politics, and breaking this cycle is one of the key challenges to mainstreaming gender and youth in politics and governance in Nigeria.

Institutional factors also add a complex layer to the matrix of women and youth marginalization in democratic governance in Nigeria. The nature of Nigeria's electoral systems is one factor that has hindered the prospect of increased women and youth representation in democratic politics. This is essentially because Nigeria operates the first-past-the post plurality system. Yet, some countries have robustly crafted some institutional provisions to enhance the prospects of women and youth participation in democratic governance. A good example is Uganda. Uganda is one of the countries where seats are reserved for women, youth and other marginalised groups in the society such as the disabled. Section 78(1) of Ugandan Constitutions provides that the parliament shall consist of one woman representative for every district, and such numbers of representatives of the army, youth, workers with disabilities and other groups as Parliament may determine (Lewis-Tamoka, 2008: 4).

Enhancing Women and Youth Participation in Democratic Governance in Nigeria

The attainment of the goals of sustainable democracy and national development depend to a large extent on the level of participation of the citizenry, irrespective of age, class or gender. Therefore, for women and youth to be effectively mainstreamed into the governance and development process in Nigeria, the paper recommends, among others, the following:

It is crucial for the Federal Government to use the opportunity expected from the planned review of the 1999 Constitution to introduce some positive mechanisms that would facilitate entry points for women and youth into key national political institutions. This could be done through constitutionally provided specific quotas or affirmative action policies in favour of women and youth in political institutions of the country, including political parties. In Liberia, for instance, the electoral regulation stipulates that 30 per cent of all parties' candidates for elections should be women (Adejumobi, 2007: 33). Although quota system has its demerits, it is still the most widely used strategy for enhancing the participation of marginalized groups in governance processes. Hence, Nigeria could enhance the prospect of women and youth participation in the institutions of political governance through formulating and implementing a programme of affirmative action that reserves certain percentage of position of marginalized group.

Further, although civic participation, political decision-making and opportunities to vote for elected officials are important channels for youth to become involved in governance and development, full political participation requires their representation in key structures and institutions of governance that affects their lives. Therefore, there is equally the need for constitutional provision of quota system for youth in some political institutions in Nigeria, especially in the National and various State Houses of Assembly.

Furthermore, women already in positions of political influence could use that platform to initiate and sustain effective networks and collaboration with fellow women and credible gender-based civil society organizations (CSOs) to produce a more unified and influential 'critical mass', capable of not only influencing and ensuring the realization of the constitutional provision for gender equality, but also undertaking constructive and sustained public enlightenment and advocacy, especially for women, to enhance women's prospects in participating effectively in politics and governance in Nigeria.

For instance, it has been noted that only very few women that ventured into politics in Nigeria enjoy the support of their fellow women. Yet studies (Galligan and Clavero, 2008; Sheri and Paxton 2005; Threlfall 2005; Waylen 2000) have demonstrated the vital role that women politicians can play in supporting and enhancing women's political representation. The Nigerian experience has not been quite positive. It is imperative therefore for gender-based CSOs to engage more in advocacy and conscientisation of women on the need to support fellow women contesting or aspiring for elective and appointive positions. Gender-based CSOs could further assist in this regard by partnering with international organizations to explore and evolve alternative funding mechanism for supporting women and youth contesting for positions. The media should equally be engaged in this respect to present and package the positive image of female politicians in Nigeria to make them more attractive to the voting public and enhance their prospect in the 2011 elections.

There is no doubt that the high incidence of poverty in Nigeria with disproportionate impact on women and youths is a key factor underlying their marginalization in governance and politics in Nigeria. Logically therefore, there is the need for the Nigerian government to initiate and partner with the private sector to implement robust and sustainable poverty reduction programmes that are gender sensitive. To this end, the Federal Government should provide adequate incentives to private sector enterprises that are labour-intensive and could contribute to more job creation. Government at all levels (federal, state, and local) should equally partner with international development agencies to establish vocational education and entrepreneurial skill acquisition centers, both in the urban and rural areas to impact practical skills on women and youths. More so, the federal government should put in place a sustainable microfinance scheme, which would be robustly organized to enhance transparency and accountability in its management, and flexibly structured to avoid unnecessary institutional bottlenecks that had prevented women and youths from accessing such institutional credit facility. This is against the backdrop that the microcredit movement has shown clearly that lack of access to capital through restrictive institutional practices is a major obstacle to giving the poor greater capacity to improve their potentials (Curtain, 2001: 6). Access to such facilities would empower women and the youth economically, thereby enhancing their prospects in participating in governance and politics in the country.

The electoral process of a state is a critical factor in enhancing or undermining the prospect of effective women and youth participation in a society. Given that Nigeria operates the first-past-the-post plurality system which undermines the chances of women getting elected in key political positions, the Federal Government should reform the electoral system to be more gender sensitive, by adopting the 'proportional representation system'. This is because more women are likely to be elected where the electoral system is based on proportional or party list systems rather than majority or first-past-the post systems.

In addition, there is the need for increased and sustained investment on human capital development in Nigeria, by way of increased provision and funding of free qualitative education, especially for the girl-child. It is therefore imperative that the Nigerian government moves decisively to eliminate all forms of discriminatory socio-cultural, political and economic practices against women in order to strengthen their participation.

Conclusion

This paper has discussed the long-standing issue of youth and gender questions against the background of a decade of democratic rule in Nigeria. It has noted that despite constituting a significant segment of the Nigerian population and contributing substantially in the economic and political process, women and the youths have remained disadvantaged socially, economically, politically and materially. Hence, if the cornerstone of the practice of democracy is based on popular participation, then it is safe to conclude that the marginalization of women and the youth who constitute a significant segment of the Nigeria population is a negation of the very essence of democracy which Nigeria claims to be practicing, including the euphoria of celebrating a decade of democratic politics in Nigeria. Therefore, to the extent that the challenge of expanding the space for women and youth to meaningfully participate in democratic governance has not been achieved, the youth and gender questions still remain unresolved in Nigeria.

References

Adebayo, M. (2007). 2007: It's do-or-die – Obasanjo. *Sun* Newspaper, February 11.

Adereti, A. (2008). Women, Politics and Elections in South West Nigeria. In Jega, A. & Ibeanu, O. (eds.), *Elections and the Future of Democracy in Nigeria.* Nigeria: Nigerian Political Science Association.

African Peer Review Mechanism (APRM) (2008). *Country Review Report: Federal Republic of Nigeria.* South Africa: Africa Peer Review Secretariat.

Ake, C. (1981). *The Political Economy of Africa.* London: Longman Group.

Ake, C. (2003). *Democracy and Development in Africa.* Ibadan: Spectrum Books.

Amali, E. (2003). Gender Economics and Women's Inclusion in Economic Policies in a Democratic Era: A Nigerian Perspective. In Ogunba. O. (ed.), *The Empowerment of the Civil Society in a Democracy: Nigeria and the United States of America.* Ile-Ife: Anchor Print Ltd.

Awe, B. (ed.) (1992). *Nigerian Women in Historical Perspective.* Lagos: Sankore/ Bookcraft.

Azuike, M. A. (2005). Women and Governance: Four Years of Democracy in Nigeria.

In Gana, A. T. & Omelle, Y. B. (eds.). *Democratic Rebirth in Nigeria, Vol. 1, 1999-2003.* AFRIGOV: Abuja.

Balle, S. (2007). Youth, theatre and sports: Creating 'Conscious' citizens within the Senegalese Nawetaan Movement. *African Insight, Vol. 37, No. 3,* pp. 376-387.

Bomoi, Y. (2007). Youth Empowerment and National Development. A lecture delivered to Participants of Course 16 of the National Defence College, Abuja, on 16 October.

Diamond, L., Kirk-Greene, A., & Oyediran, O. (eds.) (1997). *Transition without End: Nigerian Politics and Civil Society under Babangida.* Boulder Co: Lynne Rienner Publishers.

Eboiyehi, F.A., Bankole, A. O. & Eromonsele, A. (2006). Work, women employment and Feminization of Poverty in Nigeria. *Gender and Behaviour, Vol. 4, No. 1,* pp. 642-658.

Ezumah, N. (2003). Gender Awareness in Reproductive Health with some Example from Nigeria. *Nigerian Journal of Social Sciences, Vol.* 2, *No. 1.*

Federal Ministry of Health (2005). *Technical Report 2005 National HIV Sero-prevalence Sentinel Survey.* Abuja: Department of Public Health, National AIDS/STDS Control Programme.

Federal Ministry of Women Affairs (FMWA) (2006). *2006 Nigeria Gender Statistics Book.* Abuja: Federal Ministry of Women Affairs.

Galligan, Y., & Clavero, S. (2008). Prospects for Women's Legislative Representation in Post-socialist Europe: The Views of Female Politicians. *Gender and Society, Vol. 22, No. 2,* pp. 149-171.

Gavin, M. (2008). Africa's Restless Youth. *Global Dialogue, Vol. 13, No. 1,* pp. 24-29.

Giwa, S. (2008) "Nigeria: Youth Development and Challenges Ahead", *Leadership,* 18 April.

Gore, C., & Pratten, D. (2003). The Politics of Plunder: The Rhetoric of order and disorder in Southern Nigeria. *African Affairs, Vol. 102,* pp. 211-240.

Human Right Watch (October 2007). Corruption, Godfatherism and the Funding of Political Violence. Retrieved on January 12, 2008: <http://hrw.org/reports/2007/nigeria1007/5.htm>

IFAD (2006). *Enabling the Rural Poor to Overcome Poverty in Nigeria.* Rome: IFAD

Karunmi, A. (2003). Gender, Politics and the 2003 Elections. In Remi Anifowose and Tunde Babawale (eds.), *2003 General Elections and Democratic Consolidation in Nigeria.* Lagos: Frankard Publishers.

Kehinde, B. A. (2008). Youth Mainstreaming in Nigerian Democracy: Challenges and Opportunities. Paper presented at a Two-Day International Conference on *Youth and National Development* organized by the Centre for Democratic Research and Training, Auditorium Complex, Mambayya House, Bayero University Kano, Nigeria, August 5-6.

Kenniston, K. (1971). *Youth and Dissent – The Rise of a New Opposition.* New York: Harvest Books.

Lawson, T., & Heaton, T. (1999). *Crime and Deviance*. New York: Palgrave.

Leadership (2008). Nigerian Youth in Despair [Editorial]. 17 July.

Lewis-Tamoka, T. (2008). The Broader Context – Gender. Paper presented at a 2-day workshop on *Government and Opposition: Roles, Rights and Responsibilities* organized by the Commonwealth Secretariat and the Commonwealth Parliamentary Association in co-operation with ECOWAS at Nicon Hilton, Abuja, 16-18 June.

Ligali, T. (2008). Men Don't Believe We'll Do Anything Right. *Sunday Tribune*, 28 September.

Merkle, C. (2003). Youth Participation in El Ato, Bolivia. *Environment and Urbanisation, Vol. 15, No. 1*, pp. 205-214.

Nasir. M. N. (2008). Youth Unemployment Rate Disturb FG. *New Nigerian* Newspaper, 26 November.

National Bureau of Statistics (NBS) (2006). *Annual Abstract of Statistics 2006*. Abuja: NBS.

National Population Commission (NPC) (2001). *Nigeria Population Census 1991 Analysis: Gender and Sustainable Development*. Abuja: NPC.

National Youth Policy. Abuja, Federal Government of Nigeria, February 2001.

Ofong, I. (2002). Women's Participation in Politics in Nigeria. Paper presented at the 8th International Women's World Congress in Kampala, Uganda, July 21-26.

Okpanachi, E. (2008). Youth Participation, citizenship and Development in Nigeria. Paper presented at a 2-day International Conference on *Youth and National Development* organized by the Centre for Democratic Research and Training, Auditorium Complex, Mambayya House, Bayero University Kano, Nigeria, August 5-6.

Oluyemi-Kusa, D. (2006). Gender, Peace and Conflict in Africa. In Best, S. G. (ed.). *Introduction to Peace and Conflict Studies in West Africa*. Ibadan: Spectrum Books.

Omotola, S. J. (2008). Engendering the Legislature in Nigeria: Faltering Prospects and New Hopes. In Saliu, H. A., Taiwo, I.O., Seniyi, R. A., Salawu, B., and Usman A. (eds.), *Nigeria beyond 2007: Issues, Perspectives and Challenges*. Ilorin: Faculty of Business and Social Sciences, University of Ilorin.

Onimode, B. (2001). The Economic Basis of the National Question. In Osaghae, E., & Onwudiwe, E. (eds.), *The Management of the National Question in Nigeria*. Ibadan: PEFS.

Onuoha, B. (2001). The Role of the Youth in the Democratisation Process in Nigeria. In Olugbemi, S., & Anifowose, R. (eds.), *The Youths, Democracy and National Development in Nigeria*. Lagos: Department of Political Science.

Onuoha, F. C. (2008a). Youth Unemployment and Poverty: Connections and Concerns for National Development in Nigeria. Paper presented at a 2-day International Conference on *Youth and National Development* organized by the Centre for Democratic Research and Training, Auditorium Complex, Mambayya House, Bayero University Kano, Nigeria, August 5-6.

Onuoha, F. C. (2008b). Vandals or victims? Poverty, risk perception and the vulnerability of women to oil pipeline disasters in Nigeria. *Gender and Behaviour, Vol. 6, No. 2*. Pp. 1897-1924.

Pogoson, I. A. (2008). Women and Development in Nigeria. A lecture presented at the National Defence College, Abuja, 8 October.

Richter, L., and Panday, S. (2007). Youth in Africa: Participation and Protection. *African Insight,* Vol. 37, No 3I, pp. 299-307.

Sam, V. (2008). 61% of new HIV/AIDS infections recorded in Women – NACA. *The Punch*, 27 March.

Sheri, K., & Paxton, P. (2005). Pathways to power: The role of political parties in women's national political representation. *American Journal of Sociology* Vol. 111, No. 2, pp. 505-522.

Soares, C. (2000). Aspects of Youth, Transition and the end of certainties. *International Social Science Journal,* Vol. 164, pp. 209-217.

Stenning, H. J. (1926). *Selected Essays by Karl Marx*. New York: Leonard Parsons.

Swamy, A., Knack, S., Lee, Y., & Azfar, O. (2001). Gender and Corruption. *Journal of Development Economics,* Vol. 64, No. 1, pp. 25-55.

Threlfall, M. (2005). *Gendering Spanish democracy*. London: Routledge.

United Nations Development Report (UNDP) (1986). *Human Development Report 1986.* New York: Oxford University Press.

United Nations (2007). *World Youth Report 2007: Young People's Transition to Adulthood - Progress and Challenges.* New York: UN.

Vijayalakshmi, V. (2008). Rent-Seeking and Gender in Local Governance. *Journal of Development Studies,* Vol. 44, No. 9, pp. 1262-1288.

Walby, S. (2008). Gender, Globalisation and Democracy. *Gender and Development, Vol. 8, No. 1,* pp. 20-28.

Waylen, G. (2000). Gender and Democratic Politics: A Comparative Analysis of Argentina and Chile. *Journal of Latin American Studies,* Vol. 32, No. 3, pp. 765-793.

Youth Position Paper (May 2007). Second National Economic Empowerment and Development Strategy – NEEDS 2. Retrieved on February 12, 2008: <http://www.developmentpartnership.org/dpi/downloads/NEEDS2/youth_NEEDS2.pdf>

13

Unemployment and the Challenges of Economic Reforms in Nigeria (1999-2009)

Omotosho, Babatunde Joshua

Introduction

It is no longer news that Nigeria is one of the most blessed countries of the world in terms of its array of resources. In spite of these resources, the country is regarded as one of the poorest in the world (Iyayi, 2007). Several factors have been accounted for this ranging from military dictatorship, corruption, institutional failure to mention a few (Sulaimon, 2005). The implications of these abnormalities are felt in virtually all aspects of life. In terms of health for instance, the country has high mortality rates; socially, there is high level of inequalities, loss of values, dignity and respect among league of nations; while in terms of development, there is nothing to write home about as the nation is bedevilled with high level of poverty as a result of unemployment; lack of basic amenities among others. This scenario has become the identifiable feature of the nation from one administrative epoch to the other. Several moves in terms of reforms have been carried out by various leaders in times past to address this problem, but all efforts aimed at combating this challenge have proved abortive. This paper focuses on an examination of economic reforms and its implications on unemployment in Nigeria in the last eight years (1999-2008).

How it Began

The civilian administrators in the country took off from the remains left by the military. The nation has witnessed series of social and economic trauma which needed to be corrected as a result of the dictatorial approach of the erstwhile military administrators. On assumption of duty and more especially considering the plight of the masses, the civilian government that took over quickly took upon itself certain restructurings aimed at addressing the social, economic and developmental challenges facing the nation. For instance, in the remarks of Obasanjo on assumption of duty, he remarks thus: "our infrastructure - National Electric Power Authority (NEPA), Nigeria Telecommunication Industry Limited (NITEL), roads, railways, education, housing and other social services were allowed to decay and collapse. The entire Nigerian scene is very bleak. One of the immediate acts of this administration will be to implement quickly and decisively measures for the reforms and the difficult decisions and hard work required to put the country back on the path of development and growth and restore confidence in governance..., on my part, I will give the forthright, purposeful, committed, honest and transparent leadership that the situation demands'. (Obasanjo, 2005). Going by the interesting remarks of the president on assumption of duty in 1999, his commitment in restructuring the economic policies of the nation with a view to giving hope to the citizens were obvious to all and sundry.

As a starting point in this discourse, there is need to understand some of the economic reforms that took place in the country more especially with a view to addressing the issue of unemployment. It must be stated that there were reforms long existing before that of 1999 and which still operated when the administration took over. These reforms shall not be considered here as they are not within the scope of this chapter. Basically, the new sets of reforms put in place upon assumption of duty by the government were the following: National Economic Empowerment and Development Strategy (NEEDS) established in 2003 which was aimed at addressing the structural and institutional weaknesses of the economy as a medium-term strategy to be released between 2003 and 2007. Summarily, NEEDS was aimed at ensuring wealth creation, poverty reduction with a view to generating environment (Amadi and Ogwo, 2004; Sheidu, 2004). Some of the key areas also include the pursue of anti-corruption in line with other anti graft agencies, establishment of the state and local version of the programme with the establishment of small and medium term scale enterprises development agency of Nigeria (SMEDAN) and National Agency for Poverty Eradication Project (NAPEP). Also, it was aimed at financial reform and privatisation of public sectors through Bureau for Public Enterprises, among others.

Taking a further look at these structural reforms more especially as it relates to privatisation of public organisation, which came up as a result of some observed anomalies within the sector. It was observed that the need for privatisation of these organisations became necessary based on poor management, corruption and repeated losses. For example, it was estimated that from the period 2000-2003, government had spent about N74.3 billion to operate Nigerian Ports Authority (Adam Smith International, 2006). Thus between 1999 and 2006, about 116 enterprises were privatised (Okonjo-Iweala and Kwaako, 2007).

Other areas of reform which shall be considered based on their relevance to this discourse are civil service reform, banking reform and trade policies. The civil service was reformed based on the need to ensure an increase in efficiency and increase in workers' remuneration. The reason for the reform was better captured by Okonjo-Iweala and Osafo-Kwaako (2007: 16) when they opine:

> Rapid public sector recruitment under military administration resulted in an oversized and under skilled work force in which employees often did not have the appropriate technical skills needed for their assignment. For example, about 70 percent of workers in the Ministry of Finance were low level staff clerks, cleaners with secondary education or equivalent

It was estimated that in the process of privatising some of these establishments, an estimated 8,000 ghost workers were removed while about 1,000 workers were recruited (Okonjo-Iweala and Osafo-Kwaako, 2007). In the banking sector, it was also restructured on the basis of what the government termed 'weak financial base', thus, the central Bank of Nigeria ordered that banks should merge in order to consolidate and meet the new capital requirement.

Trade reform was also considered an important aspect of economic reform in the country. The country adopted the Common External Tariff (CET) of the Economic Community of West African States (ECOWAS) in order to ensure a more sophisticated tariff that will be transparent and predictable (Okonjo-Iweala and Osafo-Kwaako, 2007; National Population Commission, 2004). In order to understand the gravity of issue under consideration here, there is need to take a look at unemployment and the dimensions it take in Nigeria during the period under study.

Unemployment in Nigeria

ILO defines unemployment as numbers of the economically active population who are without work but available for and seeking work, including people who have lost their jobs and those who have voluntarily left work (World Bank, 1998: 63). Even though there is divergence on the application of United Nations' definition across countries (Obadan and Odusola, 2001), unemployment has become a serious challenge in Nigeria. For instance, Okigbo (1986) and Obadan and Olusola (2001) while describing the pattern arising from labour submitted that most people below the age of 15 years and those above 55 years who are actually engaged in economics are excluded in the statistical survey. Douglass and Gbosi (2006) further define unemployment as a situation in which people who are willing and ready to get jobs are not able to do so. From the definitions considered above, certain issues become critical. They are lack of jobs for those people expected and willing to take jobs. First, this may indicate that there is unemployment for people in their active years that are expected to take to be in active service whether at the private or public place. Second, it may also suggest that individuals who are laid off from their jobs for one reason or the other but are still willing to take up

Table 13.1: National Unemployment

Survey period	*Composite*	*Urban*	*Rural*
December 1985	6.1	9.8	5.2
December 1986	5.3	9.1	9.6
December 1987	7.0	9.8	6.1
December 1988	5.1	7.8	4.8
December 1989	4.5	8.1	3.7
December 1990	3.5	5.9	3.0
December 1991	3.1	4.9	2.7
1992 (annualised)	3.5	4.8	3.0
1993	3.4	4.0	3.2
1994	3.2	4.0	3.2
1995	1.9	3.6	1.6
1996	2.8	4.4	2.4
1997	3.4	5.7	2.8
1998	3.5	4.5	3.1
1999	17.5	11.6	19.6
2000*	18.1	14.2	19.8
2001*	13.7	10.3	15.1
2002*	13.7	10.3	15.1
2003*	14.8	17.1	13.8
2004*	11.8	11.0	12.1
March 2005	11.9	10.1	12.6

Source: Federal office of statistics (FOS) and National Bureau of statistics.
N.B: * Data obtained from statistical fact sheet.

new jobs. These definitions may aptly describe the situations of Nigerians as far as this issue is concerned. Taking a historical review of trends in unemployment in Nigeria, studies revealed that there is a sharp decline in unemployment in the period under study compared to other periods as it fluctuated between 3.4 and 4.7 percent between 1996 and 2000 (Douglass et al, 2006) and in 2003 it reduced to 2.3 percent due to contributions from the informal sector (Ajibefun and Daramola, 2003). The tables below describe the trends of unemployment between the periods under study.

Table 13.2: Unemployment Rates in Nigeria 2005

States	%
Nigeria	11.9
Akwa ibom	14.4
Anambra/Enugu	9.8/27.4
Imo/Abia	16.5/7.9
Kaduna/Taraba	21.4/3.4
Katsina	23.8
Kwara/Kogi	2.9/8.7
Lagos	6.5
Niger	0.2
Ogun	2.5
Ondo	6.2
Oyo/Osun	5.3/1.9
Plateau	2.8
Rivers	7.0
Sokoto/Kebbi	4.1/19.9

Source: Federal Office of Statistics, 2005.

A look at the tables above shows the trends of unemployment in the country from 1985 to 2005. The trickle-down implications on other areas of life are better imagined than said. The data shows that unemployment became worse at the beginning of the millennium where it doubled the size of subsequent years. This was as a result of several policies made by the erstwhile administration in downsizing the number of employed people in public employment.

Table 13.3: Registered Unemployed and Vacancies Declared in Lower Grade Professionals and Executive

Year	Lower grade Unemployed	Vacancies	Placement	Professional and executive Unemployed	Vacancies	Placement
1987	85158	13050	2378	6123	606	148
1988	116162	13502	4988	15100	444	175
1989	145084	14154	2506	16293	591	281
1990	96055	14052	3474	14281	3091	678
1991	89752	7637	1917	10182	3695	986
1992	10513	14529	2926	12624	3989	164
1993	75143	3864	985	22206	30188	10
1994	75387	3735	1251	108153	12605	79
1995	72277	3786	859	28123	3307	8
1996	81730	4182	1119	32942	3708	49
1997	85441	7873	2020	67252	250	91
1998	85832	7831	2134	66461	83	2
1999	84727	6895	1352	99376	38	15
2000	86102	7313	1611	63669	138	75
2001	85368	6583	923	104960	115	110

Source: CBN, 2002.

Unemployment and Economic Reforms in Nigeria

One of the major challenges of this reform was that it has failed to fully address the needs of the common man, in other words, it has not been able to translate to welfare programme (Okonjo-Iweala and Kwaako, 2007). This was further described by Okonjo-Iweala and Osafo-Kwaako, 2007:19) when they opine:

> the institutional reforms as articulated in the document are that it amounts to privatisation and liberalisation without a programme that addresses the huge social cost of transition. This is unbecoming in the avowed claim of 'poverty alleviation'. The programme does not speak in real terms about social programme that will address the dislocation and hardship which an ordinary Nigerian worker suffers under comprehensive privatisation as the programme advocates.

Evidences regarding this assertion are not far fetched within the society considering the implication of the reforms on the life of the common man in terms of unemployment which of course translates to poverty. Most of the programs did not clearly spell out how the life of the common man can be improved upon. For instance, the poverty alleviation programme as articulated by Okonjo-Iweala and Osafo-Kwaako (2007) did not make provision for such plans; it only painted a gory picture of what an average Nigerian go through without a concern for how such problems could be solved (Amadi, 2004). This was buttressed further in his statement as he opine thus:

> what are we to make of this statement in view of the absence of poverty reduction programmes or approaches in the proposal? We can give the architect of the programme the benefit of doubt that they truly consider poverty as a real threat to economic growth and its drastic reduction a big boost to development but why fail to provide a pragmatic process of reducing poverty? (Amadi, 2004).

We shall however take a look at how these reforms have implications on the level of unemployment in this nation.

One of the challenges that confront economic reform in Nigeria is its failure to include labour in the growth sector (ILO and UNECA, 2004). The inability of the nation to employ its teeming population in this sector constitutes a great challenge to the programme. Several young and old citizens in their active years do not have access to decent employment. Agriculture which has always been the mainstay has been underdeveloped thus unable to provide decent employment for the people. Majority of the people working in this sector do so at the subsistence level. In places where these opportunities exist, they are unevenly distributed (Rama, 1998; Ali and Thornbecke, 2000; Fosu, 2005). The poor often lack the opportunity to have access to contribute their quota to the economy more especially as there is a correlation between employment performance and poverty prevalence (Taratino, 2005; ILO, 2004). This assertion was corroborated by ILO and UNECA (2004) when they remarked:

> Decent employment is the main escape route. A major route out of poverty in Africa is decent employment, a concept that encompasses the quality of employment rooted in productive and secure jobs that provide adequate income and reasonable work conditions and quality of employment. Policies set up by the government lack issues that relate to employment. Most times, the belief is that good economic policies on the long run would translate to the provision of good jobs. (ILO and UNECA, 2004)

In Nigeria, reverse is usually the case. Lack of consideration of the labour sector has been considered as one of the serious impediment to the progress of the nation (UNECA, 2007). It is documented that the impact on the man power resources, welfare and output cannot be overemphasised (Akinboyo, 1987; Raheem, 1993). Developed nations across the globe usually rely on its workforce scattered across different fields for the realisation of its long and short term objectives. In Africa, more especially Nigeria as a case, the belief is that policies and reforms without an inclusion of this sector in its plan would still yield the desired results. This is usually not the case however. As a matter of fact, it has been seen as a major challenge to Africa and more especially Nigeria (Vandemoortela, 1991, Rama; 1998; Oladeji, 1994; Umo, 1996).

In the last political dispensation, it could be argued that all the reforms in the civil service and banking sector could be regarded as doing more harm than any good. Several innocent workers were laid off on the pretence of restructuring without any serious attempt at providing better means of survival to these people. It was reported that in 1999 Obasanjo claimed he provided two million jobs which of course never happened. Manufacturers Association of Nigeria reported that in 2001 alone more than 100,000 jobs were lost in the industry; in 2002, it reduced to 50,000; and it stood at seventy percent of what obtained in 2003 (Ogwu, 2008) The question is what is the relevance of economic reform that fails to translate to the provision of decent jobs both at the formal and informal levels? What the administration succeeded in doing was to render so many people jobless without any alternative for them. Some have not collected their gratuities and entitlements and yet they were laid off. The administration laid off so many workers without tertiary education as reported by Okonjo-Iweala and Osafo-Kwaako (2004) without any tangible means of survival. Anti-poverty agencies established to address these problems became toothless dog due to financial challenges and other generic problems. In the process, several laid off workers became motorbike transporters popularly referred to *'Okada riders'* in Nigeria based on the need to survive and the health implications are evident in all parts of the country. Several people have become disabled and some eventually died in the process due to the unconcerned attitude of the administration to the issue of employment under the pretence of economic reforms.

The implications of unemployment as a result of poor economic reforms are multifaceted. The well-being of the masses in the country have been at jeopardy. Studies have showed the relationship between psychological, personal well being and employment (Machin and Manning, 1998; Clark, 1990). The psychological trauma an unemployed person goes through is better imagined than experienced. When an unemployed person considers an array of responsibilities from family and other important people hanging on his shoulders with no realistic means of lifting them which could be through a decent job, it becomes a mental torture which could generate into other physiological and psycho-social abnormalities. It is also evident that unemployment would translate to poverty. The level of poverty in the country is on the increase on a daily basis. Taking a look at the distribution table above on the unemployment levels and dimensions in the country, one could infer without words that poverty is a by-product of unemployment. This has in the long run pushed so many youths into criminal activities based on lack of gainful employment. Unemployment is a cycle, if not properly handled; it brings about endless chains of negative effect both on the economy itself and on the innocent citizens of the nation. All these without doubt have implications on the growth and development of the nation.

Unemployment and Economic Reforms: Some Causative Factors

Efforts have been made to consider the relationship between unemployment and economic reforms in the country. There is need to consider briefly some key factors that have hindered the smooth sail of these reforms, more especially as they translate to unemployment whether on the short or long run. A major flaw on the economic reforms under study was that these programmes were only relevant and useful at the top without a proper and genuine replication at the state and local levels. For instance, NEEDS was popular and seriously implemented at the federal level, whereas states SEEDS and the local level LEEDS did not take such issues seriously in terms of implementation (Okonjo Iweala, 2007).

On the area of privatisation, experts have argued that the process was not complete due to its failure in following the reform process as obtained in other parts of the globe. It is asserted:

> in fact, although privatisation conceptually in part of the components of global public management reform, in the Nigerian sector case, it ought to not to be referred to as public sector reform because its articulation fails to connect to the usual characteristics and increased productivity. (Kettl, 2001 and Amadi, 2004)

The government has justified the establishment of privatisation programme based on the need for efficiency. But according to Amadi (2004), there are no structures put in place to justify this need. The expected institution associated with privatisation like capital market, labour law, a strengthened regulated capacity, social securities are not there (Amadi, 2004). He further highlights failure to clarify the power relationship between the Bureau of Public Enterprises (BPE) and the National Council on Privatisation (NCP) (Amadi, 2004). For instance, Demery and Square (1996), Chinsman, (1997) and Oladeji, (2000) attributed lack of efficient programme and absence of enabling policy environment as responsible for failure of these reforms.

Leadership problem constituted another major challenge to the issue of economic reforms in the country. Majority of the country's leaders have not been credible and visionary as far as the issue of governance is concerned, hence, their lackadaisical attitudes regarding its teeming work force. There were several labour unrests during the period under study. These were as a result of empty promises made based on the restructuring that took place at that period. The dictatorial tendency and lack of focus of our leaders played a serious role in hampering the actualisation of these reforms. A majority of them still 'carried-over' their military background and experience into civilian administration. Most of the statements made by the leadership are not usually followed with sincerity.

Aside these, most of the leaders in political offices are lacking in terms of competence and willingness to learn. All the factors identified as keys to the success of economic reforms in literature are in fact dependent on effective political leadership. These include the government's level of understanding of economic issues, its commitment to reform, the insulation of key technocrats, and its ability to build coalition on behalf of reform (Gyrmad-Boadi and Walle, 1996). Obasanjo himself who came up with these reforms later became a victim of leadership challenges. For instance, it was reported that he failed to communicate as expected with important stakeholders of the society. According to Ogbonna (2004): "Obasanjo's autocratic disposition is ineffective because it is not sufficiently underlined by a transparent patriotism and commitment to the Nigerian dream, a commitment that is contagious." (Amadi, 2004)

There has been a commendation about Obasanjo in terms of harnessing human resources together, but whether he has actually the requirements of a good leader in terms of commitment and visions have become debatable (Willemson, 1994; Gray and McPherson, 1999).

The roles of the entire citizenry cannot be ignored as one of the major challenges to economic reforms in the country. Nigerians were 'always in haste' as they wanted result without going through the process involved in getting results. This lifestyle on the part of an average Nigerian impacted negatively to the programme. Several Nigerians were sceptical about the workability of such reform programme based on past experience. This might not be far from the past activities of the government in terms of their lack of their commitment to such reforms. For instance, it was reported that Obasanjo regime was seriously challenged by the masses under the auspices of labour and civil societies (Amadi, 2007).

Corruption has remained an unsolved problem for the nation more especially in the area of the economy (Ayobolu, 2006 and Obayelu, 2007). Several efforts have been made in this regard to make the reform work (African Outlook, 2006). What appeared to be yielding result in terms of anti graft laws among others were not so; but it appears the nation has not succeeded in tackling the menace (CBN, 2006; EFCC Report, 2006; Molier, 2005). Anti-graft agencies set up to address the issue of corruption between the periods under focus changed its focus as it was reported that some of these agencies later became instrument of politics harassing and threatening the so-called detractors and enemies of the administration. Some of the policies that would have worked in the country were thwarted due to implementation lapses as a result of lack of transparency in managing and implementing the policies.

Conclusion

This chapter has tried to consider the relationship between unemployment and economic reforms under Obasanjo administration. On a concluding remark, it becomes important to examine the expectations of the economic reforms of the administration as highlighted by Okonjo-Iweala and Osafo-Kwaako (2004) as follows:

1. Restore the confidence of the citizenry in their government, its policies, programmes and activities;
2. Restore confidence within the international committee of nations in Nigeria's commitment to good governance and sound economic programmes;
3. Ensure greater stability and better understanding within the polity;
4. Guarantee efficient and effective service delivery;
5. Accelerate political and socio-economic development;
6. Result in a better and happier existence for the average Nigerian.

The question one may ask at this juncture is how far was the administration able to meet these expectations within its tenure? Without mincing words, all these expectations are laudable and achievable, but the administration could have done better more on the aspect of ensuring that the issue of employment was handled with seriousness in terms of harnessing it into their reforms. While it may be too early to assess the tenure of the new administration in terms of employment, there is need to submit that efforts should be made by the administration to chart a new course that will take this issue into consideration

References

Adam Smith International (2006). Analysing Financial Flows between FGN and Public Enterprises. *Economic Policy Position Paper 4, No 4*. Published as part of the support to the Bureau of Public Enterprises.

African Economic Outlook (2006). Nigeria Africa Outlook 2005-2006. Retrieved from http://www.oecd.org/dev/publications/africanoutlook.

Ajibolu, J. (2006). *EFCC, Corruption and the Due Process*. U.S.A.: Segun Dawodu.

Akinboyo, G.B. (1987). Job Creation as a Productivity Measure for Employment Problems in Developing Countries: The Nigeria and Holland Experience. *Increasing Productivity in Nigeria*, pp. 404-411. Lagos: Industrial productivity Centre.

Ali, A.A and Thorbecke, E. (2000). The State and Path of Poverty in Sub Sahara Africa: Some Preliminary Results. *Journal of African Economics,* Vol. 9. (supplement) pp. 9-40.

Amadi, S. (2004). Contextualising NEEDS: Political and Economic Development Report of Civil Society Policy Dialogue on the National Economic Empowerment and Development Strategy (NEEDS). In Amadi & Ogwo (eds.). *Human Right Law Services (HURILAWS)* Lagos: Centre for Public Policy and Research (CPPR).

Amadi, S. (2004). Privatisation Without Reforming: The Case of Nigeria Report of Civil Society Policy Dialogue. The National Economic Empowerment and Development Strategy (NEEDS). In Amadi & Ogwo (eds.), *Human Right Law Services (HURILAWS*). Lagos: Public Policy and Research (CPPR).

Amadi, S., & Ogwo, F. (2004). Contextualising NEEDS. Economic and Political Reforms in Nigeria. Lagos: HURILAWS & CPPR.

Central Bank of Nigeria CBN (2006). 2006 Annual Report. Abuja: Central Bank of Nigeria.

Chinsman, B. (1997). Poverty Alleviation for Sustainable Human Development. Paper presented on behalf of the United Nations Development System in Nigeria at the *Workshop on Poverty Alleviation in Nigeria* organised by the Vision 2010 Committee.

Demery, L., & Squire, L. (1996). Macroeconomic Adjustment and Poverty in Africa: An Emerging Picture. *The World Bank Research Observer, II,* 1 February, pp. 39-69.

Douglason G.U., & Gbosi, A. (2006). *The Dynamics of Productivity and Unemployment Nexus: Implications for Employment Generation in Nigeria. NES 2006*. Annual Conference, Ibadan, Nigeria.

Economic and Financial Crime Commission EFCC (2006). *Nigerian Government EFCC Reports*. Abuja: EFCC Communication Technology Department.

Gbosi, A.N. (2006). *Modern Labour Economics and Policy Analysis*. Abakaliki: Pack Publishers.

Gray, C., & McPherson, M. (1999). The Leadership Factor in African Policy Reform and Growth Development. *Discussion Paper No 703*, p. 20. Harvard Institute of International Development.

Gymadi-Boadi & van de Walle (1996). The Politics of Eeonomic Reform in Africa. In Benno Ndulu & Nicholas van de Walle (eds). *Agenda for African Economic Renewal,* pp. 294-332. Washington DC: Overseas Development Council.

Imolie, E.E. (2005). Nigeria Progress in Curbing Corruption. Paper Presented at a Forum Organised by the Society of Government Economists, Washington DC on September 27.

International Labour Organisation (ILO) and United Nations Economic Commission for Africa (UNECA) (2004). Employment-Friendly Macroeconomic Policies. Joint ILO-ECA Position Paper for the Extraordinary Summit of the African Union on Employment and Poverty Alleviation, September 3-9 Ouagadougou.

Iyayi, F. (2007). Institutional Failure, Democracy and Development in Nigeria. *NESG Economic Indicators*. January-March.

Kettl, D. (1997). The Global Revolution in Public Management Driving Themes, Missing Links. *Journal of Policy Analysis and Management, Vol. 16, No. 3,* pp. 446-462.

National Planning Commission (2004). *The National Economic Empowerment and Development Strategy (NEEDS)*. Abuja: National Planning Commission.

Ndebbio, J. (2005). *Fiscal Operations, Money Supply and Inflationary Development in Nigeria*. Abuja: African Economic Research Consortium.

Obasanjo, O. (1999). Presidential Inaugural Speech. May 29, Abuja, Nigeria.

Obayelu, A.E. (2007). Effects of Corruption and Economic Reform on Economic Growth and Development: Lessons from Nigeria. Paper Submitted for 2007 Africa Economic Conference. Retrieved from http://www.afdb.org/pls/ur// ITEM/3DB26A120CEOACE4E040C00A0C3369.

Ogbonna, H. (2004). *2004 NEEDS: Building on Four Pillars Report of Civil Society Policy Dialogue*. In Amadi & Ogwo (eds.). The National Economic Empowerment and Development Strategy (NEEDS). Lagos: Human Right Law Services (HURILAWS) Centre for Public Policy and Research (CPPR).

Ogwu, C.A. (2008). Developing Nigeria's Economy: The New Challenges of Industry Policy-Making. *Nigeria Matters*. Retrieved on December 2008: <http:// www.nigeriansinamerica.com>.

Okonjo-Iweala, N. & Osafo-Kwaako, H. (2007). Nigeria's Economic Reforms Progress and Challenges. *Brookings Global Economy and Development Working Paper 6*. Washington DC: The Brookings Institution.

Okigbo, PNC (1986). Theoretical and Methodological Issues Relating to Unemployment in Nigeria. *Unemployment and Underemployment in Nigeria*. Annual Conference Proceedings of the Nigerian Economic Society, Kaduna, May 13-17.

Oladeji, S.I. (1994). Absorption of Educated Manpower into Nigeria's Informal Sector. *Diagnostic Studies Series*. Lagos: INMB.

Oladeji, S.I., & Abiola A.G. (2000). Poverty Alleviation with Economic Growth Strategy: Prospects and Challenges in Contemporary Nigeria. *Journal of Social Development, Vol. 15, No. 2*. pp. 33-53.

Raheem, M.I. (1993). Nigeria for Africa: A Case for Labour Export. In Oyejide T.A & M.I. Obadan. *Applied Economics and Economic Policy* (In Honour of Emmanuel C. Edozien). Ibadan: Ibadan University Press.

Rame, M. (1998). How Sad is Unemployment in Tunisia? Assessing Labour Market Inefficiency in a Developing Country. *Research Observer, Vol. 13., No. 1.* The World Bank.

Sheidu, A.D. (2004). Harnessing Nigeria's Resources for the Successful Implementation of the National Economic and Empowerment and Development Strategy (NEEDS). 2004 Annual Lecture of the Chattered Institute of Bankers of Nigeria, Lagos.

Sulaimon, T. (2005). *Rebuilding Institutions in Report on the Eleventh.* Nigerian Economic Summit, 2005. Lagos: NESG.

Taration, G.C. (2003). Imputation, Estimation and Prediction Using the Key Element of the Labour Market (KILM) Data Set. *World Employment Report 2004-2005.* International Labour Organisation, Employment Strategy Department, Geneva, ILO.

Umo, J.U. (1996). Introductory Overview. In J.U. Umoh (ed.), *Toward Full Employment Strategy in Nigeria.* Lagos: National Manpower Broad.

Vandermoortele, J. (1991). Employment Issues in Sub-Sahara Africa. *AERC Special Paper, No 14, August.* Nairobi: AERC.

Williamson, J. (1994). *The Political Economy of Policy Reforms.* Washington DC: Institute of International Economy.

World Bank, (1998). *World Development Indicators.* Washington DC: The World Bank.

14

Constraints and Prospects of Democracy in Nigeria

Emmanuel O. Ojo

Introduction

As rightly collated by Decalo (1992: 7), the events in Africa took scholars by surprise, since most doubted Africa could move towards democracy. Even in the mid-1980's, one argues that by reason of their poverty or the violence of their politics, African states were unlikely to move in a democratic direction (Huntington, 1984: 214), another adding that "to have expected democracy to flourish would have been historical blindness" (Chabal, 1986: 5), since "outside the core (industrialized states) democracy is a rarity, support for Tilly's thesis 'Why Europe will not occur again', with a few exceptions, the limits of democratic development in the world may well have been reached (Huntington, 1984:218).

However, despite the doubts and skepticisms openly expressed by scholars, Nigeria, like several other African countries became democratic. On May 29, 1999, Nigeria became a 'democratic' state. Prior to 1999 political transition, Nigeria was under firm military autocracy and absolutism for close to 29 years since 1966, when the military made their first incursion into Nigeria's government and politics, following the collapse of the first republic (see Ojo, 2006: 3). It is vital to note that authoritarian governments were interrupted only by a brief period of civilian rule in the Second Republic (1979-1983) (Lewis, 1994: 323-340 see also, Welch (Jr.), 1998: 593-614). Thus, Nigeria's march to constitutional democracy was a chequered one marked by anti-colonial struggles, crises, coups, counter-coups and a thirty-month agonizing civil war between 1967 and 1970. So far, Nigeria has passed through several phases in her democratization bid, viz.: (a) era of colonial autocracy and absolutism, that is, period of formal colonialism till October 1st, 1960, when the country gained 'flag' independence; (b) emergence of constitutional democracy – (1960-1966), (c) the return of military autocracy and absolutism – (1966-1979); (d) restoration of constitutional democracy – (1979-1983) and (e) the second coming of military autocracy and absolutism – (1983-1989) (Nwabueze, 1989).

Since 1989, that Nwabueze made that observation, the polity has added more phases to her democratization bid. With the inglorious 'stepping aside' of General Ibrahim Babangida's administration in 1993, an Interim National Government (ING) was put in place, headed by Chief Ernest Shonekan, handpicked by an unelected military President (General Babangida) thereby making the ING suffer a serious legitimacy crisis a*b initio* (Ojo, 2003: 103-130). The interim contraption collapsed after eighty-two days following the declaration that it was illegal by a Lagos High Court in a suit instituted by the assumed winner of June 12, 1993, presidential election, Chief M.K.O. Abiola. Cashing in on the court verdict, General Sani Abacha staged a coup d'etat, dissolved all the extant democratic structures retained by the ING, and once again returned the country to a full-blown military dictatorship. It was in this state of confusion that Gen. Abacha died in June 8, 1998 in a mysterious circumstance. Gen. Abdulsalam Abubakar, who took over after the demise of Gen. Abacha had a transition programme reputed to be the shortest in the annals of military-midwife political transitions in Nigeria. Eventually, defying all odds, Gen. Abubakar handed over the reins of government to Chief Olusegun Obasanjo (a retired General) in 1999.

With the inauguration of Chief Obasanjo's civilian administration in 1999, hopes were high once again that democracy would be sustained and consolidated. But alas! The military background of Chief Obasanjo became a serious liability on the system when the supposedly democratic government became a replication of dictatorship in its entire facet. By 2003, after the expiration of his first term, his administration conducted a general election, and handed over to itself. This election was generally perceived to have been massively rigged (Ibeanu, 2007: 49-63). In 2007, at the expiration of his administration's constitutionally mandated second term, another general election was conducted to usher in another civil government. This election was remarkable in a number of ways. First, it was after eight tumultuous years of democracy – the longest period since independence from the United Kingdom in 1960 (*The Nation*, 3 August 2007: 8). Secondly, for the first time in the history of the country, there was a civilian-civilian transfer of power. It would have been even more remarkable if there had been a transfer of power from the ruling party to the opposition (Ojo, 2007: 19).

Meanwhile, the thrust of this paper is an in-depth analysis of the major challenges facing the nascent democracy in Nigeria to prevent it from the threats of authoritarian repression or what David Beetham (1994: 157-172) calls "reverse waves". It is to these anti-democratic forces that could lead to democratic reverse which had taken place in Mauritania and Guinea Conakry recently via a military coup d'état that we now turn to. We begin with the strength of the economy.

Strength of the Economy

As I have argued elsewhere (Ojo, 2006: 9), quantitative cross-national research on the economic determinants of democracy and democratization generally, consistently reveals that a country's level of economic development is associated positively and strongly with the extent to which the political systems manifest properties of democracy. There is therefore a two-way causal relationship between the economy and sustainable democracy; the state of the economy is the determinant of enduring democracy, but democracy is a key pre-requisite for sustainable economic transformation. The message is: broad-based economic prosperity sustains democracy, whereas widespread poverty and ignorance undermine it. To mimic President Clinton of US, when he was running for the presidency office in 1992, *it is the economy, full stop!* (Soludo, 2005: 10). No doubt, Nigeria is potentially Africa's largest economy. Every year, the country produces over 200,000 graduates of tertiary institutions (including 93 universities both public and private ones), has the 6th largest gas reserves in the world, tenth largest oil producer; with abundant but largely untapped natural resources – gold, limestone, among others and with 60 percent of its arable land lying fallow. In the words of Soludo (2005), Nigeria has also millions of its citizens in Diaspora (with estimated 100,000 Nigerian medical doctors and scientists abroad). Unfortunately, was not lucky in the first 40 years of its independence with sustained good political governance (Soludo, 2005).

In his perceptive public lecture, Charles Soludo, Nigeria's Central Bank Governor (2005), noted further that democracy has not been endured in Nigeria simply because the economic numbers did not add up. Whereas democracy and, indeed, any form of government must deliver tangible economic benefits to the generality of the citizenry to be credible and sustainable over a very long time period.

In a seminal article on 'What makes Democracy Endure', Prezeworski (1996: 39-59) found the empirical evidence:

> Once a country has a democratic regime; its level of economic development has a very strong effect on the probability that democracy will survive ... democracy can be expected to last an average of about 8.5 years in a country with per capita income under \$2,000; 33 years between \$2,000-\$4,000 and 100 years between \$4,000-

> $6,000 ... Above $6,000 democracies are to live forever. No democratic system has fallen in a country where per capita income exceeds $6,033.

Be that as it may, most African states have few economic potentials of any significance (many literally nothing) that could attract foreign risk capital which is why entrepreneurs did not flock into them in the past, irrespective of ideology or level of democracy! And to rely on local capital to fuel development is to foredoom many to perpetual marginality (Decalo, 1992: 29-30).

Taking a cue from the same line of argument, Akintunde (1967: 6-8) while rationalizing the reasons for the demise of democracy in the first republic, postulated that a democracy which is not founded upon a secure economic base is not likely to succeed because it lacks an essential condition of efficiency. It is unable to fulfill the expectations of its citizens; in the common parlance, it cannot deliver goods. So significant is the economic base that many people have surmised that even communist countries, as they become wealthier, will come to resemble western democracy more and more (Faure, 1958, qtd. in Akintunde, 1967). Unfortunately, in Nigeria as in most of the developing countries, due largely to the poor economic base, the middle class is a very small minority of the population. Western democracy is therefore not securely founded because it lacks one of the essential ingredients of success – an influential middle class. This fact, which is sometimes a surprise to African leaders (see, Nyerere, 1961: 39), was well known to Aristotle more than two thousand years ago. According to him, 'when democracies have no middle class and the poor are greatly superior in number trouble ensues and they are speedily ruined' (Barker, 1952: 82). The nexus between democracy and the strength of the economy reveals that those who are not rich usually confined to mere voting, political career thus become the privilege of those who are wealthy enough to afford the leisure to devote to politics in most western countries, until the advent of Trade Union M.Ps (Guttsman, 1963; qtd. in Akintunde, 1967). Thus, while blaming the politicians, it is worth repeating that by embarking on western democracy on an inadequate economic base the Fourth Republic was set on a death course - it was bound to be corrupt (Akintunde, 1967). The same scenario is playing itself out in Nigeria presently.

No doubt, it is a daunting task in the face of the aforementioned historical evidence to sustain democracy in an economy like Nigeria where per capita income has been below the $1,000 mark. That, according to Prezeworsk (1996: 39-59), poses a serious threat. Considering the nexus between democracy and the economy vis-à-vis the expectation of an average African, Claude Ake avers:

> The ordinary people of Africa are supporting democracy as a second independence. This time they want independence not from the colonial masters, but from indigenous leaders. They want independence from leaders whose misrule has intensified their poverty and exploitation to the point of being life threatening. And

> they are convinced that they cannot now get material improvement without securing political empowerment and being better placed to bring public policy closer to social needs. [Nonetheless] democracy is being interpreted and supported in ways that defeat those aspirations and manifest no sensitivity to the social conditions of the ordinary people of Africa. Generally, the political elites who support democratization are those with no access to power and they invariably have no feeling for democratic values. They support democratization largely as a strategy of power... The people can (only) choose between oppressors and by the appearance of choice legitimize what is really their disempowerment (Ake, 1995: 39-40; also qtd. in Saul, 1997: 349).

In line with the above postulations, Jerry Gana (a one-time Information Minister) admitted too:

> You know the mentality of our people. If democracy does not produce clean water, if democracy does not produce good roads, transform agriculture, cultivate industrial development, sanitise society, give us power supply, democracy will lose credibility and they may say, na democracy we go chop? (Jerry Gana in *The Guardian*, May 12, 2000: 1)

The caveat is that where democratic processes do not yield economic returns, a regression to dictatorship cannot be ruled out. This point is clearly stated by Larry Diamond thus:

> ... many new democracies in Latin America, Eastern Europe, Asia and Africa will probably breakdown in the medium to long run unless they can reduce their often appalling levels of poverty, inequality, and social injustice, and through market oriented reforms lay the basis for sustainable growth (Diamond, 1994 and 1995: 13).

When this is juxtaposed with the admittance by the Central Bank in its 2008 first quarter report released to the public (see, *Nigerian Tribune*, June 23, 2008, pp. 1, 4 & 11), it is established that the economy is in perpetual crisis. The apex Bank attributed the high rate of inflation in the country to the erratic power supply. According to the report, the inflation rate on a year on year basis was 7.8 per cent compared to 6.6 per cent and 5.2 per cent recorded in the preceding quarter and the corresponding period of 2007. The report noted further that inflation rate on a 12-month roving average basis for the first quarter was 5.8 per cent compared with 5.4 per cent recorded in the preceding quarter (*Nigerian Tribune*, 23 June, 2008: 4). Indeed, nothing can be more soothing to the nation's debilitating power crisis, largely fingered for stunting the economy, rendering it comatose and occasioning a declining industrial sector whose capacity utilization nose-dived to a paltry 20 per cent by the end of 2006. Epileptic power supply, a very prohibitive business climate and in consistency in government policies, have combined to smother the country's industrial sector leading to the closure of multinationals like Michelin, Panalpina and other notable firms. The shrinking of the textile sector from 170 in the 60's, 70s and 80s, to 10 in the 90s, also evinces the acute nature of the problem (see, Compass Editorial, *Nigerian Compass*, August 21, 2008: 16). The recent disclosure by the House of Representatives Committee on Power, which probed the power sector, that the country now generates less than a pitiable 1,000 megawatts, makes mockery of the country's vision of becoming one of the 20 largest and most resilient economies by 2020, compared to South Africa, a country of 42 million people, which generates over 42,000 megawatts. Much of Nigeria's investment in the power sector has been enmeshed in corruption and enthralled in the lust of the political elite for primitive accumulation (*Nigerian Compass*, August 21, 2008: 16).

The concomitant effect of poor economy is lingering poverty problem. Nigeria's poverty conundrum has assumed a frightening dimension. In the words of Dr. Magnus Kpakol, Senior Special Assistant to the President and National Coordinator of National Poverty Eradication Programme in a public lecture entitled "Poverty Solution: The Role of Government in Poverty Eradication" declared that:

> The number of poor Nigerians could be put at an estimated figure of 70 million ... in 1980, the figure was 28.1 million. 1985, 46.3 million; 1992, 42.7 million; 1996, 65.6 million and 1999, 70.0 million, 2004, 54.4 million (*National Life*, September 13, 2008: 8).

He gave the statistical breakdown along the six regional levels to be "North-East, 72.2 per cent; South-East, 26.7 per cent; South-South, 31.5 per cent; South-West, 43.1 per cent; North-Central, 67.0 per cent; and North-West, 71.2 per cent" (National Life, September 13, 2008: 8). Undoubtedly, something must be wrong somewhere, for a critical official poverty statistics which revealed that over half of Nigeria's 150 million population are poor is unexplainable going by the abundant human and material resources in the country. The economy is gloomy that 2007/2008 United Nations Development Programme (UNDP's) Human Development Index, HDI, ratings placed Nigeria at 158th position out of 177 countries (*National Life*, September 13, 1002: 8.). No doubt, democracy is endangered in Nigeria more than ever before. Poverty, want and squalor are anti-democratic forces in the polity.

The only exception is Indian democracy which has long baffled theorists of democracy. Democratic theory holds that poverty, widespread illiteracy and a deeply hierarchical social structure are inhospitable conditions for the functioning of democracy (Varshney, 1998: 36). But the historical novelty of Indian democracy was noted by Barrington Moore:

> Economically (India) remains in the pre-industrial age ... But as a political specie, it does belong to the modern world. At the time of Nehru's death in 1964, political democracy had existed for seventeen

> years. If imperfect, the democracy was no more sham ... Political democracy may seem strange both in an Asian setting and one without an industrial revolution (Moore, 1966: 314).

To avert recapitulation, my earlier work glaringly with empirical data proved the pathetic downslide of Nigeria's economy over the years with the attendant threat to democratic sustenance (Ojo, 2006). Bruce Baker too in his perceptive piece emphasized much the strength of the economy and sustainable democracy (Baker, 2000: 9-34; see also Shaw and MacLean, 1999: 257-264).

Strengthening the Soft State

As a corollary to the afore-stated, that is, weak economy, the state in terms of being weak or strong matters to the study of threats to democracy both from within and without, as well as one of the common modes of failure of democracy and democratization (see, Nzongola-Ntalaja, 1989). Perhaps, the greatest manifestation of a weak state vis-à-vis sustainable democracy is that it cannot successfully administer a true and fair credible election which is the kernel of democracy. No doubt, one of the fundamental problems that post-colonial African states are facing is that of how to sustain and consolidate democracy through credible elections (Kolawole, 2007:15). In the whole continent of Africa, few states could lay claim to having genuinely conducted free and fair elections as universally perceived. Hence, election administration that will attain governmental legitimacy after polls has always been a serious concern to electoral scholars (Elklit and Keynolds, 2000: 1-37). The reason for this is not far-fetched. It is well known that most new states in Africa, Asia and Latin America are too weak for the assignment. This is why state capacity is one of the major prerequisites for democratic nurturing, sustenance and consolidation. In the extant literature on democratization and state capacity generally, five elements are crucial to the strength of the state viz.: (a) monopoly of the coercive power of society, that is, control of instrument of coercion; (b) the right to improve tax and collect revenue; (c) the power of legal enactment, that is, power to make laws; (d) sovereignty over territory and society; and (e) control of the institutions of the state or state apparatus, i.e., bureaucracy (Onyeoziri, 2005: 3). These five elements taken together constitute the basis of state power and they endow the state with the status of statehood.

However, it needs be emphasized that nation states which qualify for the status of statehood may differ in their degree of stateness, some are strong states, others are weak. No doubt, Nigeria falls into the category of weak, or soft states. Like others in her category, Nigeria runs a system, one in which formal rules (laws, officially stated administrative rules and practices, etc.) are applied copiously and in a lax manner rather than rigorously and consistently. It is one in which private advantage can be gained and private bargains struck concerning the enforcement or non-enforcement of the rules as when a businessman bribes a tax official. Besides money, another inducement is kinship sentiment while another is the favour of superiors. The consequential effect is that in several cases, individuals may be too powerful than the state in which the rule of law is abused with impunity. Cases of such were too numerous to be mentioned during the last Nigeria's general elections in April 2007 (see, Ojo, 2007b). In a nutshell, the stronger the state in all ramifications, the better for deepening of democratic values in Nigeria. This can be achieved via the entrenchment of state institutions cum congruent political behaviour by the political elite.

Imbalance Federal Structure

Perhaps the most crucial of all imperatives for the consolidation of Nigeria's nascent democracy is the restructuring of the lopsided and structurally imbalance federal arrangement. As rightly noted by Emeka Anyaoku, former Secretary-General of the Commonwealth:

> At the heart of the several conflicts plaguing the Nigerian state today is the consequence of the failure of the practice of true federalism. The power shift debate that characterized the politics of transition from military to civil rule and which has persisted several months after, rose largely out of the frustration of large segments of the population with the structure of the political system that has shut significant sections out of the corridors of power for most of the post-independence period. (Anyaoku, 2001: 40)

Nigeria being one of the most complex societies in Africa, federalism was adopted to integrate the plural and divided societies. This is in line with the perception of early generation of students of inter-group relations or plural societies, which considered federalism an effective way of achieving and preserving both integration and stability in deeply divided societies. Whenever events seemed to demand that a compromise be effected between the necessity for unity and cooperation on a wide territorial basis, "the temptation is to proffer catch all management formula, such as federalism ..." (Osaghae, 1998: 1-24). This tendency to see federalism as a magic wand that can channel irreconcilable inter-ethnic hostility into conciliation and federal cooperation was subscribed to by Carnell, thus: "in tropical area characterized by extreme cultural and ethnic diversity ... federalism comes as something of a political panacea" (Carnell, 1961: 21). In a nutshell, federalism is considered the most appropriate framework for governing multi-ethnic societies. However, recent events in Nigeria clearly demonstrate that the polity is far from being a federation or alternatively as has been suggested that Nigeria is not a true or real federation (Dudley, 1963: 95-103). Since 1954, when the foundation of classical federation for Nigeria was laid (*The Guardian*, June 16, 1997), the system is still far from being problem-free. The story is that of both 'political and governmental instability' (Ake, 1998: 28). Worst still, Nigeria's ethnic make-up remains what Furnival calls "in the strictest sense a medley (of people) for they mix but do not combine" (Furnival, 1948: 304).

While the system has survived many turbulent periods like census crises, electoral crises, social and economic unrest, with coups, counter-coups and a devastating civil war, however, the genesis of the convoluting nature of Nigerian federalism has been itemized in a recent public lecture by Adebayo Adedeji (*Nigerian Tribune*, 11 April 2001: 24) thus:

- Lack of structural balances.
- Replacement of federalism of coordinate governments by federalism of subordinate governments (since 1966).
- Centralization of power and persistent lack of respect for the principle of subsidiarity.
- Inadequate attention to the need for economy in governance.
- Lack of adequate measure to protect the rights of ethnic minorities and guarantee their right of self-determination.
- Monopolization since 1966 of the power to control national and human resources by the federal government.
- Persistent breach of the principles of fiscal federalism.
- Pursuit of short-term political expediencies to the detriment of the development of proper constitutional development and practices in the long term.

Commenting on the negative impact of over-centralization of the federal structure, J.S. Coleman, observed that "excessive centralization and statism of most developing countries ...not only means greater vulnerability as a result of non-fulfilment of populist expectations, it also means heightened inefficiency" (cited in Peil, 1976:115). Also, in a perceptive essay, Fallers, observed that "centralization leads to authoritarianism" (Ibid). No doubt, persistent military rule has affected the structure of the polity. This is not unconnected with the fact that the military is both *commandist* and paternalistic in orientation (Ojo, 2000: 1-18). As perceived by Isawa Ellaigwu (1977: 6-7), the system is more of a unitary one than being federal. This negative trend must have motivated Akindele to canvass the argument this way:

> What we need today is a non-centralised federal system in which the State governments are politically virile, legislatively strong, financially resilient, and indeed, constitute self-confident and self-assertive centres of respect by and loyalty for the citizens they serve and over whom they exercise authority (qtd. in Ojo, 2005: 55).

Without gainsaying, Nigerians need to seek a solution in either "fiscal federalism", "confederation", "political restructuring", "derivative revenue sharing", or "whatever except the present warped union where there is too much power and resources concentrated at the centre". In the words of Jide Osuntokun (2000: 25), "more than anything else, we need an entirely different approach based on a different philosophy". This is imperative because democracy can only thrive where federalism is properly managed. Centralized authoritarian system is indeed antithetical to democracy.

Manifestations of Corruption in the Nascent Democracy

Indeed, corruption under the new democracy has been pervasive, open and shameless. The spate of corrupt practices was spearheaded by Alhaji Salisu Buhari, former Speaker of the Federal House of Representatives. Barely a year of Nigeria's nascent democracy, the young speaker was exposed by a News Magazine of certificate forgery and perjury. In his bio-data which he submitted for election, Buhari had purported to be 36 years and to have attended the University of Toronto, Canada. Whereas, he was neither up to that age nor ever attended that University, talk less of holding the qualification he claimed to have. In an exclusive report entitled "The face of a liar" (*The News*, Thursday, August, 1999), it was reported that the speaker was a cheat. After much controversy and investigative journalism, at the end of the day, the former speaker admitted that he forged both his birth and academic certificates. He was removed as the Speaker of the House for the fact that he had padded his age to surmount the 30 years minimum age requirement, the constitution places in the way of candidates contesting election into the House of Representatives. While the degree he faked was an egocentric misadventure, both are a criminal perfidy. He was eventually tried and convicted of forgery and perjury and sentenced to jail in August 3, 1999 by an Abuja Chief Magistrate Court though with an option of fine (*Tell*, June, 19, 2000: 19).

Immediately, after the removal of the former speaker, another privately owned news magazine *Tell* ran an exclusive, scandalous and equally corrupt story about the Senate President, Evans Enwerem. He too was accused of questionable past which ought not to have given him the privilege of becoming a number three man in the polity. Like a child's play, he too was removed as Senate President. Chief Enwerem was replaced by Dr. Chuba Okadigbo. According to the famous dictum, 'what is morally wrong cannot be politically right'. The mass media quickly discovered financial recklessness on the part of the new Senate President too (*Tell*, August 9, 16 and 13 editions). In view of persistent media 'war' against him, the house set up a probe panel to investigate him and off he went like his predecessor having been found guilty of corrupt practices too. In less than two years of democratic experiment, Nigerians had three Senate Presidents and two Speakers of the House of Representatives for no other reason than corrupt charges. As rightly put by a news magazine – from Evan(s) Enwerem to Chuba Okadigbo and now to Anyim Pius Anyim, the upper legislative house has become a laughing stock over allegations of impropriety (*Tell*, June 19, 2000).

Allegations of corrupt practices is not only limited to the legislative arm of government alone. In November 2000, a member of the House of Representatives, Adams Jangaba, Chairman of the Anti-Corruption Committee, had tendered some four million naira (N4ml) packed in eight bags, claiming it was a bribe offered some members of the house by the trio of President Obasanjo, Vice President Atiku Abubakar and Governor Peter Odili of Rivers State. His words are these: "We gathered that the money is from President Obasanjo, Governor Peter Odili of Rivers State and Vice President Atiku Abubakar and channeled through the President Liaison Officer (PLO) Dr. (Mrs) Esther Uduachi". The money according to Jangaba was to be shared among eight representatives with the sole aim of quickening the exit of Ghali Umar Na'Abba as Speaker of the House of Representatives. The allegation caused a commotion and, for over one hour, the law makers engaged in a free-for-all fight (*Tell*, November 20, 2000).

Nigerian mass media were awashed with the rumours of sharp practices which informed the dissolution of Federal Executive Councils too frequently, within the first two years of democracy, thereby resulting into governmental instability. If the federal tier of government appears so stinking, the State governments are not left out in the immoral act. In an exclusive report by (*The News,* June 4, 2001), three Governors may soon face serious problems over corruption. One of them, according to the magazine sources is in the South-West and he has been spending money like confetti, buying houses in Florida in the United States. Over $100 million was allegedly found in the personal account of one of the governors, who calls the shots in one of the States, East of the Niger. Likewise, at the state level, that tier of government is not immune from corruption too. In February 2000, the Speaker of the Oyo State legislature was declared wanted by the police for defrauding the State government of 6.5 million naira (about $60,000) (Suberu, 2001:207-212).

It needs be emphasized that corruption is a child's play at the upper echelon of government when compared to what obtains at the grassroots level. Presumably, closer to the people an assumed catalyst for rural development, the performance of local government functionaries seem opposed to what they were elected to be doing. At a public function recently, Mr. President delivered his verdict, indicting the local government administrators for lack of focus and indifference to the socio-economic needs of their people. Their governing styles he said, had "engendered so much cynicism that the federal government is being warned that this may be a particularly difficult front for the war against corruption" (cited in Tell, May 21, 2001:30). When it comes to corruption at the third tier of government, the President is putting the situation mildly. Nigerians have for long, moved from, 'cynicism' to indignation and outrage. Their 'verdict', is more strident than the President's and has resulted in heaps of petitions submitted to the state and federal legislature, the Inspector General of Police and more recently, the Anti-corruptions Commission (ICPC.) headed by Justice Mustapha Akanbi. Quoting the news magazine *Tell* (May 21, 2001: 30) thus:

> many of the chairmen have learnt well the lessons of corruption of the Gen. Babangida and Abacha regimes that span some 13 years. They are following the same formula for kickbacks, security votes and outright thievery that served the dictators and their cronies so well. And they are publicizing extravagance, flagrantly flaunting the ill-gotten wealth accumulated through ingenious, innovative way which ultimately short-changes the people they swore to serve.

Nevertheless, it needs be emphasised that the incumbent civilian administration is ever conscious of the pervasive 'culture' of corruption in the polity and perhaps definitely doing something possible to curtail it. In his inauguration broadcast to the nation, President Obasanjo identified corruption as the greatest single bane of Nigeria. Although, he admitted that the vice is incipient in all human societies, he agreed that it must not be condoned. To achieve the aim of having a corruption-free country, the President began his crusade from his own house when he ordered the arrest of his cousin, Dr. Julius Makanjuola, a Permanent Secretary, in the Ministry of Defence, who allegedly misappropriated N400 million.

On June 7, 1999, he externalized his crusade by inaugurating the Christopher Kolade Panel to review contracts and licences from 1st January 1999 to 28 May, 1999. It was also to determine whether or not the procedures for such were in conformity with existing regulations and ascertain the relevance and priority of such contracts. Apart from ascertaining whether the expenditure involved was justifiable in the light of economic realities of the country, the panel was to determine the propriety of appointments into top echelon of federal ministries and extra-ministerial departments, including whether the principle of federal character was adhered to.

The Kolade panel reviewed a total of 4,072 contracts valued at N639.62 billion, 576 licences and 807 appointments which the General Abdulsalami Abubakar regime handled. Kolade and his team revealed that the Federal Capital Territory Ministry rushed 266 projects worth over N44.5 billion. The panel also condemned the contract agreement between the Nigerian Ports Authority and Intel Services Limited, which "was packaged solely to serve the interest of Intel thus creating a monopoly situation that would exclude other companies from participating in Port activities". Consequently, President Obasanjo suspended all contract awards, licences and appointments made between 1st January and 28th May 1999, leading to renegotiations and contract re-awards (*The News*, June 4, 2001: 17).

To give legal teeth to its anti-corruption crusade, the Obasanjo administration presented to the National Assembly, the "Prohibition and Punishment of Bribery and Other Related Offences Bill", six weeks after the inauguration of his government. The two federal legislative chambers subjected the bill to their own crucible, injecting the clause that the President, the Vice President and State Governors are not immune to probe.

After a long delay, the National Assembly finally passed the bill and it was signed into law by Mr. President on 29th September, 2000. Section 3 of it establishes the "Independent Corrupt Practices and Related Offences Commission", consisting of a Chairman and 12 others (two from each of the six zones of the federation). Some of the highlights of that bill are: "Any person who asks for, receives or obtains any benefit before doing his or her duty is liable to imprisonment for seven years; fraudulent acquisition of property shall on conviction be liable to seven years imprisonment; any person who corruptly gives or procures any property or benefit to a public officer or any other person shall be liable, on conviction to seven years imprisonment (*The Corrupt Practices and Other Related Offences Bill*, 2000). The anti-corruption law is expected to be the most popular 'gospel' for the administration if the determination of the President is anything to go by (*Tell*, November 20, 2000: 22).

However, one cannot easily forget too that shortly aftger handing over to a new civilian government of Umaru Musa Yar'Adua, the Speaker of the new House of Representatives – Patricia Olubunmi Etteh – was engrossed in a six hundred and twenty eight million Naira (N628m), house contract scam. She was probed and forced to step down in 2007. Same year, it was reported too that the Ministry of Health had defied the presidential order that by December 15, 2007 all unspent monies from the 2007 budget should be returned by all government departments to the treasury. This is in keeping with existing regulations. But faced with a N300 million naira unspent part of the Health Ministry's budget, Professor Adenike Grange and her officers were said to have immediately deployed about N106 million naira to the award of last minute contracts. The sad revelation is that these contracts were for services and equipment which seem not to be immediately relevant to health care service delivery: purchase of refrigerators, photocopies, security devices, smoke detectors, fire extinguishers, equipment for protocol unit, a caustic ceiling tiles and cooling systems. The remaining amount was then allegedly shared out among the officials as "Christmas bonus". Member of the National Assembly Committee on Health also got a handsome share of the money (*The Guardian*, Editorial Comment, April 2, 2008: 16). This action cost the Health Minister and her Minister of State for Health, Gabriel Yakubu Aduku their along with 14 senior civil servants in the Ministry, including Permanent Secretary, Prof., Simon Ogandi their jobs (*The Guardian*, Editorial Comment, April 2, 2008: 16).

Similarly, in October 2008, the Chief of Staff to Rivers State Governor, Rotimi Amaechi, Mr. Ezebunwo Wike was arraigned before an Abuja High Court for allegedly converting over five billion naira (N5bn) belonging to the state into personal use (*The Punch*, October 10, 2008: 12). Also, a former Minister of Aviation, Dr. Babalola Borishade, and an erstwhile Managing Director of the Nigeria Airspace Management Agency, Mr. Roland Iyayi, were arraigned before an Abuja High Court for their roles in the N6.5 bn naira aviation fund scam (The Punch, October 10, 2008:12). Government parastatals, agencies and extra-ministerial departments are not left out in the corruption charges. Shockingly, the Senate was informed of how N453.589 billion naira was squandered by the Nigerian Ports Authority (NPA) between 1999 and 2008. The Senate also queried the N9.450m billion naira extra-budgetary allocation to the Ministry of Transportation. Members of the Senate ad hoc committee probing the management of funds and implementation of policies in the transportation sector during the period were stunned when the Minister of State for Water Transportation Prince Okechukwu Emeka, disclosed that N453.589 billion naira was spent by the NPA without proper authorization nor were there genuine documents to back it up (Nigerian Tribune, October 10, 2008: 4).

This survey of manifestation of corruption in the new democratic era is far from being exhaustive. Presently, seven of the governors that ruled their states for eight years (1999-2007) are presently serving as Senators. Of these, seven, of them are facing trial over allegations of money laundering. Some other contemporaries are also facing trials in various courts. About 11 of them are in their way to jail, if found guilty. With former Kebbi State Governor, Adamu Aliero, now added to the list, the big question is, who is next? (*Nigerian Compass*, October 19, 2008: 8-9).

From the foregoing, empirical data revealed that much as the government is waging a 'relentless' war against corruption, the more political elite appears receptive to the war. This informed General Muhammadu Buhari (rtd)'s observation that "once again, leadership in Nigeria has become a total stranger to transparency and accountability...corruption which, back in 30 May, 1999 they promised to eliminate is nowadays enjoying unprecedented prosperity" (*The News*, Nov. 4, 2002).

The snag however is that neither the politicians nor the military top brass who were opportune to be at the helm of affairs have proved to be better alternative in terms of brazen corruption. This position has been buttressed by the late Justice Pius Okigbo's report (Executive Summary of the Report, qtd. in *The News*, May 23, 2005: 39). As much as the anti-corruption law is good for Nigeria's nascent democracy, the wide gap between intents and actual practices is another hurdle for the civilian government.

The Military as Potential Threat

Unlike the position of Andreas Schedler (1998) that "as students of democratic consolidation have been quick to recognise, focusing on the military and on classical coup politics as privileged objects of research may be morally, politically and empirically questionable ...", empirical data which emanates from Nigerian government and politics is quite antithetical to his observation which is only relevant in advanced democracies alone.

In Africa, Asia and Latin America, the military has become 'political gladiators' in the battle for the control of the state through incessant intervention in politics and government, thereby making that institution of the state the most potent threat to democracy. For instance, in eleven different occasions as a result of the military's desire to control the state, Nigeria went through the 'labour pains' of coup d'etat which either failed, were aborted, or succeeded (Ojo, 2000: 1-20). Between 1966 when the military made their first incursion into politics and 1999 that they handed over to their retired boss – Gen. Olusegun Obasanjo – Nigeria has had seven military heads-of-state, with a lot of coup victims in the bargain. At last count, over one hundred and seventeen (117) persons both military and civilians have been executed over coup charges. The death toll in 1976 was 39, 10 in 1986, while the aborted coup in 1990 recorded the highest casualties of 60 (*Nigerian Tribune*, 20th July, 1995: 4). As a result of the frequent coups and counter coups, the military has ruled Nigeria for a much longer time than their civilian counterparts. The civilians have held office for 10 out of 39 years of Nigeria's flag independence, excluding the spell of the Interim National Government (ING) of Chief Earnest Shonekan between 27th August 1993 and 17th November 1993.

Though, it is a settled matter in the extant literature on civil-military relations that the military is a *sine qua non* to the continuing existence of the civil society; for any human collectivity without a standing army may easily go into extinction. As articulated by Plato in *The Republic* (qtd. in Otubanju, 1989, 1999), soldiers constitute a vital element of the ideal structure of the society. All societies require a body of men whose sole occupation is that of protecting them from the dangers of external invasion, internal subversion, or irredentist claims that may tear a society into shreds. It is against this background that in all regions and climes, human societies are faced with the problem of taming the military. It is not surprising therefore that 17th century political thinkers all took a dim view of the military.

Considering the nexus between the military and democracy, Claude Ake notes:

> ... the military and democracy are in dialectical opposition. The military is a taut chain of command; democracy is a benign anarchy of diversity. Democracy presupposes human sociability; the military presupposes its total absence, the inhuman extremity of killing the opposition. The military demands submission, democracy enjoins participation; one is a tool of violence, the other a means of consensus building for peaceful co-existence (Ake, 1995: 34).

The new political actors were ever conscious of the potential danger the military poses to the nascent democracy when in a sweeping retirement exercise, the federal government pulled out of the military a total of well over 100 soldiers including Generals and Senior military officers who were suspected to be 'political', most especially those of them that have held political appointments between 1985-1999 (*ThisDay*, June 13, 1999: 15-18). The primary reason for this official action barely a month after the formal inauguration of democracy was not unconnected with "the threat of a military coup that has long been a feature of political life in the third world ..." (Hague, Harop and Breslin, 1993: 367). In an attempt to ensure stable civil-military relations, sweeping retirements and re-organisations have been a continuous exercise. In May 2001, just as the polity was preparing for the second anniversary of democracy, General Victor Malu, the Chief of Army Staff, as well as the Naval and Air Force Chiefs, Victor Ombu and Ibrahim Mahmud Alfa were relieved of their positions and quickly replaced too. Thus, since the first spate of retirements, re-organisations of the armed forces continued to be a recurring occurrence.

It would be recalled that until 1966 the Nigerian Army was a normal/ professional force. The officers and men occupied themselves with training, peace-keeping efforts in foreign lands and other sundry military activities. But that changed when major Kaduna Chukwuma Nzeogwu and his cohorts struck in January 15, 1966. Their coup, apart from sounding the death knell of the First Republic, effectively brought the men in 'khaki' into the murky waters of Nigerian politics. Having tasted the 'forbidden fruit', the army lost its innocence, and treachery, ethnic loyalty and power mongering became its hallmark. By the time the second coup of July 29, took place, the army had become a force of "anything is possible" (*The News*, May 14 & 28, 2001). For most observers, Major-General Aguiyi Ironsi was killed not because the *coupists* disagreed with his policies, but they wanted to avenge the killings of their kinsmen in the January coup (Otubanjo, 1999). And to show that the Northern soldiers were in charge, Colonel Yakubu Gowon, a junior officer who had ten superiors ahead of him, was forced on the country as head-of-state. Matters got to a head when some non-commissioned officers and other very junior officers refused to take orders from Brigadier Babafemi Ogundipe – a Yoruba officer – just because he was not from the Northern part of the country. At that point, esprit de corps and professionalism were gradually becoming discarded concepts (Oluleye, 1985: 38-44).

Furthermore, because of their short stint in power, the barracks could no longer contain them. They struck again in 1983 thereby truncating the second republic. With persistent military rule from Generals Buhari in 1983 to Sani Abacha in 1998, the military had begun its descent into the abyss. Under these Generals, "professionalism was completely eroded. Soldiers were so enchanted with political office that their promotion had to be put on hold for the period they were serving as governors and ministers, and in other plum political positions" (*Tell*, January 22, 2001: 26,27). While it may be impossible in Nigerian context to follow the Tanzanian example, where the whole army was disbanded, the current administration can still take certain steps to save the Nigerian army from itself and the nation from another misadventure.

As I have argued elsewhere (Ojo, 2006a), the Nigerian military should be restructured, professionalized and generally re-orientated to quit politics for the politicians, so that it will be able to defend democracy. This becomes imperative because "civilian control of the armed forces is an essential aspect of government of, by and for the people. In a democracy, public policy is decided by the majority, subject to the rule of law, instead of brute force" (Trask, 1998: 12). In essence, civilian control of the military as obtained in America (Janda, Berry and Goldman, 1992: 743), a model of advanced democracy is a sine qua non to democratic sustenance. It needs be emphasized that the military should be kept busy without which their idleness may tempt them to stage another come back. This fear was expressed by Claude Welch (Jr.) too, long before the transition to civil rule. In his words, "were the armed forces of Nigeria to disengage, they would in fact be equally likely to hasten back. They are subject to contradictory pressures, meaning both countervailing efforts for restructuring and depoliticization and considerable pressures for renewed political involvement. The tension between these, neither one fully congenital to senior officer, helps explain the back-and-forth movements of Nigerian civil-military relations (Welch (Jr.), 1995:593-594). Thus, any effort at professionalizing and restructuring the military should fashion their roles in a democratic dispensation to keep them engaged and dissuade them from dabbling into politics.

The Judiciary and Sustainable Democracy

The judiciary is a cardinal institution in our established democracy. This is not unconnected with the fact that constitutional government must in part be judicial government (Hague et. al., 1993: 279). As the third organ or branch of government, the constitution vests it inter alia with the powers to interpret and apply all laws in the country in relation to both criminal and civil matters and disputes between individuals and groups, between individuals and political authorities as well as between political authorities in a parallel relationship or in a vertical relationship such as between one state and the federal government in a federal system (Awa, 1996: 8). Thus, it is the guardian of the rule of law and the upholder of justice, fair play and equity. This is the reason why in Nigerian constitutions it enjoys the greatest measure of independence from both the executive and legislative arms of government, except during military interregnum (Ojo, 2000: 1).

Meanwhile, beyond mere theoretical postulations, the Nigerian judiciary has manifested a number of shortcomings making the organ dysfunctional and eminently qualifies for reform and total overhauling and this is what qualifies it to become one of the threats to democracy. In a relatively complex society, like Nigeria, people are appointed even into Supreme Court not on merit but on such nebulous grounds of religious and ethnic balance, federal character, seniority, zonal representation and old school ties (Oshuntokun,

2008). Similarly, what obtains at state level is indeed more worrisome. In a perceptive essay, Fashikun (2008: 56) notes:

> Allegations in the media in the last few weeks are worrisome and could be a sign that the judiciary could be the greatest threat to Nigerian democracy. Add the Osun State allegation to the events taking place in Oyo and Kwara States, you will agree with my conclusion that very soon the development could threaten our democracy.

Quoting copiously from the valedictory speech of retiring Justice Olabanji Olagunju, he says:

> It is disheartening and most unfortunate that today judicial appointments have been politicized and are no longer based on merit. It is who you know, whose son or daughter you are and where you come from in Kwara state that are the main considerations for appointing High Court judges. This will lead to lowering of standards and as time goes on, a situation will come when the blind will be leading the very blind (qtd. in Fashikun, 2008: 56).

He adds:

> In 2004 or thereabout when two candidates were nominated, recommended and proposed for appointment as High Court judges in Kwara State, indigenes of a particular section of the state petitioned and complained that the two nominees were from Kwara south senatorial district and should therefore not be appointed. These two candidates were then dropped. But only recently, six new High Court judges, all of them from Kwara Central senatorial district, were appointed and nobody raised an eyebrow. Needless to say that all the new appointed judges are from Ilorin. (Fashikun, 2008:56)

Speaking on the composition of the Kwara State Judicial Service Commission, Orilonise said "in Kwara State, there are seven members with the Chief Judge as chairman. Other members are the State Attorney General and the Grand Khadi of the Sharia Court of Appeal. All these three ex-officio members are indigenes of Ilorin". One out of the two lawyers of more than 10 years post call is also an Ilorin man. This adds up to four Ilorin indigenes out of a seven-member commission. The Secretary to the Commission is also an indigene of Ilorin. Other two members are non-lawyers but nominees of the Governor. They are people, who, in the opinion of the governor, are of unquestionable character. Invariably, the two nominees of the governor are politicians but very few politicians are of unquestionable character (cited also in Fashikun, 2008:56).

This picture is a replica of what obtains in most states of the federation, where governors manipulate the judiciary to soothe their whims and caprices. The concomitant effect of this kind of scenario vis-à-vis the judiciary is divided loyalty and inability to uphold the solemn principle and ethics of judicial independence. This is one of the constraints of the judiciary in Nigeria. Secondly, as long as there is no fiscal or financial independence of the judiciary, it will continue to be subject to the control of the purse. This is not ideal for judiciary that worth its salt. In a profound work on Nigerian judiciary not long ago, Davies (1990: 125-136) identifies two major problems with the judiciary which to a great extent has cumbered its performance. First, Nigerian judges are in most cases unable to interprete the laws to accord with the progressive aspirations of the people. Secondly, some of the judges are even said to belong to some secret societies which are very powerful and feared by their members by imposing serious sanctions on them. Judges who belong to such secret societies are believed to have double loyalty, that is, loyalty to the state and its laws and loyalty to the secret societies and their obnoxious norms and dastardly acts. In the circumstances, therefore, it is most probable that a judge will, naturally tilt his loyalty to his society which can impose sanction on him with disastrous consequences than the judge is ordinarily willing to bear. It is possible therefore for a Nigerian judge to adjudicate on a dispute between two parties in a manner that is against the weight of evidence of the parties to the dispute moreso, if a party to the dispute is a relation, a member of his ethnic group or a member of his secret society. Finally, there are widespread allegations of corruption against members of both the bench and the bar. Whereas, it is only transparency and accountability that can boost the confidence of the masses of the people on the judiciary. By extension therefore, transparency boosts the democratic claim of any government (Davies, 2003: 5). From the foregoing, a democratic polity can never evolve without transparency on the part of the judiciary. This is because democracy is about government being freely chosen by the governed. In case of electoral dispute, it is the judiciary that adjudicates a government that had been freely chosen that can be responsible to the governed (Sagay, 2008: 24).

Concluding Remarks

This study has shown that the nascent democracy in Nigeria is facing daunting challenges which makes it imperative to be properly nurtured and managed. It is however significant to mention that all the issues discussed in this paper are far from being exhaustive but for constraints space. A number of other equally salient issues which are of great concern to scholars of democratization and democratic consolidation includes abuse of both human and groups' rights (Nwosu, 2000: 151-166; Mohan and Holland, 2001: 177-196; Ilesanmi, 2001: 529-539; Ojo, 2006: 15-29), Democracy is about liberty with an expanded political space. A choked system where human, religious and groups' rights are glaringly truncated is inimical to sustainable democracy. That the character of gender politics in Nigeria, in terms of the unwarranted discrepancy between the locations of men and women in the state and society, in almost all facet of life, places particular emphasis on the oppression and marginalization of women at all levels is indeed antithetical to democracy (see Nzomo, 1994:203-215, Omotola, 2007: 33-46, Lawal and Ojo, 2008: 330-346). Another anti-democratic issue is perpetual legitimacy crisis occasioned by the inability of the state to conduct a free, fair and credible election (Ojo, 2007; Iwu, 2008). Finally, other twin issues are dysfunctional political parties and the media which equally suffered a lot of limitations too (Adejumobi and Kehinde, 2007: 95-113, Ojo, 2003). The sheering news however is that Nigerians, in a nationwide opinion survey, funded by the United States Agency for International Development (USAID), in January 2000, eighty per cent of respondents agreed that democracy is preferable to any other form of government, a level of support unequalled in recent surveys in Ghana (74 per cent), Zambia (63 per cent) and South Africa (56 per cent) (see Browns, 2001). This kind of support for democracy if matched by a congruent political culture and behaviour may eventually translate to a consolidated democratic polity.

References

Abiola, A.G., & Olaopa, O.R. (2006). Economic Development and Democratic Sustenance. In Ojo. E.O. (ed), *Challenges of Sustainable Democracy in Nigeria*. Ibadan: John Archers (Publishers) Ltd.

Adedeji, A. (2001). Mastering Nigeria's Conflict: The Imperative of Restituting True Federalism. *Nigerian Tribune*, April 11.

Adejumobi, S., & Kehinde, M. (2007). Building Democracy Without Democrats!: Political Parties and Threats of Democratic Reversal in Nigeria. *Journal of African Elections, Special issue, Nigeria's 2007 General Elections*, Vol. 6, No. 2. October.

Aiyede, E. R. (2007). Electoral Laws and the 2007 General Elections in Nigeria. *Journal of African Elections*, Vol. 6, No. 2, October.

Ake, C., (1995). A Plausible Transition. *Tell*, September 25.

Ake, C. (1998). Governmental Instability in Nigeria. *Nigerian Forum*, January-March, Lagos; NIIA Publication.

Akintuñde, J.O. (1967). The Demise of Democracy in the First Republic of Nigeria: A Causal Analysis. *ODU: Journal of African Studies*, Vol. 4, No. 1, July.

Anyaoku, E. (2001). South Africa and the Challenge of Divisive Pluralism. A Convocation Lecture delivered at Rhodes University, South Africa. *This Day*, April 16.

Awa, E. (1996). Democracy in Nigeria: A Political Scientist's View. In Oyediran, O. (ed.), *Governance and Development in Nigeria – Essays in Honour of Prof. B.J. Dudley*. Ibadan: A publication of Oyediran Consult International.

Baker, B. (2000). Can Democracy in Africa be Sustained? *Commonwealth and Comparative Politics*, Vol. 38, No. 3, November.

Barker. E. (ed.) (1952). *The Politics of Aristotle, Part IV, Chi XI, Column 14*. Oxford: Clavendon Press.

Beetham, D. (1994). Conditions for Democratic Consolidation. *Review of African Political Economy*, No. 60.

Browns, M. (2001). How USAID is Assisting the Democratic Transition in Nigeria. *Development Policy Centre's Eminent Personality Seminar Series*, Ibadan, June 26 (unpublished paper).

Carnell, F.G. (1961). Political Implications of Federalism in New States. In Ursula Hicks et. al. (eds), *Federalism and Economic Growth in Underdeveloped Countries*. London: Allen and Unwin.

Chabal, P. (ed.) (1980). *Political Domination in Africa: Reflections on the Limits of Power.* Cambridge: Cambridge University Press.

Davies, A.E., (1990), 'The Independence of the Judiciary in Nigeria: Problems and Prospects', *African Study Monographs,* Vol. 10, No. 3.

Davies, A.E., (2003), 'Reflections on the Imperative of Transparency and Accountability for Good Governance', *Journal of Business and Social Sciences*, Vol. 8, Nos. 1 & 2.

Decalo, S., (1992). 'The Process, Prospects and Constraints of Democratization in Africa', *African Affairs*, Vol. 91.

Diamond, L., (1994), 'Rethinking Civil Society: Towards Democratic Consolidation', *Journal of Democracy,* Vol. 5 (July).

Diamond, L., (1995), 'Rethinking Civil Society Towards Democratic Consolidation', CROSSROADS, A USIS publication, Lagos (April).

Dudley, B.J., (1963), 'The Concept of Federalism', *Nigerian Journal of Economics and Social Studies*, Vol. 5, No. 1.

Elaigwu, I., (1997), 'Federal-State Relations in Nigeria's New Federalism: A Review of the Draft Constitution', in Suleiman Kumo and Abubakar Aliyu (eds), *Issues in the Nigeria Draft Constitution*, published by the Department of Research and Consultancy, Institute of Administration, Ahmadu Bello University, Zaria.

Elklit, J. and Reynolds, A., (2000), 'The Impact of Election Administration in the Legitimacy of Emerging Democracies: A New Research Agenda', being a paper prepared for delivery at the 2000 Annual Meeting of the American Political Science Association.

Fashikun, O., (2008), 'Threat to Democracy in Kwara', *Nigerian Compass*, (Lagos), August 5.

Federal Government of Nigeria, (2000), *The Corrupts Practices and Other Related Offences Bill*, Government Printers, Abuja.

Furnival, J.S., (1948), *Colonial Policy and Practice: A Comparative Study of Burma and Netherlands,* Cambridge University Press, Cambridge.

Hague, R., Harop, M. and Breslin, S., (1993), *Comparative Government and Politics,* 3rd Edition, Macmillan, London.

Huntington, S., (1984). 'Will more Countries become Democratic?', *Political Science Quarterly*, Vol. 99.

Ibeanu, O., (2007), 'Stimulating Landslides: Primitive Accumulation of Votes and the Popular Mandate in Nigeria', in I.O. Albert, D. Marco and V. Adetula (eds),

Perspectives in the 2003 Elections in Nigeria, Stirling Hurden Publishers Ltd., Ibadan.

Ilesanmi, S.O., (2001), 'Constitutional Treatment of Religion and the Politics of Human Rights in Nigeria', *African Affairs*, No. 100.

Iwu, M., (2008), 'The April 2007 Elections in Nigeria: What Went Right?', being the text of Public Lecture delivered at the University of Ibadan, Department of Political Science, Faculty of the Social Sciences (15th April).

Janda, K., Berry, J.M. and Goldman, J., (1992), *The Challenge of Democracy: Government in America,* 3rd Edition, Houghton Mifflin Company, Boston, Toronto.

Kolawole, D., (2007), 'Democracy, Elections, Majoritarianism and the Nigerian Factor', *The Nation*, Lagos (July 13).

Kofmel, E., (2009), "Fighting Capitalism and Democracy", in Erich Kofmel (ed), Anti-Democratic Thought, Imprint Academic Publishers, UK.

Lawal, E.E. and Ojo, R.C., (2008), 'Politics of Gender Inequality in Nigeria' in Ojo, E.O. (ed). *Challenges of Sustainable Democracy in Nigeria*, John Archers (Publishers) Limited, Ibadan.

Lewis, P.M., (1994), 'Endgame in Nigeria: The Politics of a Failed Democratic Transition', *African Affairs*, vol. 93.

Mohan, G. and Holland, J., (2001), 'Human Rights and Development in Africa: Moral Intrusion or Empowering Opportunity?', *Review of African Political Economy*, No. 88.

Moore, B., (1966), *Social Origins of Dictatorship and Democracy: Lord and Peasant in the Making of the Modern World*, Boston, Beacon.

Nwabueze, B., (1989), 'Our March to Constitutional Democracy', *The 1989 Guardian Lecture*, delivered on July 24, 1989, Guardian Press, Lagos.

Nwolise, O.B.C., (2007), "Electoral Violence and Nieria's 2007 Elections", in Journal of African Elections, Vol. 6 No. 2 (Oct.).

Nwosu, N.I., (2000), 'Thirty-six Years of Independence in Nigeria: The Political Balance Sheet', *AFRICA*, LV, 2.

Nyerere, J., (1961), 'The African Democracy' in James Duffy and Robert Manners, Africa Speaks, D. Van Nostund Co. Inc. Princeton, Toronto, New York.

Nzomo, M., (1994), 'Women in Politics and Public Decision-making', in Himmedstrand, Kinyanjui and Mburgu (eds), *African Perspectives on Development, Controversies, Dilemmas and Openings*, James Curray Ltd., London.

Nzongola-Ntalaja, G., (1989), 'The State and Democracy in Africa', in Ntalaja and Margaret C. Lee (eds), *The State and Society in Africa*, Harare, Zimbabwe, AAPS Books.

Ojo, E.O., (2000), 'The Judiciary, Phenomenon of Corruption and Sustenance of Democratic Values in Nigeria: A Prognosis', being a paper presented to the Faculty of Business and Social Sciences Seminar Series for 1998/1999 Academic session, University of Ilorin (February). (Monograph).

Ojo, E.O., (2000), 'The Military and Democratic Transition in Nigeria: An Indepth Analysis of Gen. Babangida's Transition Programme (1985-1993)', *Journal of Political and Military Sociology*, Vol. 28 (Summer).

Ojo, E.O., (2003), 'Governance and Legitimacy Crisis in Nigeria', *Research for Development,* Vol. 18, Nos. 1 & 3 (Dec.).

Ojo, E.O., (2003), 'The Mass Media and the Challenges of Sustainable Democratic Values in Nigeria, Possibilities and Limitations', *Media, Culture and Society*, Vol. 25.

Ojo, E.O., (2005), 'Federalism and National Cohesion in Nigeria', in Ebere Onwudiwe and Rotimi T. Suberu (eds), *Nigerian Federalism in Crisis: Critical Perspectives and Political Options*, A publication of Programme on Ethnic and Federal Studies (PEFS), Department of Political Science, University of Ibadan, Nigeria, John Archers (Publishers) Limited, Ibadan.

Ojo, E.O., (2006a), 'Human Rights and Sustainable Democracy in Nigeria (1999-2003)', *Journal of Social Sciences*, Vol. 13, No. 1.

Ojo, E.O., (2006b), 'Imperatives of Sustaining Democratic Values', in Ojo, E.O. (ed.). *Challenges of Sustainable Democracy in Nigeria*, John Archers (Publishers), Ibadan.

Ojo, E.O., (2006c), 'Taming the Monster: Demilitarization and Democratization in Nigeria', *Armed Forces and Society*, Vol. 32, No. 2 (Jan.).

Ojo, E.O., (2006), 'Vote Buying in Nigeria', in Money, Politics and Corruption in Nigeria, IFES-Nigeria, (May), Abuja, Nigeria.

Ojo, E. O., (2007), 'EDITORIAL', in Journal of African Elections (Special Issue: Nigeria's 2007 General Elections), Vol. 6 No. 2 (Oct.) EISA, Johannesburg.

Ojo, E.O., (2007), 'Nigeria's 2007 General Elections and the Succession Crises: Implications for the Nascent Democracy', in *Journal of African Elections (Special Issue. Nigeria's 2007 General Elections*, Vol. 6 No. 2 (Oct.). A publication of EISA – (Electoral Institute of Southern Africa), Johannesburg.

Ojo, E.O., (ed.) (2006), 'Imperatives of Sustaining Democratic Values', in Emmanuel O. Ojo (ed.). *Challenges of Sustainable Democracy in Nigeria,* John Archers (Publishers) Limited, Ibadan.

Oluleye, J.J.' (1985), *Military Leadership in Nigeria (1966-1979)*, UPL, Ibadan.

Omotola, J.S., (2007), 'What is this Gender talk All About After All?: Gender, Power and Politics in Contemporary Nigeria', *African Study Monographs*, Vol. 28, No. 1 *(April)*.

Onyeoziri, F., (2005), 'Federalism and State Capacity in Nigeria', *Ibadan Journal of the Social Sciences*, Vol. 3, No. 2 (September).

Osaghae, E.E., (1998), 'Managing Multiple Minority Problems in a Divided Society: The Nigerian Experience', *The Journal of Modern African Studies*, Vol. 36, No.1.

Osuntokun, J., (2000), 'The Struggle for Nigeria', *The Comet*, Lagos, (July 27).

Osuntokun, J., (2008), 'Judiciary and the Sustenance of Democracy', *The Nation*, Lagos (serialized between March 20-April 3).

Otubanjo, F., (1990). 'Soldiers in Ethnic Quagmire', *Sunday Tribune*, (3rd June), Ibadan.

Otubanjo, F., (1989), 'Illusion of a People's Army', *Sunday Tribune*, Ibadan, (June 11).

Otubanjo, F., (1990), 'Military and Revolution', *Sunday Tribune*, (April 29(, Ibadan.

Peil, M., (1976), *Nigerian Politics: The Peoples View*, London, Cassell.

Przeworski, A., (1996), 'What Makes Democracy Endure', *Journal of Democracy*, vol. 7, No.1.

Sagay, I., (2008), 'Election Tribunals and the Survival of Nigeria Democracy', *Nigerian Compass*, Isheri, Ogun State, (August 21).

Saul, J.S., (1997), 'For Fear of Being Condemned as old Fashioned Liberal Democracy vs. Popular Democracy in sub-saharan Africa', *Review of African Political Economy*, No. 73, Vol. 23.

Schedler, A., (1998), 'What is Democratic Consolidation?', *Journal of Democracy*, vol. 9, No. 2 (April).

Schedler, A., (2002), 'Elections without Democracy: The Menu of Manipulation', Journal of Democracy, Vol. 13 No. 2.

Shaw, T.M. and MacLean, S.J., (1999), 'Civil Society and Political Economy in Contemporary Africa: What Prospects for Sustainable Democracy?', *Journal of Contemporary African Studies*, Vol. 14, No. 2 (July).

Soludo, C.C., (2005), 'The Political Economy of Sustainable Democracy in Nigeria', *New Age*, (June 2), Lagos.

Suberu, R.T., (2001), 'Can Nigeria's New Democracy Survive?', *Current History*, (May), Philadelphia.

Trask, D.F., (1998), 'Civilian Control of the Military in the United States', in CROSSROADS, a publication of USIS (May), Lagos.

Varshney, A., (1998), 'Why Democracy Survives', *Journal of Democracy*, Vol. 9, No. 3 (July).

Welch, C.E., (Jr.) (1995), 'Civil Military Agonies in Nigeria: Pains of an Unaccomplished Transition', *Armed Forces and Society*, Vol. 21, No. 4 (Summer).

Welchi, C.E., (Jnr.), (1998), 'Civil-Military Agonies in Nigeria: Pains of an Unaccomplished Transition', *Armed Forces and Society*, Vol. 2, No. 4 (Summer).

Newspapers and News Magazines

Nigerian Compass, (Isheri)

Nigerian Tribune, (Ibadan)

Sunday Tribune, (Ibadan)

Tell, (Lagos).

The Comet, (Lagos)

The Guardian, (Lagos).

The Nation, Lagos.

The News, (Lagos).

This Day, (Lagos).

SECTION - IV

REFORMS AND POLICIES

15

The Decade of Democratization in Nigeria: Between Tumultous Trends and Deferred Dividends

Muhammad Zaiyan Umar

Introduction

One of the topical issues that keep drawing the attention of commentators and other observers is whether or not there is the evidence that Nigeria, after almost a decade of democratization, has been able to meet the desires of the people in both the realms of politics, economy and society. This preoccupation is fuelled in part by the widespread recognition that the democratic system, or at best, the democratic process the country embarked upon, possess the necessary hallmarks that could not only ensure a clean departure from the difficult and inglorious years past, but also improve the state of being of the individual and the society at large.

It is not by happenstance, therefore, that as with other parts of the world, there seems a dominant concern with and about governance issues in the country. The specter of issues that appear in the contemporary discourse on development, including the cravings for more accountability, fulfillment of citizens' needs, provision of adequate security, improvement of infrastructure and assurance of the general well-being of the people, confirms the centre stage which the governance framework has occupied and thus the needs that the state must address as it seeks to justify the mandate society thrusts in its care.

Yet the loud outcry that resonates in the society over the failure to meet these lofty goals and the resultant deprivations – social, economic, political, and cultural – it wrought on the great mass of the people remains a testimony to the failure to attain even the modicum of good governance in these societies. Perhaps, the worldwide preoccupation with the Millennium Development Goals (MDGs) further lends credence to the truism that for Nigeria and perhaps, the rest of the contemporary world, the greatest challenge remains the ability to reverse these deprivations and channel available resources – human and material – towards the goals of societal change and development.

Democracy and Development: A Theoretical Framework

The above preamble, if anything, draws attention to the relevance of democracy and good governance in the resolution of the myriad of problems that have dotted the world landscape over the years. Indeed, the governance paradigm has not only generated an uncommon scholarly interest, but has also enlisted a broad spectrum of individuals and groups that have since made it a mandate area in the quest for societal transformation. Democracy and good governance had, in other words, become the blossoming agenda for both the individual, civil society and a number of agencies in the international arena.

At the theoretical level, the concept of democracy has been utilized in highlighting issues and ideas with predominant concern over unimpeded citizen access to governmental institutions and personnel, the flourishing of fundamental rights and liberties, ascendance of the rule of law and the general accountability of the political leadership. The relevance of the aforesaid to the governance process across space and time could be seen in the near frenzied preoccupation of both democratic theorists and practitioners in regards to the utility of the form of government to the furtherance of both the political and economic goals of states.

Notwithstanding the global appeal of the aforesaid, a number of scholars have held the view that in both theory and practice, liberal democracy is essentially a western product, rooted in western history and culture (Sartori, 1995; Van de Walle, 1995, Rudebeck, 1992, Zabadi, 1995). According to this view, the contemporary push for democratic openness, championed by the west, is meant to extend to the recipients a system that is valued at home with its assumed superiority over non – democratic models.

In spite of the allure of democracy, often generated by the unprecedented frenzy of its advocates, over its capacity to guarantee the flourishing of the fundamental values of freedom, participation and accountability, however, it is evident that the system is inherently limited as a governance paradigm that is workable or even acceptable in all parts of the world. The reasons for this state of affairs are not far fetched: because of the cultural and other peculiarities within which it develops, the system (and its practice) has to contend with a bevy of "traveling" issues including cultural variability, weak social and political institutions and a low level of economic development. Faced with these realities, often conveniently ignored by its advocates, its ethos have met with obstacles and dead walls, thereby ending up with far less than its practice expected, reducing it to no more than a process involving minimalist applications. As Adedeji (1997: 6) writes:

> Nowadays, democracy is more often than not identified with the ballot box and a pluralistic political party system. Indeed, some well known theorists have gone as far as defining democracy as the "competitive struggle for the people's vote". There has been so much emphasis on elections that even dictators can now claim to be democratic because they have gone through the motion of holding rigged multi – party elections. The ease with which the international community has conferred its seal of approval on any semblance of free and fair elections in Africa has validated the equation of democracy with elections and multi-partyism.

The implication of the above is that there exists a sort of confusion about whether the recipients of the liberal democracy are indeed on track as to the appropriateness of the model that is thrusts upon them by the proponents of democracy (Momoh, 2006). Questions have been asked: are these states truly engaged with democracy? Given the cultural and historical specificities of democracy, would African and other third world states fair well in its practice? Yet still did countries engaged with the liberal form of governance returned a verdict of performance in effective representation and empowerment of the people?

Democratic performance essentially waters the fountain of a country's political development. Yet, as with democracy, the concept of democratic development has also generated a lot of scholarly attention and even controversies. Clearly, the definitional contours of development have as yet remained uncertain and complex. Yet, that this is so is no excuse for abandoning the search for meaning. In this regard and at the micro-level, development involves the creation and nurturing of opportunities that would effectively empower the citizens to meet up with their basic needs and thereby enhance their lives prospects.

At the macro-level and its economy, development entails the engendering of those conditions that generate economic growth, raise personal and group income and lift people out of the poverty line. Generally, development in the view of many analysts transcends the preoccupation with such economic indicators as the growth in per capita income to more and perhaps, realistic concern with issues that relate to "quality of life measures", including concerns over the state of health care services, educational development and generation of employment opportunities (Moss, 2007).

Suffice to argue that important as these are to the developmental pursuit of states and the people, evidence in Nigeria, for example, suggests that there is growing gap between expectation and actual attainment of stated goals in these and many areas.

At the level of politics, development may be seen or conceived in terms of changes at the levels of both the individual and the institutions of the society. It is about the degree of democratic openness and other such perquisites. Indeed, any attempt at defining development in this regard must contend with the need to establish the interface at the micro – macro levels. Thus as Chilton (1998: 9) writes:

> Political development cannot be defined solely in terms of either individual or institutional change. A concept of political development must show how both individuals and institutions change in the process of development. Institutional development clearly cannot take place without some associated change in individuals, nor can a theory of individual development without associated institutional change be regarded as political development

In other words, political development is concerned with the appreciation of the kinds of change in the state of being of both the individual, as an actor, and the institutions of the society as agencies of interaction between the individual and his/her state. It is concerned with the evolution, development and prospects of both the civic and political institutions of society and how these shape the quality of the political process of any given society.

In the long run, the utility of democracy resides in its ability to usher in a new lease of life in the body polity, one that is bereft of authoritarian, illiberal and unrepresentative credentials, as most military and other forms of government have unleashed on the peoples of the third world. Equally important, however, in the measurement of the utility of democracy is the capacity of any democratic system to ensure the flourishing of the good life among the citizens in the mould of enhanced living conditions at the social, economic and political spheres of the society as well as the entrenchment and the safeguarding of the citizens basic rights and liberties.

Trends in Nigeria's Political Development

Any account of the political development of Nigeria will, necessarily, be replete with a catalogue of change and reversals in the realms of the state, economy and society, often interspersed by crises of varying dimensions and degrees. Broadly and for convenience, two epochs could be identified in the post-independence Nigeria's political development. These are the civilian and military eras. At independence in 1960, the country experimented with the parliamentary form of government, fashioned after the British model, with a provision for the office of the prime minister and a ceremonial president. The government led by the prime minister, Sir Abubakar Tafawa Balewa, was soon beset by a number of problems, including elite unrest, political bickering between and among regions, inter- and intra-party crises, election crisis among others. These placed ominous strains on the state leading to its eventual collapse on 15th January 1966, with the overthrow of the government by the military during which the prime minister, the premiers of northern and western regions, Sir Ahmadu Bello and Chief Ladoke Akintola respectively, along with several political and military officers were assassinated.

The scuttling of the post independence civilian government remained a watershed in Nigeria's political history. Not only did it stop the civilians in their track, but it also effectively brought the military, for the first time, to active engagement in the realm of political governance of the society. Coming from the background of acute divisions in the polity, the take-over and handling of power by the military was anything but smooth. Essentially, ethnic and/or tribal meanings were soon read into the motive of the coup, given that 27 out of the 32 junior officers who were identified as master minds of the coup were "igbos of eastern and Midwestern regional origins" (Sklar, 1997: 20). In a tactical, even if shrewd move, the officers rather than hold onto the reins of power, handed same to Major-General Johnson Aguiyi Ironsi. The new leader's first actions in changing the federal system to a more centralized or unitary one remained his greatest undoing, leading to his overthrow and assasination on 29th July 1966, by elements of the military, many of whom were of the northern origin. Lieutenant colonel Yakubu Gowon thus assumed power as Nigeria's new and second military ruler.

Perhaps, taking a lesson from the blunder of his predecessor, Gowon wasted no time in reaffirming the federal system for the country. Unfortunately, however, the seed for inter - group and interpersonal hatred and mistrust sown by the coup and counter - coup has sunk deep in the society such that recriminations and acts of violent reprisals among the key eastern and northern ethnic groups became widespread and intense, culminating into threats of secession by the Igbos, under the platform of Biafran state, spearheaded by Lieutenant colonel Chukwuemeka Odumegwu Ojukwu. On 30th May 1967, Ojukwu announced the creation of the republic of Biafra thereby setting the stage for confrontation with the federal government and eventually the prosecution of a bitter civil war that lasted 31 months from May 1967 to January 1970.

The war having ended, Gowon announced his government's readiness to cede power to the civilians by 1976 whereupon some of the wounds inflicted on the polity might have healed. He was soon to recant. The decision to push the handover date forward soon became his greatest undoing as it soon became evident that the government's new position on the handover lacked popularity across the country. This, coupled with other acts of bad governance paved the way for the easing out or toppling of Gowon from the saddle in a bloodless coup that saw the emergence of Brigadier Murtala Ramat Muhammad as the country's new and third military ruler on 29th July 1975.

Murtala's rule as revolutionary as it was, considering the government affront on and zero tolerance for laxity and maladministration, including corruption and nepotism, as evidenced by his regime's purge of the country's civil service, did not last long. He was cut down in a hail of bullets by attempted coup makers led by Lieutenant colonel Bukar Suka Dimka on 13th February 1976. The assassination of Murtala foisted Lieutenant general Olusegun Obasanjo, the erstwhile second-in-command and chief of staff supreme headquarters as Nigeria's fourth military ruler. On Obasanjo's ascension to power, he promised to complete the transition programme which aimed at handing power to elected civilian leaders on 1st October 1979.

To the credit of the government, the leadership baton was handed over to the civilians in 1979 following the conclusion of the transition programme. The new civilian government, the second after independence, initially dogged by legal challenges, tried to enlist the cooperation of other parties in the task of governance. This innovation represents a substantial departure from the winner-takes-all pattern of politics. However, only the Nigeria Peoples Party (NPP) obliged and accepted to join the government. The "accord" subsequently broke down over a number of irreconcilable differences especially the NPP accusations over what it as gross violation in matters as appointment of the Presidential Liaison Officers (PLO), passage of the revenue allocation act, politicization of the police, destabilization of non National Party of Nigeria (NPN) state, etc (Nwabueze, 1985). Indeed, these perceived altercations and the bitterness, rancor and torrents of instability that occurred during the "second election" in 1983 facilitated the collapse of Shagari's NPN led government on 31st December 1983 through yet another military coup.

The collapse of the Second Republic set the stage for a long period of military rule in Nigeria. It involved the ascendance of such regimes as that of General Muhammadu Buhari (1984 – 1985), General Ibrahim Badamosi Babangida (1985 – 1993), General Sani Abacha (1993 – 1998) who took over from a hurried Interim National Government (ING) led by Chief Ernest Shonekan and General Abdulsalami Alhaji Abubakar (1998 – 1999) who assumed power after the death of Abacha on 8th June 1998. Each of these governments, notably, had its defining character, including repression, corruption, disposition to cling to power and deployment of orthodox and unorthodox methods or strategies geared at the militarization of the polity and the shrinking of the political space.

Significantly, however, while the governments from 1985 – 1999 initiated and implemented transition programmes, albeit with varying degrees of success, Buhari's remained the only exception. His 20 months (December 1983 – August 1985) reign focused on the implementation of a scheme of moral reorientation and the War against Indiscipline (WAI). Yet, the programme turned out to be a platform upon which the widely acclaimed brutal antics of the government were anchored, including arrests, detentions, long jail sentences for some elements of the political class and the muzzling of the press through the promulgation of draconian military decrees.

Both the Babangida (1985–1993) and Abacha (1993–1998) governments could not, however, be said to depart from the illiberal paths treaded by Buhari in dealing with the political class and subsequently, with the elements of the civil society. In the particular case of the Babangida regime, it promulgated the Participation in Politics and Election (Prohibition) Decree no. 25 of 1987 which banned and/or disqualified a number of would – be contestants. Exclusions, interpolations and outright tinkering with every aspect of the political transition programme were thus the hallmark of the two regimes. In the case of Babangida's tortuous transition, Joseph (1997: 140-141) observes as follows:

> In 1989, the political associations being formed were allowed to seek registration as political parties. The requirements for registration were grossly unreasonable. They included the number of offices each would-be party had to open and operate and the list of their supporters – with photographs! All this had to be amassed and submitted in just three months. The regime set the rules and it could impose any criteria it wished. After the mountain of materials were delivered to the Electoral Commission in Lagos, the verdict soon followed: none of the associations has met the test and government was going to create its own political parties, name them, write their manifestoes, and oversee their development.

Gradually and even though there was official claim to the contrary, these actions cut the picture of carefully scripted ploys aimed at the elongation of the tenure of both governments. This was given added credence with the June 23rd, 1993 annulment of the 12th June 1993 presidential election, variously considered as the fairest election in the history of the country.

The General Abacha led successor military government which eased out the ING contraption hurriedly put in place by IBB also had its own deceptive script coming in the shape of yet another transition programme. The programme which involved the convening of a constitutional conference and the formation of new political parties also suffered the now familiar antics of the military, including close supervision and subsequently reversals on some key aspects of the programme, particularly the handover date which was moved from 1996 to 1998. In all, five parties were cleared to contest and these were the United Nigeria Congress Party (UNCP), Democratic Party of Nigeria (DPN), Congress for National Consensus (CNC), Grassroots Democratic Movement (GDM) and the National Center Party of Nigeria (NCPN). In regards to the new parties, Umar (2008: 13) had cause to observe as follows:

> The composition of the party leaderships and importantly too, the brazen manner by which the government continuously interfered

> with their activities, including the determination of who vied for which offices and under what platform, eroded any confidence in their independence. Accordingly, the parties were seen as mere government fronts set up to pursue a hidden agenda. In fact, as the transition gathered momentum, the true character of the parties became manifest with all of them deciding to fill the incumbent ruler, Sani Abacha as their sole pallbearer. The hidden agenda suspicion was given added impetus when all manner of pro – Abacha groups emerged all over the country, culminating into the convening of the "two (sic) million man march" in Abuja in support of the Abacha candidacy. A counter march at Lagos tagged the "five million man march" was scattered by the police.

It was amidst these controversies, confusions and uncertainties that Abacha was pronounced dead on 8th June 1998, thereby abruptly ending another era in the political development of Nigeria.

Abacha's death necessitated the appointment, by the military top echelon, of General Abdulsalami Abubakar as the country's successor head of state. Abubakar's initial decisions, not unlike the predecessor regimes, included the dissolution of the political parties and the cancellation of all elections contested and held under their platforms. He also ensured the release of political detainees and the determination to hold new elections that would ensure the ceding of power to civilians by 1999. It came to pass as the government organized elections involving three registered political parties, the Peoples Democratic Party (PDP), All Peoples Party (APP) and Alliance for Democracy (AD). The former, (PDP) at the end of the elections, formed the government at the Center, while each of the parties secured governorship slots in a number of states and a number of representations at the National Assembly. Chief Olusegun Obasanjo, alongside elected governors in the states of the federation was sworn in as Nigeria's president on 29th May 1999. His ascendance thus marked the commencement of what came to be known as the country's Fourth Republic.

The significance of the above historical must not be lost. The twist and turns witnessed in the country's governance realm had had far reaching implications on the patterns and dimensions of its developmental processes. In effect, the instability the personnel and institutions of governance helped blocked or even truncated the development of such democratic institutions as the political parties, the parliament as well as other structures of governance. At the economic level, official corruption, waste and embezzlement as well as the limitation or even lack of sound policies at the macro and micro levels added further strains. Naturally, any departure from these ills, which many Nigerians hoped the new civilian government will ensure, raises some glitter of optimism. Whether or not such hope was realistic will be seen in the sections that follow.

The Fourth Republic: Gains and Losses

The assumption of office by Obasanjo in 1999 naturally elicited a lot of expectations among Nigerians. The belief was that the dark years of bad leadership will be halted and the country would be back on a pedestal that could ensure the speedy resolution of the problems bedevilling the people. This heightened optimism is understandable given that the democratic system, compared to all others, is reposed with those qualities that make the realization of the goals of societal development possible.

The first few years since 1999, however, left much to be desired as far as the dividends of democracy were concerned. Nigerians, naturally, were disappointed that the fruits of the democratic struggle they waged were as yet not realized. What they envisaged in form of the speedy amelioration of the grinding poverty, expansion of national output and income as well as the resuscitation of the industrial and other service sectors was not forthcoming. The few gains provided by the relatively new air of freedom that democracy ensures were equally dampened by the total lack of achievement in the resolution of the myriad of problems in both the socio-political and the economic realms. Not even the teething problems of unemployment, widespread poverty, scarcity of fuel and unreliable power supply were effectively handled. As a commentator writes of the first two years of Obasanjo:

> Fundamental questions are being posed on the commitment of the government to reversing the tide of economic decline. The government has admitted that its amateurish attempt to increase employment through providing monthly emoluments to ruling party faithfuls has failed. The campaign they launched to justify the increase in fuel prices collapsed. The policy of abandoning the pursuit of social welfare and the privatization of virtually all services has caused much consternation. More ominously, the confidence the government has placed on international financial institutions rather than its own people creates doubts as to their commitment to economic development (http://www.nai.uu.se/publication/news/archvies/013ibrahim)

Indeed, by 2003, the initial euphoria has considerably waned. The old signs of the dismal past persisted. The dream of better days was never realized. By 2007, Nigerians must have realized the folly of hinging their hope on any dividends. With the debilitating challenges that marked the regime, especially the spates of ethno - religious crises, official corruption and the rancorous electoral process, none seems forthcoming (Akwani, 2007). Perhaps, the controversies, dissensions and turmoil in both the political and economic realms were unprecedented. Since the commencement of the preparations of the 2007 polls, the polity remained charged and the political waters were turbulent. The debacle that trailed the elections has been fully captured by analysts as well as the local and international observers and included the selective indictment of prospective candidates in both the ruling and opposition parties, the politically motivated assassinations and the generally flawed primaries conducted by the political parties (*Human Rights Watch*, 2007; *This day*, 2007; *Daily Trust*, 2007)

The electoral process itself was compromised by such flaws as late or even non arrival of INEC staff and election materials, heavy presence of security personnel, missing names of prospective voters, discovery of fake and already stuffed ballot boxes, missing logo of some political parties and limited accreditation of especially domestic observers (*Nigerian Tribune*, 2007). As Umar (2007: 100) observes in this regard:

> These avoidable flaws, not unexpectedly, led to bitter condemnations, inflamed tension and even violence in some parts of the country. They also raised questions about the credibility of the entire exercise. For example, a preliminary report released by the International Republican Institute (IRI), a United States based non governmental organization, adjudged the poll as being below the standard set by previous Nigerian elections and international standards witnessed by IRI around the globe and that the elections up to those observed by members of the IRI delegations in other countries whether in Africa, Asia, Europe or the Western Hemisphere.

Suffice to note, however, that in spite of these debilitating shortcomings, there was palpable elation that at least the country was able, for the first time in its political history, to record the much elusive civilian to civilian transition. With the entry of the new government, led by Umaru Musa Yar'adua, hopes that were hitherto dashed became rekindled. The brash regime of Obasanjo having ended, Nigerians once again expectedly looked up to the new government for the speedy resolution of the issues that seem to strangulate the polity. The harsh economic conditions being faced largely due to deregulation and other unpopular economic policies pursued by the government, it was hoped, would be reversed.

Perhaps, not unmindful of these expectations, the new president, on assumption to power, openly acknowledged the rot he inherited, especially the circumstances of the elections that brought him to office. He promised to reform the electoral process and do many other things including addressing the vexed issue of the Niger delta, pursue the privatization policy, wage anti-corruption war and promote efficiency as pivot of good governance. These and other soon became encapsulated into what is now known as the 7-point agenda. Almost two years after, not many Nigerians remain optimistic that their lot will be bettered. There seems little or no sign that the goals in the president's agenda in the energy, agriculture, wealth creation, or even the Niger Delta could be attained. The much anticipated dividend of democracy, in light of this governance deficit and the current global economic meltdown, will obviously be deferred.

Nigeria's Political Development: Further Strains

A number of other issues, besides the ones raised in the foregoing discussion, must necessarily take centre stage in the attempt to grapple with the obstacles to political development of Nigeria. Drawing from the preceding sections, therefore, it seems crystal clear that the country has been mired in substantial structural and institutional summersault in its journey to nationhood. Among other factors, governmental instability, occasioned by abrupt changes in government through coups and counter coups, the subsequent ascendance of the military as a governing body and the governance deficit it wrought, the wave of political crises and violence that permeate the polity, all account for the character of the state of affairs in contemporary times.

Persistent changes in government and, with it, the abrogation of the structures of governance do not in anyway help the task of development. If anything, such events only serve to disrupt the process of the institutionalization of most of the institutions and structures that under gird any stable polity. Military takeovers, essentially, place strains, if not totally obliterate such political institutions as the political parties, the parliament, the bureaucracy and even the elements of the civil society, through the suspension of the constitution and the scrapping of the institutions of political participation. Military decrees, often with retrospective powers and ouster clauses become the new policy frameworks.

An issue that generated a great deal of attention as far as the impact of the military on the political development of the country is concerned has been in the area of the federal structure of the country. The military through its centralizing tendencies, not only encouraged dependence of the federating units on the center, but also effectively stunted the development of the federal principles as the guiding pillars of unity for the diverse peoples of Nigeria. Yet, nothing to the contrary should be expected since by its very character, the military is not suited to promote the federal principle. The strict hierarchical and other centralizing ethos of the military ensured that the central government, even though referred to as the *federal military government*, dwarfs and obliterate whatever autonomy the constituent units may lay claim to. This was further reinforced by the military initiation and supervision of the processes of constitution making that granted overwhelming powers to the federal center to the detriment of the other federating units. Federal system in the country was therefore cast in the image of the military with all its attendant consequences.

A classic illustration of what strains a perverted federal system could portend for a country is the current and ever deepening crises in the Niger

Delta part of Nigeria. Over the years and particularly since the onset of the latest democratization drive, the region has posed great danger to both the society and its economic sector, leading to not only armed confrontations, kidnappings and senseless killings of innocent souls, but has greatly affected the country's oil production and export. As the New York Times (April 21, 2007) report shows, in 2007 alone, over 150 foreign oil workers were kidnapped by the militants who in most cases ask for huge ransom for them to be released. Other debilitating challenges to the country's economic mainstay include the persistent blowing up of pipelines and disabling of pump stations. In quantitative terms, the Niger Delta unrests had led to over 25% of output shutdown and a loss of $12 million (NESG, 2006).

Constitutional Violations and the Governance Process

Constitution making, necessitated in part, by the need to lay down new ground rules of governance as the military prepares to exit and perhaps guarantee it certain perquisites, has been an area in which the military has left its mark. Indeed, all but two (1960 and 1963) of the five post independence constitutions (the others being the 1979, 1989 and 1999 constitutions) of the country were midwived by the military. The process that led to their promulgation, especially the non representative nature of the membership of the committees or panels that at various times superintended them, renders the product suspect. The constitutions were also not subjected to the ratification of the citizenry, but the approval of the members of the military governing body, which have come in different shapes and sizes.

In effect, constitution making in Nigeria had been criticized as mere charades not unlike many features of the political process. Essentially, the lack of public ownership of the documents, occasioned by some of the failures alluded to earlier, had served to deny the constitution the respect and reverence expected by it from the citizens. The pertinent question here remains: Has anything changed in the last ten years?

Answer to the above question is not hard to fathom. Essentially, attempts at constitutional reform during the second (2003-2007) tenure of Obasanjo were as half-hearted as they were self-serving. They did not seem to depart from the general trend in the other sectors of the polity. An important measure of this, perhaps, remains the sanctioning of the National Political Reform Conference which enlisted the participation of delegates from all the states of the federation and the FCT, professional groups, representatives of other interest groups as the media, the religious groups, women, and students, amongst others.

It seems the conference from the beginning was jinxed. It was trailed by bitter criticisms and contestations over the skewed composition of its leadership, unequal representation of varied interests, especially religion, and more importantly the legality of the exercise in the presence of an elected parliament that ideally should carry out any reform in the country's laws. Similar and perhaps more chaotic scenario is in the air with the current attempt at the constitutional review pitting the country's two national legislative in a battle of wits over matters of leadership of the joint panel and other protocols. Yet it remains a truism that these ills are merely reflective of the broader abuses or onslaught that afflicted the country's political and other institutions.

The character of a country's political and other institutions necessarily affects the health of the political system that thrives in the society. Inferring from this premise, it then becomes obvious that a number of actions taken by governments in Nigeria during the prolonged military rule affects the governance process in at least two varied ways. In the first instance, the ambush laid on the constitution, the obliteration or banning of political parties, the sacking of the legislature and the affront on the judiciary all combine to jettison the development of the country's established structures of governance. The gains that their existence provided were therefore lost, sequel to the actions of the "barrack boys". Yet all evidences stemming from the methods employed by the successor government never seem to depart from the course charted by the preceding regimes. This, needless to stress, has had a long lasting effect on the development of a viable political culture built on the pillars of tolerance, compromise and consensus.

Furthermore and coupled with the failure of the various governments to remedy the ills that they purportedly set out to correct, raised a number of options for the citizenry. Smarting from the apparent failure to arrest the drift to heightened economic difficulties as well as the intensification of the repressive character of the government in securing compliance to the often unpopular policies, ensured that the citizens withdrew from the state to the safety of the nets provided by the gamut of associations or organizations popularly referred to as the civil society groups, including community-based organizations, occupational and professional groups, pro-democracy groups, etc. It was not by circumstance, therefore, that these organizations gained in number around the mid 1980's when the bitter pills of SAP were ravaging the economy and as well, the programme of transition becomes mired in controversies and uncertainties. Thus, the loss of the institutions of the political society became the gain of the civil society institution, with lots of implication for the push for democratization in the country.

At the other level, the shrinking of the state also facilitated the resort to actions that are at variance with the laws of the land, but which provided avenues for remedying the penury that envelops the society. Activities such as smuggling, oil bunkering, armed banditry and trafficking in drugs and persons gained in momentum with disastrous consequences for both the state and its society. Indeed, the rising tide of the militant agitation in the Niger Delta region of the country which Ikelegbe (2001: 438-439) correctly refers to as a "terrain of violent protests, disruption of oil production, seizures of oil platforms, installations and equipments, kidnapping of multinational oil companies (MNOC) staff, confrontation with state security forces and militarizing of the region" had had serious effect for the state and its international partners especially in relation to oil output and pricing.

Conclusion

Following this discourse, it is obvious that Nigeria's engagement with the democratization process is historically rooted. Since independence in 1960, the country, in spite of the obstacles posed by among other things the persistent intrusion of the military into the political domain, with lots of implication for the development of democratic institutions and structures, could be said have made some positive moves towards liberalizing the political space. Notwithstanding these attempts, however, the citizens have as yet not benefited from the fruits that democratic openness supposedly provides. The ills of corruption, nepotism, violation of the rule of law and the general lack of good governance have continued to have far-reaching effects on the capacity of the state and its agencies to provide the much needed succor to the citizens who have continued to suffer from all kind of deprivations.

Considering that the euphoria generated by the return to civil rule in 1999 is hinged on the presumption that the country will witness some sanity in its governance realm, the lack-lustre performance witnessed in the one decade of democratization (1999-2009) has left much to be desired. For the citizens, the hopes raised have seemingly been deferred, giving way to gloom and despair.

References

Adedeji, Adebayo (1997). Popular Participation, Democracy and Development: Is there a Dialectical Linkage? In Adabayo Adedeji and Onigu Otite (eds.), *Nigeria: Renewal from the Roots? The Struggle for Democratic Development*. London: Zed Books.

Akwani, Obi O. (2007). Changing of the Guard: The Development of Democracy in Nigeria, An Assessment of the Obasanjo Era. Retrieved from http://www.imdiversity.com/Villages/Global Politics/ChangingTheGuardInNigeria.

Daily Trust, 17 May 2007.

Human Rights Watch Report 2007. *Nigeria*.

Ikelegbe, Augustine (2001). Civil Society, Oil and Conflict in the Niger Delta Region of Nigeria: Ramification of Civil Society for a Regional Resource Struggle. *Journal of Modern African Studies*, Vol. 39, No. 3, pp. 433 – 469.

Joseph, Richard (1997). Democratization under Military Rule and Repression in Nigeria. In Paul A. Beckett and Crawford Young (eds.), *Dilemmas of Democracy in Nigeria*. Rochester: University of Rochester Press.

Momoh, Abubakar (2006). Democracy and Sustainable Development in Nigeria. In Sani L. Mohammed (ed.), *Civilian and Security Agencies Relationship: The Role of Military in Consolidating Democracy in Nigeria*. Abuja: Friedrich Ebert Stiftung.

Moss, Todd J. (2007). *African Development: Making Sense of the Issues and Actors.* London: Lynne Rienner Publishers.

Nigerian Economic Summit Group Economic Indicators, October – December 2006

Nigerian Tribune, 16 April 2007.

Nwabueze, B. O. (1985). *Nigeria's Presidential Constitution 1979 – 83: The Second Experiment in Constitutional Democracy.* New York: Longman Group Limited.

Rudebeck, Lars (ed.), (1995). *When Democracy Makes Sense: Studies in the Democratic Potentials of Third World Popular Movements.* Akkut: Upssala University.

Sartori, Giavonni (1995). How Far Can Free Government Travel? *Journal of Democracy*, Vol. 6, No. 3, July.

Sklar, Richard (1997). Crises and Transitions in the Political History of Nigeria. In Paul A. Beckett and Crawford Young (eds.), *Dilemmas of Democracy in Nigeria*, Rochester: University of Rochester Press.

Thisday, 23 April 2007.

Umar, M. Z. (2007) *Nigeria and the Challenges of Democratic Consolidation* (Sokoto: Ijabah Press).

Umar, M. Z. (2008). Transitions to Democracy in Nigeria: Lessons Learned. Unpublished.

Van de Walle, Nicholas (1995). Crisis and Opportunity in Africa. *Journal of Democracy*. Vol. 6, No. 2, April. http://www.nai.uu.se/publications/news/archives/013ibrahim

Zabadi, Istifanus (1995). Economic Reforms and the Transition to Democracy in Africa. Paper presented at the Institute of Governance and Social Roundtable Conference, Jos, Nigeria.

16

Poverty Eradication Efforts in Nigeria: the Missing Links

Folashade B. Okeshola

INTRODUCTION

Despite its plentiful resources and oil wealth, poverty is widespread in Nigeria. The situation has worsened since the late 1990s, to the extent that the country is now considered one of the 20 poorest countries in the world. Over 70 per cent of the population is classified as poor, with 35 per cent living in absolute poverty (Hellandendu, 2002).

Poverty is especially severe in rural areas, where social services and infrastructure are limited or non-existent. The great majority of those who live in rural areas are poor and depend on agriculture for food and income. About 90 per cent of the country's food is produced by small scale farmers cultivating tiny plots of land who depend on rainfall rather than irrigation systems. Surveys show that across the country 44 per cent of male farmers and 72 per cent of female farmers cultivate less than 1 hectare per household. Women play a major role in the production, processing and marketing of food crops. A high proportion of rural people suffer from malnutrition and other diseases related to poor nutrition. The HIV/AIDS pandemic has also taken a heavy toll among the rural population (IFAD, 2007).

This chapter will examine poverty as a concept, poverty in Nigeria, programmes put in place to address poverty in Nigeria, factors responsible for the failure of the programme, and finally suggestions on poverty reduction in Nigeria.

Poverty as a Concept

Defining poverty has always been a very difficult thing to do. Even though various ways of conceptualising poverty has been proposed by scholars. There are three types of poverty. These are absolute poverty, relative poverty and material poverty.

Absolute poverty is defined as the lack of sufficient resources with which to keep body and soul together. It can be seen as the state of existing below the income that secures the basic essentials of food, clothing and shelter. According to a United Nations Declaration that resulted from the World Summit on Social Development in Copenhagen in 1995, absolute poverty is a condition characterised by severe deprivation of basic human needs, including food, safe drinking water, sanitation facilities, health, shelter, education and information. Absolute poverty depends not only on income but also on access to service.

Relative poverty is the inability of certain sections of the society to meet their basic needs. Sometimes the situation is best described as when income cannot meet basic essentials, like simple clothing, good health, transport cost, house rent, school fees, etc. Material poverty is taken to imply lack of ownership of physical asserts such as land, livestock and savings (Hellandendu, 2002).

Poverty is hunger, lack of shelter, being sick and not being able to see a doctor. Poverty is losing a child to illness brought about by unclean water. Poverty is powerlessness, lack of representation and freedom. Poverty is a call to action for the poor and the wealthy alike – a call to change the world so that many more may have enough to eat, adequate shelter, access to education and health, protection from violence and a voice in what happens in their communities. Poverty is the state of being without, often associated with need, hardship and lack of resources across a wide range of circumstances.

Poverty is, undoubtedly, today's most maintained problem. It's very serious because it comprises children too. Many young and smart people are forced to refuse education because they just don't have opportunity to have it. According to Dimitrovski (2006), eradicating the extreme poverty and hunger is one of the essential problems in the world which must be solved in the near future.

Aigbokhan (2000) defines poverty "as the inability to achieve a certain minimal standard of living". With severe economic shocks that rocked the Nigerian economy during the early 1980s came real and perceived increases in the level of poverty. Among the factors contributing to the shocks were declining prices of oil, the country's main export, and rises in real international interest rates that compounded the external debts. Aderounmu (2007), defined mass poverty "as the poverty that affects the masses of a population who have extreme want of necessities.

Poverty in Nigeria

According to Dike (2003), the absence of true federalism in Nigeria is a stumbling block to the nation's ongoing democratic enterprise. The Federal government is very overbearing as it controls about eighty (80) per cent of the resources in the country, leaving State and Local governments at its mercy. Therefore, true federalism would enable each region, state or geopolitical zone to control their resources and to have access to the necessary funds for community development programmes. It is only true federalism that can guarantee fairness and justice in the society. It will also enable each locality to progress according to the aspiration of the people.

Also, illiteracy and ignorance is an obstacle to the Nation's quest for true democracy. More than one half of the Nigerian population is illiterate. Thus, a certain level of education would enable the citizens to differentiate right from wrong and evaluate the principles of political leaders and political office seekers so as to make an informed political decision. It has been observed that political parties and politicians in the society are not ideologically ingrained (Dike, 2003). It has been observed that some political parties and those elected to manage the affairs of the nation do not represent the interest of the populace but rather engaged in bribery and corruption, which make the sustenance of true democracy impracticable.

Dike (2003) finds that continued poverty is reinforced by mass unemployment. This is a barrier to the Nigeria's quest to true democracy. The Federal government had announced a war on poverty, but joblessness has not lessened. It is believe that any individual deprived of the basic necessities of life cannot participate effectively in a democratic political process.

In Nigeria, discrimination, ethnicity, tribalism and poverty are closely related, as they affect the people's ability to secure employment and earn a living. Many people are concerned more of their daily struggle for economic survival than the concept of democracy, which they believe cannot feed them. In view of this, the government need to embark on social policies to gear up economic growth. Through the provision of basic education, health care and equitable distribution of resources. This will go a long way to reduce poverty.

Nigeria's reward system is one of the poorest in the world, which is among the cause of poverty. Workers work for months without getting their salaries and the retired are not paid their pension benefits. Unfortunately, hard work is not rewarded, but rogues and thieves are glorified. These attitudes adversely affect the lives of the citizens thereby making the attainment of true democracy a difficult task. For a country to prosper there is need for an individual, group or nation to provide shelter, nutrition and other material goods that will enable people to live a good life (Dike, 2003).

According to Sudharshan and Saji (2001), poverty in Nigeria is overwhelmingly rural and regional in characteristics. It is also strongly influenced by education, age and the nature of employment. Those without an education constitute a large fraction of the poor and the extreme poor.

IFAD (2007), found that rural infrastructure in Nigeria has long been neglected, while investments in health, education and water supply have largely been focused on the cities. As a result, the rural population has extremely limited across to services such as schools and health centres, and about half of the population lacks access to safe drinking water. Limited education opportunities and poor health perpetuate the poverty cycle.

Also, neglect of rural infrastructure has reduced the profitability of producing for the markets. Nigeria's rural road network is one of the least developed in sub-Saharan Africa. The poor tend to live in isolated villages that can become virtually inaccessible during rainy seasons. When there is a post harvest marketable surplus, it is not always easy to reach the markets. Limited accessibility has also cut off small-scale farmers from sources of inputs, equipment and new technology. Crop yields are low because farmers lack these inputs.

Due to the population explosion and the pressure on diminishing resources, escalating environmental problems further threaten food production. Land degradation, as a result of extensive agriculture, deforestation and other grazing, is already at an alarming level in many parts of the country. Drought has become common in the north, while in the South and South-East erosion provoked by heavy rains, floods and oil pollution is a major problem (IFAD, 2007).

Poverty and violence are often closely interconnected. Both religious and ethnic tensions continue to brew in different parts of Nigeria, erupting into outbreaks of violence and leading in turn to a situation of escalating poverty and malnutrition. The move towards political liberalisation has allowed militants from religious and ethnic groups to express their frustrations more freely and with increasing violence.

In the Niger Delta, where the oil industry is based, a vigorous trade in stolen oil has led to a serious breakdown in law and order in that area. A number of acts of sabotage have been carried out against the multinational oil companies by groups seeking a grater share of the oil resources for the Niger Delta population (IFAD, 2007).

Dike (2003), observed that one of the most pressing problem facing Nigeria is leadership. The society will continue to have problems realising its dreams until its political leaders are capable of making tough decisions with vigorous enforcement of the laws of the land to deter anti-social and anti-democracy behaviours. The democratic enterprise will not be fruitful until the leaders begin to initiate activities that promote progressive values and attitudes. Another predicament is the absence of basic democratic values in the society. Some of the political leaders have often left many in doubt about their respect for democratic norms. Ethical crisis and fraud perpetrated mostly by the law makers are approaching an alarming proportion. This includes politics of greed and lust for power, electoral frauds, political intolerance, thugs and political assassinations. To attain a true democracy, everyone in the society must have equal political opportunity to participate in the political process. Political differences and disagreements among citizens should be tolerated and protected.

Aderounmu (2007) observes that poverty in Nigeria has many indices. Nigeria is a country with over 140 million people, therefore, the dimension of mass poverty in Nigeria is both dreadful and shocking. Many citizens of Nigeria cannot afford to live a decent life. Several millions of Nigerians do not have the usual or socially acceptable amount of money or material possessions. Only a few people are comfortable. He also observes that common drinking water does not flow in Nigerian homes. People have to buy water as many boreholes have run dry and the public taps have virtually disappeared.

There is prevalence of hunger in Nigeria. Foodstuffs are the cheapest things you can lay your hands on in some other countries: in Nigeria, common and staple foods are now very expensive and many people have devised different formula to survive daily, weekly or monthly. There has not been efficient or functional power supply even if you can conveniently pay for it. There may be no fuel to run the noisy and environmentally unfriendly generators. Nigerians have no known options to persistent blackouts. It is a hard reality of life. It depicts cruelty. This deficiency of power supply has aided the mass poverty as thousands of people have been put out of job since many companies can no longer sustain their operations in the absence of it. The Nigerian masses and elites cannot travel on safe roads. The masses are more affected because there is constant chaos in the public transportation methods. The conditions are dehumanising to say the least. This is further displayed in the health schemes. The cost of getting good treatment at the hospital is prohibitive and the access to modern health facilities it greatly hindered. The poor and helpless masses are always at the receiving end of all the misgivings of the politicians and policy makers (Aderounmu, 2007).

Poverty Alleviation Programmes in Nigeria

In the light of the devastating suffering by the Nigerian economy during the past decade, a consistent pattern and incidences of poverty was initiated and maintained. The commutative effect of the country's economic problem is more clearly reflected in the likes of desperately poor rural and urban slum dwellers (Hellandendu, 2002).

In trying to deal with the problem various institutional measures were taken by the government. Consensus effort by government towards poverty alleviation began in Nigeria during the era of Structural Adjustment Programme (SAP). The severe economic crisis in Nigeria in the early 1980's worsened the quality of life of most Nigerians. The government made determined effort to check the crisis through the adoption of SAP. However, the implementation of SAP further worsened the living conditions of many Nigerians especially the poor who were the most vulnerable group (Ogwumike, 1998). The Federal Government designed and implemented many poverty alleviation programmes between 1986 and 1993. According to the Central Bank of Nigeria reports, more poverty reduction programmes were put in place.

Table 16.1: Anti-poverty Programmes by the Government of Nigeria

Programme	*Year Established*	*Target Group*	*Nature of Intervention*
Directorate for Food, Roads and Rural Infrastructure (DFFRI)	1986	Rural areas	Feeder Roads, rural water supply and rural electrification
National Directorate of Employment (NDE)	1986	Unemployed youths	Training, finance and guidance
Better Life Programme (BLP)	1987	Rural women	Self-help and rural development programmes, skill acquisition and health care
People's Bank of Nigeria (PBN)	1989	Underprivileged in rural and urban areas	Encouraging savings and credit facilities
Community Banks (CB)	1990	Rural residents, micro enterprises in urban areas	Banking facilities
Family Support Programme (FSP)	1994	Families in rural area	Health care delivery, child welfare, youth development etc.
Family Economic Advancement Programme (FEAP)	1997	Rural areas	Credit facilities to support the establishment of cottage industries.

Source: Oladeji and Abiola, (1998).

(a) Directorate of Food, Roads and Rural Infrastructure (DFFRI): This programme was a radical departure from the previous programmes. According to Ogwumike (1998), DFRRI recognised the compliment associated with the provision of basic needs such as food, shelter, portable water etc. The programme has a tremendous impact on the rural areas. From the CBN reports, since inception in 1986 and 1993, DFRRI had completed over 278,526 km of roads. Over 5,000 rural communities benefited from its rural electrification programme. This integrated approach to rural development provided for the necessary basic infrastructures that can stimulate the growth of agro-allied small scale enterprises in rural areas. It was also observed in the CBN Statistical Bulletin of December, 1998 that DFRRI impacted positively on food production as there was a steady and significant rise in agricultural output.

Unfortunately, DFRRI could not achieve many of its objectives due to many factors such as lack of standards for project harmonisation and effective mechanisms for coordination among the three tiers of government. With time, DFRRI could not sustain the rigour with which it started. It later became defunct National Planning Commission in 1994.

(b) The National Directorate of Employment (NDE): It was meant to be the main organ for employment creation during this period. The objectives of NDE were to design and implement programmes to combat mass unemployment, articulate policies aimed at developing work programmes with labour intensive potential. According to Ogwunike (1998), the directorate has four main programmes that not only create jobs but also enhances the productivity and income earning potentials of the youths and other beneficiaries. These programmes include: the Vocational Skills Development Programme (VSD), the Special Public Works Programme (SPW), the Small Scale Enterprises Programmes (SSE) and the Agricultural Employment Programme (AEP).

Although the programme has achieved remarkable progress of training people in open apprenticeship scheme, some have benefited from the resettlement scheme, the special public works programme as well as the Schools on Wheels Schemes engaged by the youths. NDE is one of the institutions that survived the SAP era and has continued to articulate development policies and programmes with labour intensive potentials aimed at solving the unemployment problems in the county. Just like any other programme, NDE has not been adequately funded as such, could not cope with the needs of the ever increasing number of job applicants in the country.

(c) Better Life Programme (BLP): The programme was set up to enhance the quality of life of rural women. It has been observed that poverty in Nigeria is a rural phenomenon and the rural women are worst hit by the dreadful incidence of poverty. This is due to lack of basic skill and education necessary for gainful employment (Ogwumike, 1988).

(d) People's Bank of Nigeria (PBN): It was set up to encourage savings and provide credit facilities for the underprivileged in both urban and rural areas. Also, **Community Banks (CB)** were established to provide banking facilities for rural dwellers as well as to support micro enterprises in urban areas (Oladeji and Abiola, 1998). The two banking schemes were established in recognition of the indispensable role of finance in poverty alleviation. It was found that the two banking schemes had some success, but many of their goals and objectives were never realised. The schemes were bedevilled by corruption and gross mismanagement.

(e) Family Support Programme (FSP): It was set up to provide health care delivery, child welfare, youth development, and improved nutritional status to families in rural areas.

(f) Family Economic Advancement Programme (FEAP): It was established to provide credit facilities to cooperative societies to support the establishment of cottage industries in both rural and urban areas. The programme was also designed to create employment opportunities at ward levels, encourage the design and manufacture of appropriate plants, machinery and equipments, and provide opportunities for the training of ward-based business operators (Oladeji and Abiola, 1998). Findings reveal that Family Support Programme (FSP) recorded several remarkable achievements such as the establishment of many nursery and primary schools, construction of many public toilets and the setting up of many vocational schools. However, these projects were not properly executed and could not be sustained. Also, many of the poor in several communities did not actually benefit from these projects while they lasted.

It is important to note that most of the poverty alleviation strategies adopted in Nigeria were well focused on rural areas and on the agricultural sector. This is because poverty in Nigeria is largely a rural phenomenon with agriculture accounting for the highest incidence over the years. We should bear in mind that poverty reduction depends to a large extent on the agricultural sector, because the sector not only provides food for consumption as well as raw materials for manufacturing activities, but it is the main employer of labour especially in the rural areas (Ogwunike, 1998).

There were other programmes that were implemented in the health, education and housing sectors aimed at poverty reduction.

(g) Primary Health Care (PHC) and the Guinea Worm Eradication Programme (GWEP): Findings show that although the guinea worm eradication programme recorder a tremendous success, the effectiveness of the primary health care programme was grossly reduced due to inadequate funding, lack of equipment, essential drugs and trained manpower (Egware, 1997).

(h) The National Housing Policy: This has brought about the national housing fund, which was managed by Federal Mortgage Bank of Nigeria. The Federal Housing Authority and various state governments were involved in the direct construction of housing units. Despite the efforts put in place in the housing sector, it is a common knowledge that many Nigerians do not have decent accommodation. Many people live in congested rooms. Many Nigerians lack adequate accommodation and some are homeless as they sleep under bridges at night in many part of the country (like Lagos) due to lack of adequate housing facilities or high cost of accommodation. Therefore, the National Housing Scheme needs to be re-focused so as to make it accessible to majority of Nigerians (Kankwenda et al., 2000; Ogwumike, 1998; Egware, 1997).

Factors Responsible for Failure in Poverty Alleviation Programmes

At the inception of the current democratic government, many Nigerians were meant to believe that poverty alleviation is the ultimate goal of the present government. However, many Nigerians were yet to feel the impact of government poverty alleviation programme. Several reasons may be responsible for this. The failure to identify the poor and the nature of their poverty, domestic policy mistakes, the politics of personal rule, top-down approach and corruption (Ogwunike, R.O. and Aromolaran, A.B. 2000, Maduagwu, 2000).

Domestic policy mistakes: Economic reforms were introduced by the government of Nigeria in the mid 1986 in a Structural Adjustment Programme that included exchange rate devaluation, trade and financial reforms, budgetary and monetary contraction. These reforms were expected to revitalise the economy's growth. In turn, growth was expected to contribute noticeably to improved equity in the country. The question that readily comes to mind is to what extent has the structural adjustment reforms alleviated poverty in Nigeria? Do we say SAP has led to increase or decrease in inequality? Is there a widening gap between the poor and the rich?

The politics of personal rule: This is where there is rivalries and struggles by the poverty and wilful men to be in power for his own selfish interest. It is a big man politics where the ruler is of a considerably distance from the ordinary people (the ruled). In this type of politics there are constant practices of conspiracy, factional politics, clientelism, no accountability, transparency, corruption and secession manoeuvres. As such, the poverty alleviation programme which is meant to better the life of the ordinary people are often hijacked by the big men whose aim is to enrich their pockets (Maduagwu, 2000).

Top-Down Approach: Poverty alleviation programme should originate from the poor themselves. This is because it is the poor that understands the type of poverty they have and how their poverty could be alleviated. Many programmes have failed because the poor were not involved in the design and implementation. This is because, the poor usually have good prceptions of their own needs and goals and of what could be required to satisfy and make progress toward them.

Corruption: According to Onimode (2001: 36):

> The contribution of poverty to corrupt behaviour is with respect to unliveable salaries and wages, high unemployment and difficulty of physical survival. Each of these can drive officials to misappropriate public funds and receive gratification, in order "to make ends meet". The unemployed are often prone to offer gratification in order to secure very limited jobs, while the starving poor have a weakened capacity to resist corrupt temptations such as gratification and nepotism.

Suggestions on Poverty Reduction in Nigeria

Empowering rural people is an essential first step to eradicating poverty. It respects the willingness and capability that each of us has to take charge of our own life and to seek out opportunities to make it better. The government has tried to reduce poverty in recent time through upward review of salaries and wages. This is because people that have been pushed into temporary or transitory poverty especially in the civil service are gradually being moved out of poverty through this process.

Agricultural and rural development constitutes an important factor in alleviating poverty in any economy where poverty is a rural phenomenon like in Nigeria. A successful agricultural factor should provide the bulk of food requirement, supply agricultural raw materials to the manufacturing sector, and provide adequate employment and income to the farmers.

Basic education can lay the foundation for human capital formation through the process of skill acquisition.

Basic health services can enhance the health status of the populace and hence their participation in the production process.

There is need for creation of employment. This will help to eliminate underemployment of human and material resources. It will also provide sustainable employment to those who are openly unemployed. We should know that the rate of growth and pattern of growth is important to poverty reduction. Therefore, the participation of all (including the poor) in the growth process should be the goal of government.

There is need for skill development and provision of adequate vocational training centre to equip youths in particular for self-employment, and facilitate maintenance of community level projects. The activities of National Directorate of Employment (NDE) need to be constantly appraised and effort should be made to link up more with both the informal sector where apprehenticeship activities are carried out without proper basic structure of sustaining the apprehentice when they finish learning the job.

There is need for community based initiatives. Poverty reduction especially in rural areas will require strengthening the management capabilities of community based initiatives such as community based organisations and community development associations through seminars and workshops to enable them participate effectively in poverty reduction activities at that level. There is need for effective coordination and avoidance of duplication of efforts especially in States and Local governments where ruling political party is not in control.

There is need for decentralisation of social expenditure. The Federal government should relinquish most of its responsibility in the social sector to the State and Local governments. This will give the State and Local councils more autonomy to evolve and execute poverty alleviation programmes or projects that will take their peculiar circumstances into consideration (Maduagwu, 2000).

In conclusion, poverty reduction will need a holistic approach, which will involve both the government (Federal, State and Local levels), non-governmental organisations (NGOs), civil society and private sectors. The institutional framework of poverty alleviation in the country need to be revised. There is need to look at the various laws and regulations governing assert ownership, access to the labour markets and government social programmes in education and health sectors in particular.

The present efforts of government and international agencies like UNDP and UNICEF, etc. aimed at employment creation, provision of credits, skill acquisition, enhancing income earning opportunities of the vulnerable groups among others are very germane to poverty reduction. But they need to be properly focused on the poor.

References

Aderounmu, A. (2007). Thy Glory, O Nigeria! Mass Poverty in Nigeria. Retrieved from http://www.geocities.com.

Aigbokhan, B. (2000). Poverty, Growth and Inequality in Nigeria: A Case Study. *African Economic Research Consortium (AERC).*

Dike, V.E. (2003). Barriers to True Democracy in Nigeria. Retrieved from http://www/nigerdeltacongress.com.

Egwara, L. (1997). Poverty and Poverty Alleviation: Nigeria's Experience. *Poverty Alleviation in Nigeria.* Selected Papers for the 1997 Annual Conference of Nigerian Economic Society.

Hellandendu, J.M. (2002). The Vicious Circle of Poverty in Nigeria: Any Way Out? A Paper Presented at the National Confernece on Politics and Political Power Relations in Nigeria in Ahmadu Bello University, Zaria.

IFAD (2007). Rural Poverty in Nigeria. Millennium Project.

Maduagwu, A. (2000). Alleviating Poverty in Nigeria. *Africa Economic Analysis.*

Ogwumike, F.O. (1998). Poverty Alleviation Strategies in Nigeria. *Measuring and Monitoring Poverty in Nigeria.* Proceedings of the Seventh Annual Conference of the Zonal Research Units of Central Bank of Nigeria.

Oladeji, S.I. & Abiola, A.G. (1998). Poverty Alleviation with Economic Growth Strategy: Prospects and Challenges in Contemporary Nigeria. *Nigerian Journal of Economic and Social Studies (NJESS)*, Vol. 40, No. 1.

Onimode, B. (2001). Overview of Corruption and Organised Crime in Africa. In Lame Ibrahim & Odekunle Femi (eds.), *Fighting Corruption and Organised Crime in Nigeria: Challenges for the New Millennium.*

Sudharshanm, C. & Saji, T. (2001). Poverty in a Wealth Economy: The Case of Nigeria. *JAE Search At ECO*, Vol. 10, pp. 143-173.

17

Health Inequalities in Nigeria

Jimoh Amzat

Introduction

Diseases slow economic growth and development. This is because illness is associated with loss of productivity, income associated with prevention, treatment or death, physical, social and psychological damages. Expenditure on health is justified on the ground that society needs healthy individuals to fulfill its functional imperatives/needs in order to survive. Unfortunately most countries (especially developing nations) are experiencing poor health conditions with high prevalence of HIV/AIDS, malaria, TB, child and maternal mortality, resulting in increasing morbidity, mortality and forms of neurological and other damages. Nigeria is one of such countries that is in critical health situation. The country is one of the developing countries of the world. The critical health situation is a result of its underdevelopment, so also its underdevelopment is a partial result of its poor health condition. This is the dual-cord of health influence on the country. Health condition has been a good indicator of development. Even so, health problems contribute immensely to underdevelopment as resources ought to be channeled towards other developments efforts are utilized for treatment of disease as other related expenditures. Even though such expenditures are worthwhile, the situation of Nigeria is that monies are spent without projected outcomes. Health reforms are merely on papers. Country still wallows in various forms of health problems. Diseases that are ordinarily preventable account for high toll of morbidity and mortality in Nigeria.

One major vital explanation for the prevailing health crisis in Nigeria is the social production of health and disease also known as the political economy perspective of health. This is not only relevant or just to maintain a critical stance, but to explain the health realities of a developing country like Nigeria, it is central to look at the dynamic of health inequalities with the social system. This projects a case for alienation from health or exploitation through health provisioning or lack of responsiveness or political resolve, or weak status of the state in health provision. The approach provides a milieu for consideration of health indicators in the country and how inequality is widespread and responsible for deprivation of health among the major segments of the society.

Furthermore, it is also important to make it clear that there have been tendencies towards self-responsibility of health i.e. blame-the-victim approach which most TB, malaria, HIV campaigns fundamentally rely. Unfortunately, this micro analysis of health issues is so deficient. Health as an individual (micro) or social (macro phenomenon has been a subject of great debate). The essence of this chapter is not to further the debate but to make a clear polemic that indicates a macro approach to health and examine the health indicators and inequality in Nigeria. The basis is that it is a macro approach that could alleviate the prevailing health crisis because such approach is holistic, comprehensive dynamic and will cater for all inter-related and interdependent factors (such as socio-economic and political factors) that influence the health condition of the country.

Over the years, different administration in Nigeria has made frantic efforts to alleviate the preventing health crisis in the country. Despite years of generally efforts, the country is still singing the 'old song' of limited accessibility, availability and affordability to health care. There are numerous health problems in the country. The task of this chapter is to examine the prevent situation despite redemocratization which has attracted lot of hope and aspiration in the last ten years. Since 1999-2009, there are numerous health- care projects in the bid to deliver the goods to the populace. Then how has the Nigeria fared in terms of health problems and reforms.

Health Indicators in Nigeria

Most of the health indicators are parts of development indicators. This is because of the reciprocal relationship between the two. The DHS 2003 and several other documents from international agencies (such as WHO, DFID) provide the basic health indicators in Nigeria. The FGN also recognizes the inter-play between health and development when it asserts that it will commit itself to intensify action to attain the goal of health for all citizen by the year 2000 and beyond which will permit citizen to lead socially and economically productive lives at the highest possible level (FGN, 2003). The FGN expresses difficulty in gathering data about health indicators in Nigeria because the process (of data gathering) is still weak. Some of the basic health indicators are below:

Table 17.1: Demographic and Health indicators in Nigeria

GNI	*930 (US $)*
Infant mortality rate	90 per1000 live births
Childhood mortality rate	189 per 1000 children (1-5yrs)
Maternal mortality rate	8 per 1000
Crude death rate	18 per 1000 population
Life expectancy at birth	47 years
Total fertility rate	5.4
Population growth rate	3.2%
HIV/AIDS prevalence	4.4%
Total population	148 million
Malaria incidence	over 70 million cases per year
Number of children orphaned by AIDS	Over 1 million

Sources: UNICEF, 2009; NPC, 2006; FGN, 2007.

With a total population of over 148 million, Nigeria is the most populous in Africa, one of the most blessed, the 6th largest producer of oil, yet one of the poorest, as GNI is currently $930 dollars. The country's GDP is above that of Ghana ($590) and below those of Egypt ($1580) and South Africa ($5760). It has been reported that more than 70% of Nigerians are living below the poverty line of $1 a day (World Bank, 2007). The level of poverty impairs the ability of the majority to afford health care. There is population pressure in Nigeria, as the growth rate is currently 3.2%. The government in 2006 reaffirmed its desire to reduce it to 2%. Unfortunately, the contraceptive prevalence rate is still less than 10%. The fertility rate is currently 5.8. This fertility rate is considerably high compared with other countries. It is also very high when compared with the carrying capacity (socio-economic condition which supports the population of the country). It is in this light that the government reformulated national population policy as a development strategy in 2006.

The population policy was reformulated in 2006. The strategies for ensuring sustainable population growth were outlined but they are more on paper than in practice. More importantly, the document recognized population issued as multi-dimensional with enormous multiplier effects on the general well-being of the population including health. This signifies that population control is a core tactic in achieving improved standard of living in a less developed country like Nigeria. Such control will provide the opportunity to ensure quality rather than mere quantity of the human resource. The policy also has plans for different health programs especially contraceptive use, abortion, reproductive health and rights, family planning, safe motherhood, child health and HIV/AIDS.

Nigeria (like every other nations in the world) is confronted with the scourge of HIV/AIDS since the first case in 1986, millions (up to 4.4% of the population) have been infected. This is apart from numerous millions that are

Figure 1: HIV Prevalence by Zone in Nigeria

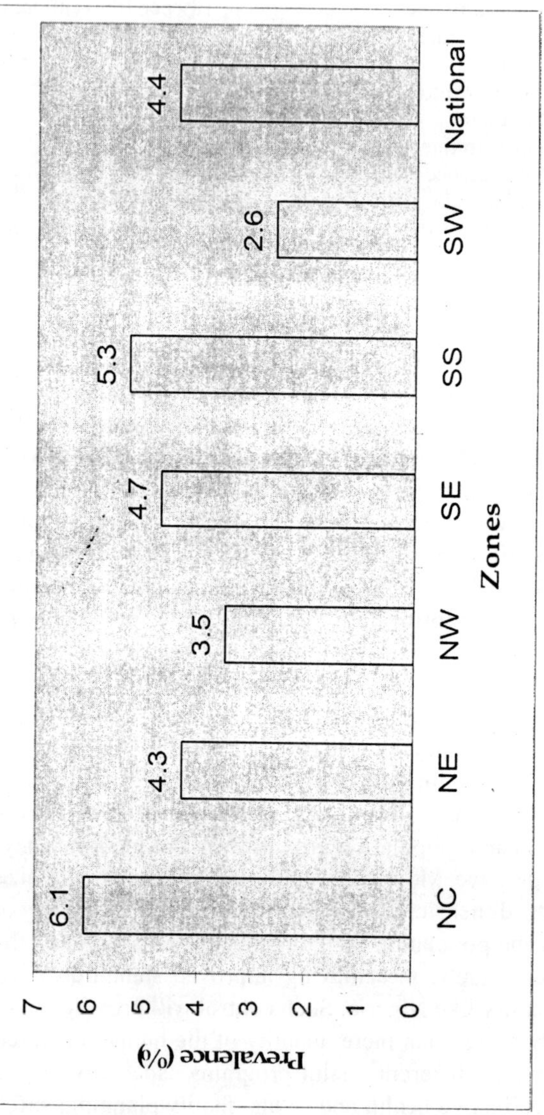

Source: 2005 National HIV Seroprevalance Sentinel Survey. Abuja: Federal Ministry of Health.

Table 17.2: Estimated Burden of Malaria Estimated Cases and Deaths (2006)

	Age group	*Numbers*	*Lower*	*Upper*
Fever suspected of being	All ages	155,556,000	95,978,000	217,205,000
malaria	< 5	92 231 000	15 447 000	years 178 057 000
Malaria cases	All ages	57,506,000	35,481,000	80,297,000
	< 5 years	34,096,000	5,710,000	65,825,000
Malaria deaths	All ages	225,000	116,000	354,000
	< 5 years	219,000	110,000	337,000
Malaria case -fatality rate	All ages	0.39		
(%)	< 5 years	0.63		
Reported malaria	All ages	2,969,950		
Cases (2007)	< 5 years	1,004,392		
Reported malaria	All ages	10,289		
Deaths (2007)	< 5 years	2695		

Source: World Malaria Report, 2008:99.

affected by the deadly diseases. Figure 17.1 shows prevalence of HIV/AIDS by region in Nigeria. The prevalence varies from one geopolitical zone to another. Socio-economic and education development also vary from one zone to another. Several interwoven factors could explain the variations. Meanwhile, the prevalence of 4.4% translates to millions of Nigeria. Despite the high prevalence of HIV/AIDS in Nigeria, several challenges are still evidence. Voluntary counselling and testing (VCT) is still a major challenge. Because of the incurability of HIV/AIDS and other factors (such as stigmatization and inadequate personal motivation) many people stay ignorant of their HIV status. There are still inadequate HIV treatment centres. Another health problem in Nigeria is high prevalence of malaria. Jegede et al. (2006) report that at least 50% of Nigerians record an episode of malaria yearly. WHO (2008) also reported that Nigeria records the highest incidence of malaria in the world. Malaria is said to account for more 50% of all hospital attendance and admission. Table 17.2 shows the burden of Malaria in Nigeria. Malaria contributes to underdevelopment as it slows down development as a result of treatment and prevention costs. This is apart from the other forms of neurological damages and mortality due to malaria.

The foregoing signifies that Nigeria is enmeshed in severe health problems which constitute a major challenge to development process. It is rather unfortunate that the world's poorest region (sub-Sahara Africa) is also the worst hit by HIV/AIDS, malaria, TB and other preventable diseases.

Explaining Health Inequality in Nigeria

Individuals operate within certain social structures which explain their health status. It is within this realm that health inequality can be explained. Differential social opportunities translate to varying levels of vulnerabilities to diseases or infirmities. It is for this that Amzat (2008) observes that the epidemiological triangle of host agent and environment is supportive of the notion that social determinants play vital role in the production of diseases. This represents a departure from what Fee and Krieger (1993) describe as biomedical individualism or self-responsibility of health. Vulnerability (to disease) is conceived as a function of the socio-spatial, political and economic conditions. The state of health indicators in Nigeria suggests that the country is enmeshed in critical heath problems which could be situated within its political economy.

Because there is high level of poverty in Nigeria most people could not afford appropriate health care services. Health is thus an expensive commodity. It is not only that poverty adversely affects people is health condition, people's health condition also induces poverty. A lot of household resources are usually earmarked for prevention and treatment of diseases. WHO (2000) observes that a poor household in SSA may spend up to 25% of its income on malaria treatment alone. These are resources from most households that live below the poverty-line (less than a dollar a day). The effect of poverty on health status is alarming. Studies have advocated for the socio economic causes of HIV/AIDS (Fassin and Schneider, 2003; Amzat, 2008). This is premised on the assumption that poverty fuels AIDS pandemic in sub-Saharan Africa (SSA). Many youths are idle without hope of securing employment, there is growing number of street children, feminization of poverty: all these may cause low priority on sexual and reproductive health and increase exposure to HIV risk behaviour (Bankole et al., 2004). Most acute diseases like malaria and cholera are diseases of the poor. Such diseases account for high level of morbidity and mortality in poor households and further pauperize them. When a poor household is affected by a chronic disease, it will be a case of poor management which induces series of complications and eventual mortality. There are many cases of Nigerians turning to street begging (exposing sores, wounds and other very poor health conditions) for charity to procure themselves medical care.

Poverty affects health not only in monetary terms but also in terms of access to information and education regarding health services - especially preventing and treatment options. The poor always demonstrates low level of awareness of effective preventive measures. They are generally alienated from organized medical care. They form substantial majority of the underserved. In a weak state like Nigeria, most infrastructure (including health) are grossly inadequate and where available, not functional. The poor are the worst hit by the problem of inadequate and non-functioning health facilities. The have's, especially the political office-holders are fond of going abroad, the western countries particularly, for medical check-up and treatment. This is another reason why there is no political resolve to resuscitate the dilapidated health infrastructures in Nigeria. The health facilities are mostly meant for the indigenous middle class, the upper class go abroad, the poor are left to consult traditional healers and empty primary health care (PHC); empty in terms of personal and equipment (where available).

Jegede (2002: 217-218) observes that 'physician ratio in Nigeria is about 1 to 10,000 persons. Even the very few one available are concentrated in the urban areas at the neglect of the rural areas where more than 65% of the Nigerian population resides. It is further observed that inadequate physicians at the rural areas make most rural dwellers resort to trado-magical practitioners, quack doctors and spiritual homes. Apart from personnel, the physical structures (i.e. health centres) are not available in most rural areas. Hence, majority of them might travel more than 5 kilometres to access health facility. Travelling a long distance contributes to the delay that is responsible for high maternal mortality in the rural areas. The problem is compounded due to poor infrastructures in the rural areas: the road network is poor, no electricity, no portable water in rural areas. All these further exacerbate health problems and make few available health centres non-functioning. Jegede (2002) observes that there is a ratio of one health facility to about 10 rural communities. The situation is getting worst as the few available health facilities in most rural areas are collapsing due to under-utilization or total lack of pàtronage which mostly results from non-availability of personnel and equipment. At least, patronage is not expected when the facility has no personnel and equipments.

The condition in the rural communities and ghettos (in the cites) are similar. Such conditions greatly explain vulnerabilities to different disease. Most dwellings do not have basic facilities like good sanitation, toilet, decent bathroom, and water supply. Congestion is the order in the ghetto or poorly planned neighbourhood. Only about 60% of Nigerians have access to good sanitations and portable water (FGN, 2007). It is in line with this that Amzat (2008) observes that in a weak state like Nigeria almost every structural component is too weak or non-functioning. This problem also explains inequality in health.

The acute and chronic infrastructural problems and weak capacity of the state to supply structural needs reflect in the poor health status in Nigeria. One of the major features of Nigeria as a developing country is the poor health status. The health problem is one of national questions which are among the seven point agenda of the new political dispensation. Unfortunately, there has not been adequate political resolve commitment to alleviate the health problems in Nigeria. Health issues also appear as one of the millennium development goals (MDGs) but adequate progress towards achieving the goals has not been recorded. That is why Amzat (2009) observes that the goals might not be met in most sub-Saharan Africa (SSA), including Nigeria

Table 17.3: Under-five Mortality Rankings

Countries	*Value*	*Rank*
Sierra Leone	262	**1**
Afghanistan	257	**2**
Chad	209	**3**
Equatorial Guinea	206	**4**
Guinea-Bissau	198	**5**
Mali	196	**6**
Burkina Faso	191	**7**
Nigeria	189	**8**
Rwanda	181	**9**
Burundi	180	**10**
Niger	176	**11**
Central African Republic	172	**12**
Zambia	170	**13**
Mozambique	168	**14**
Democratic Republic of the Congo	161	**15**

Source: UNICEF, 2009.

by 2015. The FGN (2007) reported that there is slow progress towards meeting the goals. UNICEF (2009) has just rated Nigeria as 8th among the countries with high maternal mortality rate (see table 17.3).

The foregoing discussion shows that Nigeria is still enmeshed in series of health problems and the healthcare system is not (adequately) responsive. The overall problem is a reflection of the political economy of the state. Inequality of health is entrenched in Nigeria. The poor and the rural dwellers are under-served. The health care system is almost non-functioning. (Gereje, 2005) notes that the failure of the PHC in Nigeria is reflected in the poor and continuing deterioration of the basic health indicators in Nigeria. The capacity of the Nigeria state is too low in healthcare provisioning. Health status is a major indicator of development. The development challenges in Nigeria are enormous and they effect in all infrastructures in the country. Because poverty is very high in Nigeria, many people cannot afford appropriate health care services. There are inadequate health facilities. The inequality in health is deteriorating.

The Problem of Health Care in Nigeria

Most of the primary health care (PHC) centers are non-functioning. Gupta et al. (2003) reports that about 90% of PHC did not have malaria smear or expertise to test malaria and 95% did not have urine test strip. The national health policy (2003) summarized some of the major problem of health services in Nigeria thus:

The coverage (of health services) is inadequate. It is estimated that 54% of the population now has access to modern healthcare services. The rural communities and urban poor and not well served.

The orientation of the services is inappropriate with a disproportionately high expenditure on curative services as compared to promotive and preventive health services.

The management of the services often shows major weaknesses resulting in waste and inefficient, as shown by the failure to meet targets and goals.

The involvement of community is minimal at critical points in decision making process. Consequently, communities are not well informed on matters affecting their health.

The lack of basic data is a major constraint at all stages of planning monitoring and evaluation of health services.

The financial resources allocated to the health services, especially at some priority areas, are inadequate to permit them to function.

The basic infrastructure and logistic support are often defective owing to inadequate maintenance of buildings, medical equipment and vehicles, inadequate and unreliable supply of portable water and electricity, and the poor management of drugs, vaccines and supply system.

Over the years, the government has made some efforts in alleviating the health problems in Nigeria. The launch of primary healthcare in the 80s has really helped but most of the PHCs are now non-functioning. Most of the structures are collapsing. Between 2003 and 2007, the federal government upgraded some of the facilities in the teaching hospital, but the upgrading has not matched the required level. Most of the rural health facilities were not touched. In 2005, the federal government launched national health insurance scheme (NHIS). Unfortunate, the scheme is yet to cover the informal sector and not all formal sectors have joined the scheme. The NHIS can boost of 3.5 million enrollees as at the end of 2008 (out of over 140m Nigerians) (Abdulkadir, 2008).

More so, there is usually over reliance on donor agencies in the fight against HIV/AIDS, malaria and TB. There is need to establish more HIV treatment centers and voluntary counselling and confidential testing (VCCT) centers. There is still the need to ensure availability of new malaria drugs (Artemisia combination therapy) at affordable prices and scale up distribution of insecticide treated bednets (ITN).

Conclusions

There is entrenched health inequality in Nigeria. Efforts to improve the health of Nigerians must follow holistic perspectives. There is need to address numerous socio-economic issues which have profound influence on the health of the nation. More importantly, there is need for strong political will and considerable increase in health care financing coupled with effective implementation of policies and programs. The problem of the country is not usually at policy level but at the levels of implementation and sustainability. There is need to mobilize resources (material as well as non-material) in improving the health of Nigeria.

References

Abdulkadir, S. (2008). National Health Insurance Scheme Records 3.5m Enrollees in 3 years. *National Pilot*, Vol . 9, No. 23, p. 11.

Amzat, J. (2008). Curbing the Web: An Analytical Explanation for HIV/AIDS Mitigation among Youth in Nigeria. Paper presented at International Conference on *The Nigerian Youth, Political Participation and National Development* at Center for Democratic Research and Training, Mambayya House, BUK, August 5-6. 2008.

Amzat, J. (2009) (forthcoming). Assessing the Progress towards the Millennium Development Goals In Nigeria. In Ogundiya I. S., Olutayo O. A & Amzat, J. (eds.), State and Civil Society Relations in Nigeria. Ibadan: Hope Publishers.

Bankole, A., Singh, S., Woog, V. and Wulf, D. (2004). *Risk and Protection: Youth and HIV/AIDS in Sub-Saharan Africa.* NY: The Alan Guttmacher Institute.

Fassin, D. and Scheneider, H. (2003). The Politics of AIDS in South Africa: Beyond the Controversies. *British Medical Journal*, Vol. 326, pp. 495-497.

Federal Republic of Nigeria (FGN) (2007). *Nigeria 2006 Millennium Development Goals report*. Abuja: National Planning Commission.

Federal Republic of Nigeria (FGN) (2007). *Nigeria 2006 Millennium Development Goals report*. Abuja: National Planning Commission.

Fee, E. & Krieger, N. (1993). Understanding AIDS: Historical Interpretations and the Limits of Biomedical Individualism. *American Journal of Public Health*, Vol. 83, pp. 1477-1486.

FGN (2003). *National Health Policy*. Abuja: Federal Ministry of Health, Abuja.

Gupta, M. D., Gauri, V. & Khemani, S. (2003). *Decentralized Delivery of Primary Health Services in Nigeria: Survey Evidence from the States of Lagos and Kogi.* Washington DC: World Bank.

Gureje, O. (2005). *The De-facto Health of Nigerians.* Ibadan: University of Ibadan, Postgraduate School Interdisciplinary Research Discourse.

Jegede, A. S. (2002). Problems and prospect of Health Care Delivery in Nigeria: Issues in Political Economy and Social Inequality. In Isiugo-Abanihe, U. C., Isamah, A. N., & Adesina, J. O. (eds.), *Currents and Perspectives in Sociology.* Ibadan: Malthouse Press Ltd.

Jegede, A. S., Amzat, J., Salami, K. K., Adejumo, P. O. & Oyetunde, M. O. (2006). What Women Do to Prevent and Treat Malaria in Ibadan. *African Journal for the Psychological Study of Social Issues*, Vol. 9, No. 1, pp. 14-25.

National AIDS/STDs Control Program (NASCP) (2005). *2005 National HIV Seroprevalance Sentinel Survey.* Abuja: Federal ministry of Health.

National Population Commission (NPC) (Nigeria) and ORC Macro (2004). *Nigeria Demographic and Health Survey 2003.* Calverton, Maryland: National Population Commission and ORC Macro.

Owumi, B. E. (2002). The Political Economy of MCH in Africa. In Isuigo-Abanihe, U. C., Isamah, A. N. & Adesina, J. O. (eds), *Currents and Perspectives in Sociology*. Ibadan: Malthouse Press Ltd.

WHO (2008). *World Malaria Report 2008*. Geneva.

WHO, (2000a). *The African summit on Roll Back Malaria.* Geneva. WHO/CDS/RBM/2000.17.

World Bank (2007). *World Development Indicators, 2007.*

UNICEF (2009). *State of the World's Children 2009: Maternal and Newborn Health.* Geneva.

18

Institutions, Governance, Poverty, Inequality and Vision 2020 in Nigeria

Musibau Adetunji Babatunde

Introduction

In the simplest terms, Vision 2020 is the objective of Nigerian government to grow the size of Nigeria's economy from its current position of 40th to the 20th in the world by the year 2020. It was meant to make Nigeria one of the twenty most industrialized economies in the world by the year 2020. In achieving such a gargantuan objective, economists have become increasingly aware that institutional arrangements, good governance, very low inequality and poverty rate play key roles in explaining long-run economic performance (Hall and Jones, 1999; Rodrik, 2003; Acemoglu et al., 2004; Sala-i-Martin, 2002; Easterly and Levine, 2003; Glaeser et al., 2004).

Governance and institutional factors play major roles in stimulating economic growth in many developing and developed countries and cannot be overemphasized. In recent times there has been a resurgence of interest in this subject, including research into the sources of institutional differences across countries, the channels through which institutions may affect economic performance, and the quantitative importance of these links. Vision 2020 is a long term development plan. If Nigeria desire to be among the top twenty economies in the world by the year 2020, there is a great need to reduce inequality and poverty to the barest level in order to achieve higher productivity from its citizen. The context under which the vision is achieved is dependent upon the institutional arrangements and governance factors put in place to ensure high level of equality and poverty dimension in Nigeria.

This study therefore examines the role of institutions and good governance with respect to poverty and inequality in Nigeria as the basis of achieving the vision 2020 in Nigeria and the implication for policy making. Thus, the next section discusses institutions. It highlights the meaning of institutions, how and why institution affects growth. Section three discusses governance capacity in Nigeria. Section four discusses the reality on the ground since 1999. Issues on how vision 2020 could be realized are suggested in Section five. The conclusion is drawn in Section six.

Institutions

An institution is a concept that has been defined in many different ways. Unfortunately, no clear, measurable and broadly agreed-upon definition has yet emerged. North (1990) defines institutions as the rules of the game in a society, that is, they are the limitations to free behaviour imposed on the individual by the society, shaping the relationships among individuals. He believes that institutions have great implications for society because institutions determine the fundamental structure of human exchange, whether such exchange is political, social or economic. In a similar manner, Scott (1995) defines institutions as cognitive, normative and regulative structures and activities that provide stability and meaning to social behaviours.

Schotter (1981) reveals that institutions do not only represent legal and governmental structures and regulations, they also represent the different interests of organisations and the regularity in social behaviours that specify action in recurrent situations. However, in the view of Hare (2001: 483) institutions have four major characteristics: "(a) they regulate economic behaviour in ways which, in the short run, often conflict with individual preferences; (b) they are based on shared expectations, derived from custom, trust, legal provisions, etc.; (c) they make most sense if the economy is thought of as a repeated game in which most types of transaction occur many times; and (d) anonymity, in the sense that the functioning of a given institution should not be dependent upon the identity of the economic agents seeking to conduct the types of transaction to which this institution relates."

Economic institutions mould the economic environment in which firms and individuals act. They matter for economic growth because they shape the incentives of key economic actors in society. In particular, they influence investments in physical and human capital and technology, and the organization of production. Political institutions, similarly to economic institutions, determine the constraints on and the incentives of the key actors, but this time in the political sphere. Examples of political institutions include the form of government, for example, democracy vs dictatorship or autocracy, and the extent of constraints on politicians and political elites. Social institutions can be regarded to cover a broad group of formal and informal institutions. Examples of formal social institutions include many institutions that are directed towards increasing the quality of life, for example, the organization of primary healthcare, hospitals and support for poor citizens unable to earn an acceptable income on their own.

Efficient institutions create the right incentives which encourage productive activities such as investments in machinery and the development of new skills and production techniques. Inefficient institutions, on the other hand, create a market for non-productive activities, such as diversion, rent-seeking, corruption etc. But how do institutions create the right incentives? Let us start with an example. Consider one of the most important economic institutions, namely, the structure of property rights in a society. By protecting property rights, guaranteeing sanctity of contract, and providing law and order, they create an environment in which business and private investment can flourish. Another prominent economic institution is the presence and quality of markets. Institutions regulate and/or substitute for markets. The need for these functions arises from some kind of market failure and/or other social objectives such as income distribution that societies wish to fulfill, that is, when markets fail to deliver what is socially desirable.

In addition, institutions, such as the central banks, stabilize markets by ensuring low inflation and macroeconomic stability and helping to avoid financial crises. Finally, institutions legitimize markets through mechanisms of social protection and insurance, and importantly, through mechanisms for redistribution and managing conflict. Democracy is, of course, the institution par excellence for legitimizing markets. The most interesting evolution has been the market-regulating/ownership role of institutions. There are many examples of societies with weakly developed or missing markets. When markets work improperly or are non-existent, people do not have incentives to trade. As a result there exist unrealized gains from trade implying that resources are not allocated where they provide the highest economic contribution. Hence, economic institutions determine who receives the revenues and the profit from production and other activities and, therefore, have a significant influence on the income distribution in a society.

Governance

Governance relates to decisions that define expectations, grant power, or verify performance. It consists either of a separate process or of a specific part of management or leadership processes. That is, the process of decision-making and the process by which decisions are implemented (or not implemented). Governance can be used in several contexts such as corporate governance, international governance, national governance and local governance. Sometimes people set up a government to administer these processes and systems. Thus, governance can then be defined as the manner in which authority is exercised in the management of a country's socio-economic resources. Kaufmann et al. (1999) extend the last definition by including three core dimensions of governance, namely (i) the process by which those in authority are selected, monitored and replaced, (ii) the government's capacity to effectively manage its resources and implement sound policies, and (3) the respect of citizens and the state for the country's institutions.

As a process, governance may operate in an organization of any size: from a single human being to all of humanity; and it may function for any purpose, good or evil, for profit or not. A reasonable or rational purpose of governance might aim to assure (sometimes on behalf of others) that an organization produces a worthwhile pattern of good results while avoiding an undesirable pattern of bad circumstances. Perhaps the most moral or natural purpose of governance consists of ensuring, on behalf of those governed, a exemplary pattern of the good while avoiding an undesirable pattern of the bad. The ideal purpose, obviously, would ensure a perfect pattern of good with no bad. A government comprises a set of interrelated positions that govern and that use or exercise power, particularly coercive power. Consequently, a good government could consist of a set of interrelated positions exercising coercive power that assures, on behalf of those governed, a worthwhile pattern of good results while avoiding an undesirable pattern of bad circumstances, by making decisions that define expectations, grant power, and verify performance. Politics provides a means by which the governance process operates. For example, people may choose expectations by way of political activity; they may grant power through political action, and they may judge performance through political behaviour.

According to UNESCAP (2008), good governance as expressed through factors like reliability, predictability and accountability is increasingly seen as a key factor in ensuring national prosperity. Good governance has eight major characteristics. It is participatory, consensus-oriented, accountable, transparent, responsive, effective and efficient, equitable and inclusive and follows the rule of law. It ensures that corruption is minimized, the views of minorities are taken into account and the voices of the most vulnerable in society are heard in decision-making. It is also responsive to the present and future needs of society.

Measuring Governance

Over the last decade, several efforts have been conducted in the research and international development community in order to assess and measure the quality of governance of countries all around the world. One of these efforts to create an internationally comparable measure of governance is the Worldwide Governance Indicators Project, developed by members of the World Bank and the World Bank Institute (WBI). The project reports aggregate and individual indicators for more than 200 countries for six dimensions of governance: voice and accountability, political stability and lack of violence, government effectiveness, regulatory quality, rule of law, control of corruption.

Formal and informal traditions and institutions for the common good, thus encompasses: (1) the process of selecting, monitoring, and replacing governments; (2) the capacity to formulate and implement sound policies and deliver public services; and (3) the respect of citizens and the state for the institutions that govern economic and social interactions among them" (Kaufman, 2008:p7). For measurement and analysis, the WBI has translated the three dimensions above into six concepts with their corresponding measure:

(1) Voice and accountability includes indicators related to political participation and civil liberties.
(2) Political stability refers to indicators measuring the perception that a government might be overthrown and the relative prevalence of political violence and terrorism.
(3) Government effectiveness covers indicators related to the quality of bureaucracy, political independence of the civil service, and credibility of the government's commitment to public policies (including the ability to pass legislation and stay in office).
(4) Regulatory quality refers to indicators of the quality of the public policies themselves (excessive regulation, unpredictability, etc).

Table 18.1: Nigeria-Governance Indicators

Governance Indicator	*Year*	*Percentile Rank (0-100)*	*Governance Score (+2.5 to -2.5)*	*Standard Error*
	2007	31.7	-0.54	0.12
Voice and Accountability	2006	32.2	-0.49	0.12
	2005	24.5	-0.75	0.15
	2004	26.4	-0.72	0.15
	2003	27.4	-0.72	0.15
	2002	25.5	-0.76	0.17
	2000	27.4	-0.72	0.22
Political Stability	2007	4.3	-2.07	0.21
	2006	3.4	-2.05	0.21
	2005	4.8	-1.73	0.23
	2004	4.8	-1.81	0.23
	2003	6.7	-1.65	0.23
	2002	7.2	-1.71	0.23
	2000	9.1	-1.58	0.26
Government Effectiveness	2007	14.7	-0.93	0.16
	2006	17.5	-0.89	0.15
	2005	22.3	-0.84	0.15
	2004	14.7	-0.94	0.15
	2003	16.6	-0.90	0.15

(Contd.)

(Contd. Table 18.1)

Governance Indicator	*Year*	*Percentile Rank (0-100)*	*Governance Score (+2.5 to -2.5)*	*Standard Error*
	2002	11.8	-1.04	0.16
	2000	12.8	-1.02	0.18
Regulatory Quality	2007	19.4	-0.89	0.16
	2006	18.5	-0.96	0.16
	2005	18.5	-0.89	0.16
	2004	8.3	-1.30	0.16
	2003	12.7	-1.16	0.17
	2002	10.7	-1.20	0.19
	2000	23.4	-0.67	0.21
Rule of Law	2007	8.6	-1.20	0.13
	2006	11.0	-1.19	0.13
	2005	6.7	-1.41	0.14
	2004	4.3	-1.54	0.14
	2003	3.8	-1.65	0.14
	2002	3.8	-1.50	0.14
	2000	11.4	-1.17	0.14
Control of Corruption	2007	12.1	-1.01	0.13
	2006	8.7	-1.14	0.13
	2005	8.7	-1.21	0.14
	2004	4.9	-1.32	0.14
	2003	4.4	-1.26	0.16
	2002	2.4	-1.38	0.16
	2000	6.8	-1.17	0.17

Source: Kaufmann et al (2008).

(5) Rule of law measures the extent to which agents have confidence and abide by the rules. The degree of protection of property rights, judicial independence, and crime are some of the elements included.

(6) Control of corruption measures perceptions of the prevalence of corruption (Kaufmann et al., 2008).

As can be seen in the figures in Table 18.1, Nigeria fares extremely poorly in the WBI indexes. Statistics are shown in percentile rank, the best being the 100th percentile. In 2004, the country was well below the African average in all six indicators. In particular, Nigeria is in the 4th percentile in terms of political stability. As can be seen, the percentile rank of Nigeria has declined in the last eight years (this measure was first calculated in 1996). Other variables that have been shown to be good predictors of economic growth are rule of law and control of corruption. Nigeria fares very poorly in both, with percentile ranks of 8.6% and 12.1% respectively. Similarly, in the government effectiveness, Nigeria is in the 14.7 percentile rank. If one accepts these indicators as valid, then these should explain a large portion of the economic underperformance of Nigeria. Consequently, these performances have implication for achieving economic growth, poverty and inequality as will be highlighted in the next section.

Nigeria: The Story So Far

Nigeria is one of the leading oil producers in the world and as a result has a huge natural resource base and the potential to translate this into sustained economic growth that would drastically reduce inequality and poverty and make the country a strong partner in the global economic scene. At the core of the myriad of Nigeria's development problems is a fundamental crisis of governance. The present problem of development in Nigeria can be linked to a history of poor governance characterized by inefficient institutions, corruption, social injustice and political instability. The importance of good governance is not lost on the Nigerian people despite the numerous disappointments of the past administrations in the country. Responding to the need to reverse past trends, the quest for good, transparent and accountable leadership is at the core of efforts to reform the social, political and economic order and to mobilize the population in support of democracy. Nigerians are mindful that socio-economic development cannot take place without stable political and civil conditions, which depend on good governance. The experience of long periods of military rule has shown that basic rights tend to be subjugated when people have no say over how they are governed and when their governments are not accountable to them.

The military, which often came into power through coup d'etat, did not feel accountable to anyone but to themselves. The military everywhere in the world hardly promotes good governance. Military regimes are often characterized by the absence of citizens' influence and oversight. In most cases they promote unresponsive and irresponsible political leadership. When the people are not empowered to participate in the political process and have no means to hold political leaders and their administrations accountable for their decisions and actions leaders tend to disregard the needs of the people and subject them to arbitrary rule. Under these conditions good governance becomes a rare commodity.

Thus, prolonged military rule has greatly undermined democratic institutions in Nigeria. It has prevented the country the opportunity of developing a democratic culture characterized by transparency and accountability. Nigerians, in the current democratic dispensation recognize the need to build institutions that would secure private property rights, ensure personal liberty, and provide responsive, transparent and accountable governments. The country could be said to have seen a number of ineffective governments (military and democratic) with various leaders betraying the trust of the people. Despite its numerous potentials the country has not been particularly successful in transforming its resources for the general good and ensuring sustainable development due to lack of good governance and responsive leadership in the past. The result has been the continued marginalization of the Nigerian people, intensification of the incidence of poverty and the underdevelopment of the economy and society.

The challenges facing the country today are enormous requiring democratic forces in society to have to battle with numerous obstacles against good governance. The culture of political and administrative arbitrariness has been a major characteristic of the Nigerian condition, which has generated persistent crisis of governance in the country. The occasional frictions between the executive and the legislature constantly manifested itself. A continuous decline in the quality of governance since the First Republic calls for building political leadership based on competence, commitment and patriotism. The decay of the institutional framework and declining capacity for sustained economic development requires urgent institutional reforms to build up economic management capacity. The long period of concentration of power in the hands of a few, which gradually resulted in the collapse of the rule of law, has to give way to broad participation in governance. The trend of the ruling class and in particular the rulers seeing themselves above the law must give way to the rule of law. The increase in lawlessness has weakened the security situation in the country for years. All these were manifestations of the crisis of governance.

Consequently, the Nigerian experience is an illustration that lack of democracy and good government can impoverish a people. The return to democracy in 1999 after several years of military rule made the government to take certain steps in restructuring the economy. For example, the government embarked on the process of privatization and liberalization of certain sectors of the economy to achieve economic efficiency. In addition, certain restrictive policies and laws on enterprises were reviewed and incentives granted in order to boost investment in line with its development strategy. Specifically, the Obasanjo led administration launched the NEEDS (National Economic Empowerment and Development Strategy) to empower the vulnerables. NEEDS according to its document rests on four key strategies: reforming the way government and its institution works; growing the private sector; implementing a social charter for the people and re-orientation of the people with an enduring African value system (NEEDS document, 2004).

Following these reforms, there was an upsurge in growth. As shown in table 1, whereas real GDP growth rate averaged 2.9% in 1993/99, it doubled to 6.1% in 2000/2006. Noteworthy is that in 2003/2005 period, the growth rate exceeded the prescribed 6.5% under the Millennium Development Goals (MDGs). Also noteworthy is that the growth was driven by the non-oil sector. As shown in the table, except for 2000 and 2003, during the period, oil GDP growth was lower than aggregate GDP growth. Non-oil GDP growth, on the

Table 18.2: Aggregate and Sectoral Real GDP Growth

Year	*Total GDP*	*Oil GDP*	*Non oil GDP*	*Agric.*	*Manu-facture*	*Tele- comm*	*Edu. Serv*	*Buss. Other serv*
1982/85	-0.4	0.9	-0.4	4.7	-2.0	7.4	2.3	9.5
1986/92	4.5	4.3	4.7	5.0	4.0	1.5	2.3	2.6
1993/96	2.1	1.8	2.2	3.3	-2.4	3.6	1.8	3.7
1997/98	2.9	1.9	3.4	4.1	-1.8	5.5	1.7	19.9
1999	2.8	-7.81	4.2	5.3	3.4	5.2	1.7	19.9
2000	5.4	10.99	3.0	3.0	3.4	6.1	1.6	8.0
2001	4.6	5.2	4.2	3.9	14.48	29.9	1.6	10.0
2002	4.63	-5.61	7.96	4.2	10.09	13.3	7.9	13.1
2003	9.57	23.70	4.44	6.64	5.66	85.1	7.0	13.1
2004	6.58	3.37	7.50	6.50	10.00	85		19.8
2005	5.63	-4.67	8.93	7.14	9.51	31.88		7.67
2006	5.63	-4.67	8.93	7.14	9.51	31.88		7.67

Source: Aigbokhan (2008).

other hand, was much higher than aggregate GDP growth. This is particularly noticeable for 2002, and 2004/2006. To appreciate the new sources of non-oil-led growth, Table 18.1 shows sectoral growth profile. Two sectors stand out, namely Telecommunications, and Educational Services. Following the liberalization of the telecommunications sector in 2001 which witnessed the entry of three major private operators – Econet/V-mobile/Celtel, Mobile telecommunications network (MTN), and Global Communications (Globacom), and the public sector MTEL, the country's teledensity rose dramatically from 0.62 to 19.96 (Aigbokhan, 2008).

However, this high economic growth can be said to have failed in yielding a commensurate rate of poverty reduction since it is not accompanied by a rapid growth of productive and remunerative employment. One of the most difficult challenges facing Nigeria in achieving sustainable socio-economic growth is poverty. The resurgence of interest in the issue derives from the effect of growth on poverty. The poverty-reducing effect of a growth pattern which is inequality-neutral would be different from one which is accompanied by rising inequality. It also follows that even if growth has resulted in a decline in poverty incidence, the decline would have been larger if it was accompanied by declining inequality. As revealed in table 18.2, inequality, as measured by the Gini coefficient, has been rising since 1985, except for slight decline in 1992. It declined from 0.43 in 1985 to 0.41 in 1992 and rose to 0.49 in 1996, and remained unchanged at 0.48 in 2004 at the national level. However, at the sectoral and regional levels, in addition to there being variations around the national average, there seems to be a more marked increase in inequality between 1996 and 2004. Thus, the national average may have concealed rising inequality across states and sectors since the mid-1990's.

Table 18.3: Inequality Trend by Sector and Zones

	1985	*1992*	*1996*	*2004*
National	0.43	0.41	0.49	0.48
Sector				
Unrban	0.49	0.38	0.52	0.54
Rural	0.38	0.42	0.47	0.51
Geo-political zone				
South South	0.48	0.39	0.46	0.50
South East	0.44	0.40	0.39	0.44
South West	0.43	0.40	0.47	0.55
North Central	0.41	0.39	0.50	0.39
North East	0.39	0.40	0.49	0.46
North West	0.41	0.43	0.47	0.37

Source: NBS (2006).

Poverty is defined today as a state of long-term deprivation of well-being, a situation considered inadequate for decent living. There is, however, much debates on how well-being should be measured and what indicators should be used. There are two broad approaches to defining well-being. These are the welfarist approach and the non-welfarist approach. The welfarist approach defines well-being in terms of the level of utility attained by an individual. The approach attaches great importance to the individual's perception of what is useful to him or her. The non-welfarist approach defines well-being independently of the individual's perception of it. The approach relies on what planners consider desirable from a social point of view (Aigbokhan, 2008). In qualitative terms, the manifestation and dimension of the resulting poverty includes high rate of unemployment, high and rising debt profile, economic dependence at adult age, lack of access to primary health care, food, clothing, shelter, adequate nutrition and basic education.

Analysis of poverty incidence by zone reveals that compared to 1996, the incidence has dropped in the three southern zones of the country. This is because the non-poor in the South-south, South-east and South-west which were 41.8, 46.5 and 39.1 percent in 1996 rose to 64.9, 73.3 and 57.0 per cent respectively in 2004. However, in the three northern zones, except for North-west in which the incidence dropped marginally in 2004, the situation has worsened for the other northern zones (table 18.3).

Table 18.4: Poverty Trend by Zone, 1996 and 2004

Year/zone	*Core Poor (%)*	*Mod. Poor (%)*	*Non-Poor (%)*
		1996	
South-south	23.4	34.8	41.8
South-East	18.2	35.3	46.5
South-west	27.5	33.4	39.1
North central	28	36.7	35.4
North-East	34.4	35.7	29.9
North-west	37.3	39.9	22.8
Year/zone		**2004**	
South-south	17	18.1	64.9
South-East	7.8	19	73.3
South-west	18.9	24.2	57
North central	29.8	37.2	33.1
North-East	27.9	44.3	27.8
North-west	26.8	44.4	28.8

Source: NBS, 2005 Poverty profile.

In Nigeria, poverty incidence increases over time. Poverty incidence which was just 28.1 per cent in 1980 rose to 65.6 per cent in 1996 before it fell to 54.4 per cent in 2004 (table 18.4). Nevertheless, it can be deduced from the table that the number of people in poverty increased as the population of the country increases. Thus, as the estimated population increased from 65 million in 1980 to 126.3 million in 2004 the poor also increased from 17.7 million to 68.7 million over the same period. More insight into the challenge of poverty in Nigeria is gained by considering the dimension of poverty. Urban poor rose from 17.2 percent in 1980 to 58.2 percent in 1996, but declined remarkably to 43.2percent in 2004. Rural poor rose from 28.3 percent in 1980 to 69.3 percent in 1996. The value declined again although less remarkably to 63.3 percent in 2004 (see table 18.5).

Table 18.5: Poverty Head Count by Year (1980-2004)

Year	*Poverty incidence (%)*	*Estimated Pop (million)*	*Pop. in poverty*
1980	28.1	65	17.7
1985	46.3	75	34.7
1992	42.7	91.5	39.2
1996	65.6	102.3	67.1
2004	54.4	126.3	68.7

Source: NBS (2005) Poverty profile.

Table 18. 6: Poverty Trends by Sector

Year	*Urban (%)*	*Rural (%)*
1980	17.2	28.3
1985	37.8	51.4
1992	37.5	46
1996	58.2	69.8
2004	43.2	63.3

Source: Source: NBS (2005).

Table 18.7: Poverty Incidence by Economic Group in Nigeria

	1980	*1985*	*1992*	*1996*	*2004*
No schooling	30.2	51.3	46.4	72.6	68.7
Primary	21.3	40.6	43,3	54.4	48.7
Secondary	7.6	27.2	30.3	52.0	44.3
Post secondary	24.3	24.2	25.8	49.2	26.3
All Nigeria	27.2	46.3	42.7	65.6	54.4

Aigbokhan (2008).

Since the start of the 2000's, schools enrolment has risen sharply at all levels. Primary school enrollment increased by about 36% from 19,246,000 in 2001 to 26,160,000 in 2005 while enrollment at the tertiary level increased by about 34% from 696,000 in 2001 to 930,000 in 2005. The number of educational institutions also witnessed a modest improvement. Primary school institutions increased from 50,518.0 in 2001 to 59,340.0 in 2005 while secondary school institutions increased from 10,570.0 in 2003 to 12,610.0 in 2005. The relative improvement in performance of the sub-sector could be attributed to the large sums of money spent by government at all levels in building and marketing infrastructure and the acquisition of learning tools. The rehabilitation of schools under the Universal Basic Education (UBE) Programme could also be said to be responsible for this modest result. In addition, the encouragement of greater private sector participation in the educational sector can be attributed to the increased number of private primary, secondary and tertiary institutions.

However, the pupil/teacher ratio in both primary and secondary school has been fluctuating. While the pupil/teacher ratio in primary school fell from 54 to 56 between 1998 and 2001, the ratio increased from 40 to 32 over the same period for secondary school. The marginal increase recorded in the secondary school ratio could be that a substantial number of teachers were employed during the period. However, the ratio improved for both primary and secondary to 52 and 30 respectively in 2005 (See Table 18.1). Adult literacy rate increased marginally which has consistently stood at 57% rose to an all time value of 62.0% in 2004. The percentage of females in educational institutions in the primary from 2001 consistently stood over 50%. The value is still below 50% in the secondary and tertiary institutions. This suggests that females are still under-represented at both secondary and tertiary level. While the Federal government budget allocation to education has increased in absolute terms, the percentage of annual Federal budget on education fell from 11.0% in 1999 to 7.0% in 2001 but improved slightly to 7.9% in 2004. Performance of the sector in some cases have been constrained by industrial actions by primary and secondary school teachers as well as University lecturers in the process of negotiating better welfare for themselves.

Ensuring good health not only requires the availability of medical treatment and citizen's ability to pay for this treatment, it also requires that government regulate industry and individuals to limit the levels of pollution. Official data indicate mixed situation in recent years, with the limited resources available being channelled into personnel rather than buildings: there was one hospital bed per 1,806 people in 2005, compared with one per 1,651.6 in 2001, whereas the population ratios of doctor and nurse deteriorated from 3376:1 to 3,059:1 and from 1082:1 to 714:1 respectively over the same period. The number of children who receive immunization increased from 55.1% in

Table 18.7: Social Indicator in Nigeria

Sub-Sector Indicator	*1998*	*1999*	*2000*	*2001*	*2002*	*2003*	*2004*
1. Population per Physician (No.)	4977.0	4479.0	4529.0	3,373.6	3,190.3	3,141.3	3,100.0
2. Population per Nursing Staff (No.)	1044	906.0	920.0	1082.1	951.8	922.5	818.0
3. Population per Hospital Bed (No.)	1738	1564.0	1611.0	1651.6	1685.5	1722.7	1764.4
4. Life Expectancy at Birth (Years)	54.0	54.0	54.0	54.0	54.0	54.0	54.0
5. Children Immunization							
(i) Fully Immunized (Overall)	55.1	51.9	72.7	73.3	75.0	75.0	75.0
(ii) Tuberculosis (%)	54.6	51.7	72.4	72.7	73.0	73.0	73.0
(iii) DPT (%)	55.3	53.8	75.3	67.1	70.0	70.0	70.0
(iv) Poliomyelitis (%)	57.5	51.8	72.5	61.0	68.0	68.0	68.0
(v) Measles (%)	53.0	50.3	70.4	92.3	90.0	90.0	90.0
6. Health Institutions							
(i) Primary Health Care	8958.0	8970.0	10149.0	10,393.0	15,266.0	17,012.0	17,752.0
(ii) Secondary Health Care	882.0	892.0	936.0	982.0	1,976.0	2,418.0	2,509.0
(iii) Tertiary Health Care	51.0	51.0	51.0	51.0	219.0	2,21.0	221.0
1. Adult Literacy Rate	57.0	57.0	57.0	57.0	57.0	57.0	62.0
4. Crude Birth Rate (per 1000 Persons)	49.0	49.0	49.0	39.6	39.6	38.6	42.0
5. Crude Death Rate (per 1000 Persons)	14.0	14.0	14.0	14.0	14.0	14.0	11.1
6. Marternal Mortality (per 1000 live births)	10.0	10.0	10.0	10.0	10.0	10.0	10.0
7. Infant Mortality (per 1000 live births)	114.0	75.1	75.1	80.2	78.8	77.3	76.0

Source: Central Bank Nigeria Annual Report and Statement of Accounts, 2005.

1998 to 72.1% in 2001 and stood at 75.0% in 2002.The increased immunization rate was due to repeated house-to-house visits by medical staff to immunize children against the six childhood killer diseases such as tuberculosis, poliomyelitis, and measles among others. There were, however, no major variations in the number of children who receive specific vaccinations between 2002 and 2005. For example, the overall percentage of children increased slightly from73.3% in 2001 to 75.0% in 2002 and has remained constant since then. Although the Federal government budget allocation to health has increased in absolute value (for example it increased from N11,291.9 million in 1998 to N40,741.1 million in 2001), the percentage share of the health sector in the annual Federal budget has been quite low. The percentage share is consistently below the 5.0% minimum standard recommended by the World Health Organization (WHO). The performance of the sub-sector has also been constrained by prolonged industrial action by doctors, nurses and mid-wives.

Finally, evidence reveals that fertility rate on the average between 2001 and 2005 stood at 5.02 per woman while maternal mortality rate remained unchanged between 2001 and 2005. There was, however, a steady decline in the infant mortality rate (per 1000 live births) from 80.2 in 2001 to 76.0. This could be attributed to the increased effort of the government by providing immunization assistance against polio and other childhood killer diseases. In addition, while the crude birth rate (per 1000 persons) has witnessed a steady increase from 39.6 in 2001 to 45.0 in 2005, crude death rate (per 1000 persons) witnessed a declined from 14.0 to 12.0 over the same period.

Can Nigeria Achieve the Objectives of Vision 2020?

The question of whether Nigeria can or cannot achieve the objective of the Vision 2020 is a crucial one that should agitate the minds of politicians, government bureaucrats, and the entire populace. There may, however, be no straightforward answer. It can be answered either in the negative or the affirmative. However, it is obvious that certain issues have to be put in place to realize the objectives of the vision of making Nigeria to be among the top twenty economies in the world by the year 2020.

It must, however, be recognized that achieving development plan is a complex issue and goes beyond economic growth in the immediate period. Achieving development plan such as the vision 2020 requires growth and structural change, some measure of distributive equity, modernization in social and cultural attitudes, good governance, efficient institutions, a degree of political transformation and stability, an improvement in health and education so that population growth stabilizes, and an increase in urban living and employment. Consequently, social transformation will require good change and progress in the following areas:

Transparency and accountability: Several analysis of the challenges of development in Nigeria has identified lack of transparency and accountability as a major obstacle.

Tackling institutional constraints: To deliver services to the people require effective and efficient institutions that follow due process and standards.

Pro-poor Growth: It is clear that there has been economic growth in Nigeria in the last few years above 5 percent. But economic growth alone cannot lead to achievement of the vision 2020 unless the growth is pro-poor. The attempt is not the pursuit of a high growth rate in statistical terms with a failure to reduce the social and economic deprivation of a substantial number and group of our people.

Structural Change: To achieve the vision 2020 in Nigeria, there is the need to change the structure of the economy in such a way that the economy is not dependent on only one product but diversified economy and expanding the industrial sector.

Distributive Equity: Deliberate efforts and policies must be put in place to redistribute income. The vision 2020 will be met if the poor and excluded in society are empowered to meet their basic needs and be more productive.

Sustained Political Transformation: The political system and the way it engenders commitment, participation and patriotism by the people contributes immensely to national cohesion, peace and stability and development.

Human Development: Development implies the fulfillment of basic human needs including those for education and health.

Concluding Summary

Institutions shape the economic environment in which firms and individuals act. More specifically, the economic environment provides the incentives for firms and individuals in the economy. Efficient institutions create the right incentives which encourage productive activities. Inefficient institutions, on the other hand, create a market for non-productive activities, such as diversion, rent-seeking, corruption, etc. Statistical evidence reveals that Nigeria has fared poorly in World Bank Institutes governance indicators.

Inefficient institutions, bad governance and corruption cause poverty because it significantly impedes the most effective tool in reducing poverty: economic growth. As a result of the mismanagement of the oil resources, economic growth has been stagnated while poverty and income inequality have become deep-seated in the Nigerian context owing to the impact of corruption. For Nigeria to realize vision 2020, there is the need to formulate and implement policies that will promote transparency and accountability; overcome institutional constraints; promote pro-poor growth; bring about structural change; enhance distributive equity; engender social and cultural re-orientation; engineer political transformation; and promote human development.

References

Acemoglu, D., S. Johnson, & J. A. Robinson (2004). Institutions as the Fundamental Cause of Long-Run Growth. Philippe Aghion & Steve Durlauf (eds.). *Prepared for the Handbook of Economic Growth.* Retrieved from http://elsa.berkeley.edu/~chad/handbook9sj.pdf.

Aigbokhan, B.E. (2008). Growth, Inequality and Poverty in Nigeria. Economic Commission for Africa. ACGS/MPAMS Discussion Paper, No. 3.

CBN (2005). *Annual Report and Statement of Accounts.* Abuja: Central Bank of Nigeria.

Easterly, W., & R. Levine. (2003). Tropics, Germs, and Crops: How Endowments Influence Economic Development. *Journal of Monetary Economics*, Vol. 50, pp. 3-40.

Glaeser, L.E., Rafael La Porta, Florencio Lopez-de-Silanes, & Andrei Shleifer (2004). Do Institutions Cause Growth? National Bureau of Economic Research Working Paper 10568. Retrieved from http://www.nber.org/papers/w10568.

Hall, R. E., & C. I. Jones, (1999). Why Do Some Countries Produce So Much More Output per Worker than Others? *Quarterly Journal of Economics*, Vol. 114, February, pp. 83-116.

Hare, P. (2001). Trade Policy during the Transition: Lessons from the 1990's. *The World Economy*. Vol. 24, No. 4, pp. 482-512. Blackwell Publishing.

Kaufmann, D., Kraay, A., Mastruzzi, A. M. (2008). Governance Matters VII: Aggregate and Individual Governance Indicators 1996-2007. *World Bank Institute Global Governance Program,* June.

Kaufmann, D., A. Kraay, & P. Zoido-Lobaton (1999). *Governance Matters.* World Bank Policy Research Working Paper, No. 2196. Washington.

National Bureau of Statistics (2005). *Poverty Profile for Nigeria*. Abuja.

North, Douglass C., (1990). *Institutions, Institutional Change and Economic Performance.* New York: Cambridge University Press.

Rodrik, D. (2003). Institutions, Integration, and Geography: In Search of the Deep Determinants of Economic Growth. In Dani Rodrik. *Search of Prosperity: Analytic Country Studies on Growth.* Princeton, New Jersey: Princeton University Press.

Sala-i-Martin, X. (2002). The Disturbing Rise of Global Income Inequality. Discussion Paper. US: Department of Economics, Columbia University.

Scott, W. R. (1995). *Institutions and Organizations.* US: Sage, Thousand Oaks, CA. UNESCAP (2008). *What is good governance?* Retrieved from http://www.unescap.org/pdd/prs/ProjectActivities/Ongoing/gg/governance.asp.

Schotter, A. (1981). *The Economic Theory of Social Institutions*. New York: Cambridge University Press.

19

Privatisation and Deregulation: The Gains and the Loses

Emeka Emmanuel Okafor

Introduction

It is on record that all over the world, the public service as has not been known for their capacity to create wealth. Consequently, public enterprises have usually been perceived as drain pipes for government budget, thus creating budgetary strains and avoidable burden on the economy. It became a national policy imperative, therefore, to disengage the public sector from those areas where the private sector has the comparable advantage to perform, while letting the state concern itself with the provision of infrastructure, security and the enabling environment for business to thrive through enhanced wealth creation. It is important to observe that for many developing countries like Nigeria it was perhaps unavoidable for the government, in an earlier epoch, to promote the initial investments in the early phase of national development when the private sector was almost non-existent. Unfortunately, the government got herself so involved in business that could best be tackled by the private sector she could no longer perform her traditional functions, the provision of infrastructure and security through the maintenance of law and order, as well as the promotion of an enabling and conducive environment for investments and wealth creation (Clarke and Pitelis, 1995; Savas, 1987; Ezeani, 1995).

Privatisation and deregulation as tools for economic management came to the front burner when Chile became the first country to turn public assets/ businesses to private operators in the early 1970's. Since then, over 140 countries (both developed and developing) have embraced privatisation as a route to economic growth and prosperity. While the details and strategies of the privatisation exercise may vary in each of these countries, the ultimate objective is to liberalise the economies through increasing private sector involvement and capacity utilisation. A critical aim is to free enterprises from control by rigid and bureaucratic structures and makes the management of such enterprises more flexible in their management and investment strategies. In Venezuela, it is termed *Capitalisation* while Brazilians call it *Flexibilisation*. In other countries such as Argentina, United Kingdom and Mexico where it has worked, different tags have been adopted but the aim and purpose have remained the same. It is worth noting that over 120 countries have embraced the idea of privatisation and deregulation. In the process of privatisation and deregulation, more investible capital have been injected into the various economies through local and foreign investors to the benefit of the country at large. In the process, funds that would have been committed to the maintenance of otherwise inefficient enterprises have been freed into more productive sectors of the economy (Moe,1987; Galal, 1994; Nightingale and Pindus, 1997; Bayliss and Fine, 2008).

Against the background of the above discussion, this paper, therefore, attempts to critically examine privatisation and deregulation in the last ten years by highlighting some of their gains and losses.

Understanding the Concepts of Privatisation and Deregulation

Simply put, privatisation is the incidence or process of transferring ownership of business from the public sector (government) to the private sector (business). In a broader sense, privatisation refers to transfer of any government function to the private sector including governmental functions like revenue collection and law enforcement (Chowdhury, 2006)

The term "Privatisation" also has been used to describe two unrelated transactions. The first is a buyout, by the majority owner, of all shares of a public corporation or holding company's stock, privatizing a publicly traded stock. The second is a demutualization of a mutual organization or cooperative to form a joint stock company (Bayliss and Fine, 2008).

Privatisation has a long historical past. It has been claimed that the term was first used in the 1930's by The Economist in covering German economic policy. In Ancient Greece, the government contracted out almost everything to the private sector. In Roman Republic, private individuals and companies supplied nearly everything, including tax collection, supply the army, religious sacrifices and construction. However, Roman Empire created state-owned enterprises. For example, much of the grain was eventually produced on estates owned by the Emperor. Some scholars suggest that the cost of bureaucracy was one of the reasons for the fall of Roman Empire (Edwards, 1995; Bel, 2006; Bayliss and Fine, 2008).

In the modern times, Winston Churchill's government in Britain privatised British steel industry in the 1950's. West Germany's government started a large-scale privatisation, including selling its Volkswagen majority share to small investors in a public share offering in 1961 (Boubakari and Cosser, 1998).

According to Savas (1987) there are three main methods of privatisation. These include:

- Share issue privatisation (SIP) - selling shares on the stock market
- Asset sale privatisation - selling the entire firms or part of it to a strategic investor, usually by auction
- Voucher privatisation - shares of ownership are distributed to all citizens, usually for free or at a very low price.

Share issue privatisation is the most common type of privatisation. Share issue can broaden and deepen domestic capital markets, boosting liquidity and potentially economic growth, but if the capital markets are insufficiently developed it may be difficult to find enough buyers, and transaction costs (e.g. underpricing required) may be higher. For this reason, many governments elect for listings in the more developed and liquid markets. Euronext, and the London, New York and Hong Kong Stock Exchanges are popular because they are highly developed and sophisticated.

As regards asset sale privatisation, as a result of higher political and currency risk deterring foreign investors, asset sales are more common in developing countries. Furthermore, voucher privatisation has mainly been used in the transition economies of Central and Eastern Europe, such as Russia, Poland, the Czech Republic, and Slovakia.

A very substantial benefit to share or asset sale privatisations is that bidders compete to offer the state the highest price, creating revenues for the state to redistribute in addition to new tax revenue. Voucher privatisations, on the other hand, would be a genuine return of the assets into the hands of the general population, and create a real sense of participation and inclusion. Vouchers, like all other private property, could then be sold on if preferred by what companies are offering.

The largest privatisation in history was *Japan Post*. It was the nation's largest employer and one third of all Japanese government employees worked for Japan Post. Japan Post was often said to be the largest holder of personal savings in the world. Also, Nippon Telegraph and Telephone's privatisation in 1987 was the largest share offering in financial history at the time. Fifteen of the world's 20 largest public share offerings have been privatisations of telecoms. Moreover, the United Kingdom's largest public share offerings were privatisations of British Telecom and British Gas. The largest public share offering in France was France Telecom. Privatisation in Europe has led to genuine competition: the former state-owned enterprises lost their monopolies due to legislation and technological change, competitors entered the market, and prices for broadband access and telephone calls fell dramatically (D'Souza and Megginson, 2001; Bayliss and Fine, 2008).

At this stage, it is important to state that not all privatisation is successful. There are instances of reverse privatisation. In other words, a reversion from contracted ownership of an enterprise and/or services to governmental ownership and/or provision is called reverse privatisation or nationalisation. Such a situation most often occurs when a privatisation contractor fails financially and/or the governmental unit has been unable to purchase satisfactory service at prices it regards as less than state-ownership or self-operation of services. Another circumstance may occur when greater control than viable under privatisation is determined to be in the governmental unit's best interest (Momoh, 2002; Medupin, 2002).

National security concerns may be the main reason for reverse privatisation actions when the most likely providers are non-domestic or international corporations or entities. For example, in 2001, in response to the September 11 attacks, the then private airport security industry in the United States was nationalized and put under the authority of the Transportation Security Administration. When a state-owned enterprise or service has been nationalized or privatised and then is reverted to state-ownership or service provision, the process of reverse privatisation may be called denationalisation (Ogunde, 2004; Ikejiani-Clark, 2006; Bayliss and Fine, 2008).

On the other hand, deregulation, a term which gained widespread currency in the period 1970-2000, can be seen as a process by which governments remove, reduce, or simplify restrictions on business and individuals, often ostensibly with the intent of encouraging the efficient operation of private markets, but also with the intent of opening up new areas of trade for speculators. In Western society this practice is generally supported by right-leaning politicians and neo-liberal economists and businesses, and heavily criticized by other economists, as well and the anti-globalization movements and activist because of perceived negative outcomes of such as practice on the workers and consumers, ecological damage and anti-competitive practices by large market players unrestrained by regulation. Usually the stated rationale for 'deregulation' is that such will lead to a raised level of competitiveness, better services with higher productivity, more efficiency and lower prices on the long run (Bello,1994; Olawale, 2005).

Deregulation is different from liberalization because a liberalized market, while often having less and simpler regulations, can also have regulations in order to increase efficiency and protect consumer's rights, one example being anti-trust legislation. However, the terms are often used interchangeably within deregulated/liberalized industries (Bello, 1994; Momoh, 2000).

In order to capture very well the concept of deregulation, it may be useful to relate briefly the history of regulation. Many industries in the United States became regulated by the federal government in the late 19th and early 20th century Entry to some markets was restricted in order to stimulate and protect the initial investment of private companies into infrastructure to provide "public" services, such as water, electric and communications utilities. With entry of competitors highly restricted, monopoly situations were created, necessitating price and economic controls to protect the public. Other forms of regulation were motivated by what was seen as corporate abuse of the public interest by businesses already extant, such as occurred with the railroads following the era of the so-called robber barons. In the first instance, as markets matured to where multiple providers could be financially viable offering similar services, prices determined by competition were seen as more favourable than those set by regulatory process.

One problem that encouraged deregulation was the way in which the regulated industries often controlled the government regulatory agencies, using them to serve the industries' interests. Even where regulatory bodies started out functioning independently, a process known as regulatory capture often sees industry interests come to dominate those of the consumer. A similar pattern has been observed with the deregulation process, itself often effectively controlled by the regulated industries through lobbying the legislative process. Such political forces, however, exist in many other forms for other "special interest" groups (Ayodele,1999; Ogunde, 2004).

Between 1970 and 2005 several countries have undergone deregulation process. For instance, Argentina underwent heavy economic deregulation, privatisation, and had a fixed exchange rate during the Menem administration (1989–1999).Furthermore Australia was an early leader in deregulation with a broad program of deregulation beginning in the early 1980's. Having announced a wide range of deregulatory policies, Labor Prime Minister Bob Hawke announced the policy of 'Minimum Effective Regulation' in 1986. This introduced now familiar requirements for 'regulatory impact statements' but it took many years before the policy was complied with by government agencies. Australia experienced deregulation of their labour market during the late 1980's under Hawke/Keating Labour government's. The country saw extensive deregulation of the labour market beginning in 2005 under John Howard's Liberal Party of Australia through their Work Choices policy. However, it was reversed under the following Rudd Labour government. In Canada, natural gas is deregulated in most of the country, with the exception of some Atlantic provinces and some pockets like Vancouver Island. Most of this deregulation happened in the mid 1980's. The province of Ontario began deregulation of electricity supply in 2002 but pulled back temporarily due to voter and consumer backlash at the resulting price volatility. The government is still searching for a stable working regulatory framework (Ikejiani-Clark, 2006; Bayliss and Fine, 2008).

The current status is a partially regulated structure in which consumers received a capped price for a portion of the publicly owned generation. The remainder of the price is market price based and there are numerous competitive energy contract providers. There is price comparison service operating in these jurisdictions. The province of Alberta has deregulated their electricity provision. Customers are free to choose which company they sign up with. However there are few companies to choose from and the price of electricity has increased substantially for consumers because the market is too small to support competition. In Japan, since the economic bubble in 1990's collapsed, the Japanese government has seen deregulation as an effective way to lift its economy because it has a huge deficit and cannot make a large tax cut. Also New Zealand has had extensive deregulation since 1984. Originally instigated by the Labour Party, it was later continued by the erstwhile opposition National Party. As a result, New Zealand, from having a reputation as an almost socialist country, is considered one of the most business-friendly countries of the world, next to Singapore.

However, critics charged that the deregulation has brought little benefit to some sections of society, and has caused much of New Zealand's economy (including almost all of the banks) to become foreign-owned. Moreover, Russia went through wide-ranging deregulation (and concomitant privatisation) efforts in the late 1990's under Yeltsin, later partially reversed under Putin. The main thrust of deregulation has been the electricity sector with railroads and communal utilities tied in the second place. Deregulation of natural gas sector is one of the more frequent demands placed upon Russia by the United States and European Union. Also, the United Kingdom has developed a programme of better regulation since 1997. This has developed to include a general programme for government departments to review, simplify or abolish their existing regulations, and a "one in, one out" approach to new regulations (Savas, 1987; Moe, 1987; Boubakri and Cosset, 1998; Ikejiani-Clark, 2006).

Privatisation and Deregulation: The Case of Nigeria

In Nigeria, it will be impossible to discuss privatisation and deregulation without first of all understanding the reasons for establishing public enterprises. Ezeani, 1995; Adebusuyi, 1999; Adeyemo (2001) have adduced some reasons as the justification for creating public enterprises in Nigeria as in other African countries. The most important ones are:

The first of these, especially in the context of developing countries such as Nigeria, is the development emphasis. In many developing countries, the resources available to the private sector are not adequate for the provision of certain goods and services. For example, the investments required in the construction of a hydroelectricity-generating plant or a water scheme for a large urban center are quite enormous and the returns on such investments will take a very long time to realize.

Secondly, political considerations influence governmental involvement in the provision of certain social and economic services. In many African countries, development is closely associated with the provision of social services; consequently, the performance of the government, in many of these countries, is evaluated on the basis of its ability to provide different types of public services in areas where such services do not exist.

The third reason for governmental intervention in the provision and management of goods and services in many parts of the world is the fact that no person should be permanently deprived of the access to such facilities because of lack of finances or by reason of geographical location.

A fourth reason relates to the need to protect the consumer, which may not be of interest to the private sector. For example, government intervenes in the provision of education in many countries to protect children, who are not capable of making important decisions for themselves, by making education up to a certain age compulsory and free.

The fifth reason for governmental intervention in the provision of certain goods and services relates to the indivisibility that characterizes such services. Some facilities, such as bridges, tunnels, roads, streetlights, and waste disposal facilities, cannot be divided or partially provided. Either streetlights are provided for the benefit of everybody in the community or they are not. Facilities of this type must therefore be provided publicly and financed through taxation.

The sixth reason for governmental intervention is the consciousness of the national security. Certain facilities, like the National Ports Authority and the police, are too vital to be left at the mercy of private citizens.

At this point it will be useful to give a brief historical background on the development of Public Enterprises in Nigeria. Adamolekun (1986); Okafor, (1998; 2007a); Ayodele, (1999) and Ikejiani-Clark (2006) have given more or less the same regarding the historical account of development of Public Enterprises in Nigeria. According to these scholars, the private sector was the traditional structure of the world's economies. The Nigerian economy is largely private-sector based. The public sector emerged in Nigeria as a result of the need to harness rationally the scarce resources to produce goods and services for economic improvement, as well as for promotion of the welfare of the citizens. The involvement of the public sector in Nigeria became significant during the period after independence.

The railways were probably the first major example of public sector enterprises in Nigeria. At first, conceived mainly in terms of colonial strategic and administrative needs, they quickly acquired the dimension of a welcomed economic utility for transporting the goods of international commerce, like cocoa, groundnut, and palm kernels. Given the structural nature of the colonial private ownership and control of the railways in the metropolitan countries, it would hardly be expected that the Nigerian Railways Corporation could have been started as any other project than as a public sector enterprise for such mass transportation.

The colonial administration was the nucleus of necessary economic and social infrastructural facilities that private enterprise could not provide. Facilities included railways, roads, bridges, electricity, ports and harbors, waterworks, and telecommunication. Social services like education and health were still substantially left in the related hands of the Christian Mission. But even at this initial stage government itself moved positively into some of the direct productive sectors of the economy: the stone quarry at Aro, the colliery at Udi, and the sawmill and furniture factory at Ijora. Those were the early stages.

The emergence of the crude oil industry into the Nigerian economy, after the civil war in the 1970's, with the associated boom intensified governmental involvement in production and in control of the Nigerian economy. One major aim of government at that time was to convert as much as possible of the growing oil revenue into social, physical, and economic infrastructural investments. The Nigerian Enterprises Promotion Decree of 1972, which took effect on 1 April 1974, with its subsequent amendment in 1976, provided a concrete basis for government's extensive participation in the ownership and management of enterprises. Given these developments, public enterprises at the federal level had exceeded 100 in number by 1985; and these had spread over agriculture, energy, mining, banking, insurance, manufacturing, transport, commerce, and other service activities. Before long, the range of Nigerian public enterprises had stretched from farm organizations to manufacturing, from municipal transport to mining, from housing to multipurpose power, and from trading to banking and insurance. At the state and local governmental levels, the range of activities that had attracted public sector investment also had become quite large. Thus, a variety of enterprises-with public interest in terms of majority equity participation or fully-owned by state and local government as well as other governmental entities - became visible in various parts of Nigeria. Between 1975 and 1995, it was estimated that the Federal Government of Nigeria had invested more than $100 billion in public enterprises.

In the 1980's, Nigeria witnessed steady economic deterioration and seemingly faulty economic policies. At the beginning of the 1980's, the country had entered difficult times. Scarcity of foreign exchange had set in. By the mid-1980's, reality had dawned on the nation's economy. Retrenchment of workers was rampant in both private and public sectors. There were inflation, very high levels of unemployment affecting both skilled and unskilled workers, and low levels of plant capacity utilization. The origin of the socio-economic difficulties was generally traced to the global economic recession which opened with the decade of the 1980's. Earlier, these socio-economic problems had forced the Federal Government, under President Shehu Shagari, to embark on an economic stabilization programme.

The problems of performance of the public sector enterprises in Nigeria were further complicated by the downturn in socio-economic development in the country due to the global economic recession and the collapse of the oil market. Thus, Nigeria's precarious fiscal and monetary posture could no longer sustain the requirements of its public sector enterprises, particularly since they performed below expectations in terms of their returns on investments and quality of services. Towards the end of 1980's, the public enterprises, which had grown too large, began to suffer from fundamental problems of defective capital structures, excessive bureaucratic control and intervention, inappropriate technologies, gross incompetence, and blatant corruption. With the deep internal crises that included high rates of inflation and unemployment, external debt obligations, and foreign exchange misalignment, Nigeria and many other African countries were strongly advised by the worldwide lending agencies, particularly International Monetary Fund (IMF) and the World Bank, to divest their public enterprises as one of the conditions for economic assistance. With the intensified push for economic liberalization, Nigerian and other African leaders were told that privatisation as an economic reform would help cut public sector inefficiency and waste, provide greater scope to the private sector, attract more investments, bring in new technologies, and hence revive economic growth. Thus, many countries, including Nigeria, embarked on privatisation and other market oriented reforms to pull them out of the structural imbalances (Nwoye, 1997).

It is against this background that the Structural Adjustment Programmes (SAP) proposed a kind of reform which would affect the goals, administration, and management of most of the public sector enterprises for purposes of efficiency (Federal Republic of Nigeria, 1986). One of the main objectives of SAP was, therefore, to pursue deregulation and privatisation leading to removal of subsidies, reduction in wage expenses, and retrenchment in the public sector ostensibly to trim the state down to size (Okafor, 1998).

• The combined effect of economic depression of 1980's as well as the issue of mismanagement and under-utilisation which led to huge wastage of resources and manpower potentials gave the government of the day no other option but to pursue quickly the privatisation programme. There are about 600 public enterprises in Nigeria run or controlled by the Federal Government. Many more are controlled by State Governments. These companies take a sizeable portion of the Federal Budget and account for over 5,000 appointments into their management and Board – a powerful source of political patronage. Transfers to these enterprises ran into billions of naira. These transfers were in form of subsidized foreign exchange, import duty waivers, tax exemptions and/or write-off of arrears, unremitted revenues, loans and guarantees and grants/subventions. These companies were also infested with many problems which became an avoidable drag on the economy, such as abuse of monopoly power, defective capital structure, heavy dependence on treasury funding, rigid bureaucratic structures and bottlenecks, mismanagement, corruption and nepotism. With all these problems the government had no other option but to take a positive step. In March 1988, the then Nigerian Head of State, Ibrahim Badamosi Babangida promulgated a decree establishing the Technical Committee on Privatisation and Commercialization (TCPC). The committee was formally inaugurated in July 1988 to undertake the task of reform of public enterprises, as an integral and critical component of the Structural Adjustment Programme (SAP), which was started in 1986. The reform as conceived has two interrelated components – Privatisation and Commercialisation (Ikejiani-Clark, 2006; Okafor, 2007a). The overall objectives of the privatisation exercise were:

- To improve on the operational efficiency and reliability of our public enterprises;
- To minimise their dependence on the national treasury for the funding of their operations;
- To roll back the frontiers of State Capitalism and emphasise private sector initiative as the engine of growth;
- To encourage share ownership by Nigerian citizens in productive investments hitherto owned wholly or partially by the Nigerian Government and, in the process, to broaden and deepen the Nigerian market (Federal Government of Nigeria, 1986; 1988)

During the first phase of the exercise which spanned from July 1988 and June 1993, the following programmes were executed:

- 36 enterprises were privatised through public offer of their shares;
- 4 enterprises were privatised on Deferred Public Offer method;
- 8 enterprises were privatised via Private Placement method;
- 8 enterprises were privatised via Sale of Assets method;
- 1 enterprise was privatised through Management Buy Out method (MBO);
- Sale of non-water assets of about 18 River Basin Development Authorities. (Okafor, 1998; 2007a Ikejiani-Clark, 2006).

Under the Phase I programme, about 88 public enterprises were either fully or partially privatised. These were enterprises in which the Nigerian Government invested jointly with foreign or private Nigerian investors. With the exception of the Cement and the Oil Marketing companies, the capitalisation of most of them was small. The huge capital-intensive and basic industries like the Fertiliser Companies, Sugar companies, Vehicle Assembly Plants, Paper and the Steel Mills which hold vital positions in the economy could not be privatised for various reasons ranging from financial insolvency to negative networth. Finally, there was lack of clarity of Government's policy on some critical issues associated with the Implementation of the programme. The issues include:

- Whether to privatise as "it is" or rehabilitate before privatisation.
- To relieve the Enterprises' managers of their duties before or after privatisation.
- The type of regulatory framework that will be in place.
- Whether the sales should be given to both foreigners and Nigerians.
- The valuation methods to be used.
- The role of foreign core investors in the ownership and management of the national economy.
- Loss of jobs resulting from the privatisation.
- Income inequality arising from the ownership of privatised assets.
- Whether to deregulate before or after privatisation.
- Utilization of the privatisation proceeds.
- Whether Government should go ahead and own any 'Golden Shares'.
- The level of transparency in the programme (Ezeani, 1995; Adeyemo, 2001).

The exercise had a mixture of success and shortcomings as will discussed later. For instance, unlike other countries, the privatisation exercise in Nigeria was done by Nigerians for Nigerians without any foreign technical assistance. The programme succeeded in relieving the government of the huge and growing burden of financing public enterprises, minimised the overstretching of government's managerial capacity through a redefinition of the role of the supervising ministries, created a large body of shareholders and deepened and broadened the Nigerian Capital Market to the position of being the most developed in black Africa. The market capitalisation of the Nigerian Stock Exchange (NSE) through which the shares were sold has grown from N8.9 billion in 1987 (before privatisation) to N65.5 billion in 1994 (after the Phase I) and stood at N528.9 billion as at the end of August 2006. The catalytic effect of the volume of shares released into the market via the privatisation exercise cannot be overempahsised (Okafor, 2007a).

The Technical Committee on Privatisation and Commercialisation wound up her activities and submitted a report to the President on June 5, 1993. The TCPC also transformed to the Bureau for Public Enterprises (BPE). The Bureau was to monitor the performance of the enterprise privatised in the past exercise and plan for the future phases.

Because of the perceived success of the past exercise, the military government under General Abdulsalam Abubakar promulgated the Public Enterprises (Privatisation and Commercialisation) Decree No. 28 in early 1999 (before the hand-over to a democratically elected government). The Decree kicked off the Phase II of the privatisation exercise under the Bureau for Public Enterprises (BPE). The Decree allows BPE to alter, add, delete or amend the provisions in the document in the best interest of the country. Initially, sixty-one (61) enterprises were slated for privatisation (36 partial and 25 full privatisation), but because of the new powers granted BPE, it has increased the list by 37 extra enterprises (some of which were originally meant for commercialisation). Some of the big government companies that were slated for privatisation under the second phase of the programme included: National Insurance Corporation of Nigeria (NICON), Nigerian Re-insurance Corporation, Nigerdock Plc., National Aviation Handling Company (NAHCO), Nigeria Railways Corporation (NRC), Nigerian Ports Authority (NPA), Nigerian Postal Services (NIPOST) and Savannah Sugar Company. This is an indication of the perceived enhanced interest in and the success that is expected to result from privatisation (Obasanjo,1999; Ikejiani-Clark, 2006).

In December 1999, the democratically elected government of former President Olusegun Obasanjo picked interest in the privatisation exercise and gave it a boost by establishing the National Council on Privatisation (NCP) with the Vice-President, Alhaji Atiku Abubakar, as its Chairman. The Council was empowered among other things to determine the political, economic and social objectives of the Privatisation and Commercialisation programme, approve guidelines and criteria for valuation of public enterprises marked out for privatisation including choice of strategic investors - identification of enterprises to be privatised or commercialised, and approve the prices for shares or assets of the public enterprise to be offered for sale.

Overall, this second phase was expected to help the government raise funds to narrow down the budget deficit; payback public debt; avoid new borrowings; restructure other enterprises; support social sectors as education, health, power and rural development. (Obasanjo, 1999).

Between December 1999 and May 2007 over thirty enterprises have been privatised[1], adding over 5 billion shares to the capital market while the Federal government realised a revenue of N35.6 billion from the sales. Privatisation is geared to transform the Nigerian economy. Given the size of the population (120 million) and the potential market which includes the West African sub-region, the scope for foreign investment is enormous. Given the relative transparency and technical competence that has characterised the on-going programme, the attractions of the Nigerian economy for foreign investors could prove irresistible.

Some scholars and commentators (Medupin, 2002; Ikechukwu, 2005; Ikejiani-Clark, 2006; Adegbamigbe, 2007; Okafor, 2007b) have highlighted some of the perceived gains the privatisation under the current democratic dispensation to include:

- Performance of the privatised enterprises so far has led to a considerable increase in the volume of corporate taxes accruing to the national treasury. Thus, not only has the drain on public finances been halted, it has become a positive bonus, with subsidy soaking deficits – being replaced by tax-yielding profits.
- The sale of shares and assets realised over N3.7 billion as gross privatisation proceeds from the privatisation of over thirty enterprises

whose total original investment according to the records of the Ministry of Financed Incorporated (MOFI) was N652 million. This represents less than 2% of the total value of the Federal Government's investments as at 30th November 2006 which stood at N36 billion.

- The programme of privatisation has greatly minimised the scope of political patronage in the form of Board appointments and jobs for the boys. Under the Phase-II of the programme, the Federal Government relinquished about 200 Directorship positions in the privatised enterprises. The operational autonomy enjoyed by these enterprises has put a stop to their use as dumping grounds for political appointees at management and board levels.
- Privatisation has massively expanded personal share ownership in Nigeria. Over 800,000 shareholders were created, almost twice as many as there were in 1988 when the exercise started. The programme has also intensified the operations of the Capital Market, created new awareness in the virtues of shareholding as a form of savings rather than an elitist pastime, which it was thought to be. This is a good development which enhances capital formation and economic growth.
- By reducing the reliance of public enterprises on the government for finance, the programme of privatisation has encouraged new investments in the enterprises concerned. The cold hands of Treasury Control have been replaced by the warm hands of the Capital Market which are as stimulating as they are invisible. Many of them have discovered that it is easier to raise funds through the capital market than it is to do so from the treasury, once the necessary investor confidence has been developed.
- The new operational autonomy of these enterprises and their liberation from political interference in day to day management has improved the internal efficiency of these enterprises allowing them to liberalise their purchasing as well as rationalise labour practices. This has increased massively their profitability. The negative perception of public enterprises in the minds of the general public as nobody's business has also changed.
- Flotation of shares of privatised enterprises have greatly stimulated the rapid growth of the Nigerian Capital Market and helped to deepen and broaden it. As stated earlier, market capitalisation has grown from N8.9 billion in 1987 to over 65 .5 billion by 1994 and N428.9 billion as at August 2006.
- Privatisation has allowed the management of privatised enterprises full freedom to realise their optimum potentials. This has led to more productive employment and economic growth in general terms.

Summarizing the gains of Privatisation, El-Rufai (2002), a proponent of privatisation and the former Director General of Bureau of Public Enterprises, states:

> There are about 590 public enterprises at the end of 2000 and 160 are involved in economic activities, generating goods and services. Over 5,000 board appointments are to man these gigantic white elephants with enormous patronage bestowed on high official. About $100 billion spent by FNG to establish these public enterprises between 1973 and 1999 with a return rate of meager 0.5%, employing 420, 000 workers. The quality of services from...NEPA...for instance, are deplorable and left much to be desired. These enterprises, considered by many as jewel of Nigeria, operate at sub-optimal levels of capacity and are among the most inefficient in the world. These enterprises have become the hotbed for political patronage, corruption, parasitism and rent seeking for elite... Privatisation is the only solution to remove all the maladies that are prevalent and promote efficiency, transparency and corporate governance. We should let the government do what it is suppose to do, focusing on health, education, infrastructure, environmental protection and good governance.

On the other hand, the loses and shortcomings of privatisation under the present democratic dispensation have been identified. One major shortcoming is that not all processes leading to the privatisation of these enterprise were successful thereby becoming an avenue through which government lost huge revenues. Moreover, the ones privatised were trailed by controversies as a result of non transparency that accompanied such an exercise. The cases of African Petroleum (AP); The Nigeria Telecommunication (NITEL); National Insurance Corporation of Nigeria (NICON) and many others did not follow the due process. The Nigeria Telecommunication's (NITEL) example will suffice here.

As a result of its dismal performance government was determined to privatise NITEL. Efforts by the government to reposition the organization to make it attractive to potential buyers when it is put on sale failed to achieve desired result. Earlier attempts to privatise NITEL in 2001 had proved unsuccessful as no investor found it worth the risk. The preferred bidder, Investment International Limited of London (IILL), failed to back up its bid with cash and none of the other bidder had the courage to accept the challenge. It was on the basis of this that the Dutch Company (Pentascope) was contracted to reposition NITEL for privatisation. Consequent, the company assumed responsibility for NITEL on April 24, 2003, day after the management contracted was sealed between it and Bureau of Public Enterprise to run the ailing for three years and reposition it for privatisation. However, audit report released ahead of NITEL privatisation of NITEL by March 2005 showed a big rot and the consequent dwindling of fortune of the company (Williams, 2005; Okafor, 2007b).

Highlight of the report included an inexplicable collapse of turnover by about a quarter, while overhead costs shot up to $150 million as staff emolument quadrupled. The report raised questions about NITEL's net loss, which was originally put at ₦15 billion (about $114.5 m) but turned out to be ₦19 billion (about $145 m), gross earnings falling by more than half. Other shocking revelations included the disappearance of another ₦100 m in the name 'short term investment' payment of the bonus agreed with Pentascope in spite of its failure to deliver, and the continuous payment of unmerited sum of money as Consultancy fees to the Dutch firm. According to the audit report, save for the timely intervention loan of ₦14 billion ($106.8 m) out of a total package of $290 m to cover operational cost and debt surviving, NITEL was headed for bankruptcy. Besides mismanagement, NITEL was also indebted to a number of other operators. For instance in October 2004, V-mobile Nigeria one of the four registered GSM operators in the country filed a suit against the company over an unpaid debt of more than ₦3bn ($23 m). Indeed, the total estimated owed by NITEL to Vmobile (now Zain) and other two operators, MTN and Globacom was said to be in the region of ₦11 billion(183.7 m) NITEL is also indebted to M-Tel its mobile phone arm to the tune of ₦70 million (Williams, 2005; Ikejiani-Clark, 2006; Okafor, 2007b).

In July, 2006, Bureau of Public Enterprises (BPE) selected Transnational Corporation (TRANSCORPS) to buy 75 percent of NITEL at a cost of $750 million. TRANSCORPS was given seven days to pay $500 million, thereafter 90 days to pay the balance of $250 million, failing which the offer would collapse. A day after the expiry of the seven day deadline, TRANSCORPS paid $75million and requested for a sixty day grace period to complete payment. The inability of TRANSCORPS to make the payment as at the time it was made raised some questions of trust. Second, the net worth and corporate financial standing of TRANSCORPS is not known. In August 2006, it was disclosed to the Nigerians that former President Obasanjo bought two hundred (200) million shares fully paid for, in 2004, in TRANSCORPS and are being held in blind trust by Obasanjo Holdings. This is a serious ethical question. Moreover, TRANSCORPS violated some basic principles of the bid process requiring bidders to deposit 25 per cent of their offer before being declared winner. TRANSCORPS did not do this yet it was favoured and declared winner. This process lacked transparency and policy inconsistent; a station that has made the public to view the process with suspicion (Ikejiani-Clark, 2006; Okafor, 2007).

Other losses and shortcomings of privatisation since 1999 as enunciated by the scholars and commentators (Momoh, 2002; Ogunde, 2004; Ikejiani-Clark, 2006; Adegbamigbe, 2007; Okafor, 2007a) are as follows:

- *Rising Prices:* Central to the criticism of privatisation is the fear that the private sector will exploit consumers where there is monopoly or oligopoly power such as by raising the prices of goods.

- *Creating Poverty*: At the heart of the criticism of privatisation is the perception that it has not been fair - hurting the poor and the vulnerable work force, while benefiting the rich, the powerful, and the privileged - thereby perpetrating poverty.
- *Breaking of Unions*: Workers dismissed as a result of privatisation have great difficulty finding other work; the large number of people out of jobs is forced to accept jobs with lower pay, less security, and fewer benefits. They, therefore, believe that the aims of privatisation are to reduce labour costs and numbers, and to break union power.
- *Corruption:* There is this argument that even if privatisation contributes to improve efficiency and financial performance, it has a negative effect on the distribution of wealth perhaps arising from corruption. Corruption is the single most destructive factor responsible for the pitiable state of affairs in many developing countries. It distorts the economy through waste and misallocation of resources and creates need for external assistance. Transparency International has for a long time decried the evil consequences of corruption and has identified acute corruption in many developing countries. For example, in 1999, its Annual Corruption Index rated Nigeria as the most corrupt country on earth, followed by Pakistan and Kenya. By 2003, the index moved and Cameroon displaced Nigeria as number one. Some misguided Nigerians have argued thus "...after all, corruption is everywhere, including industrialized countries." It is true that corruption is a worldwide phenomenon, and so are industrial development and technological advancement. Most Public enterprises were privatised under questionable circumstance as evidenced in the case of NITEL and failed Port Harcourt and Kaduna Refineries.
- *Injustice:* There is an assertion that it is the politicians and bureaucrats that caused the public enterprises to perform poorly but only labour is asked to carry the burden of reform. This is a clear case injustice.
- *Exploitation by Capitalist Countries*: Privatisation is seen as an imposition by foreign capitalists and agencies like the IMF and the World Bank; therefore, privatisation must be meant to exploit the developing countries.
- *Privatisation is Foreign:* Privatisation is neo-colonialism since the policy is being pushed by International Monetary Fund, World Bank, and their agencies. It is not an indigenous idea; therefore, it has pauperized the masses.
- *Labour's Demands for Job Protection*: Right from the onset, the most publicly persistent and organized opposition of privatisation in Nigeria has come from the labour movement. There always have been strikes and counterstrikes against any decision to privatize a government agency. Sometimes workers have succeeded in blocking or slowing down the privatisation of specific enterprises. In other cases the

government simply has brushed aside the labour opposition leaving a legacy of anger and political tension. What is obvious is that workers are reacting against threatened jobs or the possibility that benefits might be jeopardized under new management.

Summarizing, the losses and shortcomings of privatisation, Momoh (2002) specifically states that privatisation in Nigeria is an intension to replace state monopoly with private monopoly and described the latter as "nebulous and a big fraud". He says thus:

> The way many of the enterprises are sold off leaves much to be desired. There is the issue of lack of proper valuing, incompetent valuers, fraudulent valuers etc. There is also the issue of assets which in some instances are not taken into account...the Nigerian private sector is one of the most inhumane, insensitive, callous and exploitative to be found anywhere in the world. Many of the private sector employers neither provide insurance nor social security for their employees. They do not obey labour laws and they sack workers arbitrarily, for good or bad reasons. Many of them do not have pension schemes etc. The private sector employers do not, in some cases, permit their employees to unionize.

As regards the issue of deregulation, the benefits and losses that accompanied are best captured by examining the deregulation of downstream oil sector. To better appreciate the situation in the energy sector that gave rise to deregulation, it will be pertinent to examine briefly the situation in the Nigeria National Petroleum Cooperation (NNPC).

Table 19.1: Fuel Price Adjustment Since May 1999

Date	*Former (in ₦)*	*New Price (in ₦)*	*Percentage Increase/Decrease*
June 1, 2000	20.0	30.0	50.0
June 8, 2000	30.0	25.0	16.6
June 13, 2000	25.0	22.0	12.0
January 1, 2002	22.0	26.0	18.0
June 20, 2003	26.0	40.0	53.7
July 9, 2003	40.0	34.0	17.5
October 1, 2003	34.0	42.0	17.5
May 29, 2004	42.0	49.9	19.0
January 2005	49.9	50.5	1.0
August 26, 2005	50.5	65.0	22.3
June 24, 2007	65.0	70.0	6.2

Source: Obaaro (2005); Okafor (2007c).

The civilian government of President Olusegun Obasanjo (1999-2007) was committed to the capitalist path of development. The argument then was that the economy is to 'be market oriented and private sector-led' and made 'competitive internally and externally'. This commitment to a market driven economy was to translate to such policies as privatisation of public enterprises and attempted deregulation in the petroleum downstream sector. These had adverse affects for employment, prices and public welfare. The official policy was to divest over ₦100 billion investments in all sectors of the economy within the short and long-term periods (Okafor, 2005). The Labour through its umbrella body, Nigerian Labour Congress and Trade Union Congress respectively had severally registered its opposition to neo-liberal policies through mass actions, violent demonstrations, protests and picketing. Labour insisted that neo-liberal policies only serve the insatiable desire of oil monopolies for profits and put workers in subservient position and which ultimately accentuates poverty and cost of living.

It is pertinent to note that each time the prices of the petroleum product was increased government had given several reasons and benefits that would accrue to Nigerians from such action. According to Government it has using ₦112 billion to subsidies petroleum products - the amount considered to be too high and which could be used to develop other sectors of the economy.

Among the benefits government anticipated that would accrue form subsidy removal by deregulating the downstream sector, according to Solagbade, (2003: 18) and Williams (2003: A2-A3) include:

- Accumulation of fund for the expansion of products reception and storage facilities that are already in the process of decay and also the construction of new depots by marketers.
- Emergence of new players in the sector, which will induce competition and improve operational efficiency among all the player thereby eliminating bureaucracy and patronage with its corruptive tendencies.
- Steady procurement of petroleum products leading to stability in product supply situation.
- Immense advantage to the consumer in terms of services and his confidence and position as the "king".
- Viable border trade and foreign exchange earnings for Nigerian companies.
- Setting up of refineries in the country some of which may be export oriented.
- New investment in further down stream activities thereby creating new jobs.
- Promotion of gas consumption and freeing some products for export.
- Macro economic growth through stability in fuel supply.
- Enhancement of poverty alleviation and the empowerment of the citizens.

Perhaps the greatest benefit of deregulation appears to have come from the deregulation of the Telecommunication sub sector. The National Communication Commission (NCC) in 2001, successfully auctioned the second generation digital mobile licenses which ushered in real revolution in the sector. With the licensing of MTN (Nigeria) Celtel(Now Zain) M-Tel, Globacon and many others at the cost of over $500 million, the country has moved from about 700,000 lines in 1999 to over 35million telephone lines of which 90 percent are mobile. Also the country's teledensity has also grown progressively from 0.73 in 2001 to 15.72 and to 25.22 as at January 2007.In a nut shell the Global System for Mobile Communication (GSM) explosion has created a new class of enterprenurers who might otherwise have been unemployed. There is a nationwide network of dealers, vendors, GSM accessory sellers and the ubiquitous umbrella-stands operators (Eni, 2007).

Besides the perceived benefits that would result from the deregulation of the economy, there is strong suspicion that privatisation and deregulation actually increase kleptocracy, aversion to due process, entrenched the culture of impunity and shady deals. Following are some examples:

The deregulation of the downstream petroleum market (refining, supply and distribution) has been a key ingredient of IMF and World Bank policy advice since 1999. The most contentious of the IMF's structural benchmarks was the sale of the Kaduna and Port Harcourt oil refineries. The sale was first put on hold due to the difficulty in attracting high quality international investors. Then having been valued at $800 billion, the refineries were sold off during Obasanjo's last days in office in May 2007 for a paltry $500 million to a consortium close to the president called Bluestar Oil Service Limited. The ensuing protests which contributed to a June national strike saw Bluestar withdraw from the deal and its money refunded. The privatisation and deregulation processes of the downstream oil and gas industry has seen strong opposition from labour groups over the absence of due diligence. The government is heavily criticised for its willingness to sell state assets without ensuring the development of national refining capacity, which would eventually remove the need to import much of the refined petroleum products that Nigeria consumes. It is estimated that the federal government spent a total of $18.6 billion from 2000-2006 to import refined petroleum products (Adegbamigbe, 2007).

The failure to develop refining capacity favours the few elites who benefit from the monopoly that they hold over refined oil imports. The sale of the Eleme Petrochemicals plant, in Port Harcourt, was part of a structural reform in the Petroleum Sector in October 2005. The plant is the largest of its kind on the continent. It was sold for approximately $225 million to the Nigerian subsidiary of the Indonesian firm, Indorama Group. The National Union of Petroleum and Natural Gas Workers described this amount as "not worth the spare parts available at the plant". The International Financial Corporation

(IFC) provided a loan of $75 million and mobilized another $80 million from commercial lenders. The Eleme takeover took place following a presidential directive to commission it. The Nigerian National Petroleum Company's refusal to hand over the plant on orders from the presidency, troops took it by force. A memorandum of understanding between the government and the Bureau of Public Enterprises (set up to oversee the privatisation process) apparently agreed that the government should maintain a minimum share of 49 per cent. However, Indorama was given a 75 per cent equity stake in Eleme. Similarly, the sale of the Egbin power station to Korea Power Corporation and Energy Resources Limited for an under priced N 280 million (approximately $2 million) was protested by the National Union of Electricity Employees for the lack of consultation with stakeholders and workers (Adegbamigbe, 2007; Baker, 2008; Bayliss and Fine, 2008).

Summarising the paradox of Nigerian situation as regards energy crisis (events that preceded the sale of refineries and deregulation of down stream sector) as well as its implications for development in the country, Mazrui (2001: 5) contends:

> One had hoped that petroleum would enable Nigeria to join the more prosperous nations of the world. Following the dramatic rise of the Organization of Petroleum Exporting Countries (OPEC), Nigeria became the sixth largest producer of crude oil in the world. Yet the nature of the elite consumption and several years of misrule plunged the country into mismanagement, corruption and debt. Long queues at petrol stations and recurrent shortages of fuel became the order of the day. Commercial and other economic activities were often disrupted by shortages of petroleum products – diesel, kerosene, cooking gas and other commodities. The giant of Africa was in danger of becoming the midget of the world. Africa's Gulliver was in danger of becoming the Lilliputian of the globe.

Conclusion

In conclusion, from all indications one argue that National Council on Privatisation saying that "the people benefit as the nation privatises" is a deceptive lie. The prime beneficiaries of the privatisation and deregulation in Nigeria between 1999 and 2007 are Olusegun Obasanjo and Abubakar Atiku's friends and not the ordinary people and workers of the sold companies who have subsequently lost their jobs, and left their numerous dependants with a bleak future. A good example is the case with Alico Dangote, the billionaire merchant who donated heavily to the Obasanjo Campaign Fund in 1999 and later to his failed Third term agenda but has now bought the government's Benue Cement Company.

The mass of workers and the ordinary people have lost out from the privatisation and deregulation programme. For one, the driving force of private ownership is maximisation of profits. With this in mind, the immediate concern of the buyers of the newly privatised companies has been how to cut down overhead costs. Usually the first casualties are always the workers of the affected companies, who lost their jobs in droves and their numerous dependants who have been suffering thereafter.

Finally, the poor people in Nigeria are the ultimate and final losers. For one, the production and distribution polices of private ownership is to be geared towards maximum profit making, and not necessarily towards the needs of the people. The implication of this is that, availability of products and existing social services like electricity, water, telecommunications, health, education, petroleum products, agricultural fertilisers, recreational facilities etc., presently been produced/offered by the concerned public-owned enterprises, are now been offered at very high cost to the public. The miserable experience with maintaining a GSM line also comes to light here. Many ordinary people are already exempted from the 'GSM CLUB' because of the high cost of maintaining a line; many stay connected only to receive calls but cannot afford to make calls because of exorbitant rates.

References

Adamolekun, L. (1986). Privatisation and State Control of the Nigerian Economy. *Nigerian Journal of Policy and Strategy*, Vol. 2, No. 1.

Adegbamigbe, A. (2007). The Obasanjo Years (1999- 2007): His Legacy to Nigerians. *The News*, Vol. 26, No. 21, June 4, pp. 62-72.

Adebusuyi, B.S. (1999). *Restructuring Economies through Privatisation: A Comparative Analysis*. Ibadan: University Press.

Adeyemo, F.O. (2001). *Government Made Easy*, Fourth Edition. Lagos: FSN Limited.

Ayodele, A.M. (1999). *Issues in Privatisation of Public Enterprises in Nigeria*. Ibadan: Samlad Press.

Bel, G. (2006). The coining of 'privatisation and Germany's National Socialist Party. *Journal of Economic Perspectives*, Vol. 20, No. 3, pp. 187-194.

Bello, K. (1994). Privatisation, Deregulation and Globalisation in the Telecommunication Industry. *NITEL Journal*, Vol. 12, April - June.

Bayliss, K. & Fine, B. (ed) (2008). *Privatisation and Alternative Public Sector Reform in Sub-Saharan Africa*. London: Palgrave Macmillan.

Boubakri, N, & Cosset, J. C. (1998). The financial and operating performance of newly privatised firms: Evidence from developing Countries. *Journal of Finance*, No. 53, pp. 123-145.

Chowdhury, F. L. (2006). *Corrupt Bureaucracy and Privatisation of Tax Enforcement*. Dhaka.: Pathak Samabesh.

Clarke, T. & Pitelis, C. (eds.) (1995). The Political Economy of Privatisation. London and New York: Routledge.

D'Souza, J. & Megginson, W.L. (2001). *The Financial and Operating Performance of Privatised Firms during the 1990's.*

Edwards, R. D. (1995). *The Pursuit of Reason: The Economist 1843-1993.* Harvard: Harvard, Business School Press.

Eni, H. (2007). Yar'dua's Burden: On the Digital Train. *TELL* (Special Edition), No. 2, May 21, pp. 37-39.

Ezeani, E. (1995). Public Enterprises and the Privatisation Option in Nigeria. In Onuoha, J. & Ozioko, J. (eds). *Contemporary Issues in the Social Sciences.* Enugu: Acena Publishers.

Federal Republic of Nigeria (1986). *Structural Adjustment Programme for Nigeria. July 1986-June 1988.* Lagos: Federal Government Press.

Federal Government of Nigeria (1988). *Privatisation and Commercialization Decree No. 23.* Lagos: Government Press.

Galal, A. (1994). *Welfare Consequences of Selling Public Enterprises.* New York: Oxford University Press.

Ikechukwu, O. (2005). Beyond Service Charters. *New Age*, June 17, p. 9.

Ikejiani-Clark, M. (2006). Privatisation and Commercialisation of Nigeria.

Telecommunication Limited (NITEL). *Journal of International Politics and Development Studies.* Vol. 2, No. 1, pp. 137-146.

Momoh. A. (2002). *Privatisation as a Private Monopoly.* NEPA Review, October – December, pp. 32-36.

Mazrui, A. (2001). Shariacracy and Federal Models in the Era of Globalization: Nigeria in Comparative Perspective. Paper presented at the International Conference on Restoration of Sharia in Nigeria: Challenges and Benefits, sponsored by the Nigerian Muslim Forum and held in London, England on April 14.

Medupin, R. (2002). Privatisation in Nigeria: A Tentative Assessment. *Journal Economic and Cultural Rights*, Vol. 5, No.1, pp. 17-23.

Moe, R. (1987). Exploring the Limits of Privatisation. *Public Administration Review*, Vol. 47, No. 6, pp. 453-460.

Nightingale, S.M. & Pindus, M.N. (1997). Privatisation of Public Social Service: A Background Paper. *Journal of Finance*, Vol. 23, No. 2, pp. 56- 63.

Nwoye, M.I. (1997). Management Practices and Performance Determinants of Public and Private Sector Enterprises in Anambra, Edo and Delta States of Nigeria: A Factor Analysis. *Journal of Administration.* Vol. 5, No. 1, pp. 34-42.

Obaaro, G. (2005). An imminent showdown. *TELL,* September 12, No. 37.

Obasanjo, O. (1999). An Address Delivered during the Inauguration of the National Council on Privatisation on 20th July 1999. Abuja: Federal Government Press.

Ogunde, O. (2004). Nigeria: The Rich Profits Obasanjo's Privatisation Plans as Workers Get Poorer. *Nigerian Marxist Journal*, Vol. 1, No.1, pp. 17- 20.

Okafor, E.E.(1998). Workers' Adaptation and Work Commitment under Structural Adjustment. A Study in Lagos, Nigeria. Unpublished PhD Thesis in the Department of Sociology, University of Ibadan.

Okafor, E. E. (2007a). Privatisation Policy and Public Sector Workers: A study of NITEL Employees in Ibadan, Nigeria. *Journal of Environment and Culture*. Vol. 4., No. 1, pp. 29-41.

Okafor, E. E. (2007b). Rethinking African Development: A Critical Assessment of Overview of Developments in the Telecommunication Sub Sector in Nigeria. *Journal of Human Ecology*, Vol. 22, No. 4, pp. 327-336.

Okafor, E. E. (2007c). Rethinking African Development: A Critical Overview of Recent Developments in the Petroleum Sub Sector in Nigeria. *Journal of Social Sciences*, Vol. 15, No. 2, pp. 83-93.

Olawale, R. (2005). NITEL: Counting the loss after Pentascope. *The Guardian*, March 3, p. 15-16.

Savas, E. (1987). *Privatisation*. Chatham, NJ: Chathan House.

Solagbade, D. (2003). Fuel Prices, Silly Reasons. *The Guardian*, July 6, p. 18.

Williams, A. (2003). The failure Story of Nigeria's Refineries. *The Guardian*, July 6, pp. A2 – A3.

Williams, B. (2005). Why NITEL Is a Hard Sell. *Africa Today*, December, pp. 41- 42.

Footnote

1. Some parastatals that could not be privatised outrightly such as Nigerian Ports Authority, Ajaokuta Steel, Delta Steel Aladja were concessioned to foreign firms in controversial circumstances. The Port Harcourt and Kaduna refineries which were privatized at the twilight of Obasanjo's administration departure were reversed by the Yar'dua's administration that came to power on the May 29, 2007.

SECTION - V

NIGERIAN FOREIGN POLICIES

20

The African Peer Review Mechanism in Nigeria: The Policy, Promises and Expected Result

Kehinde A. Bolaji

Introduction

The African Peer Review Mechanism (APRM) derives its identity and conceptual design from the New Partnership for African Development (NEPAD), launched as an African response to its multiple problems in the areas of bad governance, economic disarticulation, excruciating poverty and lack of capacity to take advantage of globalisation to unleash sustainable development on the continent. It is founded on development-oriented and internationally accepted practices, including commitment to good governance, democracy, human rights and conflict resolution, and the creation of investment-friendly environment through the attraction of foreign capital and enhancement of a more robust regional economic co-operation framework. NEPAD was adopted as a programme of the Organisation of African Unity (OAU), now African Union (AU) at its 37th Summit in Lusaka, Zambia in July 2001 and has its headquarters in Midrand, South Africa. The APRM is one of the most important instruments through which NEPAD aims to achieve its good governance objective.

NEPAD itself is a consensus development agenda incorporating different programme proposals like the Omega Plan, The New African Initiative, The Millennium Partnership for Africa Recovery Programme and COMPACT for Africa Recovery[1] that were articulated by some notable Heads of States in Africa. The NEPAD initiative was predated by other development plans that derived their inspiration from Western countries and further led Africa into poverty and underdevelopment. However, NEPAD represents a departure from the previous initiatives in two respects: One, it is owned by African governments and locates Africa's problems as rooted in bad governance, and; Two, it is built upon the commitments by African leaders to good governance as a yardstick for attracting aid from the developed world.

The APRM has been described by its proponents as "a mutually agreed instrument voluntarily acceded to by member states of the African Union as an African self-monitoring mechanism …and an approach designed and implemented by Africans for Africa" (APRM, 2008). The Mechanism aims to proffer solution to African governance crisis by encouraging members to submit themselves to a non-judgmental, internally-driven, holistic, transparent, and self-corrective review process aimed at enhancing good governance and economic development. This is re-assuring to members because it prevents the possibility of using the process to undermine the stability of countries under review.

The APRM process in Nigeria is in itself a reflection of the dynamics of the Nigerian state and the challenges confronting her in her march to consolidate democracy, promote good governance and sustainable development. The process dragged, faltered and was almost truncated at a point (Jinadu, 2008). Some analysts would even argue that it was corrupted and manipulated due to what is normally referred to as the "Nigerian factor". However, it also witnessed a show of solidarity among stakeholders and a commitment by stakeholders at critical periods, to ensure the continuation of the process, irrespective of intermittent challenges and setbacks. The process led to the production of a Country Review Report, incorporating a National Plan of Action (NPoA) for Nigeria, which is expected to be implemented between 2009 and 2011. It is not that the contents of the APRM Report are new, neither is it the most comprehensive document to solve the problems of the Nigerian state. Nevertheless, it offers renewed opportunity to strengthen the country's weak governance architecture, with the support of fellow African countries and the international community.

Prior to the start of the process in Nigeria, the country played an important role in the conception, articulation and popularisation of the APRM, though she is not one of the earliest implementers of the Mechanism. She did not start the process until late 2005 and completed the self-assessment process in late 2007. The APRM Process is important to Nigeria due to its potential to allow for robust re-articulation of solutions to the country's crisis of governance since independence in 1960. This crisis finds expression in corruption, ethnic violence, and religious antagonism/fundamentalism, low human development exacerbated by poverty, illiteracy, economic disarticulation, bad leadership and lack of access to basic infrastructure by the majority of the people. In addition, it also provides an opportunity to track and evaluate the achievements that successive democratic governments claimed to have achieved since the advent of democracy in 1999. Against this backdrop, this chapter attempts to examine the APRM Process in Nigeria, review the Country Self Assessment Report, analyse the challenges of operationalising the process and suggest ways in which the APRM can act as catalyst of genuine democratic governance and sustainable development in Nigeria.

APRM: Concept, Meaning, Scope and Relevance

Peer review can be defined as the systematic examination and assessment of the performance of a state by other states (peers), by designated institutions, or by a combination of states and designated institutions for the purpose of helping the reviewed state to improve its policy-making capacity, adopt best practices and comply with certain established standards and principles (ECA, cited in Mathoho, 2008: 2). Peer review process is usually an interactive, multi-phased and comprehensive process which often involved feedback mechanism from the peer-reviewed state. It often leads to the preparation of report which is implemented and subjected to further checks from time to time by the experts and stakeholders in the peer review process. It is important to note that review in itself is not of much usefulness if there is no mechanism to ensure its effective implementation and no consequences for failure to implement reports by consenting state(s).

The principles underlining the APRM include African ownership and leadership, anchoring the development of the continent on the resources and resourcefulness of the people, accelerating and deepening of regional and continental economic integration, creating conditions that make African

Table 20.1
APRM Member States as at October 2008 (Total: 28)

Region	*States*
Central Africa	(5) Cameroon, Gabon, Republic of Congo, Rwanda, Sao Tome and Principe
East Africa	(6) Ethiopia, Kenya, Mauritius, Sudan, Tanzania, Uganda
North Africa	(2) Algeria, Egypt
Southern Africa	(6) Angola, Lesotho, Malawi, Mozambique, South Africa, Zambia
West Africa	(9) Benin, Burkina Faso, Ghana, Mali, Mauritania, Nigeria, Senegal, Sierra Leone and Togo

Source: Culled from APRM's Website: www.nepad.org/aprm, assessed on 21 October 2008.

countries preferred destination by both domestic and foreign investors, new partnership among Africans and between Africans and the international community, especially the industrialised world, and holistic and integrated development for Africa (Makoena, 2003: 4).

The APRM is a process that has designed and evolved its own distinctive features. It is voluntary, non-adversarial, and indigenous in design. The APRM has already twenty-eight African countries on board (see table 20.1) and aims to assure participants, as observed by Stultz (2007: 2), "that by subjecting themselves to such reviews, they will individually voluntarily *choose* to become better governed over time and, so choosing, will – singularly and as a group of states earn increased international respect, and the favour especially of international donors". The process has also been designed with the aim of making it free of political manipulation. The four thematic areas for review in the process are: Democracy and Political Governance; Economic Governance; Corporate Governance and Socio-Economic Development. The organizational components of the APRM include:

(a) APR Forum: This is the Committee of Participating Heads of State and Government of the Member States of the APRM (APR Forum) and has the mandate for appointing the APR Panel of Eminent Persons, considering the country review reports, making appropriate recommendations to the reviewed countries, exercising constructive peer dialogue and persuasion, and ensuring that the APR process is fully funded. The Forum also persuades development partners to provide technical and financial assistance to support the implementation of the Programme of Action of the reviewed countries.

(b) APR Panel: This is a Panel of Eminent Persons depicting regional and gender diversity and was appointed by the Heads of State to oversee the conduct of the APRM process and ensure its integrity.

(c) APR Secretariat: It provides the secretarial, technical, co-ordinating and administrative support services for the APRM. The Secretariat is currently established in the NEPAD Secretariat in Midrand, South Africa.

(d) APR Team: Also known as the Country Review Team, the APR Team visits the country to review progress with the Country's Programme of Action and produces the APRM Report on the country (Africa Governance Forum, 2006: 6-8). In addition to these four layers, there is also the Country Focal Point in consenting states, which co-ordinates the process.

The APR Process covers five stages (see Table 20.2) namely self assessment, country review mission, country review report and modification of plan of action, conduct of peer review and publication of report and plan of action.

The relevance of the APR Process to good governance and development in Africa needs mentioning. For one, it affords the widest collective of people within the political system the opportunity to air their views and opinions on critical aspects of governance through a process rich in social trust and

Table 20.2
Five Stages in the APRM Review Process

Stages	*Features*
Stage One: Self Assessment	• A study of the political, economic and corporate governance and development environment in the country to be reviewed • Country Support Mission (CSM) visits the participating country to ensure a common understanding of the rules, processes and principles of the APR. • Working sessions and technical workshops are organized with stakeholders and members of CSM signs a memorandum of understanding with the government on modalities for the country review mission. • The country starts to formulate a preliminary plan of action based on local policies, programmes and projects, with the involvement of broad array of local stakeholders and government officials.
Stage Two: Country Review Mission	• A Country Review Team arrives the country for consultation and consensus-building on contentious issues in the assessment process. • The team carry out the widest possible range of consultations with the Government, officials, political parties, parliamentarians and representatives of civil society organizations • The team includes the eminent persons, representatives of the APR Secretariat, APRM partner institutions like the UN Economic Commission for Africa (UNECA), the African Development Bank and so on.

(Contd.)

(Contd. Table 20.2)

Stages	Features
Stage Three: Country Review Report and Modification of Plan of Action	• The Country Review Team drafts a report on the country, based on primary information sources and presentations made available to it by the APR Secretariat. • The Team shares its report with government. • The Team's draft report is first discussed with the Government concerned. Those discussions will be designed to ensure the accuracy of the information and to provide the Government with an opportunity both to react to the Team's findings and to put forward its own views on how the identified shortcomings may be addressed. These responses of the Government will be appended to the Team's report. • Based on the Self-Assessment Report and the Team's Report, the country finalises its Plan of Action (NPOA), outlining policies and practices for implementation.

(Contd.)

(Contd. Table 20.2)

Stages	Features
Stage Four: Conduct of Peer Review	• The Country Review Team's Report and the Plan of Action are presented at the APR Forum by the eminent persons and to the country's Head of State for consideration. • It is also presented to other participating heads of state and government. • If the Government of the country in question shows a demonstrable will to rectify the identified shortcomings, then it will be incumbent upon participating Governments to provide what assistance they can, as well as to urge donor governments and agencies also to come to the assistance of the country reviewed. However, if the necessary political will is not forthcoming from the Government, the participating states should first do everything practicable to engage it in constructive dialogue, offering in the process technical and other appropriate assistance. If dialogue proves unavailing, the participating Heads of State and Government may wish to put the Government on notice of their collective intention to proceed with appropriate measures by a given date.
Stage Five: Publication of the Report and Plan of Action	• The Report and the Plan of Action are tabled at the AU Summit, before being made public. • Six months after the report has been considered by the Heads of State and Government of the participating member countries, it should be formally and publicly tabled in key regional and sub-regional structures

Source: Tabulated from Adele Jinadu (2008) The African Peer Review Process in Nigeria, Dakar; OSIWA/AFRIMAP P. 5 and UNECA Website http://www.uneca.org/aprm/APRMStages.asp, accessed on 27 October 2008.

transparency. Secondly, it exposes the government to feedbacks from the people on policy issues in a way that the formal processes of the political system may not have captured. Thirdly, it provides opportunity for both the government and the governed to interact on policy issues in the areas of economic growth, governance and development. In addition to these, "it affords Africans the enabling opportunity to look at themselves with objectivity and sincerity and tell themselves unambiguous truths about themselves with candour and openness for the good of the continent", (Ejikeonye, 2005: 36) and be positioned as a credible benchmark for realistic assessment of the New Partnership for African Development. It is an established fact that aids are tied to the entrenchment of democratic governance, respect for human rights, promotion of liberal economic system and respect for human rights, among other factors. The APRM benchmarks African countries on these and other indices that have long been promoted by the developed countries. In this wise, it enables performing African countries to attract foreign aid and support for their development projects. It also affords Africa the opportunity to re-position its governance architecture and earn the respect of other states among the comity of nations, without necessarily undermining established political institutions in member countries. Furthermore, it serves as early warning mechanism in order to discover potential conflict issues and address them before they get out of hand. Finally, it is a critical instrument for advancing reforms in governance and socio-economic development and also a means of identifying the countries' strength and weaknesses in governance, discussing them and helping to rectify their weak governance architecture.

The Nigerian APRM Process: An Overview and Summary of Report

Nigeria acceded to the APRM on 9th March 2003 but could not make much progress on the APR process until two years later, that is October 2006, when five Lead Research Organisations (LROs) were commissioned to kick-start the national self-assessment process (APRM2, 2008: 2). The Nigerian National Focal Point is the Office of the Secretary to the Government of the Federation (SGF) which co-ordinates the activities of the NEPAD Secretariat (Nigeria) and also that of APRM. Nigeria submitted its final Country Self Assessment Review (CSAR) and the draft NPOA to the APR Panel in January 2008. Eventually, the CRM was fielded from 3 February to 2 March 2008 (APRM2, 2008: 35). Against this backdrop, it is essential to analyse the politics and policy of the APR process in Nigeria.

(a) Summary of the Report

In the area of democracy and political governance, the report noted that the political space in the country has been opened up, with growing autonomy of the judiciary as a check on executive impunity. It also noted the tendency towards the nationalisation of political parties as having not led to a better-managed political process. It described Nigeria's traditional institutions as strong and articulates the challenge posed by an inefficient electoral system for democratic consolidation in the country. It lamented the danger posed by corruption which was described as rooted in the centralised, clientilist and patronage-based politics of the country. It suggested a review of the 1999 constitution (revisiting immunity for certain public officials, giving some roles to traditional rulers), reform of the electoral system, enactment of important laws like freedom of information bill and independence of National Human Rights Commission, independence of anti-corruption institutions and combating impunity. It called for affirmative action for women and conducive atmosphere to enable civil society contribute significantly to governance. The report also called for renewed efforts at entrenching peace in the Niger Delta and addressing the root causes of ethno-religious conflicts. It called for a more effective reform measures for the security forces, especially the police and better devolution of power to the local government. The need for employment generation, provision of basic services by the government, social welfare and civil rights was also underscored in the report.

The report noted on Nigeria's economic governance and management that the country is blessed with abundant human and natural resources, with oil and gas reserve with capacity to last beyond the next 50 years. It explained that the county can employ its resources for the task of poverty reduction, provision of basic social and economic services and building a prosperous economy. It however regretted that these resources have been used to undermine the development of the country and its peoples. It observed that the Yar'Adua's government's seven point agenda (in areas of adequate power supply, food security, wealth creation, transport sector development, land reforms and security) which is a part of NEEDS II was yielding positive results as illustrated in the decline in inflation, substantial increment in Nigeria's foreign reserves and marginal reduction in poverty. It observed the role of the legislature in passing numerous pro-reform laws, which has aided the implementation of some progressive economic ideas. Progress recorded in budget reform, debt management, transparency and anti-corruption measures, banking reform, and the fight against corruption have made a lot of difference in economic management in Nigeria, according to the report. It however pointed out areas of challenges as dominance on oil, corruption, and youth unemployment, disruption in crude oil exploration, bad leadership, and lack of transparency in resource exploitation.

On economic governance and management, the report recommends the enactment of sound macro-economic policy framework especially in agriculture, industries, and financial sector. It called for structural reform measures to mitigate the economy against external shocks. It also called on the government to ensure that the capital market is competitive, efficient, and professionally run so as to prevent corruption and facilitate economic growth. It pointed out that the implementation of sound, transparent and predictable economic policies are crucial to the success of the government. It encouraged the government to sanitise the public service so that it can help in the realisation of the economic objectives of the government. It called for political will to enforce taxation, reform the revenue allocation to favour states and local governments and fight corruption.

Good corporate governance in Nigeria, the report pointed out, has been hampered by corruption, flawed administrative and political system resulting in a lack of political accountability, complexities of regulatory framework and ineffectiveness of the judiciary and other oversight bodies as well as poor state of infrastructure. There is also a problem of inadequate awareness on good corporate governance, yet the corporate world (private sector) holds a lot of promises for Nigeria's economic recovery and development. The report recommended that efforts should be made to create public awareness of the available corporate governance codes, that the government should align local corporate laws and practices with international standards and that Information and Communication Technology, investment promotion, strong regulatory framework, basic infrastructure, efficient dispute resolution, security of lives and property, and enabling small and medium scale enterprises and operators in the informal sectors to access finance, are all key factors in creating a strong corporate sector in Nigeria.

In addition to the aforementioned, the strengthening of Investment and Securities tribunal and enforcement of corporate social responsibility for companies were also recommended. The report urged the government to intensify privatisation and investment promotion and pay more attention to the rights of workers in the private sector, many of whom are not effectively catered for under the Nigerian labour law. In this respect, the casualisation of staff, gender discrimination, and lack of access to the court by employees in the private sector should be prevented. It also called on the government to make Environmental Impact Assessment (EIA) compulsory for all categories of development projects. It enjoined the government to ensure that all the companies in the oil and gas sector work within the framework of the Nigeria Extractive Industries Transparency Initiative (NEITI) and Global Compact Network as a measure of their commitment to best practices and transparency.

The report also recommended that the government should involve trade unions, private sector employers and all levels of government in negotiations on social and industrial policy, trade and the setting of minimum wages. It called on the government to ensure that corporations treat all stakeholders: shareholders, employees, consumers, suppliers, and communities, fairly and laid more emphasis on training for corporate players in order for them to be more effective.

In the area of socio-economic development, the report outlined in spite of Nigeria's abundant wealth its excruciating poverty, in terms of human development. It decried the penchant of the government to embark on large-scale projects when more basic services like access to potable water, power supply, healthcare facilities, and educational facilities were left unattended. It also decried the tendency for the people to leave the task of development only for the government and the breakdown in positive local values that can engender good governance and self-sustaining development. It observed that the local people had limited input into the country's economic reform agenda like National Economic Empowerment and Development Strategy (NEEDS) and State Economic Empowerment and Development Strategy (SEEDS), pointing out that this has adversely affected the effectiveness of these development initiatives.

The report recommended that the government should strengthen the weaknesses noted in the NEEDS agenda namely: make it a truly national plan by allowing the people to take ownership, articulate resource profile in order to determine the capability of the country to finance the strategy, address the problem of mismanagement and corruption inherent in the implementation of economic reform, and the 7-point agenda should be transformed into a shared vision for all Nigerians. The report also called on the government to increase Nigeria's internal resource base by diversification and promotion of the non-petroleum sector. It also recommended that the government fully integrate the Millennium Development Goals (MDGs) in the national development strategy and enhance the monitoring of the programme through periodic and consistent reporting.

In conclusion, the report compressed the challenges facing the country into ten overarching issues, namely: managing diversity and promoting nation building within the framework of the federation; dependence on oil/ gas and lack of economic diversification; the scourge of corruption; ineffective policy and programme implementation and poor service delivery; the informal sector; slow gender progress and limited advancement of women; land reform policy; the role of traditional rulership in governance; Diaspora and remittance and social indiscipline; disorder and value reorientation. It added two more issues: the Lagos metropolis and the economics of the Nigerian film industry to the list of these challenges. It submitted that these issues require measured, concerted, comprehensive and sustained intervention from all stakeholders in order for the country to record progress and development. This brief review has revealed that in spite of periodic setbacks in the APR process, a fairly comprehensive report that captures some of the major challenges facing Nigeria in her quest for development was developed. The content of the report, if faithfully implemented can lead to enhanced governance and rapid development. However, there are some challenges that confront the country at the present implementation stage.

Table 20.3
Summary of Major Recommendations of the CSAR for Nigeria

Thematic Area	*Major Recommendations*	*Present State*
Democracy and Political Governance	• Constitutional Review • Capacity-building of legislature and judiciary to strengthen checks and balances • Empowerment of CSOs • Affirmative action for women • Enhanced autonomy for anti-corruption agencies	• On-going constitutional Amendment by NASS • No major capacity building programme for legislature and judiciary • Multi-stakeholder approach to train and sensitize civil society organs • Women still get below 30% of elective and appointive positions • Anti-corruption agencies still undermined by political interference
Economic Governance and Management	• Economic reform programme to be faithfully implemented • Capacity-building to deepen new budget orientation to institutionalise monitoring and evaluation by CSOs • Capacity-building of public servants to operate the new Public Procurement law • Passage and operation of the Fiscal Responsibility Bill	• Slow pace of implementation and lack of effective co-ordination • CSOs still weakened by lack of capacity in budget monitoring • Most civil servants still ignorant of the provisions of the PPL • Fiscal Responsibility Act passed and in operation

(Contd.)

(Contd. Table 20.3)

Thematic Area	*Major Recommendations*	*Present State*
Corporate Governance	• Wider jurisdiction and strengthening of the Investment and Securities Tribunal • Regulatory and enforcement agencies to insist on corporate social responsibility as a corporate obligation rather that philanthropy • Corporate integrity measures to apply to private sector also • Corporations in the oil and gas industry should be signatory to the Nigeria Extractive Industries Transparency Initiative (NEITI)	• IST jurisdiction yet to be widened • Regulators yet to enforce CSR • Corporate integrity still low • Many of the corporations yet to sign NEITI

(Contd.)

(Contd. Table 20.3)

Thematic Area	*Major Recommendations*	*Present State*
Socio-Economic Development	• Enhanced Institutional Capacity for effective implementation of NEEDS, SEEDS and LEEDS	• Slow implementation of economic reform and lack of capacity by states and LGAs
	• Better coordination of development planning at all tiers of government	• No noticeable improvement in coordination
	• Poverty reduction programmes to be better funded	• Reserved
	• Massive infrastructural development to reduce costs to business and promote private sector growth	• Being addressed through Public Private Partnership and special collaboration on power supply by states and FG
	• Sustained and more vigorous implementation of the MDG Programmes	• MDGs not yet implemented vigorously: Nigeria may miss the 2015 target on all indicators
	• Increased access to credit for small and medium enterprises	• Attempts are being made to put in place Community Economic Empowerment and Development Strategy (CEEDS)
	• Vigorous promotion of girl-child education	

Source: Tabulated from Adele Jinadu (2008) The African Peer Review Process in Nigeria, Dakar; OSIWA/AFRIMAP p. 25, with additional information from Researcher's fieldworks on progress made on each indices as at October 2008.

The Challenges of Transforming the Nigerian APR Report into Result

The most important challenge in the course of ensuring that the report is translated into result is that of institutional infrastructure at every level of government, the private sector and the civil society to set agenda and drive the process of implementing the APRM report on the country. There is no gainsaying the fact that political, economic and social institutions that are crucial to the achievements of the key targets of the APR report in Nigeria are either weak or dysfunctional. In terms of results and outcomes, these institutions have contributed little to the development of the capacity of the Nigerian people, despite having earlier information/reports similar to the APR report on the challenges confronting the country and how they are to be solved. At the local levels, most of these institutions exist in name only. There is likelihood that the APR report will not make much difference in their perception and in policy design and implementation. Another issue is that of awareness and capacity of the APRM, which is very low, especially in the rural areas, and as such lack of sufficient knowledge may hamper qualitative input by critical stakeholders in the implementation of the NPOA.

In addition to this, the country will still have to contend with the problem of leadership and the political will to implement some of the recommendations in the report. Some of the recommendations in the report deals with issues that are potentially sensitive and controversial: issues like party system reform, revenue allocation, decentralisation, fighting corruption, general economic reform, especially of the extractive industries and so on. In order to successfully implement such tasking recommendations, there is need for the leadership to demonstrate through exemplary leadership, the imperative of development-oriented reform. This will assure it of people's support and confidence. It will also give the government the moral strength to mobilise the mass of the people to effect the changes recommended in the report. However, the leadership deficit in the country stands between ideals and outcomes in the implementation process of the APR report on Nigeria.

Furthermore, for the report to impact positively on the people, they must take ownership of it and be able to link it to previous locally-driven development initiatives. This is an issue that was not raised in the NPOA. Ironically, it is a key issue in its successful implementation. Adaptability of the NPOA to indigenous and local initiatives, especially at the community level is essential to the success of the programme.

Another important challenge is that of monitoring and evaluation. The APRM process itself was not monitored and evaluated and the implementation phase is set to suffer the same setback as there are not structures on the ground for carrying out this important task. In this respect, the government is likely to toe the familiar but unhelpful path of assuring the international community and donors of progress reported on paper but on the ground the progress is nowhere to be seen. Official government sources, for instance reeled out numerous achievements under the ill-fated Structural Adjustment Programme (SAP) and Department of Food, Roads and Rural Infrastructure (DFRII) while most countrymen could not visibly feel the impact of these initiatives. This pattern is dangerous and could defeat the aims and objectives of the APRM, if allowed to continue.

The final challenge that shall be discussed here is that of implementation strategy. The government has made efforts to streamline the implementation of the recommendations with that of its Vision 2020 which is aimed at making Nigeria one of the 20 biggest economies by the Year 2020. The idea is that the Vision 2020 itself will be incorporated in NEEDS II. However, the Vision 2020 programme is being kick-started on a weak note with almost two years of inactivity by the Yar' Adua government and with daunting problems in areas of leadership, participatory governance, economy, basic infrastructure and capacity. Nowhere are these problems better illustrated than in poor natural resource governance, corruption, low capacity for small and medium scale industries, unfocused leadership, lack of political will to push radical social and economic reform, insecurity of lives and property, inadequate power supply, lack of basic healthcare and educational facilities and ineptitude of public officials threatening the implementation of this initiative. These have been compounded by the failure by the government to articulate its reform programme and sell such to non-state stakeholders. In this circumstance, the implementation of the NPOA, being subsumed under the Vision 2020 programme, may be suffer from the ills of lack-lustre implementation being presently witnessed. It may also lead to the adulteration of the original recommendation of the NPOA and such adulterated views may be passed as representing the views expressed in the NPOA.

Conclusion

Implementing the APRM Report in Nigeria is not going to be a tea party. The challenges that are going to be confronted at the implementation stage are those that led to the numerous equally brilliant, purposeful and comprehensive ideas, which were conceived before the APRM but were never implemented. But the gravest impact is that the essence of the whole APRM programme in Nigeria would have been lost in the event that it fails to impact on the lives of the masses positively through faithful implementation.

Ensuring that the APR Process positively impact on Nigeria entails following some important steps. First, there is need for stakeholders (government, civil society, interest groups, donor agencies and regional organisations) to intensify efforts towards popularising the APRM in the country and build the capacity of national institutions to play important roles in its implementation. Second, the leadership of the country at all levels should demonstrate the will to put in place far reaching reforms that will not only eliminate the risk of reversal to authoritarian governance but also facilitate sustainable human development. In addition, rather than creating big national implementation structures that will make little impact, the government is advised to focus on the use of CEEDS to implement small components of the NPOA under the effective co-ordination of a department in the National Focal Point. Monitoring and evaluation should be done collectively with the civil society and other stakeholders, with multiple channels for reporting on progress to the Midrand Headquarters of the APRM. The strategy of implementation presently adopted is still mainly driven by the government and tied to the incumbent government's Vision 2020. Since it will be difficult to totally extricate the APR process from the government due to the need for Nigeria to take ownership of implementation, the APR report implementation should be made a segment in the NEEDS II document, with more visible roles for the private sector and civil society.

References

Africa Governance Forum (2006). *Implementing the African Peer Review Mechanism: Challenges and Opportunities.* Kigali: AGF.

African Peer Review Mechanism (2008). What is APRM? Retrieved on 21 October 2008: http://www.nepad.org/aprm.

African Peer Review Mechanism (2008). *Country Review Report: Federal Republic of Nigeria.* Midrand: APRM Secretariat.

Ejikeonye, Ugochukwu (2005). APRM: Will the Dragon Dance in Abuja? *Vanguard*, July 8.

Jinadu, Adele (2008). *The African Peer Review Process in Nigeria.* Dakar: OSIWA/AFRIMAP.

Makoena, Smunda (2003). *The African Peer Review Mechanism.* Paper presented at the 4th Pan African Conference of Ministers of Public Service, Stellenbosch, South Africa, 6th May.

Mathoho, Malachia (2008). An African Peer Review Mechanism: A Panacea for Africa's Governance Challenge? Retrieved on 27 October 2008: <http://www.afrimap.org/english/images/documents/APRM Panacea.pdf>.

Stultz, Newell (2007). African States Experimenting with Peer Reviewing. Retrieved on 27 October 2008: <http://www.watsoninstitute.org/pubs_news/Stultz.pdf>.

Footnote

This plurality of inputs allows for the emergence of a more robust framework. For details of these programmes and how much they reflect the NEPAD Agenda, see UNECA's website, http://www.uneca.org/aprm/story081002.asp.

21

Democracy and Nigeria's Foreign Relations (1999 – 2009)

Enemaku Idachaba

Introduction

The emergence of General Abacha (1993-98) to the leadership of the country can be captioned appropriately as the dark years of Nigeria's foreign policy as the period witnessed the squandering of all the gains and hopes since 1960 (Idachaba, 2001, 2006; Amuwo, 2001; Jega, 2001). Once more, the emergence of General Sanni Abacha in Nigeria's leadership scene was neither an accident of history as described, nor a child of circumstances or necessity. Nigerians were conditioned to assume that indeed, Abacha's ascendancy to rulership was part of a rigorous design by the military to treat the country as a personal estate. According to Omoruyi, (1999: 165): quoting General Babangida:

> Sanni (Meaning General Sanni, Abacha) is opposed to a return to civilian rule. Sanni cannot stand the idea of chief Abiola, a Yoruba becoming his commander-in-chief at all. Sanni seems to have ear of the Northern leaders that no southerner especially from the southwest should become the president of this country. Sanni seems to rally the Northern elders to confront me on the matter. He is winning; the sultan and the Northern leaders are of this frame of mind. Where do I go from here? They do not trust me. Without Sanni, I will not be

alive today; without the North, I would not have become an officer in the Nigerian army and now the president of Nigeria.

The issue at stake was no more a subject of national interest consideration, but rather personal interest evaluation and sub-ethnic nationalism. It was time for pay-off for past nicety at the expense of grave national issues that could cause the disintegration of the country. This insight provided by Omoruyi is vital in understanding the behaviour of our leaders especially in the area of foreign policy decision-making before 1999.

Having embarked on politics of isolation, with exception of a few countries in the West Africa sub-region, Abacha behaved as if Nigeria could exist alone. He was not keen on undertaking any major foreign trips particularly to major countries. Even the few ones he made to some West African countries were very short visits (usually less than a day) which were only announced after he might have gone and returned. The only major country he ever visited as Head of state was South Africa in 1994 at the early stage of his regime. The Abacha years of isolation compromised all gains of previous government in the area of foreign policy. It was a step back to the Dark Age in an era of enlightenment. Apparently, the damage of those years would take quite a while to repair especially as it affects Nigeria citizenship in the eye of the world (Enemuo, 1999). Obasanjo himself realized this, hence his observation that "In a shrinking global community where no nation can go it alone, Nigeria had in the recent past found itself isolated from the international community." (*The Comet*, October 2, 2001).

Democracy occupies a central position among the values imposed upon the global system consequent upon the collapse of the Soviet Union and the mergence of a new world order. Obviously it has become pertinent that any country that is desirous of relevance in the emerging world order, coupled with intention, to enjoy the benefits associated therewith, must succumb to the dictates of the global wind of change, (Owoeye, 1993, Saliu and Omotola, 2005: 241). The inauguration of the current democratic government in Nigeria on May 29, 1999 was received with high hopes and expectations in the belief that a new dawn had eventually arrived (Vauhanen, 1990). This expectation was natural given the dismal picture of a polity riddled with myriad of problems which the new administration was mandated to immediately address. As observed by Obasanjo, (1999: 15): his administration's domestic and foreign policies are largely informed by the need to rectify the sad experiences of the nation and that his administration's foreign policy was conditioned by democracy, political stability, a strong economic growth, and a visionary leadership with the commitment and critical understanding of the globalisation process (National Concord Feb. 24, 2000).

The president further stated that the overall objective was to "shift from a virtually reactive approach to a more proactive orientation. Hence, the new "democratic government" embarked on a revitalisation and refocusing drive in order to boost the country's image abroad and to return the country to normalcy in diplomatic relations, and to strengthen foreign policy apparatus in order to make it more result-oriented, (Akinyemi; 2004: 25).

The administration underscored the strong connection between peace, development and good governance and emphasised human rights, freedoms, the rule of law and transparency as ingredients of the linkage between foreign and cosmetic policies, thus establishing a correlation between a virile and stable economy and the pursuit of a vibrant foreign policy (Pogoson, 2003:3). Consequently, the immediate concern of the Obasanjo administration that came to power in May 1999 on terms of foreign relations was articulated with a commitment to the following:

- Global orientation in foreign policy.
- How to redeem the shattered image of the country in the international system.
- How to re-affirm the confidence of the international community in Nigeria again.
- Attraction of qualitative foreign investments to Nigeria for economic development.
- A commitment to regional integration and development of the African continent (particularly the West African sub-region.)
- A focus on domestic economy as the determinant factor in foreign policy issues.

A Year of Restoration

May 29, 1999 witnessed the re-emergence of General Olusegun Obasanjo as Nigeria's Head of State, twenty years after handing over power to a civilian regime in 1979. The geometry and calculus of how this happened may not be within the scope of this paper; however, it is necessary to state that those who made the decision realized that in order to assuage the feeling of the southerners especially as it related to the aftermath of the monumental annulment of the June 12, 1993 Presidential election, a shift in power at that level of governance to the South West became imperative, sensible and strategic. (*This Day*, May 17, 1999) Akinadewo (2001: 36) presents the issue by noting that:

> Obasanjo had become one of the most known and acknowledged political figure in Africa. He had built the profile of the world statesman from Africa to such extent that his status could only be rivaled by former South African president Nelson Mandela.

On assumption of office in May 1999, Obasanjo left no one in doubt about his desire to open Nigeria's windows to the world and restore the past glory by embarking on foreign trips on regular basis. In fact, there is no major country in the world which has not witnessed the visit of the Nigerian president. Apart from visits to Britain, president Obasanjo had paid visits to the United States of America to hold bilateral talks with President Clinton and subsequently with President Bush. President Bill Clinton in and out of office has paid several visits to Nigeria. America-Nigerian relations have grown in bounds under Obasanjo's "democratic administration," (*This Day*, November 2, 1999).

There seems to have been the suppression of the hollow arrogance for desirable external assistance for development. For example, Nigeria has signed a memorandum of understanding with Britain and the USA for military officers from the two countries to help train Nigerian soldiers in peace-keeping and to assist in professionalising the Nigerian army in line with the new democratic dispensation, (Gabriel 2001: 39). This is because it is true that the military has contributed more than any other institution to the retardation of the country's progress in the recent past due to its unprofessional character. Furthermore, the US has also offered to provide specialised training and some facilities to the Nigeria police to assist in crime control and prevention. *Nigerian Tribune* (18 June 2001), in an editorial comment, lauded this gesture stating thus:

> It has now become a reasonable decision to accept help that are adjudged useful. They also signed different grant agreements with different countries e.g. Germany, Canada, France, Britain, Italy, and America. The agreements would help provide funds to support economic growth, agriculture and educational activities in Nigeria. However, one area where Obasanjo has succeeded tremendously was in his advocacy for paying the debt owed by Nigeria.

A New Orientation in Nigeria's Foreign Policy

Immediately, the Obasanjo administration was inaugurated, the government declared a new thrust in Nigeria's foreign policy. This new foreign policy posture became a landmark in Nigeria's foreign relations, being the first time such an orientation was adopted in terms of foreign policy perspective or priority (Okpokpo, 1999). This orientation sees the entire globe as the focus of Nigeria's foreign policy. However, this is not to say that Africa has been jettisoned as the centrepiece of Nigeria's foreign policy but now encompasses the entire globe as its foreign policy theatre.

Perhaps, Nigeria's new thrust in foreign policy must have been informed by the current wave of globalisation that is sweeping across the world. Arguably therefore, it was the desire of the Obasanjo democratic administration to be fully involved in the globalisation race that must have informed the new global thrust in Nigeria's foreign policy.

According to Akinterinwa (2004: 27) addressing a joint forum of the congress for South African Trade Union (COSATU), and the Nigeria Labour Congress in Abuja in the year 2000, the then minister of Foreign Affairs categorically declared on Nigeria's foreign policy as follows:

> Circumscribed by events in the world and other dominant global issues as necessary conditions for the policy's nuances and trajectory. The instrumentalist focus of foreign policy effectively

shift the thrust to a question of strategies of land mass, etc towards enhanced share of the benefits of globalization for our economy.

Announcing a fresh initiative which signaled a new foreign policy thrust, President Olusegun Obasanjo (1999) maintained:

> The administration would now be guided by a more global orientation which makes the entire globe, not just Africa as the canvas of its exertions. The immediate concern of our diplomacy is the revitalization of our economy with emphasis on the restoration of the international image of this great country, re-affirm the confidence with our friends had in us, attracting responsible and efficient foreign investments, addressing the problems of the debt burden and capital flight, and strengthen regional interactive relations.

Nigeria and Image Rebuilding Project

As implied earlier in this paper, Nigeria has become an isolated country, almost with a pariah status in the international arena, given the human rights record of the then Head of State and his agents all over the country, Nigeria was suspended from some international organizations such as the Commonwealth of Nations and isolated by such countries, as the United State (US), European Union (EU) member countries, South Africa, to mention just a few. Obasanjo immediately embarked on many overseas trips to canvass for support for Nigeria and to start gradually to rebuild the battered image of the country. Even in the pre-inauguration months, the then President elect visited countries such as Venuzuela, Brazil, Cuba, United States, France, Italy, united Kingdom, etc. all in an effort to redeeming Nigeria's image abroad.

Notably, since the year 2000, international relations profile of Nigeria saw tremendous improvement. The hallmark of this return of international confidence was the visit of the president of the United States of America, Mr. Bill Clinton to Nigeria. Nigeria has since made host to many international events and activities of which the hallmark was the hosting of the Commonwealth heads of Government meeting in Abuja. This particular event sent an enduring signal to the rest of the world that Nigeria has finally regained its place among the comity of Nations, (Nuamah, 2003).

The Queen of England was also physically present at the commonwealth Heads of Government meeting and her stay added credibility to the conduciveness of the Nigerian environment in contemporary time. In addition, all existing sanctions imposed on Nigeria were lifted when Nigeria attained democracy.

The United Nations, Canada and other corporations also earnestly relaxed their tight fitted relations with Nigeria. The president of Nigeria could easily be described as the most widely travelled president, all in an effort to project the image of the country to the outside world in a way that denotes tranquility and positivity to further encourage foreign investors and diplomats to do business with Nigeria (Democracy Coalition Project, 1992-2002).

A point of emphasis is that from all intent and purpose the international community has re-affirmed confidence in Nigeria due to the active nature of its foreign policy under the democratic rule. According to Olikarinen (2002: 63), the head of the European Union delegation to Nigeria from 1998 to 2002 described life and his experience in Nigeria thus:

> My second tour in Nigeria is drawing to a close. At the end of May (2002), I am returning to Finland... leaving Nigeria makes me feel sad. I and my wife have greatly enjoyed our stay here. Even more rewarding to me than the professional satisfaction has been the life itself in this vibrant, fascinating country, especially association with its people who have always shown only friendliness and hospitality to me and my wife.

The European Union welcomes the achievements of the Nigerian authorities and assured them of the European Union's intentions to support Nigeria in its efforts to consolidate democracy and advance socio-economic development.

The various foreign trips of the president (as earlier alluded to) is a clear indication of acceptability of Nigeria and the return of confidence in a country that was declared a pariah State in the preceding despotic military regime.

In the world of Akinterinwa (2004:365) an international relations expert:

> In diplomatic practice, all official visits are invited even if they are at times initiated by the government of the visiting Head of state. In other words, if the Nigeria's president wants to visit the United Kingdom, a request can be made by the Nigerian authorities either through the Nigerian High Commission or directly through the leaders of both countries.

This goes to signify that the international community now has strong confidence in the current Nigerian democratic dispensation which also has highly positive implication for the country, particularly in socio-economic, bilateral and multilateral advantages and gains; both short and long run.

Sustenance of Democracy in the Region

Nigeria has been a prime promoter and an unrepentant advocate of democratic rule at least in the West Africa sub-region. Ironically, Nigerian military regime was preoccupied with promotion and installation of democratic governments else where in the sub-region (Liberia) at a time it had not even attained democracy. The Obasanjo administration resisted regime changes through coup detat in Sao Tome and principe when the country's President Frederique de Menezes was in Nigeria to attend the Leon Sullivan summit. The Nigeria government ensured the return of de Menezes to power and president Obasanjo even accompanied him back to his country. The Senegalese president saddled Nigeria with the responsibility of restoring the ousted president to office by noting that "I condemn what has happened. I urge ECOWAS and President Olusegun Obasanjo to see what can be done to remedy the situation and I hope we will be able to bring president Frederique de Menezes back to his country" (Nigerian Tribune; 18 June, 2001).

The second instance was in Guinea-Bissau where the government of Kumba Yala was outsted. Although Kumba Yala was not seen as a symbol of good leadership for democracy and he himself saw the futility of returning to power, Nigeria and other countries ensured commitment to an immediate commencement of a transition programme to civil rule in Guinea Bissau. Consequently, a transition government not headed by the army chief was immediately installed. Furthermore, the government of the country, successfully hosted the all African games in 2003. In the contemporary world, sport, has assumed the position of a major instrument of foreign policy. The success of the events tagged "COJA 2003" was a credit to the foreign policy agenda of the government.

Furthermore, the Heads of Government of the commonwealth countries met at Abuja in December 2003 with the Queen of England in attendance. The basic issues of discussion at the Commonwealth Heads of Government Meeting, captioned as "CHOGM 2003", centred on the suspension of Zimbabwe, poverty reduction and world trade. In spite of the contentious nature of some of the issues, the conference was adjudged a success. The commonwealth secretary General concluded that "This year's summit was the most difficult meeting but it turned out to be successful due to the handling of the affairs by the new chairperson in office, president Obasanjo, (The Comet, 2003). Giving credit to re-democratisation project in Nigeria, the Nigerian Senate saw it as very successful and probably the best in the history of the Commonwealth." The General expectation was that the summit would be able to open the window of opportunity for foreign investment flow in Nigeria, (Yaqub, 2004)

The foreign policy and image restoration agenda of the Obasanjo regime has met with stiff opposition from some members of the domestic populace. *Tell* (May 29, 2000) present the issue:

> the president has been criticized for his frequent trips abroad. Those who frown at this would want him to stay at home to tackle the problems confronting the country. There is renewed hope of confidence within and outside the continent, more so, when most world leaders and investors see the president as one capable of turning the country around and in droves, they have been visiting for one possible relationship or the other.

But Akinyemi (2004) disagrees with this position of *Tell* Magazine. His opinion is as follows:

> necessary for a head of state to demonstrate the control of foreign policy or demonstrate the mastership of foreign policy by actually becoming the main implementer of the Foreign Policy.... They now want to demonstrate a personal involvement of the president before they embark on a state visit.

In the final analysis, the justification of the trips will be judged against the benefits.

A word on the Charles Taylor Asylum: perhaps no foreign policy action of the Obasanjo administration has generated more public interest and condemnation as the decision to grant political asylum to the Liberian Warlord, Charles Taylor. The government's position is that granting Taylor an asylum was not only in the best interest of peace in Liberia but also that it was in the interest of Nigeria which would have further borne the brunt of more Liberian refugees some of whom were quartered in Oru-Ijebu ode in Ogun State by the federal government. The problem of refugees must be understood as going beyond economic maintenance, as it also encompasses social and security problems. The terms of his asylum included the fact that he could not travel out of his place of abode without the permission of government. He was also responsible for his upkeep and that of his family while in Nigeria, while Nigeria provided him with security and was not allowed to grant press interviews without the permission of government (The Coment 2003).

As stringent as these conditions might seem, some Nigerians were not persuaded that Nigeria needed to bear the responsibility of hosting Charles Taylor in asylum. The views of such critics were adequately represented by the foremost scholar of international relations and former external Affairs Minister professor Bolaji Akinyemi who describes Taylor as "thoroughly discreditable character a kleptomaniac and a scoundal" who does not deserve the hospitality of the Nigerian nation (The Coment 2003). The Sunday Telegraph (London) sees him as a "Conceited showman and megalomania tyrant who was responsible for the death of an estimated 250,000 people in his country over the period of fourteen years."

Foreign Investments Drive

Nigeria's foreign policy under the new democratic rule is committed to attracting foreign investments into the country. Upon assumption of office, the president visited many countries, corporations and individuals in a bid to attract them to invest in the Nigerian economy. As a result of this, several countries and corporations started earnestly to invest in the country as a result of the new and improved investment climate that was created by the new re-democratisation process indicating relatively stable environment for investors.

Such corporations like Daimler Chrysler-the automobile giant, Coca-cola incorporated have invested millions of Dollars in Nigeria in contemporary times. Nigerian economy had also witnessed the presence of many trade delegates from several countries and companies abroad who having had good business proposals and discussions with the Nigerian business community, started investing their capitals in different sectors of the country (Onoja, 2001: 50-62) Such trade delegates came from countries like Turkey, Germany, Japan, Belgium, Denmark etc.

The newly incorporated global orientation in Nigeria's foreign policy, perhaps has also made it possible for component states in the Nigerian federation to go into trade relations, multilateral and bilateral agreements with corporations, and even individual business men all over the world.

This has brought about a situation where states in Nigeria such as Lagos, Abia, Cross-River among others (even in Northern Nigeria), have gone into several arrangements/agreements of educational, economic and infrastructural nature with many international corporations and individuals for the political and economic development of their states. The independent electricity generating arrangement between Lagos state and the foreign partner is an outstanding example, among others. Another, is the mini-industrial complex in Abia state being developed by Governor Orji Kalu in collaboration with a Japanese industrial giant.

In the opinion of Pogoson (2003:4):

> Realizing that foreign investment is an instrument for expediting economic development the campaign for foreign investment in the Nigerian economy has elevated economic diplomacy to the most important priority in Nigeria's foreign policy agenda.

The Debt Problem or Over Hang

Nigeria's foreign policy in contemporary time is also equally committed to reduction, reversal, forgiveness or even total cancellation of the external debts owed not only by Nigeria but those by other African countries. Chief Obasanjo the then president, was committed to this particular issue of debts in all ramifications in the new democratic dispensation.

President Obasanjo as the Chairman of the African Union and the Chairman of G77 had used his position to vigorously persuade the International Monetary Fund (IMF) the World Bank, the London and Paris Clubs and other international financial institutions to assist in developmental programmes in Africa by reversing or forgiving African nations, their external debts which had remained serious burden and bottleneck in their journey towards development. As will be demonstrated below, there is, without a shadow of a doubt an intrinsic linkage between democracy and Nigeria's new direction in foreign policy (World Bank, 2003).

As explained by President Obasanjo himself (*The Guardian*, 2004: 4):

> Beyond our concern for the well-being of our continent, the debt burden is not an exclusive African predicament. Many countries in Asia, the Caribbean and South America are facing similar problems with it. It is imperative, therefore, that the countries of these regions,

harmonize their efforts of the search for a fairer deal from the industrialized nations of the world and this requires of us a more global approach to world affairs than was previously the case.

President Obasanjo openly gave the issue of debt burden reduction, cancellation or forgiveness a high place in Nigeria's foreign economic policy agenda. The president maintained that while the debt overhang was too heavy, it was also a potential and serious threat to the fledging democracy and the socio-economic development which his administration had embarked upon.

However, while a few creditor countries and non-governmental creditor agencies have responded positively to the president's appeal, others have turned deaf ears to it, arguing that Nigeria does not deserve debt forgiveness and cancellation given it corrupt dispensation.

Commitment to Regional Integration and Development

Since 1960 when Nigeria became an independent nation and was admitted into the United Nations Organisation as the 99th member, Africa has remained the centrepiece of her foreign policy. In contemporary time, this orientation has not been reduced, but rather it has been extended in the context of the current trend of globalization (baylis and Smith, 1997). Consequently, the Obasanjo administration was committed to regional integration, corporation and development of the continent of Africa and the sub-region of West Africa. Instances of practical contributions of Nigeria to Africa's development abound particularly after the enthronement of democratic governance in the Fourth Republic – Nigeria. Senegal, Algeria, South Africa are the four major forces behind the new Partnership for Africa's Development (NEPAD), which is the new agenda for the economic development of the continent (ADB Report, 2003).

In the transformation of the Organization of African Unity (OAU) to Africa Union (AU) Nigeria played a very significant role and contributed both human and financial resources to ensure the eventual successful transformation of the regional body and to the achievement of the goals and objectives of the Union. Nigerian President, Olusegun Obasanjo was chairman of the Union and under this auspices he has assisted the African continent in many areas in resolving political crises and peaceful settlement of disputes. The recent dispute over the Bakassi peninsula is a case in point. Several efforts have been made to bring peace to the troubled Western Sudan, the Darfur region, most meetings to discuss the Sudan crises have been at the expense of Nigeria, and in Nigeria. The contribution of Nigeria to Africa's development in contemporary time is also evident in the desire of Nigeria government to canvass at the least possible opportunity for debts relief and forgiveness for the whole of Africa in his capacity as the Chairman of the G77. Nigeria's foreign relations in the sub-regional sphere is also worthy of note. Nigeria has continued his leadership role in the West Africa sub-region.

Nigeria has continued to contribute financial and human resources to the Economic Community of West African State ECOWAS monitoring group (ECOMOG), the embattled Liberian warlord, former president Charles Taylor enjoyed political asylum in Nigeria, and had granted loans worth six billion naira (N6b) to the governments of both Ghana and Sao Tome and Principe.

Nigerian democratic administration, as part of the African integration project is committed to establishing strong bilateral relations with Africa and other countries (Pogoson, 2003: 5-6).

As Obasnajo (1999) puts it:

> ECOWAS remained one of the major pillar in the architecture of a larger African integration project whose objectives would be realized as soon as our recent initiative, the African Economic community, becomes functionalism.

Accessing the benefit of globalization could be enhanced by an organized African market, single currency and an African parliament: (Bayo, 2003: 44)

Under the democratic government, the Obasanjo administration also announced commitment to conflict prevention management and resolution, particularly in the West African sub-region. The government had also maintained cordial relations with Nigeria's contiguous neighbours, as an integral part of Nigeria's African diplomacy (Babalola; 2002: 12). Notable in this respect, include: the role Nigeria played in the final restoration of peace to the war-torn Sierra Leone. The Sierra Leonean case, though an inherited one, the Obasanjo democratic administration had remained a key player in the attempts to find a lasting solution to the crisis.

Once again, the new direction in Nigeria's foreign policy under the democratic rule during the period in focus, does not suggest an abandonment of the general framework of Nigeria's foreign policy in Africa, and/or West Africa, rather, she is now being guided by a more global approach than ever before (Onoja, 2001). Suffice it to say that Nigeria is now preoccupied not only with Africa/West Africa but the entire world in its foreign relations as a spill over effects of re-democratisation.

Conclusion

President Obasanjo has so far been able to transform the character and framework of Nigeria Foreign Policy from isolation to globalization. The restoration agenda is not without cost as it has aroused criticism from a segment of the domestic population. But this is understandable since attempting to right the wrongs of the past would be accompanied by some deprivation. The posture development is that Nigeria is no longer perceived as a pariah state by international community and it views on global issues are not considered and respected. Nigeria is, therefore, once again assuming its leadership position in Africa. However, in order to keep the domestic structure supportive of the nation's foreign policy there must be quantitative, qualitative and perceivable dividends in terms of economic improvement in daily life of the citizenry. It is then that the restoration foreign policy agenda of the democratic administration can be meaningful to the generality of the people. Lastly, Foreign Policy decision making must move away from the purview of the whims and caprices of a ruling elite to the domain of enlarged and enlightened public. This is not a challenge for one administration alone; it is a challenge for the future of Nigeria's foreign policy in the spirit of democratic consolidation.

Restricting Nigeria's foreign policy thrust to Africa alone was a laudable goal before the 1990s, but its evolution is needed for Nigeria to meet the needs of today's diplomacy as we move into the next millennium. Africa as the center piece of Nigeria's foreign policy no longer suffices; there is now room for a broader perspective. This is both necessary and urgent. To play a major role in current high level diplomatic circles, Nigeria must learn not to build its foreign policy on only one pillar. Democracy and human rights, which in the recent past were considered in law and international relations as purely internal affair, are becoming important determinants in Foreign Policy.

Nigeria should re-orientate its foreign policy toward more profitable ventures like economic, scientific, cultural and technical cooperation with more advanced countries, including Asia. Nigeria's foreign policy has to produce results for the country and its citizens. Hence, economic development and well-being of Nigeria should be made the mainstay of its foreign policy. Though Africa should not be abandoned and/or neglected, the interest of Nigerians should come first in all its foreign policy analysis and decisions.

Finally, Nigeria's foreign policy should aim at creating benefits for the betterment of the people. At another level, Nigeria's foreign policy should encompass a clear opinion and strategy on major international issues such as the reform of the United Nations, bilateral relations between Nigeria and members of the European Union, etc. Furthermore, Nigeria should campaign strongly to get admitted as a permanent member of the Security Council.

Obasanjo has embarked on shuttle diplomacy, campaigning for debt relief, which has already yielded fruitful results including recovery of stolen public fund and attraction of foreign investments. Obasanjo also took over the leadership of G77 in order to reposition the country within the south-south group. Nigeria's image has already been boosted in the international arena due to anti-corruption commission including visits to Nigeria by many world leaders, like Presidents Clinton and Chirac, to mention only a few. Besides, Nigeria's foreign policy is still constrained by the complex nature of its domestic political arena bringing to the fore such questions as 'How democratic is Nigeria?'

How Democratic is Nigeria?

Any assessment of a country's democratic character will be fundamentally determined by what the observer chooses to use as a definition of democracy. Most analysts have scanned the Nigerian political scene and reached different conclusions regarding the democratic character of the country. This difference of opinion is explained primarily by the fact that each approaches his evaluation with a different conception of what democracy is.

We proposed a set of criteria for the description "democratic" which goes beyond formal political institutions, to the quality of life in the society (economic, social, psychological), beyond majority rule to a concern for minorities and beyond national boundaries to a global view of what is meant by the "the people", in that rough, but essentially correct view of democracy as "government of, by and for the people". We can measure the present against the past, so that we find that in 2009, we are doing better in these matters than we were doing in 1999 or 2003, the society will get a good grade for its democracy. Better still, we can even measure our democracy against an ideal (even if admittedly unachievable) standard because the ideal standard is the pragmatic one.

References

African Development Bank (ADB). Report (2003). Oxford University Press.

Akinterinwa, B. (2004a) (ed.). Nigeria's New Foreign Policy Thurst. UN Secretary General's Foreword in Akinterinwa, p. xxvii. Ibadan: Vantage Publishers.

Akinterinwa, B. (2004c). Concentricism in Nigeria's Foreign Policy. In Ekaterina (ed.), *Nigeria's New Foreign Policy Thrust: Essays in Honour of Ambassador Oluyemi Adeniji*. Ibadan: Vantage Publishers.

Akinterinwa, B. (2004b). *Nigeria in Global Strategic Calculation: Images and Expectations*. p. 365.

Akinterinwa, B. (2004d). "Preface" in Nigeria's New Foreign Policy Thrust. Op. cit.

Akinyemi, A.B. (1979). Muhammed/Obasanjo Foreign Policy. In Oyediran, O. (ed.), *Nigeria Under the Military, 1966-1979*. London: Macmillan.

Akinyemi, B. (2004). Let's Endue a New Flagship for our Foreign Policy. *Nigerian Tribune*, January 15, p. 25.

Amuwo, Kunle (2001). Transition as Demcoratic Regression. In Amuwo, Kunle, Bach, D.C., Lebeau, Y. (ed.). op.cit., pp. 1-56.

Babalola, S. (2002). On Nigeria's Foreign Policy. *Nigerian Tribune*, June 9, p. 12.

Background Note: Nigeria (2006). *Bureau of African Affairs*. p. 11.

Baylis, J. & Smith, S. (1997). *The Globalization of World Politics: An Introduction to International Relations*. New York: Oxford University Press.

Bayo, B. (2003). Nigeria: Africa's Big Brother. *The Punch*, September 23, p. 44.

Defending Democracy: A Global Survey of Foreign Policy Trends 1992-2002. A Democracy Coalition Project. Retrieved from http://www.democoalition.org/pdf/Nigeria.pdf.

Enemuo, F. (1999). Democracy, Human Rights and Rule of Law. In Aniforwose and Enemuo (eds.), *Elements of Politics.* Lagos: Malthouse Press.

Gabriel, A. (2001). From Balewa to Obasanjo. *The Comet,* October 1, 2001, p. 39.

Idachaba, E. (2001). Chronology of Major Political Events in the Abacha Era (1993 – 1998). In Amuwo, Kunle, Bach, D.C., Lebeau, Y. (eds.), *Nigeria During the Abacha Years (1993-1998). The Domestic and International Politics of Democralization,* pp. 341-363. Ibadan: IFRA/CEAN.

Idachaba, E. (2006). *Government and Politics in Nigeria.* Ibadan: Distance Learning Centre, University of Ibadan. pp. 39-45.

Jega, A.M. (2001). Democracy in Nigeria: Concepts, Representations, and Expectations. In Amuwo et al., op. cit., pp. 101-144.

National Concord, February 20, 2000.

Nigerian Tribune, August 4, 2004.

Nigerian Tribune, July 9, 2002.

Nuamah, R. (2003). *Nigeria's Foreign Policy after the Cold War: Domestic, Regional and External Influences.* Oxford, UK: International Peace Academy.

Obasanjo, O.A. (1999). Nigeria's Foreign Policy on the Eve of the 21st Century. The 1999 Annual Patron's Dinner Address, Nigerian Institute of International Affairs (NIIA), p. 15.

Okpokpo, E. (1999). *The Challenges Facing Nigeria's Foreign Policy in the Next Millennium.*

Olikarineu's "Farewell to Nigeria" (2001). *The Guardian*, 22 May, p. 63. (As cited by Akinterinwa, 2004, p. 361.)

Omoruyi, O. (1999). The Tale of June 12. Handson Press Alliance Network Ltd. P. 165.

Onoja, A. (ed.) (2001). Plying the Foreign Pitch: Media Portrait of Sule Lamido, Minister of Foreign Affairs, Vol. 2, 2000 – 2001. Abuja: Office of the Honourable Minister of Foreign Affairs. 50-62.

Owoeye, J. (ed.) (1993). *Understanding the New World Order*. Ibadan College Press.

Pogoson, A.I. (2003). Nigerian Foreign Policy Initiatives under the Obasanjo Administration: What benefits and to whom? 14th Beinnial Congress of African Association of Political Science (AAPS) Durban, June 26-28, p. 3.

Saliu, H.A. & Omotola J.S. (2005). Nigerian Foreign Policy Under Obasanjo. In Saliu (ed.), *Nigeria Under Democratic Rule (1999 – 2003)*, Vol. II, p. 241. Ibadan: University Press.

Tell Magazine May 28, 2000.

The Comet, August 27, 2003.

The Comet, August 4, 2001.

The Comet, August 4, 2001.

The Comet, August 9, 2003.

The Comet, Dec. 17, 2003.

The Comet, Jan. 12, 2001.

The Comet, October 2, 2001.

The Guardian, January 26, 2000.

The Punch, September 23, 2003.

This Day, May 17, 1999.

This Day, November 2, 1999.

Vauhanen, T. (1990). *The Process of Democratization: A Comparative Study of 147 States, 1980-88*. New York: Taylor and Francis Inc.

World Bank Operational Policies Manual Washington DC: World Bank July, 2003.

Yaqub, N. (2004). The Millennium Development Goals and the Sustainability of Nigeria's Foreign Policy in the Twenty-First Century. In Akinterinwa, B. (ed.), *Nigeria's New Foreign Policy Thrust: Essays in Honour of Ambassador Oluyemi Adeniji*. Ibadan: Vantage Publishers.

Index

D

E

F

J

K

L